Developments in Polynesian Ethnology

Developments in Polynesian Ethnology

Edited by
Alan Howard
and
Robert Borofsky

University of Hawaii Press • Honolulu

94 93 92 91 90 89   5 4 3 2 1

Library of Congress Cataloging-in-Publication Data

Developments in Polynesian ethnology / edited by Alan Howard and
    Robert Borofsky.
        p.   cm.
    Bibliography: p.
    Includes index.
    ISBN 0-8248-1181-X
    1. Ethnology—Polynesia.   2.   Polynesia—Social life and customs.
I.   Howard, Alan, 1934–   II.   Borofsky, Robert, date–
GN670.D48   1989   89-5029
306'.0996—dc20   CIP

University of Hawaii Press books are printed
on acid-free paper and meet the guidelines
for permanence and durability of the Council
on Library Resources.

For Jan and Nancy

CONTENTS

ACKNOWLEDGMENTS

A VARIETY of people contributed to the preparation of this book. The authors of each chapter cite individuals who assisted them. In addition, others helped in more general ways. We would like to thank Pamela Kelley, Eileen D'Araujo, and Iris Wiley at the University of Hawaii Press and the copyeditor, Linda Gregonis. A number of others also contributed valuable advice: Judy Huntsman, Allan Hanson, Jan Rensel, Matthew Spriggs, Lynette Cruz, Kalani English, and Barbara Ideta. Significant writing and editing of the book was completed while Robert Borofsky was an East-West Center Fellow. He wishes to acknowledge with appreciation the assistance provided by the Institute of Culture and Communication under the directorship of first Mary Bitterman and then Robert Hewett. David Friedman contributed the fine cover drawing and chapter opening art. Kimberly Walter played a major role in preparing the index. Finally we wish to thank our wives, Jan Rensel and Nancy Schildt, for their continued advice and support.

1

Introduction

ALAN HOWARD

ROBERT BOROFSKY

THIS book represents an attempt by a number of experienced researchers to assess the state of Polynesian ethnology today. It has been less than twenty years since the senior editor assembled the first set of collected papers on Polynesia (Howard 1971). At the time there was a dearth of suitable literature, in either article or book form, that was theoretically suggestive and relevant for contemporary perspectives. Trying to balance geographical coverage against thematic considerations was made difficult because so little work had been done in some of the archipelagoes. Today the problems of putting together such an anthology would be the reverse. In both quantity and quality the work done in Polynesia over the past twenty years has been impressive, and it would be difficult to pare down this wealth of materials to a few representative articles. The path we have taken, consequently, has been to commission the articles contained in this volume.

As each of us began the task of reviewing the recent literature, we were struck by how much had accumulated in our respective areas, and how extensive a task we had undertaken. As is perhaps usual under such circumstances, deadlines were repeatedly extended and what was to have been a two-year project has taken six years to complete. As editors, we have avoided imposing a rigid format on the authors, each of whom has contributed to the theoretical development in his or her area of specialization. Each chapter presents a review of recent materials, although some authors found it expedient to make their points by selecting a few representative cases and amplifying them, while others chose to cast a broader net. Certain key issues, such as gender, are of widespread significance and could not readily be confined to one chapter. They are therefore discussed in several, with each analysis showing the issue in a different light, illuminating a different set of theoretical connections. In our opinion this provides a better picture of the true complexity of these issues.

There are important continuities and trends that have become apparent to us as we worked on the volume. Throughout much of its history,
Polynesian ethnology has been marked by two distinct but complementary projects. One aims at reconstructing the nature of Polynesian
societies prior to European intrusion, the other at understanding ongoing societies as observed by ethnographers. These projects have taken
different shapes during different historical periods, but each has built
upon the insights of its predecessors, and each project has informed the
other. Understandings gained through intensive fieldwork have helped
to recast the problems of prehistoric reconstruction, while attempts to
bring order to what is known of precontact Polynesian societies have
raised new questions for contemporary ethnographic investigation. The
history of Polynesian ethnology therefore appears to be less a series of
dramatic paradigm shifts, in Thomas Kuhn's sense, than an accrual of
increasingly sophisticated analyses within a broadening, and increasingly complex, framework.

The first issue that fired the imaginations of Western scholars was
where the Polynesians originated, and how they got to such remote
islands. Speculation began with the explorers and has continued ever
since. Implicitly this endeavor required reconstructing precontact Polynesian societies so that comparisons, and inferences about historical
connections, could be made. The evidence for these speculations
included language, artifacts, myths, beliefs, customary practices, and
features of social and political organization. The nature of the task,
however, did not require integrated visions of how Polynesian social
systems worked. Comparisons were based on traits, considered more as
independent entities than as cohering parts of social systems. Reconstructions were thus piecemeal, and on the whole, unrevealing of societal character.

The Bishop Museum studies of the 1920s and 1930s approached the
problem with a more sophisticated research agenda. Ethnographers,
each armed with a well-defined format for collecting and organizing
data, were sent to a variety of Polynesian islands. Their materials were
published in a set of standardized ethnographies that were used in comparative studies aimed at unravelling migration routes and historical
connections between Polynesian societies. Although a continuation of
earlier diffusionist projects, the studies were enriched by materials from
ongoing societies, and consequently were more attuned to the subtleties
of social context. By contemporary standards fieldwork sessions were
relatively short, at times lasting only a number of weeks. Still, the publications of such anthropologists as the Beagleholes, Buck, Burrows, Gifford, Handy, Linton, MacGregor, and Métraux have proven valuable
to modern scholars studying continuity and change in the region. The
work of these ethnographers was supplemented by archaeological investigations confined largely to surveys of surface remains and compari-

sons of artifacts, primarily adzes. As Patrick Kirch notes (chapter 2), it was generally believed that excavations would have little to add to the ethnological record because settlement periods were presumed to be quite short.

Toward the end of the 1920s, serious ethnography of extant societies came into its own in Polynesian studies. Initially the focus was on the less acculturated societies. Raymond Firth selected the isolated outlier of Tikopia and Margaret Mead the relatively undisturbed island of Manu'a in Samoa. It would be difficult to overestimate the magnitude of Firth's achievements, or his impact on defining the nature of Polynesian ethnology. He gave us the first real glimpse of what a functioning Polynesian society was like, in sufficient detail so that alternative interpretations could be formulated, and in many instances, tested against his data. His voluminous writings, on Tikopia and the New Zealand Maori, have provided us with insights into cultural processes as well as an understanding of form and structure. Firth's later work, following his return visit to Tikopia after World War II, is remarkable for its insights into cultural process. For example, *Rank and Religion* (1970b) illuminates not only the nature of Tikopian religion, but the subtle dynamic factors involved in conversion to Christianity.

Margaret Mead's contributions have stood the test of time less well. There is no doubt that she posed important questions concerning socialization and character development. She can also be credited with initiating the rich tradition in psychological ethnography that is well documented by Jane and James Ritchie in chapter 4. But Mead's work has also been a source of controversy, and questions have been raised about the quality of her fieldwork (Freeman 1983; Holmes 1987).

The connection between ongoing systems and reconstructed Polynesian societies was presumed in Firth's and Mead's studies. Both chose "traditional" settings precisely because they were perceived as more representative of precontact conditions. In seemingly more acculturated settings, anthropologists like Felix Keesing and Ernest Beaglehole initiated studies of culture change during the 1930s and 1940s. These involved attempts to reconstruct pre-European baselines and to assess the impact of missionaries, traders, beachcombers, colonists, and other intrusive agents of Western culture. In their work, too, the reconstructionist and presentist projects merged.

The Presentist Project: Ethnographic Research into Ongoing Societies

World War II interrupted ethnological work in the Pacific, and research was particularly slow to resume in Polynesia following the war's end. Anthropology students from the United States with an interest in the

Pacific were steered toward Micronesia, where the U.S. government had new administrative responsibilities. It was not until the late 1950s and early 1960s that a new group of ethnographers moved into the region. Marshall Sahlins went to Moala, in Fiji; Alan Howard to Rotuma; Allan Hanson to Rapa; and Paul Ottino to Ragiroa, in the Tuamotus. Vern Carroll and Michael Lieber conducted research on Nukuoro and Kapingamarangi respectively, two Polynesian outliers in Micronesia, while Torben Monberg studied Rennell and Bellona, adjacent outliers in Melanesia. Douglas Oliver directed a group in Tahiti that included Ben Finney, Antony Hooper, Paul Kay, and Robert Levy. In New Zealand, Jane and James Ritchie began a long-term project in psychological anthropology among the Maori, and Bruce Biggs initiated his studies of Maori language and culture.

This group of field workers brought with them fresh perspectives and a new sense of purpose. It was a time when the assumptions of functionalist anthropology were being questioned, when cognitive, structuralist, and symbolic perspectives were being explored. But regardless of theoretical orientation or topical focus, the goals of these ethnographers were similar—to detail the ways in which contemporary Polynesian societies were integrated into coherent, functioning systems. They opted for extensive periods of fieldwork, at times ranging over several years, and much of their research was conducted in the vernacular language. In this sense they were guided by the standards for ethnographic research set by Raymond Firth.

From their research a composite picture of ongoing Polynesian societies emerged. Cognatic descent groups, which did not fit the African model worked out by British functionalists, were found to be prevalent; adoption rates were high throughout the region; land tenure patterns revealed a built-in flexibility that afforded everyone at least usufruct rights. The overarching importance of community was also noted. Whether they focused on kinship, political structures, or child-rearing practices, ethnographers remarked upon the degree to which the social commitments of individuals were channeled toward the broader community.

These ethnographers were followed by a continuous flow of students who have helped flesh out the details of social life and personal experience within Polynesian communities. Whereas previously a particular society had been studied by only one or two ethnographers, now some, like Samoa, have hosted innumerable projects. Research topics have correspondingly shifted away from broad scale efforts at portraying societies as cultural wholes toward more focused projects. Students have gone into the field specifically to study medical beliefs, the impact of tourism, the patterning of emotions, or the role of women in the domestic economy. The result has been a set of finer-grained analyses, and a movement beyond general frameworks to an appreciation for the complexities of form and process.

Contemporary ethnographers have thus shifted away from the overarching concern for describing intracultural regularities, which dominated earlier work, toward a concern for the patterning of intracultural variability. No longer do we accept an account from one village as representative of a whole archipelago, for the diversity within each Polynesian society has become increasingly evident. Diversity has no doubt increased as a result of differential acculturation and unique historical conditions, but it is also apparent that Polynesian societies were never as uniform as earlier conceptions implied. As we have moved away from a preoccupation with general forms, we have become increasingly aware of the flexibility of Polynesian social systems, of the degree to which they are able to accommodate variability.

Modern ethnographic efforts in Polynesia are marked by an emphasis on dynamics and the contingencies that shape them. Descriptions of specific events, daily encounters, negotiations, and recorded conversations are afforded a prominent place in recent accounts. The object is not to dwell on the particular or the unique for its own sake, but to use these particularities to comprehend the conditions that shape social life and personal experience. For some the search is for presuppositions and the intricacies of meaning that make life orderly and understandable to the people who live it; for others it is to discover the specific circumstances that initiate and shape observed events.

The Reconstructionist Project: Understanding Societies of the Past

Efforts at historical reconstruction have also changed considerably during the past thirty years, again in the direction of more sophisticated, more finely textured analyses. As Oliver (1974:xi) has noted, "many of the generalizations [previously] current [regarding pre-European Tahiti] . . . were in reality scholars' inventions that had come to acquire 'authenticity' more through reassertion than through retesting with primary sources." Contemporary scholars are more conscientious about consulting early documents, and many have attained a level of linguistic competence that allows them to scrutinize materials written in Polynesian languages. Furthermore, archaeologists have contributed a wealth of entirely new data for consideration.

Cultural anthropologists have come at the task of reconstruction from two directions, one emphasizing change, the other a reinterpretation of existing models. In their concern for understanding change, several anthropologists working in Polynesia have engaged in reconstructionist projects. As part of his project in Tahiti, which focused on sociocultural change, Oliver compiled available materials on the early postcontact period and published *Ancient Tahitian Society* (1974) in three volumes. Greg Dening, a student of Oliver's at Harvard with previous training as a Pacific historian, approached the early Marquesan material more boldly and produced his landmark *Islands and Beaches* (1980). Marshall Sahlins' recent essays, which bring together strands from French structuralist and post-structuralist writings, symbolic anthropology, and praxis theory, have also generated a great deal of interest in the reconstructionist project. In his provocative analysis of Captain Cook's death in Hawai'i (1981a),[1] and his collection of essays published in *Islands of History* (1985), Sahlins demonstrates the power of a theoretically informed interpretive approach to historical encounters.

Interpretive models of precontact Polynesian societies are not, in themselves, a recent phenomenon. Many early ethnologists offered bold interpretations of Polynesian beliefs, rituals, and customs. Nor did Elsdon Best (1924a, 1924b), in his reflections about the ancient Maori, A. M. Hocart (1929, 1952) in his writings about Fiji, and E. S. C. Handy (1927) in his analysis of Polynesian religion, shy away from taking interpretive plunges. But these works, and others like them, were given less recognition than they deserved by ethnologists, who preferred to stay closer to "hard facts." More recently Prytz Johansen suffered a similar fate. His daring interpretation of traditional Maori religious beliefs (1954) was all but ignored until the recent revival of interpretive reconstructionist projects. His writings, along with those of Hocart, Best, and other early interpreters of Polynesian culture, are cited with increasing frequency by modern commentators.

Prominent in the recent interpretive literature has been a reliance on myths as a source of insight into precontact Polynesian thinking. Whereas previously myths held an interest among Polynesianists primarily for their clues to migrational histories, current interest focuses more on what they reveal as symbolic structures about religious concepts and notions of political order. Thus Hanson and Hanson (1983) rely to a great extent on mythical materials to construct an interpretive model of precontact Maori institutions, Howard (1985b, 1986b) interprets Rotuman myths as a vehicle for illuminating traditional political concepts, and Valeri (1985b) interprets the legend of 'Umi in Hawai'i for a similar purpose.

The hazards of taking a bold interpretive approach are well-illustrated by the response to Valeri's (1985a) reconstruction of sacrificial rituals and kingship in ancient Hawaii. Valeri brings a strong interpretive program, grounded in the theoretical writings of Durkheim and his followers, to the Hawaiian material. The work has both been hailed as a brilliant tour-de-force and criticized severely for its alleged misuse of data (see, for example, Charlot 1987 and Valeri's lengthy reply in the same issue of *Pacific Studies;* Howard 1986a; Linnekin 1986). Whatever the hazards, however, many among the current generation of ethnologists are prepared to proceed apace, spurred on rather than deterred by the heated debates.

Out of this revitalized concern for interpretation has emerged a renewed interest in the nature of Polynesian chieftainship. The explorers, traders, missionaries, and colonists were concerned with chieftainship as a practical matter. For them it was of instrumental importance that political stability be maintained so they could get on with their work (see Borofsky and Howard, chapter 8). Hocart (1922) was fascinated by the issue of paramount chieftainship, and used Fijian materials, along with data from elsewhere in the world, to develop a comparative model of kingship. In the 1950s debates were generated by Sahlins' comparative study of *Social Stratification in Polynesia* (1958) and Goldman's (1955) analysis of chiefly status rivalry as the mechanism driving social evolution in the culture area (see Howard and Kirkpatrick, chapter 3). The subsequent publication of Goldman's landmark volume, *Ancient Polynesian Society,* (1970) and Sahlins' recent writings (especially 1981a, 1981b, 1983b, 1985), in which he has shifted from his earlier materialist perspective to one that is cultural and symbolic, have given added impetus to interest in the topic.

The Chapters

The essays in this volume reflect the trends discussed above. Writing about changes in archaeological perspectives, Patrick Kirch (chapter 2) notes that contrary to earlier opinions, stratigraphic excavations in the islands have yielded rich results. In addition to providing a much firmer foundation for inferences about migrations, archaeological materials now provide a solid basis for examining developmental changes within precontact Polynesian societies. Along with changes in archaeological methods have come changes in theoretical views. Kirch describes how Polynesian archaeology has moved from typological through developmental models to an increasing appreciation for the processes of change within such models. "It is now clear," Kirch notes (p. 17), "that the development and transformation of Polynesian societies must be comprehended not against the backdrop of static environments, but rather in the context of dynamic ecosystems that are very much the product of human actions." Human adaptation is depicted as an active process within negotiable environmental constraints. As Kirch emphasizes, the holistic approach is essential here; the study of prehistory flourishes in the interchange between presentist and reconstructionist perspectives.

   Alan Howard and John Kirkpatrick (chapter 3), tracing the history of
issues in social organization, describe a shift in research interests from a
preoccupation with the broad principles of group formation (e.g., kinship versus territoriality, patrilineality versus a cognatic emphasis), to
an examination of more focused topics such as adoption, incest avoidance, gender relations, and exchange. As a consequence, a much more
dynamic, conceptually sophisticated view of Polynesian social organization has been generated. They argue that specific events and social contexts need to be studied closely if we are to fully comprehend the ways in
which Polynesian social life is ordered, and point to a number of shifts
in this direction, singling out Shore's work in Samoa as exemplary. His
account illuminates the characteristic ways in which social forms help to
shape events, constrain relationships, and pattern tensions. Howard
and Kirkpatrick (p. 92) conclude that, "although no single vision unites
the field [of social organization], there is broad agreement among analysts of Polynesian societies on the importance of studying social
dynamics; on the need to integrate accounts of structures and events; on
exchange as constitutive of, not just reflecting or linking social groupings; and on the need to map Polynesians' definitions of situations and
the ways they negotiate meanings."

   Jane and James Ritchie (chapter 4) describe the history of enculturation research in Polynesia and reach similar conclusions. Tracing theoretical shifts through several modalities—from the naturalistic approach
of Margaret Mead, through psychoanalytical, cognitive and learning
theories to ethnopsychology—they arrive at a view that gives context
center stage. Fundamental to Polynesian social metaphysics, they
assert, "is the ease with which social worlds are subject to redefinition,
depending on circumstances" (p. 103). Polynesian cultures represent
adaptations to conflicting interests, overlapping allegiances and multiple solutions to problems, the Ritchies point out (p. 103), and "for
Polynesians any and all solutions are tentative, subject to reformulation
as conditions change." Learning about contexts, how to recognize as
well as to redefine them, is therefore among the most important lessons
a Polynesian child must master. Recent research in the area is notable
for the close attention paid to the details of interactions between parents
and children, and between children and their peers. As a result, we are
gaining fresh insights into the nature of cooperation and competition in
Polynesian communities, the patterning of emotions, reactions to
school environments, and other aspects of thought, feeling, and action.
In the Ritchies' opinion, we are now at a point where these insights
must be applied in the interest of helping Polynesians to cope with the
problems experienced as they adapt to new and rapidly changing environments.

   Underlying the problem of interpreting the nature of Polynesian chieftainship is the rather thorny matter of making cultural sense of the concepts of *mana* and *tapu*. Bradd Shore (chapter 5) reviews the usage of these and related terms in the writings of Polynesianists, and goes on to develop his own interpretation, relating them to key values in the Polynesian worldview. He helps to clarify the cultural logic behind these concepts, and along with it the meaning of rituals that implicate *mana* and *tapu*, the significance of prohibitions placed on women, and the relevance of these notions for chiefly status and performance. "Genuine ethnological insights," Shore (p. 166) notes, "have a way of transforming bits of ethnographic data into significant patterns." His thoughtful analysis is an important theoretical contribution in its own right. The clarification of such central indigenous terms provides us with one of our main avenues for advancing the reconstructionist program, since they reveal the presuppositions that underlie the Polynesian worldview.

George Marcus (chapter 6) points to another research trend, the focus on personhood as a centerpiece for cultural analysis. He describes two recurring chiefly images in Polynesia, one of the chief as a mystified, sacred being, the other of the chief as a respected and admired person. These relate to two aspects of chieftainship, labeled by Marcus as kingly and populist. By framing their studies in terms of personhood, modern ethnographers have emphasized the populist side of chiefs, an understandable trend since the sacred side of chieftainship has been considerably demystified during the twentieth century. With their sacred status diminished, contemporary chiefs are in an ambiguous position. They must situationally negotiate their status, sometimes emphasizing their chiefly prerogatives, sometimes their responsibilities to their constituents. The kinds of issues Marcus sees as important for micro-focused ethnographic research on contemporary chiefs include "How persons acquire chiefly status or office; what strategies of self-presentation they use, given the predicament of their simultaneously alienated and domesticated selves; and how possessing chiefly status maps onto the culturally constructed phases of life of any person" (p. 193). Marcus also directly addresses the reconstructionist project as it relates to chieftainship. He sees in recent research a movement away from stereotypic, and largely static, portrayals of traditional chiefs, to one that aims at uncovering the fundamental dynamics of precontact political systems. The key, in Marcus' view, lies in the dual conception of chiefs, as socially distant, mystified beings whose status was divinely sanctioned on the one hand, and as heroic but approachable persons on the other. The former image is one of chiefs as passive conduits of godly power, the latter image portrays chiefs as active politicians. Although all Polynesian societies shared these cultural notions, the ways in which they were worked out sociologically differed from island to island. As does Shore in his analysis of *mana* and *tapu*, Marcus goes beyond the published material and offers a new synthesis. In tandem, the chapters by Shore and Marcus underscore the excitement generated by interpretive anthropology as its notions and methods are applied to a revitalized reconstructionist project.

Adrienne Kaeppler (chapter 7) contrasts approaches of the past, which took definitions of art for granted and focused on artifacts and performances apart from their societal contexts, with modern approaches. The anthropological study of art and aesthetics cannot be limited to an examination of objects or artistic products, Kaeppler maintains, nor can they be confined to visual forms. Rather, in her opinion, "studies must try to show how visual and verbal modes of expression are embedded in social structure and cultural philosophy, as well as how ritual and belief systems are integrally related to artistic and aesthetic systems" (p. 220). By relating Tongan aesthetic notions to such aspects of social patterning as spatial arrangements, Kaeppler demonstrates the integral nature of underlying principles. She shows how, for example, the structuring of space in Tongan houses and villages and in kava ceremonies parallels bark cloth designs. She discusses a range of recent studies in the performing and visual arts, in which considerable attention is being paid to indigenous conceptions (ethnoaesthetics). In Kaeppler's view (p. 234), "such studies are important to the future of Polynesian studies, not just because of what we have to learn about art and aesthetics, but for what they can teach us about the nature of Polynesian societies and the ways they have changed and are changing."

In our essay on the early contact period (chapter 8), we also stress the progressive refinement of issues over the past few decades. Within the earlier Eurocentric framework of Pacific history, formally appointed agents of Western cultures were seen as the initiators of change. In comparison, the island-centered framework now in favor among Pacific historians stresses the impact of a broader range of participants, including indigenous actors, beachcombers, and traders. This has had the effect of shifting attention away from formal, often ceremonial engagements, to the processes out of which daily life was constructed. In our attempt to construct a comparative framework for understanding the nature of Polynesian-Western interactions during the early contact period, we emphasize the negotiable character of these early encounters. Clarifying the culturally patterned framework within which the various actors— Polynesians and Europeans alike—operated is the key to building an understanding of the processes at work. What was theft to European ship captains, we suggest, might well have been a matter of status rivalry to Polynesian chiefs. From this standpoint Captain Cook's death in Hawai'i was a product of conflicting agendas based on Hawaiian concerns with power and potency and Western concerns with trade and "civilized" behavior. What has been learned from studies of ongoing

Polynesian cultures during the past thirty years puts us in a much better position to interpret such events.

The State of the Art

The current mood among researchers into Polynesian ethnology is one of excitement and intellectual ferment. Virtually every issue posed in the past has been reopened recently and examined afresh, often with startling results. This appears to be one of those periods in intellectual history when previously exclusive viewpoints and approaches are finding sufficient common ground to provide a productive basis for cross-fertilization. Thus archaeology is no longer committed exclusively to unraveling migration paths and points of cultural origin, but has contributed markedly to our understanding of how Polynesian societies developed and changed over time; studies of contemporary, ongoing societies provide vital clues for reconstructionist efforts and vice versa; history vitalizes anthropology and anthropology vitalizes history.

Perhaps the place where this revitalization and cross-fertilization is most evident is in attempts to interpret the history of early contact between Europeans and Polynesians. Doing a proper job demands a thorough knowledge of what Polynesian societies were like at the time, a task that calls for the use of archaeological, linguistic, historical, and ethnographic materials. It requires a sense of the effects of culture on events and of events on culture. It necessitates attention to details and process as well as to form and structure. By closely examining the actions of Polynesians in their encounters with Europeans, and the actions of Europeans when confronting Polynesians, we are given an opportunity to explore the ways in which people from both worlds negotiated out of the fabric of their respective cultures a meaningful accommodation to ambiguous circumstances. Ethnological understanding, it must be emphasized, is by nature a comparative project.

As editors, we feel privileged to be part of this project to explore recent developments in Polynesian ethnology. As scholars, we feel even more privileged for the opportunity to pursue answers to the fascinating puzzles Polynesia presents.

NOTE

1. We use the spelling Hawai'i to refer to the "Big Island" or southeasternmost island in the archipelago and Hawaii to refer to the archipelago as a whole.

2

Prehistory

PATRICK V. KIRCH

THE prevailing attitude toward Polynesian archaeology throughout the first half of the twentieth century is capsulized in Piddington's opinion that "there are definite limits to what archaeology can add to our knowledge of Polynesian material culture," and worse, that archaeologists could provide "nothing more than a duplication of information already available" (Williamson and Piddington 1939:335). Despite the plethora of ethnographic studies that put Polynesia squarely on the anthropological map, Piddington and his contemporaries were convinced that humans had arrived in the islands only within the past few hundred years. The recent time of settlement, the absence of pottery, and the assumption that there had been no significant changes in material culture, discouraged would be archaeological researchers.

In 1947, E. W. Gifford—a veteran of Polynesian ethnography—undertook stratigraphic excavations on Viti Levu, the Fijian "gateway" to Polynesia (Gifford 1951). An abundance of pottery and unmistakable evidence of a complex and lengthy cultural sequence tantalizingly hinted at the real wealth of Oceanic archaeology. Three years later, Kenneth Emory began a trial excavation in the Kuli'ou'ou Rockshelter in the Hawaiian Islands. The abundance and variety of artifacts was surprising enough, but far more important was the dating of a sample of charcoal by W. F. Libby, using his then newly invented radiocarbon technique. The resulting date, A.D. 1004 ± 180, was surprisingly old, and it opened up hitherto undreamed of possibilities for establishing chronologically controlled cultural sequences (Emory, Bonk, and Sinoto 1959). In the same year, Duff (1950) published his study of the "Moahunter period" of New Zealand Maori culture, demonstrating that the Maori of ethnography had developed from a rather different ancestral society.

These studies ushered in the modern era of Polynesian archaeology, and the pace of research has not slackened in the decades since these pioneering efforts. By the close of the 1950s, cultural sequences had been established for many eastern Polynesian island groups (e.g., Emory, Bonk, and Sinoto 1959; Suggs 1961; Heyerdahl and Ferdon 1961; Golson 1959). The Polynesian Culture History Programme, a coordinated multi-institution research effort in the 1960s, extended modern survey and excavation work to the Marquesas, the Societies, Cook Islands, Pitcairn, Samoa, and Tonga (Green and Kelly 1970, 1971; Yawata and Sinoto 1968). Old enigmas of Polynesian origins and dispersal routes succumbed rapidly to the results of archaeological excavation, combined with parallel studies in historical linguistics (Green 1966; Pawley 1966, 1972), physical anthropology, and ethnobotany (Yen 1974). By the 1970s, research issues and questions in Polynesian archaeology had broadened to encompass settlement patterns and the nature of precontact social groupings, the development of agricultural systems, adaptation of technology, and cultural adaptation to ecological constraints. A far cry from Williamson and Piddington's view of a mere duplication of information, Polynesian archaeology has at last come into its own, offering a real diachronic perspective on the development of island cultures.

Several recent works have summarized the new wealth of Polynesian archaeological data, from both culture-historical and theoretical perspectives (Bellwood 1979; Jennings 1979; Kirch 1984a). No attempt is made here to review the cultural sequences of the various island groups, a task that has been covered in the works just cited and in several island-specific syntheses (Prickett 1982; Davidson 1984; Kirch 1985). My aim is rather to survey the major issues and research problems facing Polynesian archaeologists and prehistorians in the 1980s. Some review of current knowledge on particular issues will be necessary; however, my thrust will be on the unknowns and promising directions rather than on a recitation of current information. Before turning to the archaeological record, a brief consideration of island environments is in order.

An Island World

The Polynesian ancestors who voyaged beyond Eastern Fiji to Tonga and Samoa sometime in the late second millennium B.C. were the first people to penetrate remote Oceania and to encounter true oceanic conditions. Beyond Fiji and east of the andesite line, the islands are all pinnacles of basaltic lava, rising from great depths on the Pacific plate. Only New Zealand, one of the last landfalls to be discovered by Polynesians, is an exception to this geological uniformity (as, indeed, it is anomalous in many other facets of its environment). Erosion and sub-sidence of some volcanic mountains resulted in the development of coral atolls, where a volcanic core is capped by coral rock. Some former atolls have emerged above present sea level, creating *makatea* landforms such as Niue and Henderson islands, with their chraracteristic jagged, karst surfaces. The largest and most fertile Polynesian islands are the high volcanic archipelagoes such as Hawaii, Samoa, and the Societies. In these high islands the possibilities for cultural development were espe-cially rich.

The environmental variation that makes Polynesia a region of remarkable value for controlled comparison extends beyond the gross level of geological differences. Island size varies tremendously, from diminutive Anuta with a scant 40 hectares, up through large archipela-goes such as Hawaii (16,692 square kilometers), to vast New Zealand with its 501,776 square kilometers, which has more land than the rest of Polynesia combined. If some tiny high islands and atolls posed environ-mental constraints that were insurmountable (as the abandonment sequences of Nihoa, Fanning, Pitcairn, and some other islands sug-gest), many islands and archipelagoes offered an abundance of re-sources and fertile land. A host of physical and biotic resources are simi-larly unevenly distributed. Witness, for example, the variation in coral reef ecosystems upon which Polynesians depended so heavily for subsis-tence. Certain archipelagoes, such as Tonga, Samoa, and the Societies, have extensive barrier reef and lagoon ecosystems, with great species diversity and an abundance of fish and shellfish. The Marquesas and Easter Island, in contrast, virtually lack coral reefs, and have corre-spondingly depauperate marine biotas.

Climatic regimes likewise range from tropical, with marked wet and dry seasonality (in western and central Polynesia), to subtropical (in Hawaii, Easter Island, and the Australs), to temperate and even sub-Antarctic (New Zealand and the Chatham islands). For ancestral Poly-nesians with a horticultural subsistence base of tropical Southeast Asian–Melanesian crops, the colonization of subtropical and especially temperate environments posed adaptive challenges of great magnitude.

In short, the environmental diversity of Polynesia—geological, edaphic, hydrologic, and climatic—provided a marvelous spectrum of ecological permutations. Not surprisingly, the metaphor of adaptive radiation has sometimes been applied to the diversification of Polyne-sian cultures in contrastive ecosystems (Sahlins 1958:ix). To appreciate the processes of cultural adaptation to the Polynesian environmental spectrum, however, one must venture beyond simplistic notions of envi-ronmental determinism and crude biological analogies. For a start, individual island ecosystems must be analyzed in terms of the particular hierarchies of constraint that they posed to their human settlers. Some constraints were immediate and overwhelming, for example, the lack of potable water on equatorial atolls or the minimal resources available for life support on Necker Island (Emory 1928). Others were temporary but nonetheless severe, such as the recurring cyclones of western Polynesia and the droughts of the Marquesas. There were other limits to particular modes of exploitation and production: the temperate climate of New Zealand, and the streamless topography of Easter Island readily come to mind.

None of these local constraints determined the structure of Polynesian societies; rather, they posed limits to, or offered opportunities for, cultural development. Far from passive, the relationship between Polynesians and their islands was always one in which men and women actively shaped and restructured their habitat. Technologies were modified or invented to alleviate even severe constraints, such as the diversification of angling gear in the reefless Marquesan waters, and the development of semi-anaerobic pit fermentation and storage of breadfruit paste to overcome periodic food shortages resulting from cyclone and drought (see, for example, Barrau 1961:52–53). Landscapes were modified and transformed, often radically, through forest clearance, agricultural expansion, constuction of permanent production facilities (terraces, field systems, fishponds), erosion and deposition, land reclamation, and other activities (Kirch 1983). Often, such activities enhanced productivity and alleviated constraint; not infrequently, however, such transformations of environment set up entirely new hierarchies of constraint, which at times were more challenging than the natural conditions faced by pioneer groups.

Some of the most significant developments of recent archaeology in Polynesia have focused on the dynamic nature of island ecosystems. During the thousands of years that people have occupied oceanic islands, a variety of processes—both natural and cultural—have produced significant changes in their physical and biotic components. The results of long-term natural processes—such as tectonic uplift on Niuatoputapu (Kirch 1978) or climatic change in New Zealand (Leach and Leach 1979)—were often of dramatic consequence to island populations. Equally important, however, were the efforts of human groups in actively constituting their habitats. The deforestation of Easter Island (Flenley and King 1984), the extinction of large avifaunas in New Zealand and Hawaii (Cassels 1984; Olson and James 1984), and the varied geomorphic, edaphic, and floristic transformations of Tikopia (Kirch and Yen 1982) are only examples of widespread processes. The investigation of local sequences of environmental change, and the ascription of causality, are not simple problems. Interdisciplinary cooperation between archaeologists and natural scientists in a variety of disciplines is essential (see, for example, the range of specialist techniques applied in the Waimea-Kawaihae study of Clark and Kirch 1983). It is now clear that the development and transformation of Polynesian societies must be comprehended not against the backdrop of static environments, but rather in the context of dynamic ecosystems that are very much the product of human actions. As Yen and I recently argued on the strength of the Tikopia case, "men reach out to embrace and create their ecosystems, rather than the reverse proposition" (Kirch and Yen 1982:368).

Origins: Ancestral Polynesian Society

More ink has been spilled over the problem of Polynesian origins than on any single topic in Oceanic anthropology. Most early origin theories were promulgated on the basis of detailed trait comparisons, with one or more hypothesized migrations. One of the great achievements of Pacific archaeology has been to temper this migration mentality with the more sober view that the settlement of Oceania was actually achieved through a gradual process of generally west-to-east population movements, with continuous adaptation to the challenges of island life. The Polynesians did not suddenly migrate to Polynesia with their culture fully developed in its ethnographically attested mode. Rather, they descended from ancestral Austronesian peoples who first penetrated the western Pacific more than 4,000 years ago, and who gradually developed unique technical, social, political, and religious patterns.

The Lapita Cultural Complex

The archaeological manifestation of this early Austronesian penetration of Oceania has now been securely established as the Lapita Cultural Complex (Green 1979b), named after a New Caledonia site where it was evidenced, and distinguished by earthenware ceramics with a characteristic decorative system. Geographically, the Lapita complex spans the whole of Melanesia and extends to the western Polynesian islands of Tonga, Samoa, Futuna, and 'Uvea. Lapita sites range in time from perhaps 2000 B.C. up to about 500 B.C. (when they frequently are followed by assemblages containing "Lapitoid" plain ware ceramics). The immediate origins of the Lapita complex are as yet unclear, although the Bismarck Archipelago is a candidate for the region out of which Lapita emerged. Although pottery technology is probably the result of diffusion or influence from farther west, "the existing evidence . . . allows for the development in the Bismarck Archipelago of a widespread social cohesion before the earliest known Lapita sites" (Allen 1984:186).

Excavations in Lapita sites in New Britain, the Santa Cruz islands, Vanuatu, New Caledonia, Fiji, Tonga, and Samoa (see Green 1979b for key references) have greatly amplified our understanding of the cultural complex from which Ancestral Polynesian Society emerged. Lapita settlements, frequently found on small offshore islets or along emerged shorelines (though sometimes buried under alluvial deposits), usually consist of open middens ranging from 1,000 to 10,000 square meters in area. Earth ovens, postholes, trash pits, and scoop hearths have been identified in many sites, but the architecture of Lapita dwellings has as yet eluded archaeologists. A recent exception is my discovery in the Mussau Island Group of preserved wooded bases of a probable Lapita stilt house situated over a former shallow-water lagoon.

Lapita ceramics are well-fired, reddish earthenwares, often tempered with calcareous sand and finished using paddle-and-anvil techniques. A variety of vessel forms are represented, including shouldered pots, jars, open and carinated bowls, flat-bottomed dishes, and plates. Some of these vessel types may have had specialized functions, including use as bowls to serve kava. Although much Lapita ware is plain, the highly decorated component has received the most attention (S. Mead et al. 1973). Lapita motifs, executed with dentate-stamping, incising, and occasionally applique, can be reduced to a limited number of design elements consistently combined according to rigid transformational rules. Such a consistent design system is compelling evidence that Lapita constituted a true cultural complex (Green 1979a). Furthermore, Green (1979b) has shown that this decorative system has numerous ethnographic resonances in Polynesian bark-cloth and tattooing designs. Lapita sites also yield a variety of non-ceramic artifacts, including stone and shell adzes, ornaments, abraders and other tools, fishhooks, tattooing needles, and other items prototypic of later Polynesian material culture.

There is little doubt that the Lapita people were skilled voyagers, capable of maintaining contacts between communities dispersed over hundreds and even thousands of kilometers. Obsidian, metavolcanic adzes, oven stones, glitter rocks, and ceramics are among the materials exchanged or traded between various Lapita settlements (Green 1982; Ambrose and Green 1972). It appears, however, that the large water gap between Vanuatu and Fiji posed a barrier that surpassed even Lapita voyaging capabilities. Following the initial settlement of the Fiji-Tonga-Samoa region by 1600–1400 B.C., there is little evidence of continued contact with the westerly, Melanesian archipelagoes. A distinctive set of Eastern Lapita decorative motifs and other material traits subsequently developed in this region, the threshold of Polynesia.

The Polynesian Homeland

In 1959, Emory made the then bold proposal that the ancestral Polynesians developed their unique cultural traits and language "in a western archipelago in the Polynesian area about B.C. 1500" (Emory 1959:34). The idea was elaborated by Suggs (1960), who interpreted the meager evidence from the region in terms of a succession of settlements: Fiji to Tonga to Samoa. Subsequent archaeological work in Samoa and Tonga (Green and Davidson 1969; Poulsen 1968), as well as in Fiji, appeared to support this viewpoint, with early Lapita ceramic sites in Tongatapu, and later Polynesian Plain Ware sites in Samoa. By 1970, the concept of Tonga as the Polynesian homeland appeared to have been well tested archaeologically. As Groube (1971:313) put it, "the Polynesians became Polynesians sometime near the middle of the first millennium B.C., after over 600 years of isolation in the remote archipelagoes of Tonga. The Polynesians, therefore, did not strictly come from anywhere: they *became* Polynesians and the location of their becoming was Tonga" (Groube's italics).

This idea, appealing in its elegance, was soon shattered by the chance discovery of a submerged site at Mulifanua in Samoa that contained well-decorated Early Eastern Lapita ceramics (Green and Davidson 1974). Clearly, Samoa had not been settled more than a millennium after Tonga; rather, both archipelagoes were colonized soon after the initial Lapita settlement of Fiji. Subsequent archaeological work on Niuatoputapu Island (Kirch 1978) and throughout the Ha'apai and Vava'u groups hinted at the probable existence of early settlements. In short, the Fiji–western Polynesian region was not settled gradually, in an A to B to C manner with significant pauses between settlement events (Green 1981). Rather, the Lapita occupation of the entire region occurred relatively quickly, probably within no more than four centuries.

The concept of a regional homeland for Polynesian culture (as opposed to single island or archipelago) is reinforced by the evidence for continued contact between island groups throughout the first millennium B.C. In particular, there is amazing consistency in local sequences of ceramic change. The transition from Early Eastern Lapita to Late Eastern Lapita and ultimately to Polynesian Plain Ware has been demonstrated for Tongatapu, Niuatoputapu, Samoa, and (partly) for Futuna and 'Uvea, certainly implying substantial intercommunity contact.

Linguistics provides further support for a regional homeland. As Green (1981:152) points out, Proto-Polynesian (PPN) exhibits a large number of shared lexical and morphological innovations, suggesting a "lengthy period of unified development requiring not much less than

1000 years in which to occur." Geraghty (1983) further argues, on the basis of extensive data from the Fijian archipelago, that the simple linguistic model of Proto-Central Pacific breaking up into PPN and Proto-Fijian is inadequate. Rather, "a direct chain developed with Fiji before the settlement of Polynesia, and it was speakers of the dialect of Tokelau Fiji (Proto-Tokelau Polynesian) who settled Polynesia" (Geraghty 1983:381). Following the colonization of the Tongan and Samoan archipelagoes, this dialect chain was presumably further expanded, and persisted long enough for the development of the numerous PPN innovations. The breakup of PPN into Tongic and Samoic branches probably did not occur until at least the middle of the first millennium B.C. (Green 1981:153). In sum, current archaeological and linguistic evidence mutually point to a region—including eastern Fiji (Lau), Tonga , Samoa, Niuatoputapu, 'Uvea, and Futuna—as the homeland in which distinctive Polynesian culture and language developed out of Lapita foundations.

Ancestral Polynesian Society

Although the term Proto-Polynesian provides a handy label to designate the ancestral language from which all modern Polynesian communalects derived, there has been no common agreement on a similar label— or indeed concept—to represent the ancestral culture or society from which all ethnographically attested Polynesian groups descended. I have recently proposed the term "Ancestral Polynesian Society" to designate the social and technological complex that emerged from the Lapita Cultural Complex around 500 B.C. in the region composed of eastern Fiji, Tonga, Samoa, and various smaller islands (Kirch 1984a). I believe that Ancestral Polynesian Society is archaeologically distinguishable from its Lapita forerunner by about 500 B.C. After about A.D. 300, independent developments in various archipelagoes and islands were such that it is no longer reasonable to speak of a unified ancestral society; in other words, by the early first millennium A.D., distinctive early Tongan, early Samoan, and early eastern Polynesian societies had emerged from Ancestral Polynesian Society.

The reconstruction of Ancestral Polynesian Society is one of the more important tasks facing Polynesian archaeology and prehistory, for if we are to achieve any reasonable understanding of the regional transformation of social and technological structures, we must have a clear picture of the baseline society prior to diversification. Such a reconstruction need not be based strictly on archaeological data, and indeed, to restrict ourselves to excavated evidence would severely limit our comprehension of Ancestral Polynesian Society.

A powerful tool for reconstructing Ancestral Polynesian Society is lexical reconstruction. Polynesian linguists have already reconstructed an extensive set of PPN lexemes (Biggs, Walsh, and Waqa 1970), including lists of material culture items, crop plants and domestic animals, settlement pattern components, and more important, terms for social status, ritual practices, and other aspects of culture and society not usually recoverable archaeologically. Similarly, through the careful, controlled use of ethnographic comparison it is possible to project certain practices or social institutions back to Ancestral Polynesian Society. Such controlled ethnographic comparisons are most effective when carried out in conjunction with lexical reconstruction. For example, the principles of lexical reconstruction allow us to state that PPN included a word *qariki, with a generalized semantic referent 'chief'. Controlled ethnographic comparisons between various Polynesian societies permit one to further isolate certain features of Polynesian chieftainship that are widespread, held in common, and are thus probably ancestral in origin (Koskinen 1960).

Ultimately, the reconstruction of Ancestral Polynesian Society requires collaboration between archaeology, historical linguistics, and comparative ethnography, with careful cross-checking of the results obtained by each particular method (cf. Green 1986). Elsewhere I have reviewed the available evidence from these various approaches, and offered a sketch of the broad outlines of Ancestral Polynesian Society (Kirch 1984a). Here, I can only touch upon a few major points. It cannot be overly stressed, however, that the task of reconstructing Ancestral Polynesian Society has only just begun. Archaeologically, our knowledge of the western Polynesian region from ca. 500 B.C. to A.D. 300 is still elementary, focused primarily on ceramics, adzes, and evidence of subsistence patterns. We have yet to areally excavate or extensively sample an entire Ancestral Polynesian village site. Likewise, the potential of controlled ethnographic comparison seems to have been largely overlooked in recent decades, yet it is certain that this method has a great deal more to reveal about the nature of ancestral Polynesian social institutions (see, for example, Marshall 1984).

Material Culture. The material culture inventory of Ancestral Polynesian Society was complex, with most of the region's ethnographically documented items represented. The major exception is ceramics, a component of ancestral material culture in the late first millennium B.C. that ceased to be manufactured anywhere in Polynesia early in the first millennium A.D. Other artifact classes (e.g., adzes) are represented by distinctively early styles, such as the plano-convex sectioned (Type V) adzes. Given the absence, to date, of either dry rockshelters or waterlogged sites of Ancestral Polynesian age, most perishable aspects of material culture (e.g., fishnets, cordage, and other fiber products, barkcloth, and plaited objects) must be inferred from lexical reconstruction.

Subsistence. It now appears incontrovertible that the ancestral Polynesians were agriculturalists as well as skilled fishermen and gatherers of marine resources. Plant remains are scanty in the open middens excavated to date (although *Cocos nucifera* has been identified), but a host of other archaeological and geomorphological evidence leaves no doubt as to the importance of agriculture in the subsistence of ancestral Polynesian communities. Lexical reconstructions and ethnobotanical comparisons suggest that such early agriculture centered on the taro-yam complex (which also included breadfruit, bananas, and a variety of other tuber and tree crops). Shifting cultivation was probably the dominant cropping mode, but the concept and practice of water control (irrigation and drainage) for taro culture was certainly a part of the ancestral agronomic repertoire (Yen 1973). The husbandry of pigs, dogs, and fowl was integral to the agricultural complex.

Marine exploitation contributed significantly to the ancestral Polynesian diet. Archaeological faunal assemblages suggest that fishing concentrated on the inshore reef species, although pelagic and benthic fishes were also taken, along with occasional cetaceans and turtles. One-piece fishhooks of *Turbo* sp. shell have been recovered but are not common, and it may be that netting, spearing, poisoning, and other methods were more important than angling (Kirch and Dye 1979). The gathering of shellfish and seaweed, probably by women and children, further supplemented the diet.

Lexical reconstruction and archaeological evidence both indicate that ancestral Polynesians had developed semi-anaerobic fermentation and pit ensilage of breadfruit and other starch pastes (PPN *ma/masi*). The ability to store such seasonal surpluses provided early Polynesians with an important method of cultural buffering against the famine that frequently accompanied natural disasters such as cyclones and drought (the term for such disaster-induced famine, *onge*, is reconstructable to PPN).

Settlement Patterns. Ancestral Polynesian settlements were largely coastal, multi-household villages or hamlets, although interior settlements are known for Samoa by the early first millennium A.D. (e.g., the Falefa Valley, Green and Davidson 1974). Little is known of house architecture, although there is some evidence for round-ended houses, and for separate dwelling and cooking activity areas. Lexical reconstruction (Green 1986) specified the existence of ceremonial plazas (PPN *malae*), which may have been little more than open spaces where kava and other rituals were carried out.

Social Relations. Current archaeological evidence for ancestral Polynesian social relations is scant, and we must rely almost solely upon comparative ethnographic and lexical data for their reconstruction. Some form of hereditary chieftainship seems unquestioned, although the role of *qariki in the ancestral society is a subject that has barely been researched. Pawley (1979, 1981) offers suggestions as to the Proto-Oceanic origins of the PPN term *qariki, which is derived from an earlier contrast set distinguishing 'chief' from 'first-born of chief'. Koskinen (1960) and Williamson (1924) believed that the ancestral *qariki were more sacerdotal and ritual in their function than they were political. Further efforts to define the nature of ancestral Polynesian chieftainship will be crucial to understanding the processes of social and political transformation among the region's varied societies.

Aside from 'chief', a number of other social statuses are lexically reconstructable for Ancestral Polynesian Society. These include (1) *tufunga 'experts, specialists, or craftsmen'; (2) *toa 'warrior'; and (3) *tautai 'seaman, navigator, fisherman'.

It seems certain that Ancestral Polynesian Society was organized around the pyramidal geometry of the conical clan (Kirchoff 1955), and two kinds of social groups are indicated by the lexical evidence. The larger of these groups was termed *kainanga, presumably a land-holding descent group whose titular head was the *qariki. A closely related term, *kainga, probably refers to a much smaller residential grouping with its associated house lot and garden lands.

The nature of ancestral Polynesian ritual can only be vaguely surmised, although an historical-oriented comparative study of Polynesian religions might reveal much of the original, underlying structure. The existence of ceremonial plazas, PPN *malae, hints at formalized ritual, and several other PPN lexemes refer to ritual: *mori, *lotu, *fa'i. The narcotic *Piper methysticum*, kava, was almost certainly a part of early Polynesian ritual, and the original bowls, *taano'a, may have been ceramic as well as wood.

The Polynesian Dispersal

The colonization of Tonga, Samoa, and the smaller islands of western Polynesia, and the development there of Ancestral Polynesian Society, constituted only the first stage in the dispersal of Polynesian-speaking groups over several million square miles of desolate ocean. The sequence and timing of Polynesian colonizations have been major objectives of archaeological work for the past three decades. In general terms, the settlement of central eastern Polynesia (the Marquesas and Societies) from western Polynesia, and the subsequent radiation from central eastern Polynesia to the marginal extremes of the Triangle (e.g., Easter Island, Hawaii, and New Zealand) have been well documented, and are dealt with at length elsewhere (Jennings 1979; Bellwood 1979). Nevertheless, some enigmas and puzzles remain and deserve comment.

Eastern Polynesian Settlement: Unresolved Issues

Most recent syntheses of Polynesian prehistory accept Sinoto's model of initial colonization of the Marquesas about A.D. 300, followed by a slightly later settlement of the Society group from the Marquesas (Sinoto 1970; Emory and Sinoto 1965; Kirch 1986). Based largely on artifacts excavated from the important Hane Dune Site (MUH 1) on Ua Huka, and from the Maupiti and Vaito'otia-Fa'ahia (ScH 1) sites in the Societies, Sinoto defined an "Archaic East Polynesian Culture," which he maintains was ancestral to all other eastern Polynesian groups (Sinoto 1983). Among the artifact types diagnostic of this Archaic East Polynesian Culture are several types of untanged and incipiently tanged adzes, pearlshell fishhooks, pearlshell breast ornaments, and whale-tooth pendants.

Irwin (1981) expressed dissatisfaction with this orthodox view of the settlement of eastern Polynesia, although his arguments rest largely on negative data. Noting that the Lapita expansion throughout the south-western Pacific was extremely rapid, Irwin questioned whether the pur-ported pause or hiatus between the settlement of western Polynesia and eastern Polynesia (some 1,500 years on present evidence) is reasonable or likely. Given the possibility that early colonizing groups in eastern Polynesia might have abandoned pottery production rapidly, Irwin questioned whether our current chronology for the colonization of east-ern Polynesia is an artifact of low archaeological visibility.

My own dissatisfaction with the orthodox model of eastern Polyne-sian settlement was first spurred by results from the Hawaiian islands, where a series of radiocarbon age assessments on early sites appeared to be out of line with the Marquesan chronology (Kirch 1974, 1985). These dates suggested initial Hawaiian settlement by at least the fourth or fifth centuries A.D., which would make them coeval with the earliest Marquesan settlements, a proposition evidently unacceptable to Sinoto. More disconcerting, these Hawaiian assemblages lack certain artifact types regarded by Sinoto as diagnostic of Archaic East Polynesian Cul-ture (such as the whale-tooth pendants).

A reassessment of the Marquesan data provides ample reason to believe that the accepted date of A.D. 300 for initial settlement is as much as 500 years too late. The dating of the Hane site is more complex than has hitherto been claimed; there are differences in the radiocarbon age series obtained from two laboratories (Kirch 1984a, 1986). In my view, the initial occupation of the Hane site could be as old as 200–400 B.C., which would be consistent with the dates that Suggs (1961) had obtained earlier at the Ha'atuatua site (NHaa 1) on Nukuhiva. Fur-thermore, a site excavated by Sinoto on Hiva Oa Island (site MH-3-11) yielded a radiocarbon date of 1930 ± 80 B.P. (Sinoto, personal commu-nication, 1983). In short, based on the currently available data, a date for initial settlement of the Marquesas during the first few centuries B.C. is reasonable. Such a revision of the Marquesan chronology would also alleviate the purported problem of the Hawaiian ^{14}C age determinations as being too early.

It is also significant that in his definitions of Archaic East Polynesian Culture, Sinoto lumped the artifact assemblages from the three lowest stratigraphic layers at the Hane site. A number of critical diagnostic artifact types, including the important whale-tooth pendants, are absent from Layers VII and VI (Sinoto 1966:fig. 3). The assemblages from these layers provide a very likely prototypical material culture set for the early Hawaiian (as well as Easter Island) assemblages. Furthermore, the appearance of Archaic diagnostic types only in Layer V hints at the possibility that what Sinoto has called "archaic" may actually represent a later, intermediate state in central eastern Polynesian cultural development, not its initial form.

This last proposition is strengthened by evidence from the Society Islands, where the Maupiti and Vaito'otia-Fa'ahia sites, which both contain typical archaic assemblages, date from about the ninth to twelfth centuries A.D. The absence of earlier sites in the extensive and fertile Society archipelago is puzzling, although the probabilities of sampling error are high. The group is geologically subsiding, and it is likely that extensive alluviation has filled valley bottoms and coastal plains since initial human settlement. Such geomorphological conditions would require that any search for initial occupation deposits make extensive use of coring and other subsurface reconnaissance methods, yet nothing of this sort has yet been carried out. The probability that we have yet to discover the first third or so of Society Islands prehistory seems likely; certainly, the lessons from Samoa should engender suspicion (see Green and Davidson 1974).

In short, the orthodox scenario for the dispersal of Polynesians through eastern Polynesia is in need of rethinking along the following lines (Kirch 1986). The initial movement of ancestral Polynesians from the western homeland region probably occurred no later than about 400-200 B.C. (and possibly earlier, pending further work in the Societies). Dispersal of early eastern Polynesians to Hawaii and Easter Island occurred in the first few centuries A.D., prior to the development of the diagnostic material culture set that Sinoto has dubbed Archaic. These diagnostic artifacts reflect a later, intermediate stage in the development of central eastern Polynesian culture, from which the colonization of New Zealand was effected, about A.D. 800–1000.

The Polynesian Outliers

The eighteen small communities of Polynesian speakers scattered along the fringes of Melanesia and known collectively as the Polynesian Out-

liers have remained a backwater of ethnographic, archaeologic, and linguistic studies. Despite important early work on Outlier languages, as
well as the major ethnographic studies on Ontong Java and Tikopia,
our knowledge of the Outliers and their position in Polynesian prehistory remains dim. Even the term "outlier" connotes something apart
from the rest of Polynesia, with the subtle implication that the prehisto-
ries of these small, dispersed communities have little relevance to an
understanding of Triangle Polynesia.

This situation has improved considerably in the past fifteen years.
Linguistic studies by Pawley (1967) and others have clarified the position of the Outlier languages in the larger Polynesian subgroup of Oceanic. All Outlier languages clearly belong to the Nuclear Polynesian
subgroup (despite some Tongic borrowings in Tikopian, Anutan, and
other languages) and are further classified in the lower order subgroup
of Nuclear Polynesian that Pawley termed Samoic-Outlier. The implications of this linguistic model are that the Polynesian Outlier populations derived from the western Polynesian region sometime after the
breakup of PPN, their closest relationships being with Samoa, East
Futuna, and the Ellice islands. Such a model finds resonance in the oral
traditions of settlement voyages recorded from Tikopia, Bellona,
Anuta, and other Outliers (e.g., Firth 1961b; Thilenius 1902).

The first modern archaeology on a Polynesian Outlier was by Janet
Davidson (1968, 1971) on Nukuoro atoll in the mid-1960s. Later work
on Bellona and Anuta revealed the presence of early ceramic assemblages and unexpectedly lengthy settlement sequences. Subsequent
work on Tikopia, Kapingamarangi, Rennell, Taumako, Mele-Fila,
and West Futuna has now greatly amplified the picture of Outlier prehistory (see Kirch 1984b for a full list of references on Outlier archaeology). Although many critical gaps remain to be filled, a consistent pattern is beginning to emerge (Kirch 1984b).

The earliest known Outlier settlements are in the Santa Cruz group,
where colonization of Tikopia, Anuta, and Taumako occurred by
1000–800 B.C., by populations producing Lapitoid plain ware ceramics.
Small quantities of plain ware sherds were also recovered from one site
on Bellona, which dated to about 2070 B.P. In all of these islands, local
production of Lapitoid plain ware ceased around the close of the first
millennium B.C. In Tikopia, the sudden appearance of imported "Man-
gaasi-style" ceramics, along with other cultural traits, strongly suggests
an ensuing period of close contact with Melanesian groups to the south
(the Sinapupu Phase of the Tikopia sequence as defined by Kirch and
Yen 1982). In Anuta, this period is marked by a hiatus, possibly initiated by a major cyclone or combination of natural disasters, which left
the island uninhabited for some time. The complicated Taumako
sequence has yet to be reported in full, but preliminary indications are

that the island was continuously inhabited with some external relationships to the nearby Santa Cruz and Vanuatu groups. In all of these islands, the advent of unambiguously Polynesian traits in the archaeological records is a relatively late phenomenon, dating generally to after A.D. 1000. In Tikopia, such evidence consists of adzes of oceanic basalt, western Polynesian-type trolling lures, and architectural patterns, beginning ca. A.D. 1200. Such evidence accords well with local traditions that refer to the advent of foreign lineages, from such sources as Fiji, Samoa, 'Uvea, and Rotuma.

The prehistoric sequences of the northern atolls (Nukuoro and Kapingamarangi) and the Vanuatu Outliers (Mele, Fila, and West Futuna) have much shallower time depth. Initial settlement of these islands appears to have been by Polynesian speakers, either directly from one of the western Polynesian source islands, or from another Polynesian Outlier. In the case of Mele-Fila, the Polynesian occupation may have replaced an earlier Mangaasi occupation.

In summary, recent archaeological advances have shown the Polynesian Outliers to have varied, sometimes lengthy, and complex settlement histories. Indeed, the time depth for occupation on Tikopia, Anuta, and Taumako is virtually as long as that of the western Polynesian islands. The Outliers can no longer be ignored as irrelevant to the prehistory of greater Polynesia, and indeed, they hold clues vital to the culture history of the entire southwestern Pacific.

Models of Prehistoric Change in Polynesia

Golson (1965:90), remarking on the role of theory in New Zealand archaeology, pointed out that every scholar uses "some formulation current at his time to read the significance of the cultural data before him." These theoretical formulations influence not only how a prehistorian organizes and interprets the data base, but determine to a large degree the kinds of information sought. As Polynesian archaeology has matured over the course of three decades, the issue of culture change has been approached from different theoretical perspectives.

With the post–World War II discovery that Pacific Island sites could yield stratified assemblages of artifacts exhibiting marked changes over time, emphasis was placed on the definition of island sequences based upon a series of historical types. The Hawaiian fishhook chronology, established in the late 1950s as the Oceanic counterpart of ceramic chronology (Emory, Bonk, and Sinoto 1959), Suggs' (1961) typology and seriation of Marquesan fishhooks and coral files, and Golson's (1959) initial exposition of culture change in New Zealand typified this approach. One example of typological sequence building that depended

more upon architecture than portable artifacts is the Easter Island
sequence outlined by Smith (1961) and Ferdon (1961). Sinoto (1966,
1979) remains closely identified with the typological-sequence school of
Polynesian prehistory, particularly in his definition of the Marquesan
sequence.

The typological-sequence approach to modeling prehistoric change in
Polynesia is subject to those shortcomings or omittances that led to its
being attacked by the new archaeologists in North America and
Europe. It is essentialist and normative in theoretical outlook, oriented
primarily toward the documentation rather than explanation of change,
and has generally led to an overemphasis upon the search for rich sites
—those that yield large arrays of portable artifacts. Structural sites,
nonportable artifacts in general, floral and faunal remains, and even
nondiagnostic artifacts have largely been given short shrift (for example, large arrays of lithic debitage have in general been ignored by students of Polynesian artifact typology). Portable artifact typology in
Polynesia has furthermore concentrated on aspects of style, with questions of technological variability, raw material procurement, and the
like rarely posed. Finally, in the exposition of Polynesian prehistoric
sequences based on typology and artifact comparison, little or no
attempt has been made to correlate artifact change with demographic,
ecological, or sociopolitical change.

The typological-sequence approach basically reflects a continuation
of the old fascination with the problem of Polynesian origins, relying
upon the comparison of prehistoric artifact types just as material culture
traits and place names were used in the 1920s and 1930s. The attempt
to specify origin points and migration routes is, of course, a valid part of
archaeological activity. It is in the broader fabric of technological and
social change, however, that Polynesia's real contribution to anthropology lies, a fabric of which material culture is but one thread in an intricate weave.

Broader anthropological concerns are reflected in the work of several
Polynesian prehistorians who have espoused what may be loosely
classed as developmental models of change. This approach characterizes the mainstream of Polynesian archaeological thought and literature. One of the first explicit applications of a developmental model was
Suggs (1961:11) who criticized earlier Polynesianists for a "tendency
towards denial of cultural processes of independent invention, convergence, stimulus diffusion, and obsolescence." Influenced by the then-
prevailing American culture-historical school, Suggs (1961:21) established a four-period sequence for the Marquesas Islands, based on
"socio-political, demographical, economic, and technological factors."
His terminology (Settlement, Developmental, Expansion, and Classic
periods) was intended to convey significant aspects of development

within the Marquesan environmental setting. Although Suggs' monograph focuses heavily on portable artifacts and architecture (he did not conduct anything approaching a settlement pattern survey, and faunal-floral material were largely ignored), his proposed sequence reflected a serious concern with explaining contact-period Marquesan culture as the historical outcome of major ecological, demograhic, and sociopolitical processes. The efflorescence of Classic Period culture was attributed, for example, to three main factors, "each inextricably related to the other: (1) optimal productivity; (2) large population; (3) efficient political organization" (Suggs 1960:128; cf. Suggs 1961:184–187). Although many of the details of Suggs' work have been criticized, his overall interpretations of the internal development of Marquesan culture have not yet been repudiated.

Developmental models have been especially prevalent among New Zealand archaeologists, beginning with Green's (1963) discussion of the "Iwitini" region. His model emphasized structural evidence of settlement type, and incorporated Yen's (1961) model of the adaptation of the sweet potato to the temperate New Zealand climate. Green's approach (1963:25) was to trace the adaptation of an "Early East Polynesian" culture to the New Zealand environment, through a series of socioeconomic stages to its end result, classic Maori culture. For the Iwitini region, Green singled out three interrelated factors crucial to the process of cultural evolution: (1) innovations that were developed in isolation as the people adapted to a non-tropical environment; (2) a favorable environment, which was capable of supporting a large and dense population; and (3) the possible introduction of new traits "as a result of later landfalls by individual canoes" (1963:26). Green's model and Yen's agricultural sequence upon which it is based were subsequently debated heavily (e.g., Golson 1965; Groube 1967), although Green has consistently maintained the theme of New Zealand culture change as "the response in isolation of a Polynesian culture to a non-tropical environment" (Green 1974:38). This theme is echoed in the writings of other New Zealand prehistorians, such as Davidson (1984).

Developmental sequence models of change have been advanced for two other eastern Polynesian societies: Hawaii and Easter Island. For the Hawaiian archipelago, Cordy (1974a, 1974b) outlined a sequence of cultural adaptation and evolution with three stages: (1) an Initial Settlement Period; (2) a New Adaptation Period, in which population growth led to expansion into dry-leeward regions, with concomitant agricultural adaptation; and (3) a Complex Chiefdom Period, marked by a change in social ranking from two to three redistributive levels. Other models of cultural change in Hawaii are presented by Hommon (1976, 1986) and Earle (1978). Hommon recognized that population growth was an important variable in the total equation of sociopolitical change

in Hawaii, but his model also stresses the influence of production techniques, economic expansion, and warfare. Most important, Hommon
pays particular attention to the evidence of sociopolitical structure contained in the abundant indigenous oral traditions. Unlike Cordy and
Hommon, Earle (1978) regarded population pressure as an insignificant variable in the evolution of Hawaiian society. Rather, he stressed
the inherently developmental nature of Polynesian conical clans and
competitive political processes. Most recently, I presented a four-period
model of the evolution of Hawaiian culture, drawing upon five dominant processes of change: reassortment upon colonization, population
growth, environmental change, development and intensification of production, and competition and conflict (Kirch 1985; see also Kirch
1984a).

The cultural sequence of Easter Island, originally defined by
C. Smith (1961) and Ferdon (1961) largely on the basis of religious
architecture, was translated into a developmental scheme by Ayres
(1973:120–134), with the following phases: (1) Settlement and Developmental; (2) Expansion; (3) Decadent; (4) Protohistoric; and (5) Historic. No attempt was made, however, to explain the processes underlying change from one phase to the next.

A recent attempt at outlining a cultural sequence is that of Kirch and
Yen (1982) for Tikopia. Consciously avoiding the usual developmental
terminology, phases were named after key sites (Kiki, Sinapupu,
Tuakamali). Although the main phases were defined, in part, on the
basis of ceramic and other artifact typology, a range of other environmental and economic data were also incorporated in an effort to trace
the 3,000-year evolution of Tikopia culture. A methodological innovation was the application of matrix analysis to provide a quantitative
measure of the rate of change in artifactual and faunal sequences. Commenting on the complexities of the Tikopia cultural sequence, Yen and I
observed that "the processes of change in production patterns do not
correlate precisely with the cultural stages of the island's prehistory. To
attempt such a fit would be to over-apply the evolutionary concept from
two points of view—seeing evolution as proceeding at the same rate
over different aspects of culture, or culture as a single, unconsolidated
human trait" (Kirch and Yen 1982:355).

Developmental sequence models of prehistoric change have dominated interpretations of Polynesian prehistory for at least two decades.
Although most of these sequences have been carefully constructed on
the basis of extensive archaeological data, and as such have much to recommend them, they suffer from several shortcomings. One is the
underlying assumption that cultural evolution proceeds as a series of
successive stages, phases, or periods, a linear model of change. In fact,
as noted for the Tikopia case, different aspects of Polynesian societies

were probably characterized by variable rates of change that were not necessarily synchronized. It was precisely this point that Green and Davidson addressed with regard to the results of their Samoan research.

> We have not discovered in these data, nor found reason to impose on them, a particular scheme of temporal divisions. In large part this is because neither cultural peaks, abrupt changes in cultural content, nor significant clustering of distinctive materials are yet in evidence (Green and Davidson 1974:213).

> Change there was, and it would be wrong to deny it. . . . Still, it can be documented without recourse to a period or stage model. Without such a model, the principal feature of the Samoan sequence is its continuity (Green and Davidson 1974:224).

The prevailing developmental models have other attributes in common, such as the theme of adaptation to environmental conditions, a stressing of economic and settlement-pattern data, and an emphasis on population growth as a dominant causal variable. These attributes are certainly essential components of any informed model of Polynesian evolution. One may argue, however, that this techno-demo-environmental orientation needs to be tempered by a deeper concern with sociopolitical structures, not merely as response or adaptive mechanisms, but as causal variables of cultural change.

Development of Island Societies: Topical Issues

Although the issues of cultural origins and dispersal dominated Polynesian archaeology and prehistory in early years, and remain important research problems, the last two decades have seen a broadening of research aims and problems. The application of new methods and analytical approaches to settlement patterns, subsistence systems, land use, exchange of resources or materials, and similar issues, have added new dimensions to the study of Polynesian prehistory. Polynesian archaeologists increasingly view their data bases as directly relevant to fundamental questions of sociopolitical development and transformation. The remainder of this chapter reviews five issues of major significance to Polynesian prehistory, all the subject of active investigation. I begin with the fundamental problem of demography, for human numbers are a critical issue when considering bounded, insular ecosystems. Current research on production systems and on the impact of production and land use on island ecosystems is reviewed next. Finally, I consider the settlement evidence for social systems, and the problem of the development of social complexity.

Paleodemography

In his opus on ancient Tahitian society, Douglas Oliver (1974:1123) opined that "the principal influence upon social change in these islands was population increase, and not so much by immigration as by steady internal increase." Similar views have been expressed by a variety of archaeologists, ranging from deterministic models in which population growth is held to be an independent variable (e.g., Cordy 1974a:98), to more measured arguments in which demographic change is seen as one of several interrelated variables (e.g., Suggs 1960, 1961; McCoy 1976; Hommon 1976; Kirch 1984a). Regardless of one's position on this theoretical spectrum, several points underscore the significance of demography for an understanding of Polynesian prehistory. First, it is evident, from the prehistoric sequences of all island groups studied to date, that initial colonization was always by relatively small propagules, followed by a period of rapid population growth and expansion. Second, on the majority of islands at European contact, populations were densely settled (ranging from 11 to 120 persons per square kilometer of arable land). Although not necessarily at any maximum level of carrying capacity these populations exerted considerable pressure on local resources, especially in periods of environmental stress (e.g., after cylones and during droughts). Third, statistical analysis of the available ethnographic data indicates that degree of social stratification was positively correlated with population size and density. It would be naive to conclude that population growth somehow determined the level of stratification; on the other hand, it would be equally foolish to assume that demographic variables did not affect the processes of sociopolitical transformation.

Although there are a few scattered references to prehistoric population sizes in the early Polynesian archaeological literature, such as Emory's (1928) effort to estimate the population of Nihoa Island, serious efforts to obtain archaeological data for paleodemographic reconstruction began in the early 1970s. Shawcross (1970), developing concepts of the potential productivity and productive efficiency in the exploitation of coastal resources (an offshoot of the interest in midden analysis in New Zealand archaeology), attempted to estimate the late prehistoric population of New Zealand. Green (1973) applied a similar approach to Tonga, using estimates of arable land and a model of late prehistoric Tongan agriculture to estimate the carrying capacity on Tongatapu. Bellwood (1972) relied more directly on archaeological data, such as frequency of house sites, agricultural terraces, and food-storage pits, to estimate the maximum population of the Hanatekua Valley in the Marquesas. In all of these studies, the emphasis was on estimating maximal pre-contact populations, and no effort was made to determine sequences of demographic change.

One potentially significant source of information on prehistoric population dynamics consists of the large skeletal populations uncovered in some archaeological excavations (e.g., the large burial sites of Mokapu and Puʻu Aliʻi in Hawaii, and the *faʻitoka* burials in the Tonga islands). Techniques for the demographic analysis of skeletal populations, particularly the reconstruction of life tables, have developed rapidly in recent years, yet there are few attempts to apply these methods to Polynesian burial sites. A preliminary analysis of life tables from four Polynesian sites (Kirch 1984a) revealed differences that may prove to be culturally significant. The late prehistoric populations from ʻAtele (Tonga) and Puʻu Aliʻi (Hawaiʻi) have the lowest survivorship rates, while the relatively early Hane (Marquesas) and un-dated Mokapu (Oʻahu) series have higher survival rates. Such differences, if confirmed by further work with larger samples, might indicate the effects of increased population density and pressure on food resources in the later prehistoric sequences of many Polynesian islands.

Ultimately we must develop and refine archaeological techniques of prehistoric census-taking if we are to reconstruct sequences of demographic change over time, and be able to understand the role of population growth in the development and transformation of Polynesian societies. Such census-taking (Ammerman, Cavalli-Sforza, and Wagener 1976) generally depends upon the assumption of a proportional relationship between some class of material objects (e.g., houses, rooms, subsistence remains) and the population that created and used them. In many Polynesian islands, habitation sites are structurally discrete and are thus potentially valid sources of data on prehistoric population. To date, the only attempts to apply such a census-taking approach with settlement pattern data have been in Hawaii.

Hommon (1976, 1980), Cordy (1981), and Kirch (1984a) have all used dated series of habitation sites, from the western side of Hawaiʻi Island and from Kahoʻolawe Island, to derive first-order approximations of prehistoric population growth curves. Despite methodological problems, these preliminary results are encouraging. They suggest that a major period of population growth and expansion began about A.D. 1200–1300, and that in some areas at least, the rate of population increase had declined significantly by about A.D. 1600–1700. In the leeward region of West Hawaiʻi, which lacked the environmental conditions for pond-field irrigation, limits to agricultural expansion and intensification may have been approached, if not actually reached. This could account for the leveling-off seen in the local population growth curve. We also know, however, from recent work on other islands (e.g., in the Anahulu Valley on Oʻahu) that the limits to agricultural intensification had not been reached in many areas, especially those in which conditions favored pond-field irrigation. Further work on prehistoric Hawaiian population growth will thus have to take into consideration the possibility that different demographic sequences are characteristic of local regions within this large archipelago.

Production Systems

Despite the value of early eye-witness accounts of Polynesian subsistence practices, as well as more recent studies of production systems (e.g., Handy and Handy 1972), a thorough understanding of indigenous production systems in Polynesia can only be achieved through archaeological investigation. The pace of change following initial Western contact was so rapid in all island groups that even early historic accounts present a distorted picture of the pre-contact situation. Population decline, the adoption of steel tools and implements, and the rapid rearrangement of subsistence emphases necessitated by ships' provisioning, not to mention subsequent effects of plantation development or cash cropping, are just a few of the factors that rapidly transformed Polynesian production systems. It is not surprising that attempts such as that of Handy and Handy (1972) to characterize traditional Hawaiian agriculture, are biased or distorted when compared against recent archaeological evidence. (This is not to imply that the ethnohistoric corpus is without significance when used critically and in conjunction with archaeological data.)

In addition to providing critical data for the reconstruction of traditional end-point production systems, archaeological research provides the only avenue for tracing the development of production systems in individual archipelagoes. I should note that by production system I mean not only the technical apparatus of production (fishing gear, cultivation tools, permanent agricultural facilities such as pond fields), and the strategies of subsistence activity, but also social relations, including the organization of labor, the control of land and other means of production, and the appropriation and distribution of the product. Archaeologists are more experienced at reconstructing the technical aspects of production, yet as the prospects of a social archaeology improve (Renfrew 1984), the possibilities for understanding the development of production systems in their wider sociopolitical context seem reasonable. The complex forms of political organization characteristic of late prehistoric Polynesian chiefdoms were intimately bound up with intensive production of various kinds (e.g., irrigation and intensive field cultivation in Hawaii). Any attempt to explain the transformation of Polynesian political systems from ancestral forms must also take account of the development of production systems.

Polynesian archaeologists have made significant progress in the reconstruction of indigenous agricultural systems, and of strategies for marine exploitation. The most substantial work on prehistoric agriculture has focused on Hawaii, where the impressive structural remains of taro irrigation attracted initial investigation. The study by Yen et al. (1972) of a fifteenth-century pond-field irrigation complex in the upper Mākaha Valley on Oʻahu Island broke methodological ground with the reconstruction of field evidence for structural change and direct dating of irrigation. Subsequent work by Riley (1975) in Hālawa Valley on Molokaʻi, by Tuggle and Tomonari-Tuggle (1980) in the north Kohala Valleys, by Earle (1978) in the Haleleʻa District of Kauaʻi, by Kirch and Spriggs (n.d.) in the Anahulu Valley on Oʻahu, and other studies have refined our knowledge of the distribution, scale, intensity, and operation of taro irrigation systems in late Hawaiian prehistory (see Kirch 1977 and Earle 1980 for summaries). Important problems remain to be tackled, however, including the temporal development of large scale irrigation systems and their relation to demographic as well as sociopolitical factors.

A major contribution of recent Hawaiian archaeology has also been to demonstrate that intensive cultivation was not confined to irrigation, as often implied in standard ethnographic texts (e.g., Goldman 1970; Sahlins 1958). Notable are the vast dryland field systems of leeward Hawaiʻi Island, which on current evidence began to develop in the fourteenth century A.D. and had perhaps expanded to the limits of arable land by the time of European contact (Kirch 1984a). Investigations of these field systems by Rosendahl (1972), Clark and Kirch (1983), and Schilt (1984) have provided data that will be fundamental in tracing the development of complex chiefdoms in later Hawaiian prehistory.

Substantial progress has also been made on the nature of pre-European Maori cultivation systems, beginning with the important work of Helen Leach (1979, 1984) at Palliser Bay. That work has recently been supplemented by more investigations on field systems surrounding the volcanic cone *pa* sites in the Auckland region. McCoy (1976) added new data on the distribution of intensive garden features *(manavai)* on Easter Island, but more work will be required before a reconstruction of agricultural development for that island will be possible (Yen 1984). In western Polynesia, Kirch (1975) surveyed and excavated in Futunan taro irrigation systems that were comparable in scale to those of Hawaii, while Green and Davidson (1974) have presented tantalizing data suggesting the former presence of extensive swamp cultivation systems in Western Samoa. Throughout most of tropical Polynesia, however, archaeological studies of prehistoric agriculture have yet to be initiated.

The role of marine exploitation and hunting and gathering in the subsistence of precontact Polynesians has received substantial archaeological attention, with a plethora of quantitative faunal studies and investigation of fishing gear. Progress is especially noteworthy for New

Zealand, where the work at Galatea Bay (Shawcross 1967; Terrell 1967), Mt. Camel (Shawcross 1972), and Palliser Bay (Leach and Leach 1979) are just a few examples of the advances achieved in our knowledge of prehistoric diet and economy. In Hawaii, midden analysis is a standard part of archaeological procedure, but there has been little effort to critically review the mass of quantitative data in terms of marine exploitation strategy (see, however, Kirch 1979, 1982b; Goto 1984). Kikuchi (1976) reviewed and synthesized the surface structural evidence for the Hawaiian fishponds, a unique development within Polynesia, representing the intensification of marine exploitation in the direction of true aquaculture. Ayres (1979) addressed Easter Island fishing, while in central eastern Polynesia, I outlined the Marquesan faunal sequence (Kirch 1973), and Sinoto and his colleagues have added some data on prehistoric fishing and marine exploitation (Sinoto 1970, 1979). In western Polynesia, the studies of Davidson (in Green and Davidson 1969) and of the Utah group (Jennings et al. 1976; Jennings and Holmer 1980) on Samoa, and those of Poulsen (1968) and Kirch and Dye (1979) for Tonga, have added data both on fishing gear technology and on marine exploitation strategy. For the Outliers, substantial data on marine exploitation and fishing have come from Anuta (Kirch and Rosendahl 1973), Tikopia (Kirch and Yen 1982), Nukuoro (Janet Davidson 1968), and Kapingamarangi (Leach and Ward 1981).

Southern New Zealand (the area south of the Banks Peninsula) and the Chatham Islands offer an intriguing field of study, since these areas lay beyond the limits of Polynesian agricultural technology. In Southland and the Chathams, archaeologists have the opportunity of investigating rapid transformation of a former horticultural-based production system into one dominated by hunting, fishing, and gathering. Recent work by Anderson (1982a, 1982b), Sutton (1980), Hamel (1982), and others has done much to advance our knowledge of Archaic economic patterns, demonstrating that the diversity and complexity of subsistence strategies renders the old term Moa hunter a misnomer.

As the foregoing review suggests, archaeological work on Polynesian production systems has emphasized subsistence aspects, concentrating on the rich data provided by faunal materials and extractive and exploitative material culture. Increasingly, however, prehistorians are widening their scope of inquiry to encompass such non-subsistence aspects of production as craft specialization, procurement, and exchange of scarce or unevenly distributed resources (e.g., obsidian or fine-grained adz stone), and production to support or underwrite monumental architecture.

Although the reconstruction of economic patterns has improved our understanding of variability in precontact Polynesian production systems, the wider anthropological issues rest with attempts to trace the development of production systems over relatively long periods of time. The development of production systems can be analyzed in terms of three major components: adaptation, expansion, and intensification. Adaptation of production systems in Polynesia generally occurred early in the occupation sequence of particular islands or archipelagoes, in response to new environmental conditions and constraints. The expansion of production is a quantitative process that often appears to be directly linked to expanding populations (but which can also be related to the rise of a powerful chiefly class). Most interesting from a theoretical point of view, however, is the intensification of production (Brookfield 1972), since this involves a changing relationship between labor and the means of production. Agricultural intensification thus implies transformation of the social and political relations that structured the organization of labor, and the distribution of the increased product (often appropriated as surplus). Polynesian archaeologists have hardly tackled the complex issue of intensification of production, but instances of intensification abound throughout the region, including the irrigation systems of Hawaii, Rapa, and Futuna, dryland field systems in Hawaii and New Zealand, the substantial pit ensilage of breadfruit pastes in the Marquesas, Mangareva, and other islands, and the extensive fishponds of Hawaii. Already, it is clear that simple demographic explanations will be insufficient to account for such intensive developments, which must be understood in the context of changing sociopolitical structures. As Polynesian prehistorians turn increasingly to these fundamental issues, the potential for serious dialogue among archaeologists, ethnologists, and ethnohistorians should dramatically increase.

Human Impact on Ecosystems

Earlier generations of anthropologists tended to view island environments as static, changeless canvases—more of a backdrop than an integral part of the cultural scene. Most Polynesian ethnographies commence with a perfunctory section on the local setting, never again to raise the question of culture-nature interaction. If an environment was seriously discussed at all, it was usually in the context of cultural adaptation to environmental constraints.

A rapidly developing research area in Polynesian archaeology is the impact that prehistoric human populations have had on island ecosystems—including both physical and biotic components—and the implications of such changes for the island societies. Research to date has centered on only a few islands, but it is increasingly certain that Polynesians extensively modified virtually every island ecosystem they colonized. Future efforts to understand the evolution and transformation of island societies will have to account for the effects of a dynamic ecological context. In several recent papers, I have reviewed the rapidly accumulating evidence for human impact on island ecosystems (Kirch 1982b, 1983, 1984a). Here, I confine my discussion to four kinds of human influence: (1) the introduction to remote and fragile island ecosystems of exotic biota; (2) deforestation; (3) erosion and deposition; and (4) faunal extinction and depletion.

Fosberg (1963a, 1963b) eloquently summarized the fragility of remote Oceanic ecosystems, with their endemic, specialized, and vulnerable biota. On their voyages of colonization Polynesians carried with them a variety of domestic plants and animals, with the intention of purposefully introducing these in the new landfall. A wide range of inadvertent, synanthropic stowaways also accompanied Polynesian voyagers, and the impact of these highly competitive species (along with the domestic crops and animals) on the native biota was often dramatic. Among the transported synanthropic or anthropophilic species found in recent excavations are several genera and species of land snails (Christensen and Kirch 1981, 1986; Kirch 1973), geckos and skinks, rats (virtually ubiquitous), and various weeds. All of these species were either highly competitive or directly predatory, and quickly proliferated throughout the lower elevations of Polynesian islands. By the time that botanist David Nelson on Cook's third voyage collected the common coastal plants of Kona, Hawai'i, a variety of exotic weeds were dominant elements in the flora.

More significant was the direct replacement of native habitats through forest clearance, particularly with the use of fire. At initial European contact, most Polynesian islands had extensive tracts of terminal grass or fernland vegetation; some islands, such as Easter and Mangareva, lacked forest entirely. These were not natural vegetative communities, and human impact was clearly responsible for the extensive deforestation of these islands. The evidence is especially dramatic for New Zealand, where recent pollen work (McGlone 1983) demonstrates that something on the order of 32,000 square kilometers were deforested between the time of Polynesian colonization and European settlement. Flenley's palynological studies of three crater lakes on Easter Island (Flenley and King 1984) similarly reveal that the island was originally forested, and that the modern treeless landscape is an artifact of human exploitation and impact. Such environmental change was not without significant consequences for the human population. Consider, for example, the stress on late prehistoric Easter Island society as supplies of firewood and hardwoods for canoe building, house construction, and other uses dwindled rapidly and then disappeared. It is not too much to suggest that the catastrophic collapse of Rapanui society was intimately bound up with this rapid deforestation (McCoy 1976; Kirch 1984a).

As communities of native vegetation were altered and replaced with cultivation and savannahs, the landscape was frequently exposed to erosion and redeposition of sediments. The most dramatic evidence for human-induced landscape change in Oceania to date comes from outside Polynesia, in Aneityum, where Spriggs (1981) demonstrated massive erosion and valley infilling that made possible late prehistoric intensive irrigation. Within Polynesia, the evidence for substantial rearrangement of landscapes is rapidly accumulating. In the Canterbury region of New Zealand, extensive deforestation seems to have had a major effect on local geomorphic regimes (Molloy 1967). Hughes et al. (1979) demonstrated local erosion due to burning in the interior of Lakeba Island in the Lau Group, and I discovered the late Lapita site of Tavai on Futuna under more than two meters of erosional sediments (Kirch 1981). On Tikopia, Kirch and Yen (1982) argued that human-induced erosion resulted in the creation of the island's most productive agricultural soils. Patricia Beggerly's (personal communication, 1984) ongoing research in Kahana Valley in Hawaii promises to yield similar evidence of major valley-infilling, which facilitated the development of late prehistoric irrigation systems.

For decades, New Zealand moas, a diverse group of struthious, flightless birds, constituted the only known case of faunal extinction in Oceania. Moas were exploited heavily by the early Polynesian settlers, who were dubbed "moa hunters" as a result (Duff 1956). Recent studies have shown that the Polynesians were responsible for the extinction of species other than moas, including rails, a gallinule, a coot, geese, ducks, an eagle, a crow, and harriers (Cassels 1984). Nor is New Zealand any longer unique. The dramatic discoveries of numerous new species of extinct birds in Hawaii, including large flightless geese and ibis, but also many honeycreepers, rails, crows, and other species have opened our eyes to the effect of human-induced habitat modification on island biotas (Olson and James 1984). Even on tiny Tikopia, the early colonists quickly extirpated the megapode, and possibly a small rail (Kirch and Yen 1982). Recent finds of extinct birds on Mangaia, and on remote Henderson (Steadman and Olson 1985) hint that we have just scratched the surface with regard to human-induced extinction of island avifaunas. Similarly, human populations had substantial effects on local animal food resources, such as shellfish (A. J. Anderson 1979, 1981).

The old concept that Polynesians developed their island societies in a range of diverse, but largely static environments, is now unacceptable. The island landscapes recorded by early European voyagers had been extensively modified through the introduction of exotic biota, by forest clearance and habitat modification, erosion and deposition of sediments, and faunal and floral extinctions. Some of these effects were advantageous to the Polynesian populations, such as the creation of fertile, irrigable floodplains through erosion and valley infilling. Other modifications may have been disastrous, such as the deforestation of Easter Island and Mangareva. Only as research on the human impact on island ecosystems advances over the next few years will we gradually understand the role of changing environments in the transformation of Polynesian societies.

Space, Settlements, and Society

A vital aspect of Polynesian archaeology for more than two decades, the settlement pattern approach has virtually dominated the direction of archaeological research in the region. An explicit focus on the spatial organization and interrelationships of settlements was first applied in Oceania by R. C. Green who, as a Harvard graduate student, was exposed to the early settlement pattern studies of Gordon Willey and K. C. Chang. Green's survey of the 'Opunohu Valley on Mo'orea (Green 1961; Green et al. 1967) demonstrated the value of this approach in Polynesia, and comparable projects were soon developed in Hawaii, New Zealand, and Samoa. An impressive set of literature on settlement patterns now encompasses all of the major island groups (see Kirch 1982a:78–81 for key references).

Within Polynesian settlement pattern studies it is possible to delineate four different approaches (perhaps they should be termed emphases). The first approach focuses primarily upon the spatial distribution and organization of sites as indicators of the ecological adaptation of Polynesian populations to local environmental conditions and constraints. This approach has been especially developed in Hawaii, where differences in local settlement patterns have been interpreted in terms of the varying constraints of windward valley, leeward valley, and leeward slope environment (e.g., Kirch and Kelly 1975; Green 1980; Tuggle and Griffin 1973). The second approach emphasizes the social dimensions of settlement patterns; that is, it attempts to recognize or reconstruct patterns of social grouping in the spatial arrangement of sites and features. This was the main thrust of Green's early Mo'orea work (Green et al. 1967), and it has continued to be an important aspect of settlement pattern studies throughout the region; for example, the work of the Utah group in Samoa (Jennings, Holmer, and Jackmond 1982), and that of Kellum-Ottino (1971) in the Marquesas. Indeed, the majority of Polynesian archaeologists have tended to see both ecological and social factors as closely linked (Bellwood 1979:319), and the two approaches have often been applied in consort.

The third and fourth approaches are less developed, though they appear to be on the rise in Polynesian archaeology. Rather than an explicit social focus, the third approach is concerned with the reconstruction of economic and political structures, such as the control and distribution of limited resources (e.g., fine-grained adz stone or obsidian). The fourth approach is allied with an increasing interest in symbolic or structural studies in archaeology, and attempts to understand the semiotic value of space in ancient Polynesian communities. Clearly, this latter approach depends heavily upon the use of the ethnographic record, and on the application of a direct historical approach. Recent examples of this fourth approach to settlement patterns include Prickett's (1979, 1982) reconstruction of spatial patterning in the Maori dwelling, and the interpretations of Weisler and Kirch (1985) regarding the symbolic patterning of space in the late prehistoric community of Kawela, Moloka'i.

One of the fundamental units of all Polynesian settlement patterns is the household cluster (or, as it is sometimes termed, the household unit, HHU, or residential complex). McCoy (1976), in his analysis of late prehistoric Easter Island settlement patterns, was one of the first to focus explicitly on the household cluster. In his 19.7 square kilometer study area, households were archaeologically manifested by repetitive associations of dwelling houses (indicated by stone-curbings or pavements), earth ovens, chicken houses, and garden enclosures. Clusters associated with higher-ranked households were situated close to the coast in proximity to the major *ahu* 'statuary temples', while those of commoners were dispersed inland.

The prehistoric Samoan household cluster has also been the focus of considerable study, first by the University of Auckland group under Green and Davidson (1969, 1974), and later by the Utah group under Jennings (Jennings et al. 1976; Jennings and Holmer 1980; Jennings, Holmer, and Jackmond 1982). The household units or HHUs analyzed by Jennings and his colleagues are readily recognizable as clustered platform groups surrounded by stone walls or boundaries, with one edge frequently bordering a pathway. HHUs of higher status groups are indicated by differences in platform size and volume, and often by the associated presence of large earth ovens *(umu ti)*. The Utah group brought their study of HHUs forward into the ethnographic present with the mapping of a contemporary village, Fa'aala on Savai'i Island. As a result, they have demonstrated that "the use of space, the importance of HHU boundaries, the importance of rank in the disposition of households along the paths, and other organizing principles appear to have been stable for 500 to 600 years on both Savai'i and Upolu and to have survived large population fluctuations and changes in village size" (Jennings, Holmer, and Jackmond 1982:100); and, it might be noted, the advent of missionization.

Late prehistoric Hawaiian household clusters varied considerably in

space, and incorporated a temporary-permanent component, as indicated by the Hālawa, Lapakahi, and Mākaha projects (Kirch and Kelly
1975; Tuggle and Griffin 1973; Rosendahl 1972; Green 1980). On
Moloka'i Island, Weisler and Kirch (1985) recently completed an intensive study of household clusters in two leeward *ahupua'a* units. All
household clusters in this study area shared common architectural components, such as a primary residence unit and separate cookshed, and
usually a lithic activity area. The household clusters occupied by higher
status groups were readily distinguishable, not only by architectural
features (such as the presence of enclosed stone shrines or temples), but
by faunal and artifactual indicators (e.g., presence of pig and dog bone,
and of fine-grained adz stone).

The studies cited above are only a partial sample of works dealing
with Polynesian household clusters, but they are sufficient to indicate
the potential of a settlement pattern approach for delineating prehistoric
social groups. Unfortunately, virtually all such studies have concentrated on late prehistoric sites, and relatively little is known of Ancestral
Polynesian or Early Polynesian household units. Future efforts at tracing the development of household clusters over longer time spans may
yield essential information on basic structural changes in Polynesian
societies.

Settlement patterns, of course, are not simply redundant repetitions
of HHUs, and attention must be devoted equally to the more specialized components such as community houses, burial monuments,
shrines and temples, and fortifications. Green's Mo'orea work (Green
et al. 1967) remains a classic demonstration of the social information to
be obtained by a comparative analysis of both community houses and
marae sites. On Easter Island, a detailed structural and spatial study of
ahu promises to reveal the changing political structure of the island over
the later prehistoric period (Cristino and Vargas 1980; Stevenson 1984).
In New Zealand, a plethora of studies have focused on the fortified *pa*
sites, which dominate the archaeological landscape (Fox 1976; Davidson 1984), providing data on the origins of this unique type of settlement pattern and on the internal structuring of *pa* communities.

In many areas of Polynesia, however, the potential for settlement pattern studies has yet to be fully realized. For example, the varied artificial mounds that dot the Tongan landscape have yet to be studied
beyond the level of simple descriptive typology. In Hawaii, despite
decades of interest in the abundant *heiau* (which display an almost bewil-
dering variability), there is not yet a comprehensive spatial study of the
distribution of temple sites over even a single island. *Heiau* sites encode
a great deal of untapped sociopolitical information on the structure of
the late prehistoric chiefdoms. Certainly, the study of settlement patterns is an aspect of Polynesian archaeology that has yet to reach its full
potential.

In this brief overview of settlement pattern studies I must note two massive survey efforts that are on a scale above anything else in Polynesia. The first of these is the nearly complete survey and recording of settlement components (2,337 discrete features) on the entire island of Kaho'olawe, which for a variety of historical reasons escaped serious land modification during the historical period (Hommon 1980). The voluminous data generated by this project have yet to be published in full, let alone analyzed in any detailed fashion; they comprise a tremendous resource for understanding Hawaiian prehistory. The second major project, still incomplete, is the comprehensive mapping and recording of all Easter Island sites, an even more massive undertaking than the Kaho'olawe Project. The Easter Island survey was initiated by McCoy (1976), and has been vigorously pursued since then by the Easter Island Studies Institute of the University of Chile, under the direction of Claudio Cristino (Cristino, Vargas, and Izaurieta 1981). As of 1981, a preliminary *Atlas* published by the project gave the locations of 9,213 features in 12 quadrangles. The concept of a 100-percent survey of all archaeological manifestations on an island the size of Rapanui is unprecedented in Oceania, and when completed this data base can be expected to provide grist for the archaeological mill for decades to come.

Development of Social Complexity

The early and continuing attention paid by European savants and scholars to Polynesian societies was due in part to the aristocratic aspects of their polities. As ethnography and anthropology acquired a more systematic character, the value of Polynesia for theoretical excursions into the nature of complex, pre-State political systems continued to be evident. Although all Polynesian societies form a closely related set, demonstrably descended from a common ancestral group, they display a remarkable range of sociopolitical complexity. Atoll societies such as that of Pukapuka are barely chiefdoms (using the classic definition of the term), with little hierarchical differentiation, and a great deal of functional redundancy between household units. Most of the high island societies, however, displayed considerable stratification and functional specialization. In the most elaborate cases—Hawaii and Tonga— one discerns a structural rift between a conical clan of chiefs (itself internally ranked) and a class of commoners, as well as such institutions as hypergamy, a state religious cult, corvée labor, and numerous material symbols of status and rank (feathered headresses and cloaks, large houses, and monumental burial structures). Using the Marxist terminology of Wolf (1982), these latter societies had undergone a transition from a kin-based to a tribute-based mode of production.

Efforts to explain this differential development of social complexity in Polynesia have a long history. Early attempts such as Handy's (1930) depended upon diffusionist principles: for example, in Tahiti the *ari'i* class was interpreted as invading and conquering the early *manahune* population. Williamson and Piddington (1939) rightly criticized this approach, and Burrows (1939a, 1939b) suggested several cultural processes that might have led to the internal differentiation of Polynesian societies. The two classic studies of social complexity in Polynesia are, of course, those of Sahlins (1958) and Goldman (1970). To oversimplify their arguments, Sahlins accounted for social stratification by using an ecological model that stressed the functional role of redistribution, while Goldman emphasized the status rivalry inherent in Polynesian society. With the hindsight of nearly two decades, both models offer insights, yet both are incomplete and flawed (Kirch 1984a).

All of the above studies depended upon synchronic data—ethnographic description of Polynesian societies at the European-contact endpoints of development—in order to generate models of temporal process. Yet only archaeology has the ability to generate truly diachronic information that will permit us to trace aspects of social change in Polynesian societies through time. Indeed, now that Polynesian prehistory has moved beyond its earlier preoccupation with origin dates and migration routes, the potential for understanding the temporal development of social complexity in particular islands is becoming a reality. In these efforts, however, we need not abandon the older approach of synchronic ethnographic comparison. Rather, as several authors have suggested (Kirch 1984a; Green 1986), a tripartite approach to understanding and explaining Polynesian social complexity will be most rewarding. In brief, the components of such an approach are (1) the controlled use of ethnographic comparisons in order to define common and original structures of Polynesian societies, as well as unique developments; (2) the use of lexical reconstruction to further our understanding of certain domains in Ancestral Polynesian Society and other reconstructable nodes (cf. Green 1986); and (3) the application of archaeological methods to work out detailed temporal sequences in particular environmental settings. Such an approach, requiring cooperation and collaboration between ethnographers, linguists, and archaeologists is not without problems (such as differing analytical concepts and kinds of data), but ultimately should lead to a richer understanding of sociopolitical change in the region.

To date, relatively few Polynesian archaeological studies have explicitly addressed the problem of social complexity. Suggs (1961) paid some attention to social change in his interpretation of the prehistoric sequence on Nuku Hiva in the Marquesas, and stressed the importance of both population growth and status rivalry. Most recent efforts have, however, centered on the Hawaiian case (Earle 1977, 1980; Hommon 1976, 1986; Cordy 1974a, 1974b, 1981; Kirch 1985). Focusing empirically on the role of irrigation in the political economy of the Halele'a District on Kaua'i, Earle argued that population pressure was not a significant factor in the development of stratification; rather, he stresses the high returns of chiefly investment in irrigation infrastructure. Cordy, on the other hand, has espoused an explanation of Hawaiian sociopolitical complexity in which population growth is regarded as an independent and largely determinant variable. Hommon's model takes the middle ground, and while noting that both demographic change and chiefly competition were significant factors, also draws attention to the process of inland expansion and the formation of the *ahupua'a* system.

In a recent monograph (Kirch 1984a) I apply the tripartite approach described above to the problem of the evolution and transformation of Polynesian social, economic, and political systems. Lexical reconstruction, controlled ethnographic comparisons, and archaeological evidence each contribute to the reconstruction of Ancestral Polynesian Society, and thus help to define the baseline from which later Polynesian societies diverged. Such divergence and differentiation can be analyzed in terms of five major processes: (1) the founder effects of colonization and the adaptation of culture to new and frequently radically different environments (what Yen has referred to as reassortment); (2) the growth, frequently rapid, of large and dense populations; (3) environmental change, including long-term natural processes (e.g., tectonic shoreline change), short-term stochastic fluctuations or perturbations (e.g., cyclones, drought), and human-induced alteration of habitat; (4) the development and intensification of production systems; and (5) competition and conflict between social and political groups. In a contrastive analysis of social, economic, and political transformation in three island groups (Tonga, Hawaii, and Easter Island), I have attempted to demonstrate how each of these processes contributed to the formation of distinctive social and cultural patterns. At the same time, however, the retention of certain ancestral traits and institutions indelibly mark all three ethnographic endpoints as distinctively Polynesian.

Summary

In the preceding pages I have endeavored to sketch the modern development of Polynesian archaeology and prehistory, from its renaissance after World War II, through a phase dominated by a quest for origins and migrations, to more recent emphases on settlement patterns, sequences of sociopolitical change, the role of demography in culture change, human impact on island ecosystems, and other issues. I have also tried to point out areas of disagreement, or those which require more work. Polynesian archaeology is still young, and we have only begun to amass a sufficient data base about which truly significant questions can be posed.

Our best understanding of the Polynesian past is achieved when all of the methods and perspectives of a holistic anthropology are brought to bear. Thus, as I have pointed out, the reconstruction of Ancestral Polynesian Society depends as much upon historical linguistic subgrouping and lexical reconstruction and on systematic comparison of ethnographic patterns (of which Marshall 1984 is a superb example), as upon direct archaeological evidence. In writing this, I do not mean to imply that archaeology is dependent upon ethnography either for its conceptual development, or in order to achieve substantive results. Indeed, I would echo Flannery in his recent admonition that "if evolution is what you are interested in, then anthropology includes archaeology or it is nothing" (1983:362). My point is simply that for those of us who wish to understand the Polynesian past in all its rich detail, holistic anthropology is still the best approach.

3

Social
Organization

ALAN HOWARD
JOHN KIRKPATRICK

NEARLY all topics of interest to contemporary anthropologists are understood in relation to social organization. As a result, social organization is depicted in many different ways—as extended description, as formal models that focus on social structure or specific processes, or as capsule descriptions of central features. Social organization is thus not a neatly bounded field of inquiry in which a single theoretical scheme prevails. Rather, it is a field in which intersecting perspectives offer a variety of insights, provoking debates but at the same time offering possibilities for synthesis. Evolutionary approaches vie with synchronic ones, comparative schemes are met by particularistic rebuttals, and cultural analyses are offered as alternatives to ecological explanations. But amid the apparent turmoil we perceive some significant trends, and perhaps the emergence of a synthetic perspective that promises to yield a much finer understanding of how Polynesians ordered, and continue to order, their social worlds. To provide a basis for understanding theoretical tensions, and how recent work bears upon them, we take a historical approach in this chapter.

Attempts to grasp the fundamental features of Polynesian social organization began with the explorers. Their accounts, like those of other early voyagers, suffered from a dearth of concepts suitable for describing basic forms of social life, much less the nuances of ideology and interaction. These limitations constrained the interpretations of most early commentators, for whom forms of social organization were primarily of interest insofar as they reflected sequences of migration. Characteristically, those forms associated with commoner status were attributed to early migrations of people of inferior stock, while those associated with chieftainship were attributed to subsequent migrations of culturally or racially superior peoples. Typical was the two strata theory that hypothesized that the original Polynesians were an egalitarian people with a clan organization, but without a highly developed political system. They were presumably followed by a later wave of neo-Polynesians who brought with them well-developed political institutions complete with court etiquette, dynastic traditions (with a strong emphasis on seniority and genealogical precedence), social ceremonialism, and notions of social caste (see, for example, E. S. C. Handy 1930). A similar approach is found in the writings of Thor Heyerdahl (1950, 1952, 1958). He attributes the monumental sculptures on Easter Island and other marks of high culture to conquerors descended from Old World migrants. Such perspectives were no doubt encouraged by Polynesian myths that associate chiefs with stranger kings (Sahlins 1981b; Howard 1985b; Marcus, chapter 6, this volume).

Although fascination with Polynesian origins stimulated scholarly pursuit, interest in political structures was a practical matter for those Europeans who established trade, missions, and eventual colonial governance. They required surety with regard to who was authorized to make agreements that would hold over a period of time. To their dismay, Europeans often found it difficult to identify a clear-cut institutionalized hierarchy, but they were determined to have a recognizable form of chieftainship, and so set about creating it by elevating one of a number of rivals to a position of paramountcy wherever they could, then giving that individual material and ideological support.[1]

Descriptions of more mundane aspects of social life—kinship and kin groups, family structure and the division of labor, land tenure, and adoption practices—were generally colored by a pronounced ethnocentrism, with moral judgments as often explicit as implicit. Ceremonies were seen as amusingly barbaric, reciprocal exchanges as extravagances (or a failure to recognize the proper value of commodities), adoption practices as indications of parental indifference to the fate of their children, and so it went. It is not surprising, therefore, that nineteenth century evolutionists placed Polynesian societies well down the developmental ladder, often lower than would be warranted on the basis of technology.[2]

Early accounts of Polynesian social organization were thus biased in a number of ways, ranging from simple omissions to gross inaccuracies. But while such faulty accounts rendered the task of reconstructing traditional social life an exceptionally perilous one, it did not deter armchair anthropologists from the attempt. As standards for evidence rose, however, the need for fresh appraisals and systematically collected information soon became apparent.

The modern period of social analysis in Polynesia began in the third decade of this century with the efforts of Robert W. Williamson (1924, 1933). Williamson's major contributions consisted of compiling the relevant materials and sifting through them with an appropriately critical eye, but he was hampered by the lack of a suitable framework for interpreting them. He nevertheless recognized many essential features of Polynesian social organization, such as the optative nature of social groups. He also raised many of the right questions.

Most scholars who worked in Polynesia during the 1920s and 1930s devoted their efforts to the production of a set of standardized monographs (published by Bishop Museum). These aimed at providing a basis for understanding culture history. Social forms were examined in the same light as artifacts, myths, and other cultural elements—as traits to be compared so that judgments could be made concerning similarities and differences between the various societies. Furthermore, it was not contemporary forms that were of concern, but traditional, precontact ones. Typically the oldest members of a society were interviewed in order to elicit information about what social life was like prior to European intervention.

As fieldwork became the basis for anthropological accounts, broad comparative issues receded from view and both evolutionary and diffusionist assumptions fell into disfavor. The data collected on an island or in a single village proved to be sufficiently complex to tax the imagination. Raymond Firth set the standard for detailed ethnography and prudent analysis in his prolific publications on Tikopia, a Polynesian outlier. It is a standard that has never been surpassed and remains a source of awe for all contemporary Polynesianists. In his best known work, *We, the Tikopia,* Firth (1936b) described in vivid detail the organization of social life on three levels: households, *paito* 'houses tracing descent from a common ancestor', and *kainanga* 'patrilineal clans'.

Although social life on Tikopia had been relatively unaffected by European intrusion at the time of Firth's initial field trip, in 1929, most other Polynesian islands had undergone considerable change as a result of contact with the West. It soon became apparent, however, that there was still much to learn about traditional social forms, despite the magnitude of change. Ethnographies by Beaglehole and Beaglehole (1938, 1941), E. S. C. Handy (1923), Hogbin (1934), M. Mead (1930b), and others provided material that, when added to Firth's splendid accounts, allowed for a new consideration of Polynesian societies as functional systems adapting to changing conditions.

The functionalist view predominated from the late 1920s through the 1950s, when a post-war generation of anthropologists took a new look at some old problems. Although Polynesian societies were less affected by the war in the Pacific than their Melanesian and Micronesian counterparts, the pace of change had accelerated. The continuities between traditional and contemporary social life had to be considered in a new light, given the obvious effects of new economic and political forces. In response, postwar ethnographers took a more dynamic approach to social organization, focusing on social processes rather than the particular groupings most visible during fieldwork. Attention shifted to the cultural premises that Polynesians used in ordering their social lives, and the various ways people acted upon them. As a result, contemporary versions of Polynesian society were no longer seen as mere shadows of traditional cultures. Modern social organization came to be viewed as fascinating in its own right. Moreover, anthropologists discovered that studies of contemporary social life could contribute to an understanding of the past by helping to separate cultural principles from their material embodiments under specific ecological and historical circumstances.

Although most post-war ethnography was only incidentally comparative in orientation (with field workers citing each other's work when it served to frame issues of common interest), Marshall Sahlins and Irving Goldman undertook major comparative projects, both oriented toward accounting for the variations in sociopolitical systems in the region. Both assumed an evolutionary posture, although their perspectives differed markedly. Sahlins' viewpoint bordered on ecological determinism; he used the model of adaptive radiation, borrowed by analogy from physical anthropology, to account for similarities and differences in social forms. Goldman, in contrast, saw Polynesian social systems as grounded in a single cultural principle—status rivalry. He attributed the differences between them to the historically specific ways in which the potentials of that principle were realized. Thus, whereas Sahlins provided a view of Polynesian social organization from the ground up, so to speak, Goldman's view was from the lofty perspective of chiefs who shaped things to suit their own purposes. The contrasting perspectives of Sahlins and Goldman have strongly affected the form that explanations take in the current literature, with ecological explanations frequently counterposed to cultural ones (although Sahlins has changed his viewpoint and now champions the cultural perspective; see, for example, Sahlins 1976, 1981a, 1985).

The most recent work on social organization in Polynesia ranges from detailed studies of delimited problems such as adoption, incest prohibitions and siblingship, to broad speculative accounts. A definite shift has taken place toward a concern for the cultural principles underlying social forms, with the interpretation of symbols, metaphors, and myths playing a central role. Fueled by the possibilities of symbolic interpretation of textual materials recorded in earlier times, renewed interest in traditional, or early contact forms, has been part of this movement. So, too, has been a shift toward ethnohistorical reconstructions of the impact of European interventions on Polynesian social structures (see Borofsky and Howard, chapter 8, this volume).

The Issue of Descent Groups

The analysis of group formation has been central to Polynesian studies in this century. The issue was first raised by Williamson, who, after carefully reviewing the information available at the time, offered considered opinions and tentative hypotheses. He clearly recognized the optative nature of these groupings—that "the children and later descendants of a marriage between persons of two different groups might live and become established in the home of either the male or the female ancestor" (Williamson 1924, 2:2). Williamson treated this possibility as a source of confusion, along with adoption. He considered social groupings to be properly formed on the basis of kinship alone, a possibility obviated by such ambilineal reckoning since residential considerations inevitably must come into play under the latter circumstances. He went on to evaluate information on various Polynesian societies regarding the relative significance of kinship and locality in the formation of groups. Only for Samoa did he consider the data to approach adequacy, but he concluded nevertheless that throughout Polynesia groupings were based primarily on kinship considerations. This conclusion constituted Williamson's central finding regarding Polynesian social organization. It colors virtually all of his subsequent interpretations. For example, on the question of social classes, he distinguished four—chiefs, middle and lower classes, and a special category of priests and sorcerers—but he surmised that since kinship is the primary organizing principle, boundaries between classes are necessarily blurred (Williamson 1924, 2:356–357).

Edwin Burrows, drawing upon the Bishop Museum monographs of the 1920s and 1930s, took up the issue of social group formation in his paper "Breed and Border in Polynesia," published in 1939. Burrows held that alignments of breed (kinship-based groupings) and border (territorially based groupings) had fairly regular distributions. Coincidence of breed and border (territorially contained kinship groupings) was found either in marginal regions or on atolls with a comparatively small population. Intermingling of breed and border (groupings based partially on kinship, partially on territoriality) appeared in two separate areas, one to the west and the other farther east, between which stretched a continuous line of islands where breed and border either coincided or were aligned in unique intermediate fashions. Two isolated regions also had intermediate alignments peculiar to themselves. This situation suggested to Burrows that coincidence of breed and border was the earlier alignment, and intermingling developed later. Diffusion accounted for similarities within the area of "intermingled breed and border," he maintained, although "purely local dynamic factors" accounted for the variations in detail that give each region a unique pattern (Burrows 1939a:18).

Burrows concluded that kinship groupings were the primary form of social organization in Polynesia, but that progressive encroachment of border over breed seems to have been the rule. He postulated several processes as favoring change in that direction, including intermarriage, adoption, migration, and most important, warfare arising from rivalry over land or ambition for enhanced status (1939a:20–21).

Amidst this variability, Burrows perceived a general pattern. Polynesians reckoned kinship by means of genealogies that were primarily patrilineal, he maintained, although matrilineal reckoning was sometimes used as a means of gaining status. Furthermore, a woman did not lose usufruct rights to ancestral lands following marriage, but unless her children were raised by maternal relatives, matrilineal rights tended to lapse after a couple of generations. "In short," wrote Burrows (1939a:1) "living and recently dead kinsfolk were grouped bilaterally; but the larger, more permanent kinship groups were almost invariably based on common descent from an ancestor in the male line."

From Burrow's culture historical perspective, certain questions that might have been asked of the data were secondary. How are "mainly patrilineal" units organized, that is, are there explicit rules of patrilineal descent; if so, what factors account for the retention of filiative links in genealogies? How are the two kinds of units sketched by Burrows—bilateral groups of kinsmen and larger, more permanent patrilineal units—related? Do the members of the former depend on rights and statuses gained through affiliation with the latter? (If so, such bilateral groups may be expected to have a patrilineal core of right-holders.) How do marriage patterns affect group membership and recruitment of group leaders? Do bilateral units have a recognizable structure? When kin units are formed bilaterally individuals may have claims on more than one unit: how does this affect the functioning of these groups?

These questions became pressing as British anthropologists developed models of unilineal descent structures. In the work of such analysts as Radcliffe-Brown, Evans-Pritchard, and Fortes, groups based on exclusive descent principles were seen as basic to social continuity. Where descent is non-exclusive, allowing persons to affiliate with both maternal and paternal groups, the result might be that each group would eventually include the entire population, and each person would belong to every other person's group. Such a situation would presumably be untenable, because corporate management of estates would not be possible and individual loyalties would be hopelessly divided.

As more cases that did not fit the assumptions of unilineal descent theory were noticed, they came to be viewed as demanding their own analytical models (Davenport 1959; Firth 1957, 1963; Murdock 1960;

Barnes 1962). Since many of these cases were found in the Pacific, a regional interpretation of nonunilineal groups, based on a hypothetical original form and variant historical realizations (due largely to adaptation to different environments), was advanced by anthropologists working in the area. Thus Goodenough (1955) suggested that nonunilineal landholding kin groups, with membership open either to all descendants of a founder or restricted by residence criteria, were part of original Malayo-Polynesian social structure. For Goodenough, the patrilineal elements noted by Burrows and others did not detract from abundant evidence of nonunilineal descent groups in Polynesia. Firth agreed. Although descent groups in Tikopia are unilineal, "in most other Polynesian societies they are not" (Firth 1957:4). Firth distinguished between definitive descent groups, with members expectably recruited by clearcut rules, as on Tikopia, and optative ones, in which actors' choice in affiliating to groups is crucial to their composition. He introduced the notion of viewing descent units operationally, rather than in terms of their charters or structural models, a view he developed in his re-analysis of data on the New Zealand Maori *hapu* (Firth 1963).

In traditional Maori culture the *hapu* was a group of kin who traced their relationship to one another, with the ultimate point of reference a common ancestor. Although tracing genealogical connections through males was favored, membership was recognized if a line of descent included several females, so the *hapu* was not unilineal. In effect, a person could opt to claim *hapu* membership through his father, through his mother, or through both parents. Firth termed the system ambilateral because both parents were available in obtaining *hapu* membership. Theoretically, persons could become participants in many groups, but this was rare. In practice, membership was selective. For all practical purposes, *hapu* formed corporate units functionally analogous to lineages. Firth saw the mechanism for sloughing off potential members as the key to the effective operation of the *hapu*. Genealogical claims had to be validated by social action, notably residence and the use of the *hapu* lands. Since communication was difficult and travel dangerous in pre-European New Zealand, Firth maintained, most individuals' participation was practically restricted to one or two groups.

Ottino (1967) found the traditional descent units of the western Tuamotus (*'ati*) to be structurally parallel in most respects to lineages elsewhere, and argued that they should be classified as nonunilinear descent groups. *'Ati* were named, were located in definite geographical areas, had a guardian spirit, a *marae* 'ceremonial area', and by implication rites, rituals and priests—in short, a complete religious organization. *'Ati* were therefore corporate groups that owned rights, "if not exactly in the land itself at least in its resources and in the structures which have been erected on it" (Ottino 1967:478).

What distinguished the 'ati from lineages in Ottino's view was the lack of a unilineal descent principle and of jural rules regulating marriage, postmarital residence, and the affiliation of children. The result was that no one had a specific legal destination at birth, so that the core of each such group was composed of both men and women. Ottino's (1967:477) analysis of genealogical records also suggests that although 'ati linked by marriages formed allied groupings, compared with segmentary lineages they were "much less autonomous" and "neither self-sustaining nor functionally independent."

Two distinct approaches to resolving the problems inherent in descent group models emerged in the wake of such structural debates. One followed on the suggestion of Firth that descent units be viewed operationally. This led an increased emphasis on individual decision making, on the strategies that people followed in making choices, and on the relevance of contextual factors, including ecological contingencies. The other approach focused on the issue of corporateness. Here the task was to evaluate the fit between the ethnographic evidence on functional groupings and a reconsidered definition of corporation.

An early example of the first approach is Howard's (1963) analysis of land tenure in Rotuma. He specifically rejects the unistructural model of society in favor of seeing societies as composed of activity systems, with the relevant units being principles, or factors, that are predictive of choice among behavioral alternatives. He focuses on the dynamics of usufruct, succession, transactions, and disputes as a way of illuminating the ways in which cognatic descent groups operate in Rotuma. In taking a behavioral as opposed to a jural perspective, Howard is more concerned with the principles that determine the actual composition of groups when specific activities are being conducted, rather than beginning with a descent group typology and trying to fit indigenous concepts into it. As a concept, he maintains, the Rotuman term kainaga is better understood as a cultural principle, used in a variety of situations by individuals as a means of legitimizing their activities in certain key activities, than as a kind of group. Following in Firth's footsteps, Howard advocates a decision-making approach to group formation.

As more evidence became available on cognatic descent systems it was apparent that the simple dichotomy between exclusive and non-exclusive systems was inadequate. Allan Hanson suggested that an intermediate range be recognized that he labeled "semi-exclusive," in which most individuals are associated primarily with one descent group but also may hold secondary rights of membership in others (Hanson 1971). The Maori hapu and Tuamotuan 'ati both fit Hanson's semi-exclusive category, as did the traditional descent groups on Rapa, where he conducted fieldwork.

One of the major points of Hanson's analysis is that despite the non-exclusive nature of contemporary Rapan descent group formation, the system works adequately. There are several reasons for this, including the fact that land is plentiful in relation to the population and thus competition for its use is limited. Also, improvements to the land, around which many descent groups ('opu) form, do not last forever. Groups based on improvements dissolve after a period of time, and if things get too complicated as a result of 'opu memberships becoming too large, there is always the option of dividing the estate. Ultimately, according to Hanson, "because a Rapan is rarely called upon to act in the role of member of an 'opu, and because his commitment to it is so narrowly defined, it is unlikely that his obligations as a member of one 'opu would conflict with his obligations as a member of several others" (Hanson 1971:127).

This shift in perspective, from unistructural models of societies seen from the outside to models emphasizing choice and decision making, has gone a long way towards clarifying the manner in which contemporary Polynesian societies function, and has provided us with better conceptual tools for reconstructing traditional systems. An important point is the degree to which Polynesians seem to rely on specific contexts to organize their behavior. Attempts to discover the rules governing Polynesian social behavior have thus been much less fruitful than studies examining the processes involved in conducting activities.

Ottino's study of modern Rangiroan social organization illustrates the value of the decision-making approach. He describes a situation of non-exclusive descent, much like that found on Rapa, except that land is far more limited on Rangiroa. He answers the question of how non-exclusive groups, formed of the descendants of land title-holders, can function by examining when and how decisions are made. Usually the children of a title-holder, "not wanting to destroy kinship bonds in dividing the lands" (Ottino 1973:407, our translation), do not divide their shares. Thus the grandchildren of the original title-holder inherit a joint estate and must work out arrangements to share the land and its profits. Over time, however, such arrangements become unwieldy. As descendants of the founder proliferate, questions arise as to the rights of different descendants. The value of maintaining a single 'opu, so clear to the founder and his children, is not so obvious for second cousins whose shared activity consists of difficult discussions about the allocation of resources. Consequently, formal land division occurs about once every three generations. Although land divisions involve difficulties—they are, after all, generally occasioned by the inability of co-heirs to cooperate—they can be accomplished by drawing on arrangements for usufruct worked out in earlier generations. In other words, the working arrangements of one generation provide the basis for decisive alterations by the next. Although this form of organization may seem ill-defined, it effectively orchestrates processes of group formation and division. Moreover, it is sensitive to ecological conditions, since the more demand there is for using a particular parcel of land, the more likely it is that co-heirs will either work out arrangements to use it or divide it up.[3]

The second approach—focusing on the issue of corporateness—was employed by Webster (1975) and Tiffany and Tiffany (1978) in efforts to clarify the nature of contemporary descent groups among the New Zealand Maori and Samoans, respectively. They start by reconsidering the notion of corporateness, and attempt to demonstrate that the Maori *hapu* and Samoan *'aiga* do indeed meet the qualifications for being considered corporations. However, they point out that the terms *hapu* and *'aiga* are polysemic, referring to different things in different contexts, and that it is only in a restricted sense that they are used to refer to corporate descent groups. Both Webster and the Tiffanys take an operational perspective and make their case by analyzing specific activities central to the functioning of those groups, but since corporateness is ultimately an ideational concept, their perspective is jural rather than behavioral.

Webster begins by criticizing the notion, ascribed to Metge (1964), that the contemporary *hapu* has become nothing but an abstraction, a name without a social function and without any sign of corporate life. He argues that most authorities have been misled by supposing the *hapu* to be a localized group, but that such was probably never the case, although he agrees that close association with a particular locality has always been a focal characteristic of the Maori kin group. However, it is the close symbolic identification of land, home, and ancestry that is at the heart of this association rather than practical considerations. This has made it possible for descent groups to continue as corporate entities despite an increasing necessity among contemporary Maori to be economically independent of the land.

The local center of the kin group is usually a *marae* 'ceremonial clearing with associated meeting and dining halls' (although the households of group elders also operate as centers for group activities), and it is participation in ritual gatherings on the *marae* that is the primary indicator of kin group membership. For any given ceremonial occasion, participants are divided into two categories: *tangata whenua* 'people of the land' or 'hosts' and *manuhiri* 'visitors' or 'guests'. Those who are responsible for organizing and financing the gathering, typically resident and nearby descent group members associated with the *marae,* act in the role of hosts, while even quite close kinsmen who become involved after the initial organization has taken place are treated as guests. It is the *tangata whenua* who are the corporate core of the cognatic descent category, which consists of all those individuals who can legitimately claim descent from the founding ancestor. Admission to *tangata whenua* status requires active support, including a rather heavy commitment of time and resources, which makes it difficult (although not uncommon) for an individual to be a core member of more than one descent group.

Whereas previously land was the primary foundation of a *hapu*'s estate, emphasis has now shifted to other resources. According to Webster it has been well documented that

> kinsmen with whom one interacts on a frequent basis and members of one's kindred or *whaanau* ['extended family'], as well as the usually narrower domestic group, have a reasonable claim on the use of one another's personal property such as cars or money, and usually enter, eat, and sleep in one another's houses without formalities. In the wider descent group, local marae committees or, in the city, "family committees" and regional organizations often maintain an account which is expended in their name on the occasion of formal gatherings, or is used to offset the emergency needs of its members . . . the corporate descent group maintains a jural claim on the labour, savings, and production of each of its members, mobilised on a moment's notice for any of its assemblies (Webster 1975:137).

Although hypothetically an individual can choose to affiliate with many descent groups, practically he or she is drawn toward only one by life-cycle events, beginning with birth. This tends to put the child into closer association with one set of grandparents, who are likely to be influential in the choice of a name. Courtship and marriage may further restrict possible affiliations, depending upon post-marital residence and the ease with which multiple ties can be maintained, but perhaps the most important factor dictating primary association is the choice of a burial place—a matter of great concern for most Maori.[4] Webster concludes that the contemporary *hapu,* in at least one of its usages, satisfies the jural requirements for being considered a corporation.

Sharon Tiffany approaches the Samoan *'aiga* in a similar way (see especially Tiffany 1975a for an explicit comparison). Like the Maori *hapu,* the Samoan *'aiga* is identified by reference to its founder, and all individuals descendant from that founder are potential members. Actual membership requires, as among the Maori, active participation in the affairs of the group. In Samoa this includes some combination of the following: economic support of *'aiga* exchanges and ceremonial redistributions, residence on the estate of the *'aiga,* cultivation of land vested in the membership of the *'aiga,* and political support (Tiffany 1975a:432). It is the internal organization of the *'aiga* as a corporate descent group, however, that is of special interest to Tiffany.

Three categories of individuals have rights to make decisions on behalf of an *'aiga:* the holders of chiefly titles, the *'aiga potopoto* 'an ad hoc assemblage of *'aiga* members organized for the purpose of discussing matters pertaining to title successions or removals', and *faletama* 'constituent units of the *'aiga* composed of all those people who acknowledge common descent from a brother, son, sister, or daughter of the founder'. Descent groups generally own several chiefly, or *matai,* titles, with the highest ranking title that of the reputed founder; all other titles are ranked in relation to it. It is difficult to overestimate the importance of chiefly titles to Samoans. Not only do chiefly titles carry with them one's symbolic importance as a person, but chiefs continue to play an extremely active role in regulating their *'aiga*'s affairs. Their responsibilities include allocating *'aiga* land for cultivation, designating house sites on *'aiga* land, arbitrating and mediating disputes involving group members, assessing goods and labor for ceremonial redistributions and village-sponsored projects, representing the group politically in the village council of chiefs, maintaining corporate property such as the *'aiga*'s official house site, and possibly a savings account, maintaining the *'aiga*'s genealogy, and defending the integrity of other titles associated with the group (Tiffany 1975a:435).

When a title comes up for consideration it is the *'aiga potopoto* who deliberate. The ability to trace a consanguineal link to the descent group is the only necessary condition for attending an *'aiga potopoto* meeting, at which the relative qualifications of various candidates are considered. Failure to express interest in the decision, by not sending a representative if one cannot attend, is likely to be taken by other members as a forfeiture of the right to dissent, and is one way potential membership in the group goes unrealized. As with village councils, decisions are not considered binding unless all interested parties (including those unable to attend the meeting) consent, and for this reason some disputed titles have remained vacant for extended periods of time.

Faletama are segments of an *'aiga* that are politically subordinate units, often having their own interests in opposition to other such units. Higher order *faletama* units may be subdivided into lower order units, and each may have its own title. Conflict between *faletama* gets most intense when they offer opposing candidates for a higher level title within the *'aiga*. In the past, when a descent group grew quite large, so that relationships between members became diffuse, *faletama* would sometimes split off to form their own *'aiga*. Thus, although *'aiga* are corporate groups, important internal political divisions often play a prominent role in the way they function (for an excellent account of the way in which political factionalism operates in relation to Samoan social organization, see Shore 1982).

As with all cognatic descent systems, Samoans have the option of making claims in several *'aiga* and often in several *faletama* within an *'aiga*. Given the political nature of such units, and their frequent opposition to one another, however, individuals are forced to make choices on a variety of occasions with regard to how they will use their limited resources. In an insightful article concerning redistribution ceremonies in Samoa, Tiffany and Tiffany (1978) illuminate the way in which affiliations and alignments occur in practice. They find that individuals generally seek enhance their social position by opting to meet contribution obligations to high status groups that control desirable land, titles, and political influence. The structural implications of such cumulative choices remain to be spelled out, however.

The issue of descent group formation has served as a catalyst for moving Polynesian studies to a new level of sophistication. Analyses of the anomalies that Polynesian descent groups presented in the light of prior models stimulated a shift from rather simple structural models, which screened out the intricacies of political maneuvering, individual decision making, and the like, to much more complex understandings of social action. In the 1980s, praxis theories, exemplified in the works of such theorists as Pierre Bourdieu, Anthony Giddens, and Marshall Sahlins (see Ortner 1984), have provided a strong theoretical foundation for the latter perspective.

Attempts to explain the nature of descent groups was also of vital significance because it raised the question of whether Polynesian social formations are primarily shaped by pragmatic adaptations to ecological circumstances, or whether they are better understood as manifestations of underlying cultural principles. Clearly both processes are involved, but the differential emphasis afforded one type of explanation at the expense of the other leads to quite different perspectives and understandings. The ecological perspective seeks explanation in economic advantage, with the key to Polynesian systems being sought in the adaptive demands of island environments. Cognatic descent, from this perspective, is seen as a way of distributing individuals so that ratios of population to resource are optimized. Whereas unilineal descent, rigorously applied, leads to groups that grow at disproportionate rates as a result of demographic fluctuations, thereby creating conditions in which some groups end up with an excess of land while others are land-hungry, cognatic descent permits individuals to go where the resources are, thus evening out person-to-resource ratios. In an island environment this can be crucial to the overall survival of the population.

The cultural perspective argues that Polynesians carried with them a set of principles for interpreting the world and organizing their social lives. From this standpoint Polynesian social formations are expressions, under a variety of historical and ecological conditions, of a basic world view that includes specific notions about kinship, relationships between human beings and ancestral gods, and a host of related beliefs.

Nowhere has this basic issue of interpretation been more clearly articulated than in attempts to interpret the role of chiefs in Polynesian societies, and to account for the forms of political organization.

Social Stratification

It will be recalled that early theorists, working within the diffusionist framework, explained Polynesian political forms as the consequence of successive waves of immigrants, with an original population of egalitarian people followed by a wave of neo-Polynesians who brought with them a well-developed set of political institutions, including notions of aristocracy and chieftainship. The first significant shift in perspective was toward a functionalist view, which was introduced into Polynesian ethnography by Raymond Firth and Ian Hogbin, and to a lesser extent by Margaret Mead and Ernest Beaglehole. It was Ralph Piddington, a student of Malinowski, however, who articulated the functionalist theory of Polynesian chieftainship most fully. In his conclusion to *Essays in Polynesian Ethnology* (1939), a book based on Williamson's ethnographic files, Piddington offered a hypothetical sequence by which elaborate forms of political organization might have developed out of the simple social structures of small colonizing communities. He speculated that as population increased, pressure on food supplies led to a struggle for the most fertile and most easily cultivated lands, leading to inter-group rivalry and the eventual dominance of some groups over others. Political alliances were formed, along with them a greater centralization of authority, with some headmen becoming first chiefs, then head-chiefs. This extension of authority generated elaborate systems of etiquette and taboo, and once-ordinary principles of genealogical reckoning, prolonged through generations, merged the progenitors of the chiefly families with the ancestor-gods. These two factors led to the beliefs and practices subsumed under the general title of the sanctity of chieftainship (Williamson and Piddington 1939:206–207).

Piddington's explanation for why these various forms arose stems directly from Malinowski, his teacher and mentor: social institutions are presumed to satisfy social needs. He made no attempt to account for the variations that were to be found in the forms Polynesian political systems took, other than listing such factors as geographic and demographic circumstances, individual variations in role performance, institutional efflorescence within particular societies, and diffusion.

Some twenty years later, Marshall Sahlins (1958) presented an evolutionary explanation for the variations in political organization within the region. Sahlins reviewed data from fourteen Polynesian societies with the purpose of establishing a stratification gradient and correlating it to technoenvironmental differences. In considering traditional social structure, Sahlins focused upon two features of stratification: degree and form. He estimated degree of stratification by using a combination of structural and functional features. The major structural criterion was socially recognized categories of rank, while functional criteria included economic, sociopolitical, and ceremonial privilege and power. The result was a four-level classification, ranging from the highly stratified societies of Hawaii, Tahiti, Tonga, and Samoa to the egalitarian small islands of Pukapuka, Ontong Java, and Tokelau.

Sahlins also examined forms of stratification from the viewpoint of adaptive radiation. He distinguished three types: the ramage system, which is based on "internally ranked, segmentary unilineal kin groups acting also as political units"; the descent-line system, which is characterized by "discrete, localized common descent groups organized into territorial political entities"; and atoll systems characterized by "complex organizations of interlocking social groups different from both ramage and descent-line structure" (Sahlins 1958:xi–xii). A ramage system, in Sahlins' usage, is the working out of the principle of seniority within patrilines to its logical conclusions, without regard for territoriality (he accepted patrilineality as the dominant descent principle). A descent-line system, while based on patrilineal principles, makes important concessions to territoriality, such that titles are located in space as well as in genealogies. (Sahlins' distinction was an updated version of Burrows' breed and border thesis; see Sahlins 1958:200).

Consistent with his emphasis on technoenvironmental adaptation, Sahlins concentrated attention on systems of production, circulation, and consumption of goods. Chiefs are seen preeminently as directors of production, as central agents in large-scale redistributions of food and other goods, and as privileged consumers. They are also imbued with sacred powers and exercise political prerogatives, but these are clearly derivative, in Sahlins' scheme, from their economic roles. Ultimately, then, stratification is traced to productivity and the size of redistributive networks.

Sahlins accounted for forms of stratification by considering them as variant solutions to the problem of distributing surplus production. Thus ramified systems are postulated to be a response to familial specialization in the production of surplus strategic goods. Familial specialization, in turn, is a predictable reaction to spatial distributions of rich resource zones too scattered to be exploited by a single household, or where the range of crops is so wide as to preclude effective exploitation by a single household. Descent-line systems are presumed to be responses to spatial distributions of rich resource zones clustered in a small area, or to a narrow range of crops.

Sahlins was sharply criticized for his treatment of particular societies (Finney 1966; Freeman 1961, 1964), and a close examination of his data shows that degree of stratification can be accounted for by the single factor of population size, without regard to productivity or technoenvironmental adaptation (Orans 1966). Nevertheless, his book demonstrated the potential for ecological explanation, and it served as a model for comparative research.

While Sahlins' study was awaiting publication, Irving Goldman published an article entitled "Status Rivalry and Cultural Evolution in Polynesia" (1955), in which he proposed a developmental scheme that hinged upon the notion that status rivalry was particularly acute in Polynesian societies. He suggested a sequence of three historical phases: traditional, which referred to early stages of Polynesian cultural development; open, which referred to a transitional condition; and stratified, which referred to the culminating phases of development. Each phase is identified by characteristic forms of authority, property, kinship, position of women, sexual practices, infanticide, mourning, warfare, priesthood, dieties, afterlife, sorcery, and omens. In several subsequent papers, Goldman (1957, 1958, 1960a, 1960b) elaborated on his thesis, which culminated in the publication of *Ancient Polynesian Society* in 1970. Although Goldman's evolutionism has been greeted with skepticism (Hawthorne and Belshaw 1957; Howard 1972), his dynamic portrayal of political life has had a significant impact on contemporary views of Polynesian social organization.

Goldman took Polynesia to be a cultural unity, and attempted to explain variation in terms of a dominant pattern that unfolded in historically diverse ways. He focused on the Polynesian status system, by which he referred to "the principles that define worth and more specifically honor, that establish the scales of personal and group value, that relate position or role to privileges and obligations, that allocate respects, and that codify respect behavior" (Goldman 1970:7). In Polynesia, he maintained, "it is the status system—specifically, the principles of aristocracy—that gives direction to the social structure as a whole. Principles of status dominate all other principles of social organization" (Goldman 1970:7).

In his discussion of social groupings, Goldman acknowledges that descent groups can usefully be viewed as deriving from rules of affiliation. He also acknowledges the value of examining the way in which kinship principles functionally allocate rights and responsibilities, but he regards descent as primarily concerned with honor. In Polynesia, Goldman (1970:419, emphasis in original) insists, "descent is not really a *means* to status, it is the *heart* of status." Rather than attempting to classify Polynesian descent groups as various forms of nonunilinear types, which misses the central point in Goldman's view, a more precise designation would be to consider them as status lineages.

The status lineage in Polynesia differs from the broader class of "conventional" lineages in the lack of exogamy and in its lack of full commitment to either male or female descent lines. Or, to state the difference positively, the conventional lineage holds to categorical rules of exclusion and of affiliation; the Polynesian status lineage, to flexible rules. Polynesian flexibility . . . is primarily political, and it is for political reasons that the status lineage is so highly variable an organization (Goldman 1970:422–423).

A special feature of status lineages is that even within specific societies, criteria of descent differ in accordance with genealogical rank. Among high chiefs, unilinearity authenticates rank and authority, whereas among commoners, whose central concerns are utilitarian rather than honorific, bilaterality is the rule. In the stratified societies, according to Goldman, (1970:424), "only the upper ranks can be said to belong to a lineage organization at all. Commoners are part of both a political organization and part of small kindreds."

Chiefs are concerned with descent as a means of establishing honorable affiliation to a prestigious descent line in order to authenticate their *mana* and authority. They are likewise concerned with affiliating themselves to people who will contribute to their power. Commoners' interests, in contrast, are best served by affiliating politically with rising chiefs and those who offer the best conditions of service. Goldman thus sees descent principles as part of a set of options by which individuals can structure their affiliations.

One of the more fascinating aspects of Polynesian social stratification is that island clusters such as Hawaii, the Societies, Tonga, and Samoa developed such elaborate political systems on such a rudimentary economic base (see Kirch, chapter 2, this volume). It is on these grounds that Goldman attacks materialist and ecological explanations. "Since Polynesian societies can be similar in basic culture whether they occupy atolls or high islands, relatively rich habitats or barren islands," he maintains, "they cannot be regarded as having been molded by their different material environments" (Goldman 1970:478). For Goldman, then, the general explanation for Polynesian social forms is cultural, while the particular outcomes result from the play of historical chance and human intentions. From his perspective, growth in political centralism does not stem from the organizational imperatives of modes of production, as the cultural materialists would have it, but from the status ambitions of chiefs, and more particularly, from wars of conquest.

The character of Polynesian economies stems, in Goldman's view, from the forms of aristocracy in the area. It is not that commerce, that is utilitarian exchange, was ignored, but it was subordinated "to a greater interest in ritual circulation of goods" (Goldman 1970:477). All Polyne-

sian economies were to be considered as aristocratic economies. Production, circulation, and consumption serve to measure, allocate, and
validate honor. Thus, in those societies where the status of chiefs was
comparatively high, the economy was slanted toward the honorific;
where lower ranks dominated, the bias shifted toward the utilitarian.
From the standpoint of aristocracy, participation in a cycle of exchanges
is neither the source of status nor a test of status, but rather the prerogative and documentation of status. In a more general sense, as Goldman
(1970:496) succinctly puts it, "exchanges are the code through which
status information is communicated."

Goldman's cultural approach to an understanding of Polynesian
political organization hinges to a considerable extent on the logic of
mana 'efficacy, potency'. Theoretically *mana* is an inherited potential,
transmitted genealogically, with greater proportions going to firstborn
children. It is therefore a matter of degree—a gradient ideally coinci-
dent with kinship seniority. Ultimately it stems from the gods, who are
the source of prosperity or famine, of good or ill-fortune. The gods, as
ancestors, are incorporated into the kinship system, and those individuals who are most directly linked to them through seniority are presumed
to have the most *mana*. If *mana* were conceived strictly as an inherited
quality it would have had a profoundly conservative effect on social
organization, but such was not the case. Rather it was conceived to be
dynamic, manifest in action and in the outcomes of problematic events
(Firth 1940; Shore, chapter 5, this volume). To be effective was therefore to demonstrate the strength of one's *mana;* to be ineffective was to
reveal its weakness or absence. Since *mana* could only be validated with
results, maintaining high status required repetitive demonstrations. By
implication, then, *mana* could be lost or gained by individuals, with rises
in fortune signifying gains and declines in fortune signifying losses of
mana.

Chiefs in particular were under pressure to continually demonstrate
their *mana,* for only by doing so could they validate their status and
demonstrate their vitality. On the one hand chiefs were engaged in
efforts to defend their status against threats, for failure to successfully do
so implied loss of *mana,* and hence significance as a person. On the other
hand, there was no better way to demonstrate *mana* than by successfully
challenging, and defeating, a person of equal or higher status. It was the
impetus of this cultural logic that lay behind Goldman's (1970:12–13)
notion of status rivalry as a relentless motivator of political change in
Polynesia.

The concept of *mana* was also applicable to skilled craftsmen, whose
wares were judged by their effectiveness, and to other specialists, such
as healers, priests, and sorcerers. Successful specialists, along with successful warriors, gained status through their displays of efficacy. There

were thus multiple routes to enhanced status in most Polynesian societies, lending further impetus to the dynamism of social organization.[5]

Goldman's reconstruction of traditional Polynesian social systems constitutes a remarkable achievement. By focusing on the status system he highlighted many aspects of social and political dynamics that had been previously overlooked. The distinction he drew between the concerns of chiefs and commoners stands as a major contribution, as does his dynamic portrayal of status lineages. Yet, his account has the limitations of any grand scheme. It does not, for example, provide a satisfactory explanation for the details of political relations documented in ethnographic accounts such as Firth's work on Tikopia (1936a, 1964, 1967, 1970b). Goldman also overemphasizes the degree to which chiefs rely on patrilineal principles to authenticate rank. Since his work was published a good deal of evidence has accumulated suggesting that both paternal and maternal lines play a role in rankings, and that power stems from successfully claiming multiple affiliations. Goldman also oversimplifies the concept of *mana,* and does not deal effectively with such issues as the relationship between chiefs and priests, or between either of these and other kinds of specialists. His dismissal of ecological considerations is also a bit cavalier, but his analysis has the virtue of dramatizing the dynamic character of Polynesian sociopolitical systems.

The structural flexibility we have encountered in Polynesian approaches to group membership (insofar as descent group affiliation is optative) thus also characterizes Polynesian stratification. Prior to European intervention, the level of material development was insufficient to permit uncontested hegemony by any group. Weapons, tools, surplus food, and symbols of status were accessible to all who could mobilize the human resources necessary to produce them. So, despite the apparent structure imposed by rules of seniority and the superiority of the male line, political success required adept manipulation of interpersonal relations. It was through the dynamic processes of exchange, rather than the imposition of static structural rules, that real political power was acquired and exercized.

Ultimately, however, it may well have been the cultural logic of *mana* that lent to Polynesian political systems their volatile characteristics. Thus chiefs in power seemingly were encouraged to push their people's tolerance to the limit in order to display their potency, and aspirants to power appear to have continually tested their relative strength. The ambiguities in structural principles provided by the rules of cognatic descent permitted genealogies to be rearranged to legitimate new ascendencies, so changing fortunes could be accommodated without altering the basic structure. But in the final analysis political success, whether through the imposition of genealogical principles, the peaceful mobilization of resources, or through conquest, was its own legitimation, for to be successful was to demonstrate *mana,* to make manifest the favor of the gods. It is therefore in action and process, informed by deeply embedded cultural principles as well as by situational pragmatism, that Polynesian social organization must be understood.

In a sense, the issues we have discussed thus far—those that dominated Polynesian ethnology up through the 1960s—placed the cart before the horse. That is, compelling generalizations about group formation and political structures require cogent theories about the nature of social action. Because kinship lies at the heart of the matter, we shall begin our analysis of how anthropologists have attempted to remedy the situation by sketching out a general view of Polynesian kinship based upon its more obvious features. We then go on to consider recent attempts at clarification by ethnographers who have been studying the ways in which kinship principles are expressed in specific contexts.

Kinship

The term *kaaiga* and its cognates can be glossed as 'kin' or 'kinship' in most Polynesian languages.[6] *Kaaiga* may be used as a verb, noun, or modifier, and is capable of indicating many kinds and shades of relationship. Huntsman's analysis of the Tokelauan *kaaiga* is exemplary.

A Tokelauan uses the word *kaaiga* as a predicate *e kaaiga ki maa* "we are related"; and as an indefinite noun *ko ia he kaaiga e o oku* "he is my kinsman"; and as a definite noun *ko ki maaua e i te kaaiga e tahi* "we are in the same kin group". A word derived from *kaaiga*—*ituukaaiga* (*ituu* means side or portion) —is used to classify, sort or type animals, plants, objects or activities. The myriad varieties of fish are classified into a number of overlapping *ituukaaiga* by their appearance, habitat and behaviour; sleeping mats are sorted into *ituukaaiga* by their design and fibre; ancient songs are typed into a number of *ituukaaiga*. Both the derived word *ituukaiga* and the base word *kaaiga* denote two or more items which share distinctive attributes; but *kaaiga* is used exclusively to denote two or more human beings with common attributes, which may be as broadly inclusive as the *kaaiga* of God encompassing all humanity, living and dead, or as narrowly exclusive as the *kaaiga* of a couple and their child.

Shared ancestry conceived of as *auala* "paths" linking people to a single forebear, ancestral couple, or sibling set, makes two people *kaaiga* "kinsmen" to each other and defines a number of people as a *kaaiga* "kin group". People are *kaaiga* to each other because they have at least one common known or assumed progenitor. All the people with whom an individual is aware he shares a forebear or who he knows are linked to a kinsman of any of his forebears, he considers to be his kinsmen. This is an ego-oriented category. A number of people consider themselves a kin group because they all have a common assumed or known, forebear. This is an ancestral-oriented category. In the *kaaiga* of God, all men are conceived as related because all 'paths', if they were known, would ultimately converge at Adam and Eve [this, of course, represents the application of traditional principles to post-missionary teachings].

Today, a Nukunonu man [Nukunonu is one of the atolls in the Tokelau group] speaks about *toto* "blood" as a substance shared by *kaaiga,* but says this is something they have learned from Europeans. However, he points out that people have always been aware that *kaaiga* share some substance, otherwise why would they have similar appearance and character. Distinctive attributes of personality and behaviour are attributed to certain kin groups; members glance sideways, eat excessively, are unkempt or are good cricket batsmen (Huntsman 1971:320–321).

The Tokelau use the term *kaukaaiga* (*kau* means 'to join') in reference to

a corporate group which has common rights to property, specifically to *mataaniu* 'coconut plantations', which they jointly exploit and from which they share fruits. This property was estates inherited by a founder or founders, who were occasionally great-grandparents or grandparents of elders, were most frequently parents of elders, and are often the elders themselves. All people who can trace a "path" to the founder are *kaukaaiga* members.

A kin group is recognized as a *kaukaaiga,* entitled to representation in the elders' council, only when it controls a *mataaniu.* People are acknowledged to be a *kaukaaiga* because they are linked to its founders, but, more important, they are identified by their common rights to shares of produce from a *mataaniu.* Consequently, *kaukaaiga* may have affiliate members who do not share ancestry, but do share produce (Huntsman 1971:327).

The notion of kinship as shared substance is richer and more ambiguous than analysts' conventional definition of kinship in terms of genealogy. Substance may derive from filiative links, from shared involvement in land (that most precious of commodities), or from shared consumption of produce. In particular, those who regularly share food are seen in Polynesia as acting like kinsmen, regardless of their blood ties. Thus behavior is treated as an index of kinship, as a basis for affirming or denying it. Furthermore, acting like kinsmen is a means to creating kinship bonds between persons previously unrelated.[7]

For example, on Anuta, a Polynesian outlier located in the eastern Solomons, Feinberg documented the importance of *aropa* 'positive affect as expressed through giving or sharing of material goods and assistance in performing tasks' for defining kinship (Feinberg 1981:116).[8] The elementary property-owning, producing, and consuming unit on Anuta is known as the *patongia.* Although patrifiliation is the primary genealogical basis for membership in the group, it is defined culturally as "that group of people who share a common basket of food at island-wide distributions" (Feinberg 1981:116). Sometimes genealogically distant cousins who participate within the same unit have closer emotional and behavioral ties than full siblings who are separated. Likewise, an outsider who is adopted into a *patongia,* and who contributes to it economically, comes to be treated as a "true sibling of the same parents" by all his generation mates in the group (Feinberg 1981:117). Thus social distance in Polynesian societies is only partially determined by genealogical connection; other factors, such as residential proximity and access to resources, which can affect interpersonal commitments, also play an important part in structuring relationships. Sharing the same food regularly is perhaps the most powerful sign of relationship, that is, of sharing the same substance, although other indices are recognized.[9]

In his review of the literature on Polynesian kinship systems, Goldman (1970:especially chapter 21) concludes that they are constructed out of two fundamental principles—seniority and gender. Seniority is reflected in the precedence given to earlier generations, and to firstborn children. If it were to operate without modification, the principle of seniority would result in all of the descendants of a founding ancestral couple being ranked uniquely vis-à-vis one another. Not only would their children be ranked according to birth order, but in subsequent generations the descendants of their firstborn child would rank higher than the descendants of their second born child, and so forth. This principle, carried to its logical conclusion, results in a set of ranked lineages stemming initially from the first sibling set, but gaining further divisions from sibling sets in descending generations. The highest ranking person is the firstborn child of the firstborn parent, of the firstborn grandparent, and so on, and all other persons could be ranked accordingly.

Whereas the principle of seniority results in fine quantitative gradations of status, gender is categorical in its implications. Male is set off against female, providing the basis for dualistic divisions of kinsmen. The gender principle shows up most clearly in Polynesian sibling terms, where the main distinction is between siblings of the same sex and those of the opposite sex. In its simplest form, as in Tikopia, brother and sister call each other by the same term *(kave),* while siblings of the same sex call each other by another term *(taina).* In more complex systems, like that of the New Zealand Maori, males call their sisters by one term *(tuahine),* while females call their brothers by another *(tungane);* seniority is recognized between siblings of the same sex, with the younger calling the older by a different term *(tuakana)* than the one used by the older for the younger *(teina).* Some societies, like Pukapuka and Tokelau, are intermediate; they have a single term for siblings of the same sex but differentiate siblings of the opposite sex by separate terms for male and female (see Firth 1970c and Panoff 1965 for penetrating, comparative analyses of Polynesian siblingship).

For many years variations in Polynesian kinship systems were all but ignored by comparative theorists, perhaps because they appeared deceptively simple, but in fact, internal variation within the region requires explanation. Firth hypothesizes that the smaller the community, in numbers and in geographical circumscription, the simpler the terminological system is likely to be (Firth 1970c:275). The evidence, although there are some anomalies, seems to support this, at least in relation to the elaboration of sibling terms.

In addition to differences in sheer complexity are those that distinguish eastern and western Polynesia. Whereas western Polynesian societies appear to have elaborated the principle of gender duality to a considerable degree in structuring their kinship systems, eastern Polynesia has emphasized the principle of seniority. Thus in western Polynesian societies such as Samoa, Tonga, and Fiji the distinction between siblings of the opposite sex provides a basis for making distinctions between relatives in adjacent generations, whereas in eastern Polynesia (with two exceptions) it does not. Mother's brothers and father's sisters occupy special positions in these societies, as do their corresponding reciprocals, cross-nieces and nephews. The social significance of these gender distinctions lies in the special honorific status of women vis-à-vis their brothers. In western Polynesia, after puberty, a rule of avoidance applies between siblings of the opposite sex, and men are required to show the utmost respect to their sisters. The way this gets expressed in kinship idiom differs from one western Polynesian system to another, however.

In Tonga, although men hold formal political power, they are outweighed by their sisters in formal honors (Gifford 1929; see also Goldman 1970).[10] What a man holds in actual power over his sister he surrenders in ritual power to her children, thus balancing the relationship. A man's sister's son or daughter is known by the term *ilamutu*, the etymology of which Goldman reconstructs as "a destroyer," implying that one's sister's child is "above the law," and the symbolic destroyer of his or her maternal uncle.[11] In fact an *ilamutu* is entitled to take at will the uncle's property, and even has the right to seize his sacrificial offerings, which implies a god-like ascendant status. This relationship between sister's child and mother's brother is known as the *fahu* (*vasu* in Fiji), and plays an important role in political maneuverings (see section on political organization below). The father's sister, in contrast, is owed reverential respect, and is known by the term *mehekitanga,* which implies preciousness. This complex of relationships is summarized by Goldman as follows:

Through his sister, a man loses ritual or symbolic power and suffers a reversal. Through her brother, a woman gains an ascendancy equivalent to what a man has over his children. Through his mother, a child gains an ascendancy over a male of his parental generation. Through his father, a male submits to an awesome respect relationship before a female of his mother's generation. The key element is the concept of sex opposition as the switch-over point for status. Within consanguinity, the brother-sister pattern is the key (Goldman 1970:454; see also Bott 1981, Rogers 1977).

The Samoan pattern also derives from a heavy emphasis on restraint and respect between brother and sister, but in Samoa it is the father's sister who is known as the *ilamutu*. The term is also used in reference to the eldest sister of a man holding a high-ranking title. A man's sister has the power to place a curse of barrenness upon him, thus cutting off his line, which in Samoa (and indeed in any Polynesian society) would be an act of the utmost gravity.

In the Marquesas, within eastern Polynesia, the cognate term *i'amutu* refers to a man's sister's child or a woman's brother's child. There is no mention in the literature of sisters' power over their brothers; rather MoBr, MoBrWi, FaSi, FaSiHu act as ritual sponsors. It is the inequality between generations that is emphasized in this system.

In general, eastern Polynesian societies emphasize seniority and, although gender is important, gender is not given the same degree of prominence as in western Polynesian systems. Sibling terms provide one index of this difference. Whereas all of the eastern Polynesian societies make a terminological distinction between elder and younger sibling of the same sex, most western Polynesian societies do not. In the parental and offspring generations, on the other hand, the bifurcation that distinguishes cross from parallel kinsmen that is commonplace in western Polynesia only occurs in the eastern Polynesian societies of the Marquesas and Tongareva.

The Hawaiian case clearly shows the dominant eastern Polynesian concern for seniority. Relatives are grouped together by generation without distinctions between siblings and collaterals. Within each generation siblings of the same sex used the reciprocal terms *kaikua'ana* 'older sibling' and *kaikaina* 'younger sibling'. When required, sex distinctions were designated by adding generic suffixes for male *(kane* or *nane)* and female *(wahine* or *hine)* (see Handy and Pukui 1972:42).

Goldman (1970) interprets the differences between east and west as representing a reduction in complexity that corresponds to historical processes. Thus we find in Tonga and Samoa (and in Fiji) the oldest Polynesian societies, and the strongest brother-sister avoidance patterns. These are somewhat less emphasized, but still present, in other western Polynesian societies, and appear in an even more diluted form in the Marquesas. In the remainder of the eastern Polynesian societies brother-sister avoidance is essentially absent, and the sibling relationship in general is downplayed in favor of the husband-wife dyad. Since dualism allows for a variety of elaborations, the kinship systems in western Polynesia are more complex and variable, those in eastern Polynesia are simpler and more uniform.

In Goldman's view, all Polynesian kinship categorizations denote honors, respect, and worth, so they are sensitive to changes in concepts of status. Since he associates dualism with the domestic status system and seniority with the public status system, he interprets the simplification process as a reduction in the significance of domestic status in favor of an emphasis on political pragmatics. In eastern Polynesia, in other words, a political concern for ranking shaped the kinship system at the expense of domestic concerns for gender distinctions. Goldman's preference for rational-cognitive explanations, as opposed to materialistic ones, is made explicit when he states that "evidence for high variability of the dualism—seniority pattern, particularly in western Polynesia, points unmistakably to acts of choice" (Goldman 1970:468).

Whereas Goldman relies on the etymology of kin terms to argue that Polynesian kinship systems reflect status concerns, other scholars have looked to the ways in which kinship principles operate in specific contexts in order to clarify the issues involved. Most notable are studies of incest taboos and adoption.

Incest Taboos

In 1976 the *Journal of the Polynesian Society* published a special issue on rules and beliefs about incest in Oceania. Four of the articles deal with Polynesian societies, and help to illuminate certain aspects of kinship. For example, the essays make clear that Polynesians disdain most incest between brother and sister, seeing it as action based on desire, untempered by respect for social rules and arrangements. Since the social consequences of incest are of primary concern, it is not so much the sexual component of the relationship that arouses negative responses as the prospect of marriage (although a marriage between cousins may transform a liaison considered scandalous into a routine relationship once it is accepted by kinsmen; see Ottino 1973). The focus is on the implications of an incestuous relationship for the kinship groups immediately involved—the ones to whom both partners belong. Furthermore, and perhaps most revealing, is the degree to which kinship is defined in a pragmatic and conditional manner, so that one cannot delineate a clear set of genealogical rules that would accurately define incest. This latter point, which is central to Polynesian perspectives on kinship (and social relations in general) can be understood from both an ecological and cultural perspective. Ecologically, it is important to keep in mind that we are dealing with islands, some of which are very small and can sustain only relatively small communities. But even on the larger islands, one

must assume that founding colonies were small, and became inbred
before population expansion generated sufficient numbers to obscure
genealogical relationships. Thus Polynesian societies probably all had
to go through a period when mating was inevitable between closely
related kinsmen, and there had to be some way to make it socially
acceptable. From a cultural standpoint, the situation is complicated by
the general Polynesian preference for local endogamy, for marrying
within or near one's home community.[12] The reasons for this are multiple, and reflect such factors as bilaterality in decision making (women's
choices are given enough weight so that they are not forced to leave
their home communities for the political or economic expediency of
their male consanguines), the notion of ancestral spirits who are associated with one's home locality and who are relatively benign in comparison with alien spirits who inhabit other communities, and a senti-
mental attachment to the land that is owned by one's cognatic descent
group. It is, in fact, difficult to overestimate the importance of land as a
symbol for Polynesians, even in modernized societies like Hawaii and
New Zealand, where most Hawaiians and Maori neither exercise economic control over nor receive tangible benefits from their ancestral
lands (for an excellent account of the symbolic importance of land as
distinct from its use, see Hanson 1970). Given the potential for ambiguity in defining kinship relations within Polynesian systems, opportunities for negotiating, or renegotiating, relationships are often rather
extensive, allowing for ready circumvention of generally formulated
rules (such as those proscribing incest).

The study of Tokelau incest prohibitions by Huntsman and Hooper
perhaps best exemplifies the operation of these principles. The Tokelau
group is composed of four atolls, three of which are currently inhabited.
Despite a common language and culture, people have a strong attachment to their home atoll and a definite preference exists for marriage
within the local community. Demographic data gathered by Huntsman
and Hooper in 1967 and 1968 show rates of endogamy ranging from 79
percent on the smallest atoll (population ca. 500) to 91 percent on the
largest (population ca. 700). Despite a stated preference for atoll endogamy, however, the data suggest "that Tokelauans, when confronted
with the dilemma presented by a preference for atoll endogamy and the
prohibition on marrying close kin, do sacrifice endogamy" (Huntsman
and Hooper 1976:268).

A genealogical study of Atafu, one of the atolls, supports this idea.
Atafu was settled toward the end of the eighteenth century by two married couples, to whom members of the present population trace their
pedigree. In the early generations following settlement the genealogies
show that preference for endogamy was sacrificed in order to abide by
incest prohibitions. In intermediate generations, as the population

grew, they compromised, with some marrying out in order to maintain the ban on marrying second and third cousins, while others married within these parameters in order to maintain local endogamy. With continued expansion of the population, generation by generation, it was possible for people both to find mates within their local communities and to conform to the rules governing incest. This is reflected in the fact that the degree of cousinship among those marrying relatives has become increasingly remote (Huntsman and Hooper 1976:268–269; reporting data collected by Raspe 1973).

Tokelauan social organization reflects its close historical connection with Samoa and employs essentially the same cultural principles. The relationship between brothers and sisters is characterized by avoidance, deference, and respect. They are complementary roles, involving mutual support, and bound together in a covenant, which extends beyond the life-spans of particular sibling sets to members of succeeding generations. Thus, as in Samoa, cognatic descent groups are divided into complementary divisions, with the founders' sons and their issue comprising the *tama tane,* the daughters and their issue constituting the *tama fafine* (for a discussion of this feature of Samoan social organization, see Shore 1982:91–95).

The Tokelau term most closely approximating that of incest is *holi kāiga,* which translates roughly as the 'desecration of kinship' (Huntsman and Hooper 1976:257). Theoretically, all Tokelauans are kinsmen because they derive from common ancestors, but pragmatically kinship is defined in terms of sharing common property as part of the same descent group. A marriage between two members of a *kaukaaiga* is thus the epitome of incest regardless of the degree of relationship.

> In the Tokelau conceptual scheme, those who hold joint rights to common property are by definition "kinsmen." "Kinsmen" do not marry; those who do are "no longer kinsmen." Thus those who marry can no longer hold common rights to property. The logic which forces this conclusion is irrevocable. Either the property of any "stock" [cognatic descent group] in which a husband and wife both hold land rights must be divided, or the property is retained intact and the marrying couple banished (Huntsman and Hooper 1976:265).

The high value Tokelauans place on maintaining the unity and identity of cognatic descent groups is a source of great social pressure on members who are tempted to mate.

Another problem generated by the marriage of close kin is that it forces role reversals, as kin become affines and vice versa. There is no single term in Tokelau that can be translated as 'affinity', and "the opposite of *kāiga* 'kin' or 'related' is simply *he kāiga* 'not kin' or 'unrelated' and marriage should take place only between people who are 'not kin' " (Huntsman and Hooper 1976:260).

When an incestuous marriage occurs, individuals who were previously related as categorical brothers and sisters, for example, and therefore expected to be respectful and restrained with one another, suddenly are cast into the roles of brother-in-law and sister-in-law, which calls for sexual banter and easy-going interaction, while categorical siblings of the same sex, among whom ease and unity are called for, suddenly become in-laws of the same sex, among whom restraint and respect is prescribed. These ambiguities can only be ignored if the marriage is ignored, which sometimes happens when outmigrants to New Zealand marry kinsmen; their common *kāiga* in the home atolls simply continue to act as kin. Huntsman and Hooper (1976:270) conclude that, "since they are conceived and expressed in the idiom of social rather than genealogical relationships, Tokelau incest prohibitions are pragmatic, flexible, contingent—more attuned to social and economic realities of village life than to absolute principles of any kind."

This pragmatic, contingent approach toward the definition of kinship is also reflected in the analysis of incest in Samoa, by Shore (1976a), and the papers by Hooper (1976) on Tahiti and Monberg (1976) on Bellona, which appear in the same volume. It is further evident in *Siblingship in Oceania*, a volume edited by Marshall (1981). The contributors to the volume each made an effort to contextualize the usage of sibling terminology, and in so doing contribute to a finer understanding of these central relationships. What comes through from the Polynesian chapters (Feinberg 1981 on Anuta; Hecht 1981 on Pukapuka; Huntsman 1981b on Tokelau; Kirkpatrick 1981 on the Marquesas) is the extent to which biographic, situational, and pragmatic considerations enter into kinship designations. Kinship terms are polysemic, and are used at different levels of contrast, depending on circumstances and purposes. Thus true siblings may or may not be distinguished in ordinary discourse, and a close relative in one context may be termed distant in another.

Adoption

Although the study of incest prohibitions in Polynesia focuses our attention on the brother-sister link, the study of adoption illuminates the relationship between parents and children. Two volumes published in the 1970s (Carroll 1970; Brady, ed. 1976) contain the bulk of the literature on Polynesian adoption. They represent a major comparative effort to understand the dynamics of Polynesian parenthood, and the results have been revealing.

Both the form and the high frequency of adoption in Polynesia are remarkable, at least in comparison with Western norms. In the United States adoption is numerically insignificant, involving less than 3 percent of all children (United States Children's Bureau Division of Research 1964). Typical rates in Polynesia range from one-fourth to nearly the total population. For example, on Rangiroa atoll in the Tuamotus, Ottino (1970) reports that 35 percent of the households had adopted children resident within them and 73 percent of the households had been involved in an adoption transaction. Brady (1976b) reports that 30 percent of the households on Funafuti contain adopted children, and estimates rates of 50 to 70 percent on other islands in the Ellice group. On Kapingamarangi, a Polynesian outlier in Micronesia, Lieber (1970) found 51.7 percent of the persons canvassed to have been adopted, and on Nukuoro, another Polynesian outlier in Micronesia, Carroll (1970) was able to locate only two married adults, representing just 2 percent of the resident population, who had no experience with adoptive parenthood. Even in those Polynesian societies most affected by Western culture, such as Tahiti and Hawaii, adoption rates remain high. Thus Hooper (1970) reports that 38 percent of households in the community of Maupiti contained adopted children, and Howard et al. (1970) found this to be the case in 28 percent of Hawaiian-American households studied.

In form, too, adoption in Polynesia contrasts sharply with the practice in Western societies. Whereas adoption in European and American societies characteristically involves a formalized, legal procedure to transfer total and exclusive parental rights between unrelated persons, Polynesian adoption normally involves relatively informal transactions between consanguineally related individuals who all exercise parental prerogatives and responsibilities. Furthermore, while Westerners who give up their children for adoption are likely to be seen as incompetent at best, and are often stigmatized, prestige can accrue to Polynesian parents who give up their children, for they are looked upon as generous.[13]

The specific reasons given for adoption are multiple, and it indeed seems to be the flexibility of adoption as an institution that gives it such wide appeal in Polynesia. On a domestic level, the high value Polynesians give to completing families is a strong motivating force for adoption. Childless couples are pitied, and are regarded as both socially and economically disadvantaged. Adoption serves as a distributive mechanism, helping to equalize major imbalances in family size. It must be pointed out, however, that infertility is not a major problem in the region, and that most adopting adults already have, or have had children.

Economically, adoption often serves as means of balancing the labor needs of a household. In most island environments the domestic unit operates most efficiently with a division of labor (flexible though it may be) between men and women, and between adults and children. Children perform a variety of light chores when they are young, and move into important economic roles as they mature. They also serve as a form of long-term economic insurance (see Hooper 1970 for an instance in which this is apparently of primary concern).[14]

Adoption also serves as a means of selecting heirs for land that might otherwise revert to less favored individuals. A favored niece or nephew or grandchild can thus be given priority over other competitors. In turn, the selected individual is placed under an obligation to provide for the adopted parent(s).[15] Another economic reason given for adoption is the desire to have a child learn a skill from an expert (Handy and Pukui 1972:46).

From an ecological perspective, adoption emerges from these studies as a powerful adaptive mechanism for equitably distributing people relative to resources, including land, in island environments. Particularly where periodic droughts, destructive storms, tsunamis, and other vicissitudes of nature combined with normal demographic fluctuations to create imbalances between population and resources, adoption became an important adjunct to cognatic descent as a means of redistributing people through the use of culturally approved strategies. Although such ecological variables may have stimulated the development and refinement of these strategies, their implications for social organization were elaborated within the framework of each society's cultural logic. We find, therefore, a number of variations on dominant themes, but there are some distinctive notions that appear to be widely shared throughout Polynesia.

One such theme centers on the way jural rights are defined in relation to children. Whereas in Western cultures jural rights over children lie almost exclusively in the hands of the natural parents unless otherwise altered by legal process, in Polynesia siblings, parents, parents' siblings, and even older children share parental rights with the natural parents. Adoption of consanguines is therefore not so much the transfer of parental rights from one to another as it is a strengthening of existing rights. Adoption and fosterage are, in this sense, expressions of a more diffuse conception of parenthood than exists in the West.

As Levy (1970) first pointed out for Tahiti—and the principle holds for most of Polynesia—prevalent adoption serves to communicate to children, and indeed to everyone in the community, that all relationships, even those of mother to child, are contingent and problematic. According to Levy this has important psychological repercussions, including a tendency to avoid strong emotional attachments to anyone (see also Ritchie and Ritchie 1979, and chapter 4, this volume). On the positive side, Firth (1936b:192–193) suggests that on Tikopia adoption conveys the message that persons must have ties beyond the domestic unit; it therefore constitutes a form of social weaning that complements physiological weaning. Brooks, in her description of adoption on Manihi in the Tuamotus, draws a further implication. Although particular relationships are fragile, she points out, it is always possible to find new partners for relationship. "All individuals are replaceable. . . . Security cannot be assured through any individual, but chances for security may be maximized through the maintenance of a group of potential substitutes" (Brooks 1976:62–63). This is close to Firth's point, of course, although his functional imperative has been recast as a cultural perspective reflecting both on adoptions and the tenor of relational activity in general.[16] But perhaps the most important message, from a sociocultural standpoint, derives directly from the ecologically induced importance of maintaining cooperative relationships within potentially imperiled communities, "that relatives are interdependent and that the maintenance of this network of interdependency must take priority over the wishes of individuals, even such strong wishes as attach to one's natural children" (Carroll 1970:152).

An extreme case can be found on Taku'u, a Polynesian outlier in Melanesia. There, everyone is adopted at birth, and individuals are under great pressure to honor adoptive relationships over natural ones. The explicit reason given is that otherwise people may narrow their allegiance to their natural families at the expense of broader community involvement (B. Moir, I. Howard, personal communications, 1986).

The particular forms of adoption—who does the adopting and under what conditions—may carry even more specific messages about cultural principles.

> Adoption, as it is practiced on Nukuoro, is an especially appropriate vehicle for the expression of cultural norms of kin-group solidarity in that, by obliging parents to give up their children, the supposition that children belong exclusively to their natural parents is modified in the direction of recognizing a multiplicity of claims. The claims of particular parents and particular children on each other must give way in the face of the authority of all elders and the requirement that siblings should cooperate. To put the matter another way, "adoption" reiterates not only the principle of "group solidarity" but emphasizes the particular dimensions of this solidarity (Carroll 1970:152).

As in the case of Taku'u, Carroll points out that in practice adoption does not serve to deny the importance of biological parenthood, but in fact underscores it, while at the same time communicating the necessity of overcoming its threat of exclusivity (Carroll 1970:152–153).

Gender

One focus of the debates concerning the nature of Polynesian descent groups involved the question of a patrilineal bias. Although it is acknowledged that optation is a characteristic of most Polynesian systems, in many cases the core of corporate descent groups is composed of patrilineally related males. Succession patterns also reveal a tendency to favor males, so from a statistical standpoint evidence exists to support a case for patrilineality. Furthermore, cultural conceptions of descent widespread in Polynesia display a bias toward the male line. In Samoa and in the Ellice Islands, for example, alignments traced to an ancestor through males are referred to as "strong blood," while those traced through females are known as "weak blood," linkages (Brady 1976b: 124; Shore 1976a:177). Goldman, in summarizing the literature for Polynesia, concludes that the sanctity of the male line is a basic principle of status in the region. He considers most Polynesian societies to manifest a pro-patriliny bias, which is based on the notion that men and the male line carry more *mana* 'potency' than women and the female line. This bias is mitigated by the principle of seniority, and by other criteria associated with *mana*, such as genealogical depth and reputations for skill and valor (Goldman 1970:16). Sahlins, in his earlier comparative study, also referred to a patrilineal bias, and defined Polynesian corporate units as non-exogamous patrilineal descent groups, although he acknowledged that female links were occasionally important for tracing ancestry, and used the term ambipatrilineal to designate this mode of descent reckoning (Sahlins 1958:146).

Indeed, one could make a strong case for male dominance if one were to focus entirely on certain cultural conceptions of male and female, as these were described by earlier ethnographers (e.g., E. S. C. Handy 1927:37). More recent ethnographic accounts based on cultural conceptions likewise tend to emphasize male strengths and female weaknesses. For example, in their description of male and female in Tokelau culture, Huntsman and Hooper (1975) report a distinction between *itu malohi* 'strong side' and *itu vaivai* 'weak side'. The reference is only partly to physical strength; it also implies "that men are dignified and controlled and thereby qualified to make decisions and exercise authority," while "women are emotional, vulnerable and erratic, that they are unable to control their feelings and are prone to express themselves without caution" (Huntsman and Hooper 1975:419).

Women's activities are conceived as confined and sedentary, men's as expansive and active. As elsewhere in Polynesian societies, spatial metaphors are used to portray this difference. "The woman stays: the man goes on the path," is an expression translated from Tokelau to summarize differences between male and female activities.

In general, female activity is on land, within the village and in the domestic sphere of house and cookhouse, while male activity is at sea, on the outlying plantation islets of the atoll and in the public places of the village, known figuratively as "the path." Thus land and sea, village and outlying islets, domestic and public areas of the village are contrasted as complementary domains of the sexes. In each contrast set, it is the female who is more confined, more restricted in both social and spatial terms (Huntsman and Hooper 1975:418; see also Shore 1982:225–228, Hecht 1977).

In Samoa, men are allotted tasks defined as heavy, such as clearing the bush and planting, deep-sea fishing and preparing earth ovens, while women perform light tasks such as weeding, cleaning, taking care of children, fishing on the reef, and everyday cooking (Franco 1985). This division of labor is common throughout Polynesia, but the rigidity of task division varies from culture to culture. In some practicality dominates structure, and flexibility prevails; in others the separation of tasks is quite sharply defined. (Flexibility is not always forced on Polynesians by circumstances, of course; it also reflects a cultural assumption that persons can and will work out arrangements according to their own wishes or needs.)

Traditionally, restrictions upon women were often formalized in the form of taboos and were backed by supernatural sanctions. In many Polynesian cultures women were barred from sacred places, from contact with men's fishing gear, and from consuming certain kinds of food. Menstruating women were generally considered dangerous, and were secluded to a greater or lesser degree. The common notion was that women are especially vulnerable to capricious supernatural influence when menstruating; hence, they must be confined in order to avoid accidental disruption of supernatural-human relationships.

The literature reveals a number of other indicators of low status for women in certain Polynesian societies, including the enforced virginity of unmarried girls, a relatively high frequency of rape, and a marked subordination of wives to husbands within the domestic sphere (Ortner 1981:359).

Despite all these signs of inferiority, however, there is a good deal of evidence to suggest that women enjoyed high status throughout Polynesia. As already indicated, in western Polynesia women outweighed their brothers in formal honors, and received deference from them. More striking is the active political roles that women played. Not only did they play a critical role in cementing alliances—indeed, as recent studies have shown they played a pivotal role in mobilizing networks and converting them into political power—but they held high office with some regularity (see Bott 1982). Furthermore, although virginity was generally valued, and some women were carefully guarded, for the most part women were free to indulge in sexual relations without stigma.

The status of women in Polynesia thus appears at first glance to be paradoxical. Despite a negative ideology associating women with weakness, darkness, and an absence of control, and the overall subordination of women to their husbands, ethnographers have generally described Polynesian women as enjoying relatively high status (Loeb 1926:82; Linton 1939:162; Mariner 1827, 2:95, 119, 211; Oliver 1974:1132).

Steps toward clearing up this paradox have been taken by Schoeffel (1978, 1979) and Shore (1981, 1982) in their analyses of sexuality and gender in Samoa, and by Ortner (1981) in her overview of the topic. Schoeffel (1978:69) argues that male and female symbols in Samoa express "an opposition between the moral and secular aspects of society and [have] nothing to do with gender descriptions as such." The key concept is *feagaiga,* which refers to "a special relationship between two parties who interact in a defined, reciprocal manner and who represent opposed concepts which regulate their interaction" (Schoeffel 1979:69). *Feagaiga* relationships (which Shore glosses as 'covenant') occur in three distinct arenas: kinship and gender, religion and politics. As Schoeffel interprets them, *feagaiga* relationships involve social contracts between two parties, "one of whom represents sacred forces which impose moral order on the other, who represents the impulsive, 'natural' human animal (Schoeffel 1979:70). Sisters in Samoa are perceived as exercising such a controlling power *(mana)* over their brothers, and are thus honored and served by them. As wives, however, women are expected to serve their husbands and submit to their authority *(pule).*

According to Shore, sexuality in Samoa is associated with the concept of *āmio,* which is applied to behavior that is considered to stem from personal drives and urges. In contrast is the concept of *aga,* which refers to "social norms, proper behavior, linked to social roles and appropriate contexts" (Shore 1981:195). Shore presents these two terms as parallel to (but not identical with) the nature-culture dichotomy as it is used by structural anthropologists. Thus *āmio* implies "lack of social restraint or form, and the expression of personal impulse and spontaneity," while *aga* "suggests social constraint, dignity, and subordination of personal impulse to cultural style and social control" (Shore 1981:196).

For Shore, the key to women's status lies in Samoan conceptions of blood, which when it flows from the body in an uncontrolled manner (as in menstruation, or from a wound), is referred to in chiefly address as dirt and is a source of pollution (see Hanson 1982b for an alternative perspective). In contrast, when the flow of blood is under societal control (as in blood transfusions or during tattooing) there are no implications of pollution. The basic contrast as far as women are concerned is that between menstrual flow, over which society has relatively little control, and the hymeneal blood of a new bride, which Shore believes may symbolize societal control (Shore 1981:198; see also Shore, chapter 5, this volume).

There is, Shore maintains, a distinction that follows from this cultural logic between women as sisters, whose sexuality is restrained and is (properly) under their brothers' and father's control, and women as sexual partners, where their sexuality is an expression of personal desire. As a wife, therefore, a woman's status is lower than as a sister, although a woman whose marriage was arranged enjoys higher status than one who eloped, or one who has a reputation for promiscuity (indicating total lack of social control). Although not all Polynesian societies place such a strong emphasis on controlling female sexuality, in general this is the case, especially among women of rank.

Ortner takes as axiomatic the nature-culture distinction of Lévi-Strauss, and the tendency for women to be associated symbolically more closely with nature and men with culture. In particular, it is the reproductive capacities of women that are identified with nature, Ortner maintains, and are relegated to an inferior status. Men, in contrast, express their creativity externally and artificially, through the manipulation of technology and symbols (Ortner 1974:75), that is, through cultural means. But women are not only associated with reproduction. They are as wives, mothers, and lovers, but not when they are in the role of sisters, daughters and ceremonial virgins. Women thus have a dual nature in Polynesia; they are like men in some ways, different from them in others.

Like Schoeffel and Shore, Ortner (1981) perceives that the status ambiguity of women derives from the contrast between their roles as sisters and as reproductive beings (wives, mothers or lovers), but she goes further and relates the issue to the ranking system in general. Ortner gained inspiration from Goldman's insightful analysis of rank and status in Polynesia, and following Goldman, she sees the status system as having a dominant effect on other features of social organization, including kinship, gender, and descent group organization. She presumes the system of prestige and ranking to define the nature of personal and social value, and therefore what men and women are and should be. Ortner organizes her analysis about what men, who usually control the prestige system, are trying to accomplish, and how that project implicates the organization of their relations with women.

Ortner maintains that although the abstract principles of rank in Polynesia are based on kinship seniority, in fact the secular power of chiefs depends upon the resources they control, and in particular on the personnel under their command (see Marcus, chapter 6, this volume, for a discussion of these two aspects of chieftainship). But cognatic descent systems present a problem to chiefs, for they allow individuals to choose between descent groups, especially at the time of marriage. Descent group strength is therefore subject to manipulation, and it is here that women provide a key. For one thing, since women, as daughters, inherit rights in their descent groups' land, "sons-in-law with less substantial property stakes in their own lines may be attracted into their wives' lines, while at the same time, given the patrilineal bias in the inheritance structure, they can hold on to their own land and bring it into their affinal line's orbit" (Ortner 1981:367). Since the children of such a marriage would more likely affiliate with their mother's group, this has the potential of adding substantially to its membership. Control of women thus becomes a key factor in manipulating descent group strength, and leads to placement of values on virginity, attempts to use women as lures, and a variety of sexual "assaults" upon women.

> A girl has real value to her descent line, particularly if she sustains her affiliation with it and brings in her husband, his land, and their children. There is thus structural motivation for "holding on" to a daughter/sister. This "holding on" is symbolically expressed through control of her virginity. The virgin both displays her kinsmen's symbolic retention of her and, because virginity is defined as highly honorable, expresses her genuine value to her group. At the same time the control structure means that sex with her must be "taken," "stolen," or otherwise forcefully appropriated, even when she presents herself, as she often does, as a consenting party. Hence the prevalence of various forms of sexual theft—sleep crawling, marriage by capture, triumphal defloration of virgins, and the like (Ortner 1981:375).

Why, then, do Polynesian women have the reputation for easy, uncomplicated sexuality? And how do we explain the extensive documentation of women's intercourse with sailors during the period of exploration? Is the popular image of natural Polynesian sexuality a myth? Ortner points out that not everyone has equal stakes in the recruitment game. There is therefore a considerable differential in the degree to which young women are controlled: high-ranking women are much more closely supervised than those of low status. Low status women—those with fewest material and social resources to bring into a marriage—were unlikely to contract a marriage with a resourceful male anyway, so the stake in controlling them was relatively low. Along with widows, divorcees, and other women tainted by explicit recognition of their sexuality, they constituted a pool of available women. Added to this cultural cynosure was the anomalous status of junior male siblings in senior lines. Being both of high rank and junior to their elder siblings who stood to succeed to titles and positions of chieftainship, junior siblings were perceived as potential threats, particularly if they married early, and well, and produced a sizeable progeny. According to Ortner, the solution was to encourage them to sexual indulgence (but not to marriage or paternity), particularly with lower status women with whom marriage would be less of a threat, since their offsprings' status would be lowered accordingly. All this encourages an extended adolescence, with sexual adventures as a prime concern. As for the women who were made available to sailors during the early period of contact, Ortner surmises that here, too, they were used as bait to obtain valuable commodities, including insemination, from men who were considered to be of superior *mana* (Ortner 1981:376; see also Sahlins 1981a).

On the whole, Ortner agrees with the assessment of most previous commentators that the status of women in Polynesia is relatively high. To account for this she argues that kinswomen—specifically daughters, sisters, and aunts—have culturally defined high status, and that consanguineal kinship is the idiom upon which social status is based. It is descent rather than marriage that generates rank and prestige. Sisters are more respected than wives, and women in general are conceptually identified as sisters more than as wives. Within the political sphere patrilineal biases work categorically only against wives. Ortner (1981: 394) notes that sisters and other kinswomen occasionally succeed to public office within their kin groups.

Ortner's viewpoint, while stimulating, is too rigid and narrowly conceived to account for all the Polynesian material. Although the strategies she postulates were no doubt of importance on occasion, they almost certainly constituted only part of the Polynesian repertoire for strengthening groups. She also fails to take into account life cycle changes in sexual expectations and social status. In general, her model seems somewhat more compatible with the data from western Polynesia, where cross-sex sibling ties were most elaborated. Nevertheless she has brought into the foreground a number of important questions that should provoke fruitful research.

Other recent materials have raised questions about the image of women as inferior. For example, Tahitians are reported by Levy (1973: 236-237) as minimizing sexual dimorphism and portraying a man's lot as more difficult, rather than men as stronger. Hanson (1982b) concludes that the concept of female pollution has been misconstrued. He interprets the data as indicating that women were traditionally perceived as conduits of the sacred, and apt to attract, not repel, divine influences. He generalizes from an analysis of *tapu* removal to a broad hypothesis about women in traditional Polynesia. "Women were perhaps too close to the gods, too subject to their influence, to be able to control them. Although men were more remote from the gods—perhaps *because* they were more remote from them—they may have been thought to be more effective at relatively dispassionate manipulation of the divine for human ends" (Hanson 1982b:375). Although it does not fully address the fundamental question of how gender informs social life, Hanson's formulation places the problem of gender relations in the context of cultural conceptions that assure cultural continuity. Thus he cites Sahlins, who suggests that in Hawaii, "the sexes represented the two fundamental ways in which humanity drew the necessary conditions of existence from the gods: for the male it was to extract human livelihood from the gods in the form of food, while for the female it was to attract the gods and to transform their generative powers into children" (Hanson 1982b:371).

An increased appreciation for the complexities of gender conceptions has led contemporary anthropologists to question the validity of earlier formulations emphasizing patrilineality as a structuring principle in Polynesian societies. Although a bias in that direction certainly existed at both conceptual and pragmatic levels, to characterize Polynesian societies as patrilineal, with merely a few concessions to practicality, seems clearly erroneous. An example is provided by Webster's reanalysis of the Maori data, cited earlier. Webster asserts that previous accounts of Maori descent groups, including Firth's, neglected the egalitarian and bilateral aspects of cognatic kinship, emphasizing instead "the dogma of male autocracy and patrilineal descent" (Webster 1975: 125). In a careful study of one of the tribes reputed to be most firmly male authoritarian, he found an average incidence of 35 percent female links among all links traced by terminal descendants. The point is that female linkages were hardly trivial, and presented a genuine, and apparently culturally approved, alternative. Although there were certainly differences in the degree to which male links were emphasized in various Polynesian societies, and within the same society under different circumstances (see Linnekin 1985b concerning changing patterns in Hawaii), what evidence there is supports the view that linkages through females were both culturally important and pragmatically used to a considerable extent throughout Polynesia. They were clearly more than a residual phenomenon.

Alliance and Exchange

It is no accident that Marcel Mauss, in his famous analysis of gift-giving and exchange (1954), used the New Zealand Maori as an epitomizing case. Formalized exchange is an essential part of social life in Polynesia and operates at every level of society, from the domestic to the apically political. Although various aspects of exchange have been described by the earliest observers of Polynesian cultures (it would have been difficult to miss), recent field workers have placed the topic at the heart of their analyses. For purposes of discussion we shall distinguish two general models of exchange, those in which persons are the primary commodities transacted, either through marriage or adoption, and those in which goods or services are passed between individuals or groups. In practice, of course, our distinction breaks down, and intangibles such as knowledge, prestige, and privileges can also be counted among the commodities that enter into exchange transactions.

As pointed out previously, for most Polynesians marriage between those recognized as kin is abhorrent. Yet marital bonds that reinforce local ties or reunite long separated lines of kinsmen may be welcome. The claim that all members of a local population are 'kin', heard often in Polynesia, is testimony to a history of endogamy as well as to a high level of recognized solidarity. Yet tensions may occur, especially within small communities where marriage partners are limited, leading either to uncomfortably close marriages or to the emigration of young people in search of new marriage partners.

For the western Tuamotus, Ottino (1965, 1967) has reconstructed traditional marriage strategies involving both patterns. For most people, nearby 'ati 'descent units' formed marriage isolates based on local endogamy. A few children of chiefly status married elsewhere, into families of similar status. Such marriages not only sealed political alliances; they also helped to maintain the distinctive identities of 'ati and the prestige of chiefly lines.

It appears that the transformation of political alliances into explicit rules or preferences for marriage partners among aristocratic families had a widespread potential in Polynesia. Close unions, precisely because they would be improper or even scandalous for common folk, underscored the differences between those of high estate and commoners. Given the heroic god-like qualities ascribed to high-ranking individuals in Polynesian societies, it is not surprising that incest, one of the behaviors that characterizes gods in myths, should also occur among the ali'i. In Hawaii, for example, marriages between closely related persons of exalted descent occurred regularly, with the closest marriages (between siblings) consolidating the highest status.

In Tonga, relations of wife-givers to wife-takers were stable among the highest chiefly lines, so long as these maintained their political position. When one line supplanted another as wife-giver to the Tui Tonga, this marked, and presumably sealed, a military victory (see Bott 1981, 1982). Gifford (1929:189) reported mother's brother's daughter (MBD) marriage to be "common among chiefs, but rare among commoners." In her analysis of the data, Biersack (1982) construes Tongan society as organized through the interaction of two structures, elaborated by cross and parallel relationships. Each structure is hierarchical and becomes a conduit for assymetric exchange. She goes on to argue that the MBD marriage rule is not generated by an elementary structure (as defined by Lévi-Strauss), nor does it merely maintain the cross/parallel distinction. Instead, it is affected by both structures: wife-giving units stand as both mother's brother and younger brother to wife-takers. The result is an intensification of hierarchy and a generalization of the privileges of *fahu* (prototypically, sister's child) outside of life crisis contexts.

Biersack's analysis has some notable strengths. For example, it accounts for the cognatic emphases in the official genealogies among persons of high rank in Tonga. It also provides a rationale for marriage practices linking the highest *ha'a* units, and it helps to explain the correlation of changes in wife-giving units with changes in such units' political fortunes. In addition, it sheds light on relations between cross-siblings and between elder and younger brothers, relationships that western Polynesians have encumbered with elaborate interactional and transactional rules. And her discussion of adjacent-generation relationships brings out the patterning of relations between parents' siblings and siblings' children. One implication seems to be that parent-child relations are subsumed by structures of seniority and cross-sex kinship.

Biersack maintains that the two structures she has identified combine to produce a formation that underlies Tongan social structure. But for reasons that will emerge, we are uncomfortable with any attempt to locate fixed structures at the heart of Polynesian societies. We wonder whether the structures Biersack describes are truly fundamental, or whether they take on such clear definition only under conditions determined by the political system.

In the Marquesas, cross-cousin unions of chiefly children were seen as maintaining the rank of descent units *(mata)*, although the application of the rule was open to considerable interpretation. Thus Dening (1971) identified a marriage that Marquesans presented as following the rule despite the fact it united parallel cousins. We therefore suspect that the rule did not prescribe marriage partners so much as it provided a rationale for action in response to status considerations. Such claims appear to be only one of several ways to present a particular marriage as appropriate and momentous.[17] In fact, models of alliance that emphasize the workings of prescriptive rules appear to be of limited use in Polynesia, because exchanges tend to involve several media and to be practiced in a variety of contexts. Within this cultural area there are multiple mechanisms for forming alliances, including transactions in goods, services, and intangibles. And in addition to marriage, there is adoption.

Whereas our previous discussion of adoption emphasized its ecological importance and its implications for conceptions of kinship, here we are concerned with its significance for cementing relations between individuals and groups. As indicated earlier, adoption in Polynesia plays an important role in affirming existing relationships and establishing new ones. This is especially true since natural parents do not give up their jural rights, but rather extend them to the adopting parent(s). Natural parents and adopting parents thus become co-parents of the same children, creating a bond between them that is logically parallel to that between husband and wife, whose strongest bond is apt to be that of co-parents of the same offspring. Although most adoption transactions are between individuals or nuclear families they have the symbolic capacity for creating and strengthening ties between larger groups in much the same way that marriage does. In some respects, however, adoption is even more flexible than marriage as an alliance mechanism, because it can be transacted between families for whom marriage is prohibited by incest restrictions. Indeed, this may be one of the reasons adoption has such a high incidence in Polynesia, since, as we have already pointed out, cognatic descent systems normally extend the incest taboo to third or fourth cousins, thus reducing the possibility of using marriage as a basic mechanism for forming alliances between groups so related. In contrast, most unilineal systems prescribe or encourage cross-cousin marriage as a means of forming alliances, with incest prohibitions extending only to parallel cousins. As Brady has written, the "adoption of kinsmen in cognatic systems with extensive prohibitions on marriage may fulfill many of the same internal group support and alliance functions that close cross-cousin marriage does in unilineal systems" (Brady 1976a:290).

The implications of adoption for political maneuvering in status-conscious Samoa are ably spelled out by Shore (1976b). He documents the importance of alliances for building the prestige of particular titles, and shows how adoption is structurally parallel to marriage and the transferring of titles between groups as alliance mechanisms. By extending parenthood over a child who is not related by blood, political alliances are symbolically transformed into attachments of common descent, in this case projected into the future rather than relying on common ancestry. Thus by adopting the child of an outside chief, a group creates a common heir to the titles of both political units.

Even in localized contexts adoption may serve to ally groups who have much to gain from such transactions. Thus in one case Shore describes, repeated adoptions and acts of name-giving link a pastor's family (A) with a kin group (B) in the village of his ministry, where the pastor has no resident kinsmen. The transactions are asymmetric, with the pastor's family giving names and taking children. The result is that "while members of family B increased their status by their new kinship links with family A, the pastor's family gained strong supportive kinship ties in the village" (Shore 1976a:187).

Although adoptive ties between families are often important, adoptions may also work to avoid differentiation within a kin unit. In eastern Polynesia especially, multiple adoptions may crosscut potential divisions between generations or emergent lines, and thus work to preserve the ideal of unity. As a result, exchange, in the form of reciprocal nurturance, may not only complement genealogical ties but may actually supplant them as the perceived basis for kinship.

In reviewing the literature on transactions, particular forms of reciprocity emerge as crucial in one society or another. However, moving from the study of marriage or adoption to alliance and reciprocity as a total social phenomenon is a complex business, because even the smallest Polynesian societies maintain dense networks of exchange. In Tokelau, for example, food distributions occur within and between *kaaiga* and other local groupings, as well as among small groups of households. Much attention is paid to food exchanges, not simply to effect generalized or restricted exchange, but to involve all in a shared social fate. As Huntsman (1981b:100) relates: "That everyone shares and shares equally is 'the true Tokelau way'." (See Linnekin 1985b for a similar view among Hawaiians.)

A deceptively modest paper by Tiffany (1975b) shows how complex Polynesian exchange systems can be. She documents chiefly redistribution in Samoa, describing sixteen occasions in a single year in which a chief contributed to redistributions. *'Aiga* 'Samoan units of descent, land and rank' are described by Tiffany as pooling units, and the *matai* who lead them as the coordinators of pooling and redistribution. But *'aiga* are involved in exchanges at several social levels, and the actions of *matai,* who invariably have ties to multiple *'aiga* and villages, cannot be seen simply in terms of self-interest or commitment to a single unit.

Tiffany's analysis is a welcome corrective to the simpler model of Samoan exchange based on two forms of goods, *toga* 'women's goods, especially fine mats' and *'oloa* 'men's goods, especially foodstuffs'. Exchanges of these two categories of goods at weddings, between the family of the groom and the family of the bride, were documented early by M. Mead (1930b), and a number of subsequent commentators have accepted the wedding exchange as prototypical. Although the significance of these two types of commodities at life-crisis ceremonies cannot be denied, the closer look at exchange provided by Tiffany raises questions about the nature of these categories and their flow over time (see also Franco 1985).

In short, although models of exchange circuits such as Lévi-Strauss' models of generalized and restricted exchange focus attention on a single type of transaction, Polynesian exchanges can be mapped by such models only insofar as they take into consideration a variety of transactions that can be reduced to instances of a rule, or by noting why alliances are, in a particular sector of society, so narrowly focused. Where special value is granted to a transaction, as confirming the privileged positions of those involved, such value does not appear to follow inevitably from set rules. Rather it appears to be based on contextual definitions, complex social histories and actors' attempts to promote versions of events that suit their perceived interest.

The above considerations testify to the importance of exchange in Polynesia as well as to the gap between Polynesian practices and models based on the repetitive practices of one or another form of exchange. At a moment of heightened transaction, such as a wedding, many participants can choose to define their relationship to the major actors involved in one of several ways. At other exchanges they may give priority to a different path or linkage. Hence it is easy to view skilled transactors, such as Samoan chiefs, as calculating strategists. It should be kept in mind, however, that they are also working to maintain a network of ties that might collapse if the ambiguities of multiple connections were to be reduced.

Both the power and persistence of multi-stranded exchange in Polynesian communities is illustrated by Linnekin's description of the contemporary Hawaiian community of Ke'anae. Ke'anae Hawaiians categorically separate commercial relations with the outside from social relations inside the community, where gift exchange is governed by an ethic of generalized reciprocity. In addition to short-term exchanges based on bananas, taro shoots, and small favors, "the imperative of reciprocity also drives long-term cycles of exchange among Hawaiians, as marriage and adoption join families and localities in a network of relatedness" (Linnekin 1985b:240; also see Ito 1985b concerning the presumption of continuing relationship among modern Hawaiians).

If the complexities that confront would-be analysts of exchange in Polynesia under relatively stable conditions are not formidable enough, Polynesians have also been known to tinker with social groupings in order to produce new alignments of relationships. In Pukapuka, for example, a council of elders decided to recreate a traditional form of social organization as a means of rearranging the bases for competition and exchange (Borofsky 1987). Consequently, one must deal with a plethora of organizational forms, and confront the suspicion that such forms may be continuously generated from the traditions of the atoll. As Borofsky's analysis makes clear, there is by no means an agreement about what the traditions are, making the possibilities for realignment even greater. It may be that the dispersion and confounding of competing units, rather than stable patterns of reciprocity, are central to these transactional practices (see Glasse 1968 for a similar view of feuding).

To summarize, whereas descent group models bring to the fore discrete and continuing social units, the classic exchange model places in the foreground cycles of reciprocity through which such units are defined as partners. We see Polynesian practices as conveying a view of society in which the fact of widespread relationship is assumed, but in which the emergence of well-bounded units and well-defined circuits of exchange may also be precipitated through extensive and repeated actions. From such a perspective, a wide range of exchange strategies can be seen as operative, and under certain conditions clearcut exchange systems can be located within particular social fields.

In our opinion the challenge of developing an appropriately supple model of Polynesian exchanges remains. Although the analysis of structures or total social facts has often been revealing, the work of specifying the contexts in which such structures obtain, and the logic whereby contexts are aligned in a larger social order, has barely begun.

Toward an Understanding of Polynesian Contexts

One starting point for the analysis of Polynesian contexts is the study of formalized events, such as *fono* and chiefly kava ceremonies in western Polynesia, and settings for heightened action such as the Maori *marae* (see Bott 1972; Duranti 1981b; Salmond 1975). By identifying the parameters that define such events for participants, the potentials for variation in them, and the sense made of such variations, perspective can be gained on the ways in which Polynesians view their organization. Any perspective would be incomplete, however, unless attention to elaborately ordered situations is balanced by attention to everyday interactions. Without explicit means of relating these, analysts may find that well-enunciated views of social life, enacted and expounded in formal events, do not correspond with other realities. We may therefore be tempted to take such views as masks or illusions, but the efforts Polynesians devote to ceremonial events would make such a deduction questionable. In fact, formal events often serve to order everyday relationships. They may do so by summarizing them, by selecting out one or another aspect for mention, or even by asserting ironically what people know to be not quite the case. When dealing with dramas of status, such as chiefly kava ceremonies, or even with celebrations of youth and beauty such as those that occur at Bastille Day festivals in French Polynesia, local conventions of dramaturgy must be examined closely.

The analysis of contexts involves a search for those aspects of action and events that signal cultural interpretations of situations, and for the underlying cultural logic whereby situations are aligned or contrasted. Studies of Polynesian ideas (e.g., Salmond 1978; Kirkpatrick 1983) and interactive procedures (Keesing and Keesing 1956; Marcus 1984) touch on these issues, but Shore (1982) has confronted them most directly.

Shore identifies several key dimensions that lie behind Samoan concepts of action and of relationships. The terms of his analysis—*āmio* 'personal impulse and behavior' and *aga* 'social conduct, behavior style'; symmetrical and complementary relations; ranked and unranked relations—are used both to point out contrasts important for Samoans and to model the general principles Samoans draw on in making sense of social action.[18] Similarly, his analytical focus on social control works on two levels. He deals with the control of aggression (organizing the book around the background and responses to a murder) and with the ways in which certain types of relationships stand as complements and control mechanisms for others. The approach yields a scheme of relational types (Shore 1982:212) but, more important, it portrays the interdependencies among relationships and levels of social organization in such a way that Samoan processes of gauging and responding to crises are illuminated. In other words, he provides the materials for either a homeostatic account of Samoan society or a symbolic one, but turns away from these objectives to stress the interplay of institutions and relationships that frames Samoan political strategies.

Shore (1982:257) argues that "social contexts are always negotiated to some extent in the course of social interaction, but the range of possibilities for the tone of these contexts is sharply delimited by the logic of the culture from which they take their meaning." Oppositions of dignity and crude power and control and energy pervade presentations of self, formulations of relationships, and hence understandings of situations.

The accounts of isolable situations provided by Shore (see especially 1979) constitute only one part of a fully articulated analysis of contexts. His emphasis is on the ways social forms help to shape events; by establishing potentials, tensions, and alternatives that actors can explore. This type of analysis goes a long way toward clarifying both the significance of particular event sequences and the inherent dynamics of a social system.

Conclusion

During the past few years the standard categories and domains of social analysis have been challenged. Once the topics that came under the rubric of social organization could be easily listed; now analysts include a wide variety of issues, with differing emphases. Although this decrease in consensus makes institutional comparisons more difficult, it forces authors to specify more fully the extent and nature of the coherence they find in their data. Hence it offers the hope of a theoretically more explicit account of social organization, and for comparative understandings of entire social systems, not just of institutions that are vaguely similar in form or function.

Although no single vision unites the field, there is broad agreement among analysts of Polynesian societies on the importance of studying social dynamics; on the need to integrate accounts of structures and events; on exchange as constitutive of, not just reflecting or linking social groupings; and on the need to map Polynesians' definitions of situations and the ways they negotiate meanings. As we have indicated, a search for cultural principles that structure social life in Polynesia is yielding suggestive results. This is largely a comparative effort, but it does not lessen the need to study processes within particular societies, and to analyze them in detail. If we are to comprehend Polynesian social realities, even the most extensive and subtle models of cultural principles must be buttressed by accounts of the processes that bring them into play.

In the course of this essay we have referred to differences between cultural and ecological explanations, between structural and processual analyses, and between studies aimed at generalized models and those with a particularistic emphasis. These differences indicate that much theoretical work remains to be done. For explanations to be fully adequate, cultural analyses would have to take into consideration ecological opportunities and constraints, structural models would have to be complemented by considerations of the social processes that reproduce structures and the historical realities that transform them, and generalized models would have to be responsive to the nuances of form and process contained in the most sensitive particularistc accounts. The order is a tall one.

Currently, studies focusing on the cultural bases of social life are in vogue, but this is not to say that a single paradigm has triumphed. Rather, most analysts agree that any satisfactory understanding of Polynesian social organization must be grounded in the ways that information is systematically organized and communicated. For some, this means giving priority to views articulated by Polynesians. For others, the impetus is to discover codes implicit in artifacts, etiquette, formalized events, and myth. But regardless of the approach we take, the task of constructing compelling models of Polynesian social systems remains before us. The task is both theoretical and ethnographic, for new models raise to prominence data that have been refractory. Such data, in turn, stimulate new insights. In the light of past scholarship, prospects both for extensive debate and increased understanding appear good.

NOTES

We would like to acknowledge the extensive critiques of earlier drafts provided us by Aletta Biersack, Rob Borofsky, and Judy Huntsman. Jocelyn Linnekin and Merrily Stover also made helpful comments.

1. Later on, colonial administrators often redefined features of traditional social organization in order to make them conform to a preconceived legal order. Thus in Fiji, an attempt to codify customary land tenure rules and to record holdings led to a rigidification of descent units as corporate, and to a restriction of rights in previously accessible land. It also magnified the power of unit heads (Chapelle 1978; France 1969; Walter 1978a). Crocombe's (1964) analysis of Rarotonga landholding also reveals a pattern of streamlining complex social relations into a legally recognized unilineal descent system. It has also been pointed out that in some instances Polynesian chiefs supported the elevation of one individual to paramount status, partly to facilitate trade between themselves and visiting Europeans (Newbury 1980:47).

2. The most notable case is Morgan's (1871) view of Hawaiian kin terms as evidence for the earliest form of human marriage.

3. It should be noted that views of descent found in eastern Polynesia differ systematically from those found in societies with classic unilineal descent groups. Thus the descendants of an ancestor, X, are not necessarily "the sons of X," a phrase that implies continuing filiation. Instead they are likely to be "inside" or "in the belly of X." We see an image of pregnancy here, one that entails the eventual birth of those "inside," and hence their separation from the ancestor and each other. (Tree metaphors, whereby ancestors are "trunks" and descendants "branches" are often found in Polynesia. Interestingly, these can be read either way, stressing the continuity of trunk and branch or the differences between the two.) Terms for descendants may mark these as extensions of an ancestor, rather than as members of a group. Marquesans sometimes explain *hina* 'great grandchildren' as the gray *(hinahina)* hairs of the ascendant, a usage that signals the old age and imminent demise of the latter as well as the formation of a unit around the ancestral estate. We are not claiming that an etymological analysis of these phrases is an adequate substitute for detailed analysis of social data, but rather suggest that the view of cognatic descent as involving perpetual units may reflect preconceptions that Polynesians do not share.

4. Hecht (1976) reports a similar concern for burial sites in relation to group membership on Pukapuka. There, patrilineal groups control burial plots, and interment in a particular plot defines membership. Living persons, however, may attempt to maintain ties to several patrilines, rendering their status ambiguous until burial.

5. The importance of *mana* for competitive relations among chiefs or specialists is evident in other Oceanic societies as well. See Roger Keesing (1984) for Melanesian concepts.

6. Even where idiosyncratic terms are used (such as Tahitian *feti'i*), they are conceptual equivalents.

7. The notion of kinship as shared substance derives from a point made by David Schneider (1968). More generally, Schneider's (1972, 1976) insistence on ethnographically based concepts of kinship has been a major stimulus to studies of social organization within Polynesia.

8. The term *aropa* is cognate with Hawaiian *aloha,* Samoan *alofa,* and so on.

9. Here, sign and reality are distinguishable but of equal importance. Most Polynesians take kinship to be real and proper when sign and reality, action and filiation coincide; they take it to exist in an important way when signs abound

despite the absence of filiation; and find it to be little more than hypothetical, even shameful, when genealogy alone links persons.

10. Women sometimes do assume political office in Polynesia. In postcontact polities, Kaʻahumanu of Hawaii, Pomare IV of Tahiti, and Queen Salote of Tonga are notable.

11. One ought to exercise caution in accepting such etymological speculations. The relationship between the semantic content of currently used terms and their root forms is at best highly problematic. Such reconstructions cannot be taken as an accurate indicator of speakers' attitudes when they use a concept.

12. An exception to this rule of preference is that persons of high rank often opt to marry out in order to establish political alliances with other groups.

13. It should be made clear that the concept of adoption causes difficulties when used cross-culturally, especially since Western definitions are legalistic in orientation. It is often difficult to distinguish between temporary fosterage and long-term arrangements. Indeed, much ink was spilled in the volumes edited by Carroll (1970) and Brady (1976) in attempts to arrive at a suitable cross-cultural definition of adoption and related concepts.

14. Kirkpatrick (1983) casts doubt on the economic insurance view of adoption with regard to the Marquesas. There the hope that children, adopted or natural, will provide for their aged parents may be questioned. More important, Kirkpatrick argues that adoption serves to bolster the identity claims of adopters. Marquesans appear to be less concerned with getting eventual support from their dependents than with maintaining their roles as providers, which signifies their status as competent, mature adults.

15. Whereas adoption in Europe and the United States normally involves an adopting couple, in Polynesia transactions generally take place between individuals. Thus only one partner in a marriage is usually considered the adopting parent.

16. This is in line with Silverman's (1969) model of Banaban strategizing as a matter of maximizing options. Silverman's account of a Micronesian case can be neatly applied to Polynesian data.

17. See also Shore 1976a:294 for comments on factors militating towards alliance among a few families at the pinnacle of the Samoan status system.

18. Freeman (1984) has challenged Shore's account of the terms *āmio* and *aga*. In our view, much of his criticism fails, for he faults Shore on details that are not critical to Shore's analytical project and, in discussions of the notion of nature, seems to misunderstand Shore. As a result, while Shore's account of the two terms may not be definitive, his broader argument concerning Samoan understandings of action is upheld, or even strengthened, by such criticism.

4

Socialization and Character Development

JANE RITCHIE

JAMES RITCHIE

IT IS striking to realize that it has only been fifty years since the study of enculturation emerged in anthropology. The field, which came to be known as culture and personality, and later as psychological anthropology, has contributed much to our understanding of Polynesian culture and behavior over the intervening years. In this chapter we review the attempts of psychological ethnographers to make sense of it all. Theoreticians are still struggling with conceptualizing the complexities of emotion, cognition, and the relationship between personal and cultural organization (see Shweder and LeVine 1984, for example), so we can offer no definitive synthesis of Polynesian studies on these topics. Nevertheless, a number of high quality descriptive accounts have emerged over the years that form the basis for sketching out significant dimensions and emergent issues.

The Study of Polynesian Enculturation

An examination of the literature on Polynesian enculturation reveals both continuities (as, for example, in a respectful yet skeptical and cautious attitude towards psychoanalytic theory) and quite radical discontinuities. Because we have ourselves been part of this process we will refer to it in personal terms, but we do so with the goal of illuminating the stepwise progression of theoretical development more generally.

On a broad level, changing perspectives on enculturation reflect more general changes in the social and behavioral sciences. The earliest anthropological records consist of descriptive accounts in the tradition of natural science. The writers of these accounts set out simply to describe. Subsequently, other scholars followed with theoretically informed analyses and searched for ways of testing them. These were superseded by interpretive approaches aimed at discovering cultural logic and symbolic meanings. Today, we are seeing the acid test applied by some students of Polynesian culture, the really daring step that follows from the question, "Do we understand Polynesian cultures well enough to confidently intervene without creating serious disruptions?"

The Natural Science Approach

The earliest perspective was the naively confident one employed by Margaret Mead and others in the 1920s. It was thought that by living among a group of people for an extended period of time (that is, for months) observing, questioning, and recording, the truth could be discovered. This general view persisted without challenge for some time among anthropologists. When we were preparing to enter the field for the first time in 1952, to study the Maori at Rakau in New Zealand, Ernest Beaglehole gave us a copy of the Royal Anthropological Institute's field manual, *Notes and Queries* (1951), and Murdock et al.'s *Outline of Cultural Materials* (1950). He told us to record everything in duplicate, to count everything countable, and to take unposed photographs using the candid eye of the camera in a completely neutral way. He instructed us not to trouble ourselves with interpretation; that was a separate project and would come later. "A good natural scientist describes first. That is the real foundation of true science," he said. Even then we were aware that this was too simplistic. We had read *Some Modern Maoris* (Beaglehole and Beaglehole 1946) in which he and Pearl had broken these rules themselves, thickening their description with interpretation, and we knew why. In that volume they were out to cut through the bulk of accumulated materials on Maori, and they strove to make theoretical sense of the data. They had obviously been selective, just as Mead, in Samoa, was selective in reporting on the experience of her sample of young women in *Coming of Age in Samoa* (1928a).

The Shift toward Theory and Psychoanalysis

The format of *Some Modern Maoris* is similar to that used by the Lynds in their Middletown study (Lynd and Lynd 1929), and is organized on the basis of life tasks (growing up, making a living, and so on). Although this device carries no special theoretical baggage, it does have its own implications. Clearly the Beagleholes wanted to emphasize the present-world nature of acculturated Maori experience, and to place their data in a sociological as well as ethnographic context. This represented a deliberate shift away from the naive naturalist viewpoint. It was time for the study of native cultures to join the mainstream of sociopolitical inquiry, so that they might be understood in terms of human universals and the political framework of emerging internationalism.

The other formative idea in this work was derived from psychoanalytic theory. The Beagleholes did not concern themselves with the specifics of Freudianism as had Malinowski and Roheim (Spiro 1982), but were attracted to the model of explaining adult behavior on the basis of childhood experience. The ideas of trauma as a determinant mechanism; of culture as a compulsive, repetitive working out of childhood experience; of the compensatory nature of culture as a defense system, slip into the book almost unannounced. They nevertheless carry a considerable interpretive load. Thus Maori children, cut off from the golden years of early childhood, are seen as searching forever for that lost Eden in amiable social relations, avoidance of emotional involvement, and so forth. The Freudianism of the Beagleholes, with its emphasis on basic personality structure, paralleled that which emerged from the Kardiner-Linton seminars at Columbia University in New York (Kardiner 1939, Kardiner et al. 1945; Linton 1945).

The ethnographic task for these early culture and personality theorists was to discover those childhood events that determined cultural character, or as the Beagleholes termed it "character structure." They wrote that the "characteristic patterning of human needs and emotions of a particular group is largely unconscious" (Beaglehole and Beaglehole 1946:118), and the ethnographic problem "is that of accounting for both the character structure of the group and the differing personalities of the members of the group" (Beaglehole and Beaglehole 1946:119). In the Maori community of Kowhai they found that:

> The Maori infant and young child is petted, "spoilt," indulged, and affectionately treated, its whims gratified, its need for love and security fairly adequately fulfilled. It receives no severe toilet training. It is made to feel a welcome member of the group. Both parents and old ladies see eye to eye in this sort of treatment. Punishments and frustrations, either of a physical sort or through deprivation of love, attention, and affection, are rare and exceptional.
>
> If the prevailing picture for the infants and young children is one of indulgent care, that for the older children makes a vivid contrast. Older children should very literally be neither seen nor heard. They become extremely independent of adults; the discipline and control they receive is casual, capricious, and often very severe. Punishments tend to outweigh rewards . . . it seems clear that this transition from the overt love and affection of early childhood to the casual, capricious, and sometimes severe discipline of the middle years gives to the Maori child something of a traumatic emotional shock, which has a profound influence on his character-structure (Beaglehole and Beaglehole 1946:125–126).

Then, in one great daring leap, they move to adult and cultural character:

> We would assume that the persistent anxiety to be well-liked, to be sociable, to be generous, to be friendly, to be the eternal giver, is ultimately linked with the traumatic anxiety of early childhood when the Maori child after two years or more of warm, affectionate, friendly, and loving care is suddenly cast on his own resources and expected to be largely independent of care and affection. For most children, as we have seen, traumatic change is the usual one and it is to be expected that it should leave a profound trace on adult character.
>
> The trace that it leaves, we suggest, is that constant unconscious struggle to regain some of the security and friendliness of infancy by putting every adult one meets in one's debt by one's generosity. In other words, one buys friendship and in this way one makes oneself superior and secure. Thus symbolically does the Maori adult ever seek to recapture that golden world of love and affection which he lost irretrievably in the process of growing up. . . . His fear is to be lonely, separate, an isolated individual. His chief character-directive is to return to the warm security of the group, which thus becomes a symbol for the warm security of his early infant life (Beaglehole and Beaglehole 1946:143–144).

They proceed to explain religious and symbolic culture in terms of mechanisms of defense.

> It is not to be expected that a traumatic change of the sort we have indicated could be very satisfactorily carried through unless both the Maori child and the Maori adult were provided with some culturally respectable outlet for the hostility and aggression that would be dammed up in the process. Looking at Kowhai Maori culture we find a number of such outlets: belief in sorcerers and black magic, fear of supernatural spirits and ghosts, fear of breaking tapus. Formerly also, inter-tribal warfare was another such outlet. The Maori was able to project on to tribal enemies much of the aggressive hate and anger that was denied expression in the close-knit integration of family and tribal life. Warfare was thus not so much a sport to the Maori, it was an absolute necessity. Without it one would expect tribal cohesiveness to be split by intra-group rivalries and hostility. It is not therefore merely a matter of chance but one of underlying necessity that a belief in evil supernatural and black magic and an interest in inter-tribal competitiveness have been kept alive. These beliefs and activities are necessary supports for the basic character-structure of Maori culture (Beaglehole and Beaglehole 1946:150).

The Beagleholes then go on to use this singular approach to explain the nature of warfare, working patterns and habits, tribal loyalties—indeed everything! Furthermore, they predict acculturative disaster unless character structure changes.

One of the basic obstacles in the way of the Maoris' adapting fully and immediately to the ways of the pakeha world is at once apparent. By the very nature of his character-structure the Maori is unable to fit into a world which is organized in its chief values round the drives of quite a different type of character structure. Success in the pakeha world depends on fighting, on striving, on ambition, on aggressiveness, on thrift, on long-range planning, on individual responsibility. But ability to act in these ways in turn depends on the individual possessing the sort of character-structure to which such activities are congenial or at least not completely alien. To the Maori, however, with his own specific character development, these are activities which are alien to him, which make no appeal to him, from which he turns aside because they only serve to accentuate his loneliness and insecurity (Beaglehole and Beaglehole 1946:151).

No wonder the book caused a flurry of criticism and rejection in New Zealand and among most anthropologists, even when the manuscript was circulating prior to publication. Te Rangi Hiroa (Sir Peter Buck) reflects on this in his introduction to it. The Beagleholes' had sought prior reaction, almost as though they needed relief from their own anxieties.

By the end of 1952 they had shifted methodological ground and were now looking to apply the hypothetic-deductive methods that, in theory at least, had become dominant in social science research. As a result, when we returned from our first summer in the field in 1953, Ernest Beaglehole suggested a new direction for our Maori research. We were advised to formulate hypotheses about what went with what in Maori experience. This would serve two objectives. First, such hypotheses could be field-tested in order to validate (make more true) the original description; second, the results would reflect on the utility of the theory. It was never clear, however, how one objective might be distinguished from the other. In order to test such hypotheses we proceeded to wheel into place a set of awkward and cumbersome methodological procedures, chiefly based on projective techniques that seemed ill-suited to the task. The formality of the procedures seemed completely contrary to our initial goals of getting close to the people we were studying, getting accepted and involved, and gaining an empathetic cultural understanding.

The enterprise was completed, but the results are buried in thesis form in libraries (James Ritchie 1960); what got published were ethnographic and descriptive accounts (James Ritchie 1963). On reflection, this was not merely a reversion to a natural science approach in the face of problems encountered in operationalizing the culture and personality approach. We were reaching for a new kind of theory and method.

Developmental Continuities and Learning Theory

In the second phase of fieldwork at Rakau we had with us a team of researchers, each working on a different stage of childhood. This time it was the continuities in Maori experience that impressed us, as opposed to any simple disjunctive trauma. We now accumulated documentation on linkages, on repeated childhood experiences, and on general interactional styles—on what some scholars were beginning to call behavioral ecologies. These data were amenable to interpretation in terms of social learning theory, and anthropologists used such concepts as social reinforcement, behavioral modelling, shaping, learning styles, and preferences. It was the repetition of patterns, over and over again, at different ages and in different contexts, and its reinforcement by rewards, that focused our attention.

For example, our field observations confirmed a sharp discontinuity in adult-child relations as the child became more mobile and verbal. We could not help but notice a change in attitude toward the toddler. But it was the behavioral solution that we now saw as primary, not the emotional loss of early warmth. Older children and other adults assumed parent-like responsibilities, and children had all the socializing resources of the community around them. They were treated in much the same way by all.

We could place in overlay, observations of free-ranging peer groups, school behavior on the playground and in the classroom, and what children did in the meeting-house when meetings or ceremonies were under way. We saw two patterns. On the one hand children maintained a watchful vigilance of adults, looking for signs of their likely reactions. On the other hand there was a free and easy comradery with other children, the preferred and most constant form of behavior. From their peers children learned sociability and the "how to" of living in Rakau; from adults they learned "when to" and respect. Already we were moving out of the wilderness of endless hypothesis testing back into a search for patterns, but it was now based more in cognitive than in motivational theorizing.

Working with the new conceptual apparatus of social learning theory was complex, tedious, and anxiety-provoking. It did not provide a royal road to instant understanding; there was neither a single determining trauma nor a grand theory to give data obvious meaning. Small scale field experiments in and out of classrooms replaced the projective tests of the earlier phase. Although this approach promoted more adequate descriptions of behavior, no corresponding methodology existed for the analysis of culture. So for a while, in Polynesian studies at least, the field seemed to become a branch of child development, studied cross-culturally.

Cognitive Theory and the Move toward Ethnopsychology

The interest in cognitive theory, which gained impetus when cognitive anthropologists looked beyond the narrow vision of ethnoscience to confront questions of worldview (Shore n.d.), restored the balance. Anthropologists needed to find better ways of conceptualizing the metaphysical basis of culture than those employed by Gregory Bateson (1936, who relied on the distinction between ethos and eidos) and Clyde Kluckhohn (1951, who used the concept of values). If worldview is described in terms of basic premises and principles of action, then socialization is the process whereby such cultural assumptions are acquired. It seems to us that the task upon which psychological anthropology has now embarked is to study this process, rather than to test cross-culturally psychoanalytic, Piagetian, or some other ethnocentric theory. This is a theoretically open stance, which increasingly brings psychological anthropology into the mainstream of general anthropological inquiry.

Similarly, over the years we have watched the field of developmental psychology, in which we were trained, swing in the direction of universalistic theory and then away from it. When we were graduate students, the orthodox Freudian perspective was losing credibility. Developmental psychologists were being invited to explore various alternatives of a neo-Freudian kind, notably in the work of Erikson (1959) and others who emphasized developmental sequences. In due course these theories, which focused on emotional development and the ego construct, were supplanted by cognitive formulations, notably those of Piaget (Price-Williams 1975) and Kohlberg (1969). We were encouraged to look toward ethology, and later to sociobiology, for universals.

The literature of cross-cultural psychology has not convincingly demonstrated to us the universality of specific developmental sequences, nor are we satisfied with the prevailing theoretical formulations. We are, however, convinced that fieldwork will show that every culture conceptualizes development in terms of stages and emergent capacities—that ethnopsychologies have conceptual equivalents of a broad and possibly fundamental kind. In yet another shift in perspective, recent work in the area has moved toward an ethnopsychological approach, one that aims to discover through the analysis of talk and cultural texts how indigenous peoples conceptualize their own experience. Some of the most interesting work along these lines, and most relevant to our present concern, is based on attempts to discover area-wide patterns by comparing the ethnopsychologies of specific cultures (see White and Kirkpatrick 1985).

Although a few studies have addressed the issue (e.g., Levy 1973; Martini and Kirkpatrick 1981), we do not yet have a sufficient research base to describe with confidence how Polynesians think about developmental sequences. The scarcity of information is surprising, for one might have expected that interest in cognitive classification over the past few decades, and more recently in concepts of the person, would have logically extended into this area. Clearly the matter is both worthy of investigation and researchable. Polynesians to whom we have spoken readily discuss the principles on which they base their childrearing. Perhaps their comments are no more than afterthoughts or rationalizations, but they are freely made and could be systematically documented. They are usually offered in the form of broad formulations, or recipes for the proper growth of children. The following saying by Sir Apirana Turupa Ngata, a political revitalization leader who died in 1950, has wide contemporary currency among New Zealand Maori.

E tipu, e rea, mo nga ra o tou ao.
Ko to ringa ki nga rakau a te pakeha hei ora mo to tinana.
Ko to ngakau ki nga taonga a o tipuna hei tikitiki mo to mahunga.
Ko to wairua ki te Atua nana nei nga mea katoa.

Grow, tender shoot, for the days of your world.
For your hand the tools of the white man's world to sustain your body.
For your heart the treasures of your ancestors as a crown for your head.
For your spirit there is God to whom all things belong.

A surface analysis indicates that children grow like plants, and if given the right conditions the whole business of development takes care of itself. People, like plants, are organic. Yet the proverb implies that organic naturalism is not enough, that there must be an appropriate mixture of traditionalism (culture) with nature, of emotional commitment with pragmatism, of spirituality with mundane interests. Implicitly the saying is an ambiguous endorsement of both continuity and change. It is not addressed to parents at all, but to a child. Does this imply that Maori children are expected to bring up themselves? Certainly parents are not, in this proverb, placed under any injunction, and from this saying alone one might conclude that parenting is relatively easy for Polynesians. Obviously one proverb cannot reveal the intricacies of Maori, let alone Polynesian, thoughts on child rearing, but it is this kind of material that we will need to analyze if we are to develop a worthwhile ethnopsychological understanding of socialization in Polynesia.

Cultural Targets for Child Training

In this chapter we adopt the view that socialization is a method for attaining culturally defined behavioral, cognitive, and affective goals.

Our initial concern, therefore, is to describe certain broad features of Polynesian cultural style that have implications for the child training process. We have selected four metaphysical notions—kinship and relatedness, status and respect, sharing and caring, unity through consensus—which we believe to be central to Maori worldview. Other Polynesian cultures share these concerns, although they may be expressed in slightly different ways. The principles are interactive, so that it is impossible to rank them on a scale of cultural priorities; individual actors must take all of them into consideration when making decisions.

The Importance of Context

Even more basic to Polynesian social metaphysics than the above-mentioned principles, however, is the ease with which social worlds are subject to redefinition, depending on circumstances. This may be related to the fact that throughout their long history of migrations, Polynesians were forced to reinvent their cultures over and over again. Perhaps all colonists romanticize their homelands, their *Hawaiki,* and produce simplifications of who they are and what they are about. Such fictions provide a sense of stability while people charge ahead with explorations and innovations within new environments. Cultures with this kind of history assimilate, but are not easily assimilated. They can draw into their cultural identity (that prepotent fiction "we are the people who . . .") all manner of new ideas, techniques, skills, and people as they rework their history accordingly (Borofsky 1987).

Cultures that have the capacity to assimilate the new must contain ways of validating and valuing individual departures from orthodoxy; they must train people to have a high level of tolerance for ambiguity and to suspend judgment, as well as to educate people in the creative use of conflict. Whereas other cultures deal with conflict by seeking to dissolve differences and to find ultimate solutions, Polynesians have historically chosen to incorporate differences, and to use them as a means of keeping options open. Polynesian cultures thus represent adaptations to conflicting interests, overlapping allegiances, and multiple solutions to every problem. For Polynesians any and all solutions are tentative, subject to reformulation as conditions change.

Thus, as many scholars have pointed out, contextualization is all important for interpreting social action within Polynesian communities (see Shore, chapter 5, this volume). Learning about contexts, about how to redefine them as well as recognize them, is therefore one of the most important lessons Polynesian children must master. For example, traditionally the ridge-pole of an ancestral house must be a single log, for who would break the backbone of a *tipuna* 'ancestor'. But in present day construction, large houses require ridges longer than trees can supply. The Maori scholar Apirana Ngata confronted this problem and found an easy solution. Since the house concerned was to bear the identity of a notable historic fisherman, the ridge-pole could be joined by using a canoe-joint to interlock the beam. He provided a new chant to validate it, claiming it to be old and traditional.

Or again, a young persons' concert group in a major city had no item in their repertoire older than songs celebrating the events of World War II, yet they claimed everything they performed was traditional. No one denied it, for in a sense it was, stylistically if not historically. Of the groups' code of practice its leader said, ironically, "If something happens once around here, well, its just what happens, but if it happens twice its a tradition!"

A modern concert group may have dance dresses of tapestry needle-weave rather than the old fiber craft, apparatus painted in flourescent colors to catch black light for more dramatic display, poi balls to twirl that have flashlight assemblies built in—all of this to impress an audience and impart a sense of modernity. These are ways of demonstrating they are technologically "hip," while at the same time their songs emphasize traditional themes and concerns.

Redefining tradition is by no means confined to urban Maori. It occurs everywhere in Polynesia, having been documented for places as diverse as Pukapuka (Borofsky 1987) and Hawaii (Linnekin 1983). New contexts call for new definitions of tradition. Ngata's ridge-pole made sense in the context of the community in which it was erected. Traditional dances may look very different when performed for a Polynesian audience rather than for tourists, especially if traditional ceremonies are involved. But it is not enough to validate performances simply by claiming they are traditional; unless they are also appropriate to contexts, such claims are likely to go unappreciated. There are, of course, instances in which contexts are not redefined, where the Polynesian ways of acting are carried over into inappropriate contexts. For example, Polynesian children, having learned not to question parents, have trouble in formal school settings where questioning is almost obligatory.

Relatedness and Kinship

Over the years we have come to see how basic the bilateral nature of kinship is to social life in Polynesia (see Howard and Kirkpatrick, chapter 3, this volume). It produces an enormous range of relatedness, so that an individual is never without standing.[1] Bilaterality is even more powerfully ramified where adoption is common, as it is in most parts of Polynesia (Carroll, ed. 1970; Brady, ed. 1976). Then one not only has the descent lines of mother and father ramifying back in time, but linkages through adoptive parents as well. At the levels of both cognition and social action bilaterality means there is almost always a way of establishing kinship with someone. And if genealogical knowledge is insufficient, kinship can be established on a de facto basis by assuming the obligations of kinsmen. The kinship system is thus a model for dealing with ambiguity and multiple options. It is also a model for inclusiveness: each person in a Polynesian community can be incorporated into nearly every other person's kin network.

Status and Respect

The attention to social stratification in Polynesia, and to the importance of elites, underscores the salience of status in the region, and rivalry over it (see Marcus, chapter 6, this volume). Status considerations are so ubiquitous in Polynesian contexts that it is very easy to take them for granted. Manifestations of status are to be seen not only in the obviously competitive phenomena of oratory, gift distribution, and other status rating and ranking exercises; they are equally evident in seemingly uncompetitive acts of generosity, cooperation, and caring. What others are doing, especially those who are within what might be termed modifiable distance from one's own status, requires constant attention if one is to avoid displacement in the ever-changing status game. Those far above or below one in status are of little concern, but those who are close can become an obsession. There is no sense, however, in which status rivalry becomes a Hobbesian war of each against all. Rather, under most conditions, it is a highly structured, elaborated, cultural dynamic.

One consequence of this emphasis on status is a constant concern for respect, which is brought to one's attention in a variety of ways. Who speaks at a gathering? Who does not speak? Who precedes whom? Who defers to whom? Who does not appear until called? Who, when expected, does not appear? Who sits higher than whom? Who ducks their head, averts another's gaze and avoids eye contact? Whose name is freely mentioned and whose is referred to only obliquely (if at all)? Indeed, respect implications are deeply embedded in virtually all social behavior. Consequently, learning to recognize status and to respect it is an extremely important component of Polynesian child training (Shore 1982). Although rarely directly taught, the implicit lesson is well-learned because all of a child's relationships are so framed.

Sharing and Caring

The lessons of sharing are early learned and deeply impressed. People may joke about it ("first up best dressed"), but the banter masks a serious concern. In former times those of *rangatira* 'aristocratic' status were obliged to care for all those in their lineage, while humility, and sometimes poverty, were signs of an *ariki*'s 'high chief's' *aroha* 'love, compassion'.[2] Property was for sharing; it was in the service of relationships. The whole range of words derived from or built on the root *oha* are powerful concepts. *Koha* is a gift brought to a gathering (these days it includes money). Although often presented in a ceremonial fashion, it is sometimes offered as though by casual afterthought, depending on circumstances. *Mai oha* is a reciprocal gift; it reminds the receiver of the value the giver places on the relationship (rather than the gift). *Aroha* is a gift of emotional concern. The value of anything *oha* increases with generosity.

Unity through Consensus

To the Western mind a dual emphasis on status rivalry and consensus politics may seem paradoxical, but not so for Polynesians. Although the first objective of political process is the attainment of consensus—in Polynesia politics may be involved at every level of social life, from household to nation-state—unity is ideally achieved only after all the nuances of status have been acknowledged. Consensus is rarely a simple matter. In our own area of New Zealand, hardly a day goes without reference to the proverb *"Waikato taniwharau; he piko he taniwha, he piko he taniwha"* 'the Waikato river has a thousand water spirits, one at every turn of the river'. Simply put, this means that the political jurisdiction of every chieftain requires recognition, that everyone has a status and none may be disdained or discounted.

That may be well for chiefs, but what about the rest? The point is that the same process permeates the entire social fabric. Within each social unit, whether household, extended family, village, or political division, attributes of status are displayed and are expected to receive appropriate recognition. If a demand for immediate action does not permit this requirement full play, however, the head of the unit or a person of *mana* may show the courage and audacity to decide for the group without proper consultation. The arrogant alternative is risky, and if unwarranted or extreme may result in lack of cooperation, but it is by no means unthinkable. If well calculated, agreement follows. Thus the focus swings between a pronounced concern for status and that felt necessity for consensus. For individuals, the trick is to enhance their status vis-à-vis others (for example by sensing the disposition of the group and making appropriate suggestions) in the context of arriving at a consensus. The process is a subtle one that requires an acute social sensitivity.

Consensus is valued because it enhances community. Even these days, when the phenomenal reality of community may be fractured or in decline, particularly in urbanized areas, people still speak as though all actions should be related to a cohesive community. It matters not that most of one's relatives are elsewhere. Rhetoric reflects the sentiment that communities are the proper context within which individuality may be displayed. An entertainer may be a celebrity in Waikiki, but he validates his Polynesian status by coming home to sing at a *lū'au.*

To Polynesians one's personhood is embedded in social relations and community. Setting oneself apart through blatant displays of personal achievement, or by calling attention to one's achievements, is a sure path to disapproval. Individual achievements must be accompanied by humility, although even displays of humilty can, on occasion, appear downright arrogant. Individuals must therefore learn to communicate about their achievements in subtle and indirect ways.

We have described this social value, or target, in an abstract and rather simplistic way, but working it out in day-to-day reality is a very intricate process. Learning the techniques of balancing individual against community interests, by respecting and acknowledging the strategies of others, requires a complex and precise socialization, and continuous learning throughout one's lifespan.

Polynesians admire individuals who express a strong sense of independence while acknowledging community consensus, who can deal with the politics of status effectively, who are able to fulfill the obligations of membership in a community with generosity and humility, who accept authority but know how to manipulate it, and who can tolerate conflict and ambiguity while adapting to change. These principles are often clearly manifest in public oratory, as the following field report illustrates.

Rua had been away from his home village for a long time. He returned because the family wanted him to assume the responsibility for the family land. At least some did but others were not quite sure. The matter was generally discussed but did not become an issue until Rua, feeling the insecurity, asked that a meeting be called to discuss the matter. At it the older men spoke roughly in age order. Then it was Rua's turn. He launched into an elaborate *whaikorero,* or speech, in classic form. He greeted the ancestral house, then the earth-mother land on which it stood. He summoned the spiritual ancestors. Generally he mourned all the dead of the place, departed since he had left years ago. He confessed his dereliction in not having returned for the burial of all—asked their spirits to forgive him. He welcomed each group within the [family?] using genealogical and personal references. He spoke of the need for someone to care for the land now that it was returning from being leased out. One by one he acknowledged the superior skills of each of his relatives. Almost it seemed, he was talking them into taking the job. But not really. By the time he addressed the issue of the meeting there was no question. The purpose would be fulfilled. He would be acknowledged as the one to do it. There were other speeches but gradually they drifted off the issue. It had been solved, not by problem solving, but by a single oratorical act (unpublished field notes, 1956).

Against the commonalities of this pattern is reflected the stuff of genetic and circumstantial variation—the individuality of each person. In their day-to-day dealings with children, parents and others provide highly variable and often idiosyncratic environments, leading to significant differences in personal styles, even among siblings. The concept of personality refers to these unique aspects in each individual's makeup, while the concept of character, which will be our primary concern in this chapter, is more limited in scope. Concerned as it is with moral training, character development focuses upon consistencies in socialization that are the result of cultural intent. There may be, in addition, some unforseen consequences—the culturally determined but unintended results of directing socialization towards certain ends. We will comment on these later.

Socialization to Achieve Cultural Targets

As we see it, psychological and anthropological studies within Polynesia proceeded so rapidly that they over-ran their resources. The data are there, contained in some of the most comprehensive ethnographies in the whole of modern anthropology. But from these data ethnographic analysis progressed initially only in the area of social organization (see chapter 3, this volume). The pure analysis of cultural themes, values, basic patterns of behavior, and the rules of daily life has only begun within the past thirty years, and we have only started to make sense of it in the past decade.

It seems from our present perspective that early workers forced the issue and, at the same time, made mysterious what now seems simple and self-evident. The unity in diversity theme, the democratic process within an elitist status structure, the search for consensus, the assurance of social placing through kinship, and the obligation to care are all there and obvious. They are clearly evident in the structure and content of oratory. Any diary of a week's activity will show them. Old men, young men, women—anyone—will point toward them. And just as clearly, parents and other socializers exert pressure on children to conform to behaviors they believe will promote these values and goals.

The link is not quite direct, however. When adults are questioned about their child-training goals they usually offer second-order abstractions as answers: "They must learn respect," "I want them to be polite," "to behave properly," and so on. But the simple probe, "give me an example" (rather than "what do you mean by good manners") immediately produces two orders of information. One relates to the attributes of childhood, or sets childhood apart as a separate subculture. The other speaks of linkages between children's and adults' attributes.

Despite the abstractness of answers to such questions, we still think that one way of understanding socialization is to query socializers—children, adolescents, and adults—because what they say they are doing they often do. Much of the time they know why. They can give meaningful, within-culture, explanations. They are aware of culturally valued traits—the targets toward which socialization is aimed.

Less direct influences, those that come through participation in socializing structures and situations that no one seems to be directing, are also consistent with these targets. Thus the roughhouse of peer group decision making, the casual compliance with a peer leader's suggestions, are simulacra of formal community meetings. And they, in turn, are images of the more general system in which the values of unity, status, caring, and kinship are expressed in everything cultural.

Community: The Context for Socialization

The literature on child development, derived for the most part from social science research on Western families, provides no guidelines for dealing with the cultural realities of community settings in tribal societies. But wherever we turned, to ethnographies, to creative writing, or to our own field experience, we found that the context of community was ubiquitous and powerful. Even in contemporary Hawaii (Gallimore, Boggs, and Jordan 1974) and in urban New Zealand (Jane Ritchie 1964), where organizational structures are vastly different from those of traditional villages, community contexts have been created that have a great impact on child rearing.

> Everywhere in Polynesia [community] has a local, specific and precise meaning. For example, in Samoa it is the nu'u, the village. . . . In Niue it is everyone, for the island is small. . . . In the real sense, community is those with whom one lives, who are also one's kin with whom one shares common understandings of a moral and ethical nature that govern the ordinary course of life.
>
> At the symbolic level, community is the hook on which one's identity hangs, the group from which one draws one's membership and for whose company one longs, even when they are not around (Ritchie and Ritchie 1979:21).

Wherever one is, the community in which one was socialized retains its emotional strength. In part this is because children are always included in or, to be more accurate, never excluded from community events. For example, while community elders and representatives of a large commercial company were negotiating a multi-million dollar contract, we have seen a three-year old wander confidently among them, trying out knees for a lift. Already this child had learned how to penetrate the social space of adult activities without creating a disturbance.

Polynesian communities often comprise what Firth (1936b, 1961a) termed a ramage, or ramified lineage; they are essentially one family. In some cases the term commonly used for household and community is the same (in Maori, *whanau*). Furthermore, kinship terms are extended widely, with the words for mother and father generally applied to all relatives in the parental generation. Individuals are likely to know who their biological parents are, and to which household they belong, but they may have stronger emotional links with grandparents, or with an aunt or uncle. Since children are considered to belong to the community, everyone in it is expected to act parentally—to comfort, to instruct, to admonish, to punish. This distributed pattern of parenting leads children to develop a range of emotional ties among adults, rather than investing almost exclusively in their biological parents.

Multiple parenting reduces the strain of responsibility on individual parents and provides two important kinds of experience for children. First, because they relate so closely to such a variety of individuals, children have many models. They learn first-hand about individual differences, about each person's quirks, moods, and times of reliability and unreliability. Second, children, early on and throughout their lives, know that they are not desperately and irrevocably locked into unchangeable, punitive situations. They are able to move, not only from household to household within their community, but among kinsmen in adjacent communities, providing relief to both children and parents.[3]

From Parents to Peers

On the one hand, the ethic of community action means that trouble can be shared; on the other hand, it means that each individual enhances her or his well-being by contributing to the well-being of others. In most Polynesian languages the suffix *oha* or *ofa* expresses this idea in various forms. In Maori the word *koha* is applied to ritual gifts, *oha oha* to symbolic gifts of more special personal significance, and *aroha* to a gift of emotional warmth. These concepts are central to the Polynesian ethos. In early childhood the ethic of *aroha* has full play, and a golden world of childhood is created, which provides a basic foundation for the Polynesian worldview. Howard writes that youngsters are attended to closely during infancy.

Much of their waking time is passed in someone's arms, being cuddled, played with, and talked to. At family gatherings it is common practice for an infant to be passed from one to another; holding a baby is perceived as a privilege rather than a responsibility, so that age takes precedence. Usually it is the older women who monopolize a child, although over a period of time almost everyone—even teenage boys who may like to come on "tough" at times—is apt to be given an opportunity to indulge in fondling, looking at, and pacifying an infant. Although men, on the average, spend less time holding and cuddling an infant, the pleasure they display when they do appears no less intense than the delight shown by women. At no time did we hear any male chide another for giving attention to an infant, nor did we obtain any evidence that to do so is unmasculine. Quite the contrary—some of the hardest drinking, belligerent men openly showed the greatest tenderness.

An infant is rarely allowed to cry more than a few seconds before someone comes to provide relief. Mothers are pressured to do so; if a child is left crying other persons present show signs of distress. Speculations are made as to the cause of the baby's discomfort and other indirect cues are emitted to let the mother know that if she does not attend to the child's welfare immediately she is likely to be branded negligent. Consistent with this patter is the practice of demand feeding. Although a few women reported attempts to establish a feeding schedule, they were almost invariably given up within a few days; the cries of a hungry baby were just too much to bear. Feeding an infant is more than just the means of providing nourishment, however. It has symbolic value in the sense that it provides a public display of nurturance, or concern for the child's welfare. Food was therefore offered to crying infants even when it seemed clear to fieldworkers that the child was not hungry, but distressed for other reasons. There were even some reports of infants being fed when their distress was more than likely the result of overeating (Howard 1970:40–41).

Although this period of infant indulgence is characteristically followed by one in which parents distance themselves from their children, the warmth and attention that surrounds young children is not normally sharply withdrawn. Our view is that continuity rather than discontinuity is at the heart of the matter. By this we mean that though parents may less readily display indulgence to the toddler than to the infant, the difference is a matter of frequency and degree rather than quality. In terms of social learning theory, children need less frequent reinforcements to maintain the habit of sociability; indeed, the shift is a quite remarkable demonstration of a switch from regular to intermittent reinforcement, with all the consequences for habit strength that implies.

This is not to assert that no significant change occurs in adult behavior, for the shift in adult reaction, from being always to only sometimes indulgent, is sufficiently pronounced to have been noticed by researchers in many different Polynesian locations (Beaglehole and Beaglehole

1938, 1946; Jane Ritchie 1957; James Ritchie 1963; Gallimore, Boggs, and Jordan 1974; Howard 1974; Levy 1973; Martini and Kirkpatrick 1981).

Though in earlier writings the term rejection was used to describe this shift in parental behavior (i.e., a period of extreme indulgence was said to be followed by a period of parental rejection), subsequent work by Rohner (1975) on parental rejection and its cross-cultural consequences clearly indicates that this is an inappropriate description of Polynesian parenting. Although independence training begins early and is firmly enforced, it is not generally accompanied by the kind of adult harshness, coldness, or emotional withdrawal that the term rejection implies. And when the shift takes place, children are encouraged to turn to others to fill the gap.

The special relationship that exists between grandparents and grandchildren is of some importance in this regard. Formal or informal adoption by grandparents (a child for one's old age), although somewhat less common nowadays in urban locations, was virtually a universal phenomenon in traditional Polynesian communities.[4] Grandparents thus often buffer the discontinuity in parental attention and provide a continuity in interpersonal warmth and indulgence.

In previous publications we have emphasized two features of this shift: an increased attention to social signalling (James Ritchie 1963), and a turning from adult to peer dependency (Ritchie and Ritchie 1979). Attending to social signals, reading the signs, is so natural that it seems quite unremarkable to the people themselves. This attribute is simply the result of a lifetime of training. The consequences of not paying attention are legion—a backhand swipe from a parent, being laughed at in public or gossiped about in private, committing a faux pas or shameful breach of etiquette, being left out when one should be included, or being judged gauche, inept, or above all, disrespectful. So independence training does not produce a social isolate, someone who will go it alone, but rather an individual with skills of social vigilance, which is the other side of the coin of social caring.

Social vigilance is learned, not only in relation to the adult world of parents, grandparents, aunts, and uncles, but far more powerfully, through peer socialization. We do not know of any culture area where socialization by peers has been so well documented (Weisner and Gallimore 1977; Weisner 1982). An overview of any Polynesian community reveals age-graded peer structures that appear like regular swells in the Pacific Ocean. In cultures that otherwise seem so hierarchical, common status with one's peers represents a horizontal principle that qualifies and mitigates the harshness of what might otherwise become a very rigid authority structure. It is this socialization principle that, more than any other relates to the consensus nature of Polynesian politics. In

Growing Up in Polynesia we made the following observations concerning peer socialization.

> Boys are less involved in sibling caretaking but they too may be called upon to play their role and far from there being any disgrace in doing so, they may earn commendation for it. Like their sisters, they may be assigned the care of one special child exclusively and Gallimore [Boggs, and Jordan 1974] notes that in Hawaii older children will be made responsible not only for general care and supervision of a particular younger child, but once they are working they also have economic responsibilities to provide for that child's material needs—toys, clothes, educational necessities. . . .
>
> Weisner and Gallimore hypothesise that child caretaking by siblings will reduce or dilute the saturation and force or intensity of parental socialisation and in particular lessen attachment to the mother. On her part the attachment may not be so much lessened as become latent. A Samoan friend writes: "She stands afar and takes pride or shame in her children's interactions with their peers . . . this may be expressed to her friends in private or to the child when no one else is around". Parental socialisation does continue but is less directly, publicly and openly expressed. Thus instead of childhood seeming like a staircase with fixed and regular intervals and regular progression towards the goal of adult status, childhood is a world of equals. Child caretaking and peer socialisation certainly affects the nature and organisation of play groups as well as their sex composition. It dilutes the specialness and individuality of the particular family into which the child was born so that family and community became almost identical. It provides the development of pro-social, nurturant and responsible behaviour both in the children who mind and the children who are minded, for they too one day will mind. Where the caretaking tasks are assigned differently to boys and girls the load is likely to fall more heavily on the girls so that societies in which there is considerable child caretaking by other children probably provide earlier and stronger sex role training for the girls. And at the same time, in that situation, boys are learning that childminding is not their role.
>
> When Western children are given responsibility to mind others it is usually occasional, time specific and under adult scrutiny and ultimate responsibility. Often older children "mind" younger ones, especially in rural areas, but the allocation is not so general or extensive. It is only a temporary parent substitute, not a way of life (Ritchie and Ritchie 1979:64–65).

Status rivalry is powerfully emphasized in a situation where virtually everybody of one's age is to be regarded as a sibling. Peer justice can be harsh and immediate, but it can also lead to a powerful appreciation of consensus and a strong sense of togetherness. The rules of competition and cooperation need to be learned early and well if one is to play the game effectively. The capacity to drop yesterday's conflict for today's cooperation is learned in children's activities, is reinforced in the games adolescents play, and is carried over into the political arenas of the adult

world. It is not that conflicts do not matter, but they cannot be allowed
to persist, and certainly should not be allowed to interfere with long
term social commitments (see D'Amato 1987 for a vivid description of
peer group dynamics among a group of Hawaiian second graders; also
Boggs and Watson-Gegeo 1985).

Peer structures are not rigidly categorized by gender, but sometimes,
for some purposes, the sexes may be kept apart. Girls generally have
more domestic responsibilities and are drawn into women's work activities. Boys are permitted to roam farther from home, take more risks,
and appear to assert more authority within the peer group. In effect, the
pattern of sex role socialization is as much a consequence of peer influence as of parental modeling.

As various anthropological commentators have struggled to come to
grips with the nature of Polynesian kinship (chapter 3, this volume) or
the structures of Polynesian households (Metge 1976) and marriage
(Biggs 1960), the significance of peer groups has often been recognized,
but not always adequately emphasized. The vital functions of relating,
respecting, uniting, and caring are primarily learned in peer group contexts. Polynesian socialization cannot be comprehended as a process
applied by adults to children; it is equally (if not more so) a process
applied by children to one another. In Polynesia it is often easier to
leave one's family behind than one's peer group.

The correspondence between these principles of socialization and the
cultural targets of style and character discussed earlier is not one-for-
one, or point-for-point. Each of the themes contributes to each of the
cultural outcomes. Thus, moving in a bilateral kinship world clearly
links with multiple parenting, receiving affection from many caretakers, learning to read how and where one fits into the world of extended
relationships, and how to use that information to enhance the status of
one's group, and of oneself within it.

We have described these cultural patterns without regard for variation, not only because the present volume focuses on the region as a
whole, but because this has been the direction of our own writing and
thinking. It is astonishing to see how widespread this pattern of child
training is, occurring in locations on both high and low islands, in eastern and western Polynesia, on island outliers and in metropolitan centers. We believe that its generality can be explained by the adaptive
requirements of cultures that spread by relocation. If indeed an island
mass like New Zealand was populated by a few human remnants of a
long canoe voyage, then the sample from which cultural regrowth
began would have been very tiny, aimed at survival in a relatively
inhospitable environment, and therefore preoccupied with the essentials
of social relations.

Socialization and Learning Styles

Over the years a variety of studies concerned with questions of learning style have been conducted. About half of these come from people working in the fields of cross-cultural psychology, social psychology, or education, while the rest are anthropological in orientation. The research in this area was drawn together in the Hawaiian studies of Howard (1974) and Gallimore, Boggs, and Jordan (1974), which provided a good foundation for later research.

More recently, ethnopsychology has become a prominent research issue, and with it has come a renewed concern for indigenous theories of knowledge. Robert Levy's discussion of emotion, knowing, and culture (1984), Bradd Shore's paper on Samoan worldview (n.d.; see also chapter 5, this volume), Rob Borofsky's study of traditional knowledge in Pukapuka (1982, 1987), and many of the chapters in a volume edited by White and Kirkpatrick (1985) on Pacific ethnopsychology place theories of knowledge at the center of discussion. A renewed interest in the psychology of personhood (Kirkpatrick 1979, 1983; Shore 1982; J. Smith 1981) is an important part of this development.

To know what is worth knowing is to understand matters that lie at the very core of a culture, and this can be studied by examining what the young are taught and how they are taught it. Thus the content of learning, as well as learning styles, has become an important focus.

The traditional Polynesian learning style, as manifested in the learning of crafts, emphasizes observation with a minimum of direct instruction. Instructors demonstrate the correct way with a minimum of task-related interaction, though demonstrations are often accompanied by stories, chants, verbal horseplay, joking behavior, and gossip. Typically the novice works on a replica of the object being produced by the craftsman and makes detailed comparisons. Learning in such situations is informal in the sense in which Scribner and Cole (1973) use the term, and has been well documented in a number of Polynesian societies including Tikopia (Firth 1936b), Rotuma (Howard 1970), and Pukapuka (Borofsky 1982, 1987).

Traditionally, instruction occurred when the necessity arose. It was not separated from the context of everyday existence. One did not practice making a canoe in order to learn how to build canoes, nor were stories or legends likely to be told just for the sake of transmission. Canoes were built when they were needed and stories were generally narrated in order to define contexts for specific events.

The first point to be drawn from this is that motivation was of little concern. Children put themselves into learning situations when they wanted to learn and they stayed only as long as they remained interested. Similarly, an instructor's primary concern was with getting on with the job rather than with the attention of the learners. It was the responsibility of the observers to learn; if they did not, they were the losers. The canoe or tapa cloth still got made. Furthermore, the attitude of the novice to the craftsman or performer was one of respect, which was manifested, in part, by not asking intrusive questions. The expectation was that novices would maintain a diligent, wide-eyed watchfulness, then go and practice on their own. To ask questions was not only considered disrespectful, it also implied a shameful lack of understanding and provided an opening for ridicule. Howard (1974) and Gallimore, Boggs, and Jordan (1974) provide details of this learning style among modern Hawaiians.

The subordination of novice to teacher is explicitly acknowledged in Polynesian contexts, and is often strongly symbolized or dramatized. Thus in some Polynesian societies children are beaten until they stop crying (Ernest Beaglehole 1944b; Gerber 1975). Such punishment, Borofsky (1987) notes for Pukapuka, is not just to communicate to the child the gravity of the offense, but also to impress subordination upon it. Children rapidly learn that they must yield control of interaction to adults if they are to avoid punishment in one form or another.

One result of this pattern is a low level of verbal interaction in learning situations, and a very limited degree of questioning. Paula Levin (1978) found in Tubuai that direct questioning of the teacher was a problem for Polynesian students, a finding also reported in New Zealand (Graves and Graves 1983) and Hawaii (Howard 1974). Even adult learners ask questions in oblique and roundabout ways, taking care as they do to observe the nuances of status in their language. For example, in many places in Polynesia it is impolite to refer to a high ranking person by his or her name, and where extreme respect is required between siblings of opposite sex, or between elder and younger siblings, questioning can only take place through a third party. The attitudes involved are nicely captured by Borofsky's observations on Pukapuka. "Given that people do not like to abase themselves in front of their equals, given the issue of status rivalry, one can sense why so many people are not eager to be taught formally. It goes back to why people do not ask too many questions. It is just not worth all the trouble; it is just not worth all the humiliation. It is better to wait, to observe, to ask indirectly" (Borofsky 1987:99).

A nonassertive approach to learning is reinforced by the likelihood of ridicule for inept or incomplete performances. Thus learners are reluctant to display their newly acquired skills until they are reasonably certain of being able to perform correctly. There are no indications that this retards the learning process. Rather it encourages diligent observation and much practice. In traditional learning situations there was plenty of time for rehearsal, including mental rehearsal, and a novice's first public performance was only likely to occur after confidence was established. One of us learned to chant in a traditional Maori context with a mouthful of pebbles that were only removed when both teacher and learner were quite sure no mistakes would be made without the impediment. The pebbles allowed one to rehearse over and over, with mistakes blamed on the pebbles rather than the abilities of the learner.

Other themes in the socialization literature are a reluctance to use praise (Borofsky 1987) and an emphasis on the use of self-deprecation as a means of earning respect (Howard 1974). To praise oneself is considered despicable; to be praised by someone else may be downright embarrassing. In Maori, a person who engages in self-praise or self-exhibition is termed *whakahihi* 'braggard' and sooner or later will be required to *whakaiti* 'reduce oneself, make oneself small'. The Polynesian learning style demands that novices not draw attention to themselves, that they remain *whakama* 'passive, watchful, withdrawn' until they have mastered the tasks at hand. This results in a learning trajectory that proceeds from one competence to another, and minimizes exposure to publicly recognized failures and acknowledged incompetence. The difference between this style and that characteristic of Western educational institutions is quite fundamental.

Although information is sometimes explicitly transmitted from teacher to learner in traditional settings, directness is contrary to one of the great Polynesian cultural games, namely the game of incompleteness. Stories and legends, while sometimes fully recounted, are more often relayed in scraps or allusions. Bits of genealogy are recounted almost as though the speaker were refreshing his or her memory of parts of a family tree. Since all traditional knowledge is related, one is never in a position to tell more than a fragment of it, and storytellers are given license to free-associate their way through tales or legends, leaping about in ways that baffle Western observers, who are habituated to lineal plots and serial time. An old Maori man once explained to us that plots of legends were like *whakapapa* 'genealogies'; a skillful storyteller could start anywhere and finish anywhere by working his or her way across the lattice of motifs, as though legends were a structure of maze-like pathways, connecting each entry point with each exit.

Traditional knowledge was therefore generative in addition to being conservative. The elements may have been relatively stable, but they could be recombined in imaginative ways. The old man referred to above had a reputation for being rather more creative than others in the community thought proper. "Watch out for Pine," they said, "he makes it up." When confronted with this criticism Pine chuckled and said, "but you're supposed to make it up." His assertion is born out by a wealth of performative data, if "making it up" is interpreted not as absolute license, but as a challenge to recombine traditional elements in order to suit a narrative to the situation. As in all things Polynesian, appropriateness lies not in the action itself (a form of behavior, a legend, a song, etc.), but in the way it is contextualized. As Borofsky (1987) points out, this means that there can be no concept of absolute correctness. Once consensus has been reached, people will swear to the reality of events that could not possibly have happened and conversely may universally deny that an event of historical record ever occurred.

The metaphysical implications of this socialization pattern and learning style are evident in the recent work of two New Zealand anthropologists, Anne Salmond and Peter Cleave. Although neither directly addresses the issue of socialization and learning styles their work raises interesting questions. Salmond (1978) has attempted to elucidate the central concepts of Maori cultural metaphysics. From our point of view, it is interesting that what appears to be deepest and most profound is so inaccessible to ordinary consciousness. That it should take an outsider, in this case an anthropologist, to formulate the basic ground rules that divide the sacred from the secular, the world of the living from the world of the dead, the knowable from the unknowable, is remarkable. If these basic propositions were taught directly, and were an obvious part of socialization, we would not have had to wait until the 1980s for them to be explained. So how were they taught? It is as though the deepest messages of the culture are pushed furthest from overt consciousness, an idea that has recurred in the writings of scholars as diverse in orientation as Sapir (1929), Bateson (1979), and Laing (1965).

Cleave (1981) has begun the long delayed task of showing how Maori language structurally communicates underlying metaphysical notions. For example, he asserts that the language makes a basic distinction between that which is mutable and that which is immutable. He follows in the footsteps of Prytz Johansen (1948), who several years ago attempted to explicate the Maori sense of time in terms of continuous and completed actions. There is an approach here, derived from the Sapir-Whorf hypothesis of linguistic determinism, that looks for clues to metaphysical propositions in the grammar of a language on the one hand, and in its conceptual typology on the other. As far as socialization is concerned, the implication is that in the process of learning language, children learn culture.

Emotional Expression and Mental Health

Mead's (1929) early work in Samoa drew attention to the Polynesian pattern of suppressing strong emotions, which is one way to preserve harmonious social life in tightly knit communities. Ernest Beaglehole developed the same theme in his Cook Islands studies (Beaglehole 1957), and Levy (1969, 1973) elaborated it still further in his superb accounts of the management of anger and aggression in Tahiti. The general theme of these analyses is that overt expression of strong emotions (and negative ones in particular) is so disruptive of amiable community relations that multiple mechanisms operate to avoid its occurrence. People tend to avoid situations where overt conflict might flare up, and if forced into them tend to avoid confrontations. The commitment to group solidarity is emphasized over individual desires and needs. Whereas the early literature stressed positive reinforcements for gentleness—the emphasis on *aloha* (and its many cognates; see Shore, chapter 5, this volume)—recent studies in Samoa have raised questions about the volatility of emotions in Polynesian communities. Freeman's (1983) attack on Mead is only the most publicized, but Eleanor Gerber (1975, 1985) and Bradd Shore (1983, n.d.) have explored the issue with greater depth and subtlety. They point out that in strongly hierarchical societies like Samoa, anger can neither be vented upwards (for fear of reprisal) nor downwards (for fear of shame stemming from improper status behavior), so the pool of unresolved emotion explodes sideways (Gerber 1985). The mechanism available is personal confrontation, and while some do it, the risks are loss of community support and upsetting significant others; hence the outer affability masking the anger that so impressed Freeman (1983:216).

Although there may be differences between Polynesian communities, with small ones emphasizing solidarity and gentle behavior more strongly, one is apt to see signs of emotional distress in all of them. Polynesians are not alone in preferring affable, amiable social relations, and as people do everywhere, they become deeply angry, sad, depressed, and excited on occasion.

The bibliography of culture and mental health in the Pacific is not extensive (Rubinstein and White 1983) and has largely been concerned with the consequences of emotional suppression. Howard produced an overview in 1979 in which he discusses alcohol, suicide, rape, and forms of mental illness. He is largely concerned with the threat to mental health posed by the strains of modernization and increased cultural complexity. Although we are not aware of any culture-bound syndromes of consequence, suicide has recently become an important focus of concern, especially in Western Samoa where it appears to have reached epidemic proportions among youthful males (Bowles 1985; MacPherson and MacPherson 1985; Oliver 1985).

Wherever human emotions are subject to powerful cultural restraints the consequences are stressful for the individual. Thus the normally

bland pattern of social life in most Polynesian communities is periodically interrupted by violent emotional expressions that break through
personal constraints and create social control problems. From the same
source arises the soporific use of alcohol, though drunkeness is often
used as an excuse for rape and violent outbursts of anger. Similarly,
depressive responses are linked to patterns of emotional suppression,
and may be intensified where an outburst results in feelings of shame,
or where shame is imposed as a social sanction.

Howard (1979) is undoubtedly right in the emphasis he puts on culture contact in the genesis of mental health problems. The superficial
compatibilities and cultural convergences between Polynesia and the
colonial West mask fundamental differences that are profound and far
reaching. Westernizing pressures have become increasingly intense,
and threaten the very foundations of Polynesian social and personal
integration.

In spite of past efforts to suppress them, Polynesian folk therapies are
prolific, and they remain vigorous. Almost anyone can be a healer and
healing rituals are flexible, personal, freely adapted, and readily available. Although the literature on folk therapies in Polynesia remains thin,
studies of ho'oponopono in Hawaii are suggestive of Polynesian strategies
(Pukui, Haertig, and Lee 1972, 1979; Ito 1985b). The term ho'oponopono means "to make right, orderly, correct", and is used in reference to
meetings called to settle disputes between parties, or to uncover the
source of dissension (Ito 1985b:201). The notion is that interpersonal
entanglements are a major cause of illness and bad fortune, and that
clearing up entanglements—setting things straight again—is a necessary condition for healing to occur, especially in instances where the
malady is persistent. Whereas the contemporary metaphors Hawaiians
use to talk about the healing effects of ho'oponopono emphasize emotional
aspects of current interpersonal relations, that is, the need to clear away
anger and hostility so that the path will be clear again for binding
exchange (Ito 1985b:203–205), it is likely that in earlier times the gods
were thought to play an important role. Thus Howard (1979) describes
a situation in Rotuma in which persistent maladies are attributed to the
anger of ancestral spirits who are presumed to be upset by the inappropriate behavior of their descendants. Intra-familial conflicts are especially likely to be seen as a cause of ill-fortune, and steps must be taken
to resolve them to restore the harmony that is a precondition for health
and prosperity.

Although experiences with ghosts, spirits, visitations from ancestors,
visions, and the like—many of which still are reported to occur in more
traditional communities—are not easily distinguished from psychotic
processes in Western psychiatric practice, they take place within a different cultural framework and have to be assessed accordingly.

Contemporary Issues

We grew up in a world in which scholarship focused on the structure and function of traditional societies, viewed, if not in a steady state, at least as subject only to slow change. The history of the Pacific since World War II has changed that, and we, as residents of the culture area we study, cannot remain detached from the painful problems of our time. In the world of scholarship the landmark that signifies this change is Margaret Mead's (1956) restudy of Manus. The hidden curriculum in that book is that the people of Manus were more ready for change, more deeply involved in it, and more competent in handling it than most anthropologists or administrators had assumed. Anthropological theory at the time had no compelling way to explain this rapid accept-ance of change.

In the modern era changes in Polynesia have centered on political and economic struggles. Although there has been the rejection of coloni-alism and a quest for independent status and nationhood; there has also been the problem of building and sustaining modern economies out of quite unviable bases. Economic problems have been aggravated by rapid population increases, triggered by improved public health mea-sures and decreased infant mortality, and by extensive outmigration that has left some islands, for example Niue, depopulated to a critical degree. Urban centers have also mushroomed in most of the island groups, and now a substantial portion of the Polynesian population are confronted with adapting to the complexities of urban life. The substan-tial numbers who have migrated to New Zealand or the United States confront the problems of minority status, in addition to the problems of adapting to the complexities of modern life.

Since we are primarily concerned with socialization and psychologi-cal development, we will not review the full range of consequences these changes have wrought for Polynesians, but there are three that are of direct concern. These are the effects of population processes on family and community structures, changes in education patterns that have resulted from increased exposure to Western-style education, and pathologies that are occurring in response to acculturative stresses. Our discussion focuses on New Zealand, where we live and work.

Changes in Family and Community Structures

The rapid increase in population following World War II and the migration patterns it has fueled have generated new problems for Poly-nesian families. Traditional patterns of socialization were able to accommodate expanded family size with no trouble at all, provided community support and control systems were operative and there was enough land and resources to support subsistence. Obligatory sharing redistributed whatever resources were available, and compelled people to provide social security for everyone in good standing. But problems arise when people try to maintain large family structures without a supportive community or access to resources. Reluctance to limit family size under such circumstances then becomes highly dysfunctional, and for women in particular, a source of considerable stress.

The Samoan family now living in San Mateo County, California, may be as isolated, and thrown back to the essentials of survival, as were their ancestors when they arrived at and colonized a new island after a long canoe journey. It is far more difficult to approximate the socialization themes that form the conservative core of the Polynesian pattern in suburbia, however, than it was on a new island. To begin with, the sense of community as a setting and target for child-training becomes attenuated, lost to everyday living, although it may be romanticized in memory by older generations. Multiple parenting is often impossible to sustain in urban or suburban situations, especially where houses are small and grandparents are not present. When families are large and multiple parenting arrangements are unavailable, it is not only difficult to continue the traditional pattern of early indulgence, but the strain on parents may become intolerable, resulting in the abuse or neglect of children (Ritchie and Ritchie 1981b).

Generally speaking, childhood is harsh where mothers are required to perform both economic and domestic roles, where they have considerable responsibility for their children's conduct and its consequences, and especially, as in housing shared by a number of families, where behavior is under close scrutiny (Segall 1983). Conditions similar to this occur with high frequency among Polynesian immigrants to urban areas. For example, in our general study of child-rearing patterns in New Zealand (Ritchie and Ritchie 1970), the group of mothers under the greatest stress were Maori migrants living in a small rural town. Their attitudes towards nakedness, modesty, and sexuality were highly puritanical. Their scheduling of infant feeding was rigid, they punished harshly for toilet training accidents, shouted at and scolded children frequently, used a good deal of physical punishment, and kept children under close supervision. There was not much that resembled indulgence. The sensitivity of these mothers to community opinion forced them to adopt a stark stereotype of the Western model of child-rearing—a kind of tragic caricature.

Although early independence training persists under such circumstances it causes problems. The urban environment demands knowledge to protect oneself from a multitude of dangers, including predatory individuals, poisons, pills, motor cars, broken glass, tin cans, electricity, and disease-bearing vectors. Children who roam can fall into situations that are unimaginable in traditional settings. Furthermore, compulsory schooling removes peer caretakers of the very young, and so early independence is no longer balanced by the provision of sibling caretaking. Even when the child enters school, siblings attend other classes and are relatively inaccessible. Furthermore, peer groups of the strength and style characteristic of Polynesian communities are perceived as potentially disruptive in modern urban settings. School authorities frequently identify them as delinquent subcultures. Where communities are unable to provide the urban equivalent of peer socialization, the result is often severe generational conflict within Polynesian families. Children may accuse their parents of not doing their job properly, and parents may become befuddled about their proper roles, unaware that in traditional settings it is Polynesian children who produce Polynesian children, not Polynesian parents.

Despite strong counter pressures, peer groups do remain central to Polynesian social life in urban environments. They cross-cut the class structure of high schools and they persist in inhospitable suburbs, where they are often seen as delinquent gangs. There is no doubt that Polynesian peer groups can become venal and vicious, and the media promotes such an image (Kelsey and Young 1982), but it is also true that thousands of Polynesian youths learn the strategies of urban living through participating in peer groups without involvement in drugs, crime or anti-social behavior. We know of young people who are running their own cooperatives (Pene 1983), and throughout New Zealand there are new youth groups regularly competing in cultural festivals, operating like a substitute family for individuals otherwise isolated from kin. Two high schools in South Auckland have successfully restructured their school organization on a peer affiliation basis, calling each group a *whanau* 'family'. These examples demonstrate that there are no inherent incompatibilities between Polynesian peer socialization patterns and modern urban life.

Although population growth has slowed among most Polynesian groups, in some localities the problems associated with it are becoming increasingly acute. Despite the development of tribal-like community organizations such as village associations, church groups, and social clubs, the wave of urban dispossessed cannot be denied. It appears that reconstructing the Polynesian extended family in non-Polynesian settings would be relatively easy if governments and local authorities would take that as a starting point for planning. But in most metropolitan situations governmental agencies incorporate the model of the Western nuclear family, based on a single household, one income and all the ideology that goes with it. They therefore fail to address the adaptive problems experienced by Polynesian families.

When one listens carefully to Polynesian politicians speaking of fam-

ily it is important to know whether they are using the word in a Polynesian or Western sense, for they seem to switch readily from one to the
other. When they use the word in its traditional Polynesian sense they
often have a tendency to become vague and unrealistically romantic,
and end up supporting policies that are not as carefully considered as
they might be. For example, the decision to promote exclusively Maori
language preschools *(Kohanga Reo)* in New Zealand may have the desirable effect of providing crèche facilities and support structures, reducing the strain on women as well as providing socialization based on
Polynesian principles, but thus far inadequate attention has been given
to the quality of care given, to educational objectives, and to the transition into bilingual education when the children go to school. *Kohanga
Reo* may have the potential to assume the functions of traditional Maori
families, but they could also degenerate into poor quality child care situations, providing low levels of language stimulation, skill, and ability
development.

Education in a Changing World

During the 1970s local people throughout the Pacific began reassessing
the value of educational systems that had been developed on the Western model. Almost everywhere there was a heightened interest in vernacular language teaching and a concern for rewriting social studies
programs to reflect the history and values of local cultures. The struggle
between cultural conservation and education for modernity was much
discussed. Some of the rhetoric in which this debate has been conducted
had its origins in the ideology of neo-Marxism, and in such minority
protest movements as black power, Rastarfari, and feminism. Each
rhetoric contains a valid critique of what is happening to Pacific populations. Urban Polynesians can be portrayed as oppressed populations
still suffering from colonialism and its historical consequences. They are
exploited as a proletarian underclass and are subjected to patriarchal
structures, so the full range of anti-establishment critiques applies.

It has been within this intellectual milieu that Pacific nations have
been trying to formulate educational policies—at a time when the general objectives of formal education in Western nations are being seriously challenged. Despite evidence that metropolitan education systems, in Apia as well as in Auckland, in Suva as well as in San
Francisco, are ill-adapted to Islanders' needs, bureaucratic response
has been sluggish, indicating that no obvious solution exists. Even those
activists who advocate a return of public education to control by village
councils, cooperatives, or other local agencies are not able to show how
these alternatives will produce the people needed to run a modern economy, or to better educate the majority (for whom diplomas or certifi-
cates are irrelevant).

So colonial educative standards persist, notably in examination systems, which dominate the curriculum and require a formal means of progression through it. It is this formality, both in what the education system provides and in the means by which instruction is offered, that contrasts so strongly with the informal processes by which traditional knowledge was imparted (Borofsky 1982).

For children growing up in traditional Polynesian settings, and for those who have absorbed Polynesian epistemological assumptions elsewhere, formal schooling represents a sharp discontinuity in experience. The usual adaptation is for a rather hard line to be drawn between the two ways of codifying reality, with the world of school left behind as one leaves the playground gate. And when school is left behind, so too is much that one learned there.

Some young people are able to move between these two worlds and make a virtue of having access to, and command over, two cultural modalities. This bicultural coping strategy is most likely to occur where highly acculturated models are present, but the more unacculturated and traditional the setting the greater the conflict between the two worlds, particularly when teachers bring to the classroom their own monocultural ethnocentricities.

Research in New Zealand shows little difference between Maori and non-Maori achievement motivation, once urban-rural differences are taken into account (Ausubel 1961, Nicholls 1978), but the gulf between them in actual attainment is enormous (Ramsey 1983, Ramsey et al. 1981). Studies indicate that teachers there have low opinions of the general ability of Polynesian children (St. George 1978, 1983; D. Thomas 1979), and offer little encouragement to them. Maori students vote with their feet and simply leave a system that they often find meaningless and punitive. In contrast, Howard (1970) describes a pattern of sustained support for achievement in Rotuma that derives from a general interest on the part of adults in the attainment of children. The teachers, who are themselves Rotuman, have successfully adapted Polynesian learning styles to the classroom. Unfortunately formal educational structures elsewhere have been less responsive to such innovations.

McKessar and Thomas found low levels of verbal and direct help-seeking behavior among urban Maori children. They attribute this to "a general Polynesian pattern of child rearing in which children are not encouraged to seek help directly from parents once they are old enough to be looked after by older siblings" (McKessar and Thomas 1978:38). This tendency is even greater where teachers have low expectations of Polynesian children. It is no wonder that research has found the self-esteem of Maori high school students to be significantly lower than that of their Pakeha counterparts (Ranby 1979).

Attempts at remediation from various viewpoints have been well-documented. The earliest project of this kind was initiated by Howard in 'Aina Pumehana (a pseudonym), and has been described from a social psychological perspective by Gallimore and his associates. 'Aina Pumehana is a small Hawaiian homesteading community in rural Oahu. Over the years Howard and Gallimore studied socialization, specifically as it related to learning styles and classroom difficulties. Broadly considered, the remedial strategy that developed from this project emphasized behavioral reinforcement within group learning situations. For example, MacDonald and Gallimore (1971) devised educational strategies for young Hawaiians who found beach life within their peer group structures far more satisfying than the somewhat esoteric and attenuated reward systems of the high schools. There is no doubt that these young men knew perfectly well what the high school required of them, but they had no intention of remaining in that learning situation when the more autonomous, relaxed, and generally more attractive life outside of school was readily available. Furthermore, both legally and illegally, the out-of-school scene provided financial rewards as well. MacDonald and Gallimore set learning targets and made individual contracts to induce a return to school, at least for specified lessons, and successfully used group reinforcement strategies to induce fulfillment of the contract.

The Kamehameha Early Education Project (KEEP) arose from an intention to generalize what had been learned in 'Aina Pumehana to a wider population of Hawaiians, chiefly through the establishment of an experimental elementary school attached to the Kamehameha Schools[5] in Honolulu, and through projects on the island of Hawai'i. KEEP strove for changes in two directions: to modify a range of behaviors in young children in order to increase their capacity to learn in a Western classroom; and to modify the behavior of teachers so they would be more aware of and responsive to the Polynesian learning style. Thus, for children, the project sought to increase verbalizations, to work through concept trees and sequences, to increase questioning and to overcome the characteristic shy withdrawal behavior of school entrants. The modification of teacher behavior was chiefly directed toward an increased use of group goals and targets, the development of cooperative classroom strategies, and precise behavioral management (see Jordan et al. 1977).

Much of what the Kamehameha project endeavored to achieve was little different from the general objectives of minority education in the sorts of programs that were collectively called Head Start (Stanley 1972, 1973; Consortium for Longitudinal Studies 1983). Thus, developing a positive self-image, increasing expectations of successful performance and improving language and conceptual abilities were more central to the program than anything specifically Polynesian.

A number of individuals have developed techniques for classroom management designed to enhance the performance of Polynesian students within New Zealand classrooms. Jane Ritchie (1977, 1978), working through the Centre for Maori Studies and Research at the University of Waikatao, ran an experimental preschool program called *Te Kohanga,* which sought to overcome the disadvantages suffered by Maori children faced with the demands characteristic of Pakeha classrooms. Classroom behaviors such as sitting still and paying attention were stressed along with language skills in a structured curriculum-based program. Included in the curriculum were Maori cultural items such as songs, greetings, and language, but the major focus was on English language acquisition. At first it was thought that the low level of language use and concept development at entry was primarily the result of deprivation and poverty. But it was not only this. The families of these children had become dissociated from the social support structures typical of traditional communities. They no longer were involved in multiple parenting patterns and peer interactions were relatively impoverished. The generally low level of one-to-one interaction between adults and young children typical of Polynesians was exacerbated in this urban context, and was not compensated for by stimulating peer relations.

The major contribution of the *Te Kohanga* project to overcoming language disadvantages was the emphasis on books as tools of language development. Subsequently this approach was used by Warwick Elley at the Institute for Education at the University of the South Pacific in what has been termed The Book Flood Program in Niue and other Pacific locations (Elley and Mangubhai 1981a, 1981b). In the work of Marie Clay (1976) with Samoan migrant children, and the reading program of Donna Awatere in South Auckland, the importance of early access to and success with literary skills is also emphasized.

David Thomas (1975, 1978), using an ingenious device known as the Madsen Cooperation Board, has shown differences in cooperative versus competitive behaviors between Pakeha and Maori children, and between groups of Polynesians exposed to varying degrees of acculturation. In general, the more traditional the milieu in which Polynesian children are raised, the more cooperative and less competitive they are. Nancy and Theodore Graves (1973) explored a related dimension that they label "inclusion-exclusion." The Graves use this dimension in reference to social motivation to incorporate or exclude individuals into the group. They found Polynesian children to be more inclusive than their Pakeha counterparts and more responsive to learning in group contexts. Strategically, this suggests encouraging group learning rather than one-to-one, individualistic, competitive-style learning in the classroom.

As interesting as these studies are, it sometimes seems to us that researchers are more interested in cooperation than are Polynesians. Without wishing to endorse the extreme, competitive aspects of Western capitalism, we are not yet convinced that the Polynesian style of cooperation has been clearly identified. If we go back to the earliest discussion of this matter (Mead 1937), there is definite evidence of dispute and conflict. In western Polynesia in particular, pugnacity and status rivalry require elaborate and sometimes heavy-handed cultural authority systems to limit the disruptive effects of personal moves aimed at self-enhancement. Peer socialization does not automatically insure that individuals are brimming over with cooperative motivation, even though the enthusiasm with which collective enterprises are conducted when consensus does occur is often impressive. The blend of coexisting cooperative and competitive styles that one sees in Samoan cricket, for example, has yet to find an ethnographer. Returning to our earlier description of cultural style, we would emphasize that cooperation is a customary control on competitive propensities that are actively developed during independence training (Freeman 1983).

In New Zealand, where bureaucratic response has been especially slow, pressure has built toward the development of separatist institutions. For example, there has been a movement in one Maori tribal group to establish its own *whare wananga* 'university'. Other educational alternatives are being promoted by the Department of Maori Affairs through a series of programs known collectively as *Tu Tangata* 'stand tall'. The *Kohanga Reo* Maori language preschools already mentioned are part of this; others are *Kokiri* 'skill training centers', and pre-employment training programs. Some of these programs provide training in Maori crafts, such as carving for men and weaving for women; others focus on entrepreneurial business seminars and the stimulation of collective enterprises of various kinds. The Department of Maori Affairs provides money and advisory services to get these programs started, then leaves it to the community to handle things their own way.

There is no doubt that these sorts of programs, especially since they create employment and bring economic activity back within the cultural purview, are providing for a greater degree of cultural continuity than the general education system. The style is relaxed, informal, and Polynesian and the levels of aspiration are appropriate to the levels of attainment.

Acculturative Stress and Pathology

The key to acculturative stress among Polynesians seems to revolve around the ways in which traditional communities exert controls that are absent in modern urban settings. There are several features to note.

First, Polynesian parents tend to be swift and harsh in correcting behavior that infringes on community standards. By contrast, the urban policing system is protracted, capricious, and unpredictable, and easily fosters the expectation that one may get away indefinitely with wrongdoing.

Second, Polynesian socialization places the teaching of respect in a very central position. Respect is demanded for community authorities, for elders, for decisions reached by community consensus, and for the cultural identity of which one is a part. But there is no comparable socialization to instill respect for the policeman who comes from elsewhere, or for an alien legal system that shrouds itself in strange rituals and a seemingly arbitrary criminal justice system, in which punishment appears to have no connection to the crime. Compare a short prison sentence for sexual assault, taking the offender into the macho environment of a prison, with the shaming that would go on in a small village for years after the same crime.

Third, community surveillance of behavior and public discussion about it is a continuous and effective control system so long as one wishes, or is required, to remain part of the community. Where socialization no longer emphasizes the importance of living harmoniously with kin and neighbors, community watchfulness loses its sanctioning power.

Recent attention to the quality of child care has brought into focus the high frequency of child neglect and abuse in Polynesian families (Fergusson, Fleming, and O'Neill 1972). Our assessment of this situation (Ritchie and Ritchie 1981a, 1981b) is that acculturative stresses lead to increased risk, but as with crime, there is nothing particularly Polynesian about the patterns. Data presented by Alan Howard (1974: 185–189), for instance, indicate that Hawaiian parents who favor physical punishment score higher on scales measuring acculturation to white society than their community-mates who favor alternative strategies.

It may well be that children are exposed to greater risk where inappropriate standards of behavior are applied within a punitive framework of fundamentalist Christianity. There are many Polynesians who fall into this category. Throughout the Pacific the form of Christianity that was implanted tended more towards the evangelical and puritanical. We think it possible that child abuse as a pathology arises as much from that cultural tradition as from anything definably Polynesian.

Lack of community and child-rearing supports, social isolation, the stresses of poverty and urban alienation, along with the by no means paranoid belief that their white neighbors are watching and judging, all probably contribute to this particular pathology. Furthermore, Polynesian children are encouraged by the dominant middle class culture to question authority, including their parents, and to talk freely about topics such as sex in family contexts. Such behavior is considered rude and disrespectful in Polynesian contexts, and may lead to harsh responses from befuddled parents.

Although as far as we can tell child abuse was rare and regarded with horror in traditional Polynesian communities, corporal punishment was not uncommon (Borofsky 1987, E. Beaglehole 1944b, Freeman 1983). Polynesian reactions to our own extensive discussion of the role of corporal punishment in child-training (Ritchie and Ritchie 1981b) has generally been an incredulous, "How else can you correct children?" or an accusatory, "But it is part of our culture to hit children; how else do you teach respect?" However, we also have statements from Maori informants to the effect that physical punishment was not traditional, especially in upper status families, because it was neither necessary nor compatible with parental dignity. It is likely that no generalization is possible, that there is considerable variability among Polynesian cultures, among groups within cultures, and among individual families. But in any case, children lived primarily within the world of children. Perhaps in the traditional context what children learned from physical punishment was to avoid parents, and that is probably still the case. Like people everywhere who are tempted to use physical punishment as a disciplinary strategy, modern Polynesian parents will have to assess its implications in the light of the impact it has on their children in contemporary settings, including the fact that it almost certainly breeds violence (Straus, Gelles, and Steinmetz 1980).

Conclusion

When we began work on Polynesian families thirty years ago we wondered whether what we were recording was simply a function of large family size, low income, and a rural environment. To answer this question we undertook comparative research among Pakeha New Zealand families. But even when matched for sociological variables, we found distinctive differences between Maori and non-Maori. Twenty years of further research on both Pakeha and Maori families in New Zealand (Jane Ritchie 1978; Ritchie and Ritchie 1978) have only confirmed that finding. When we reached beyond our own data to other Polynesian locations, researched by other workers from a variety of disciplines, we found this conclusion strengthened. We have also been gratified to find that Polynesian audiences have responded to our presentations with an affirmation that we are portraying a world that they recognize as their own.

As an heuristic way of summarizing the basic model of socialization we have presented and to link it to the cultural themes or targets to

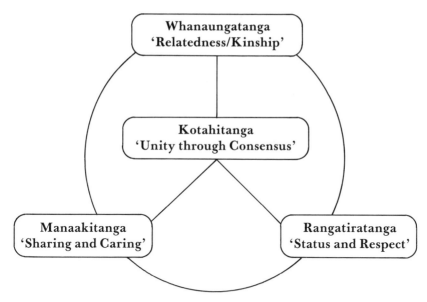

Figure 1. Themes in Polynesian socialization

which we earlier referred, we will use the device of a simple diagram (Fig. 1).

The Polynesian child is born into an omnipresent community in which all adults and many older children act parentally. Initially the child enjoys every privilege, comfort, and attention in the care of these indulgent parents and surrogates. But independence is a highly valued attribute. It contrasts with, tempers, and balances an emphasis on community goals and processes. So the young child soon becomes a caretaker of younger children, as well as a member of a peer group that plays a major role in his or her socialization.

The primary community is typically a ramified kinship group, and the centrality of family process in all cultural matters is constant. Children are put through an educative process in which the work of *whanaungatanga* is gradually revealed in all its complexity and power. Parents and their surrogates represent ancestral elders, who must be given respect. This is taught partly through affection, but also by punishment, fear, and threats. Later, in peer groups, the leadership qualities of *rangatiratanga* are recognized and may even be emulated. *Rangatiratanga* is lineage-based, but it is confirmed by accomplishment, personal achievements, style, and consistency.

With so many parental hands, children are presented with multiple models of caring. As they grow, they are required to share with and care for the whole *whanau* (and especially for younger children). Such caring, *manaakitanga*, constitutes a blending of the physical and the non-physical. Young children are especially important to old people, and their concern is reciprocated.

Independence thrusts a unique identity on the child early in development, but there are others in the same situation; thus peer groups are formed where all four themes come together. Such groups are the learning ground for *kotahitanga,* the holy grail of unity, of oneness in and with the *whanau,* in which all statuses are recognized and ordered, surrounded by the support of a caring system and ethic. What does it matter if things sometimes fall apart, if conflict and back-biting are rife. The structure of cultural character has been formed and is available for the expression of individuality; it is now open to be shaped to adult ends and purposes.

Although we have found it convenient to organize our discussion of Polynesian child-rearing around the major themes of relatedness, status and respect, sharing and caring, and unity through consensus, there is clearly more to it than that. Each of these themes appears in other cultural systems, and indeed, they are present in cultures outside the region. But they are only components of more complex patterns that convey the particulars of being not just Polynesian, but Maori, Samoan, Tahitian, or Tongan; of carrying and expressing a set of values, an interpersonal style, a political style; of deciding how to spend one's energies or resources, one's day or one's lifetime.

Directions for Future Research

We do not think it is necessary to reject any of the earlier approaches mentioned in our introduction. Basically we still find the concept of cultural character plausible and its description worthy of pursuit. The earlier conceptions of it may have been crude and simplistic (as ours might seem to a sophisticated member of any Polynesian culture), but when child development is viewed against the template of central cultural concerns, then the pressures, rewards, punishments, exhortations and injunctions, the ordering of events, and the modeling of behavior clearly fall into place.

In order to gain a well-balanced perspective on Polynesian character we need to take into consideration observed behavior, symbolic learning, cognition, emotion, and motivation—we cannot cast aside any net still capable of catching fish. We look back and see the ethnography of socialization in Polynesian cultures as a pattern of many islands and many ancestors, with each anthropologist charting a small portion of the territory. By trial and error, by successive approximations to an elusive truth behind the truths, we continue on our exploratory journey.

The basic model of Polynesian socialization described in this chapter emerged from the cumulative work of researchers who were explicitly interested in the role that socialization played in shaping adult character, and by extension, basic cultural forms. The scope of their concerns was extensive, and details were often sacrificed in the interest of defining broad patterns. The essentials of each developmental stage were well described, but much less attention was paid to the particulars of transition between stages. Concern for interpersonal interaction focused on behavioral regularities, while the subtleties of verbal and nonverbal communication were given short shrift. A good deal of research was done on parent-child interaction, but there were few comparable descriptions of peer group interaction. In general, emphasis was placed on intracultural regularities at the expense of diversity within cultures and communities. And few systematic studies have been conducted that compare socialization patterns within various Polynesian communities. The (often implicit) comparative case against which each description has usually been reflected is one or another version of mainstream western patterns.

Much of the current socialization research being conducted among Polynesian populations aims at filling these gaps. For example, several recent fieldworkers have initiated studies of early interactions between caregivers and young children, aided by video and high quality tape recorders, which facilitate detailed microanalyses of interactions. Their work is helping to flesh out the more general patterns. Martini and Kirkpatrick (1981), for example, analyzed film sequences of caregiver-infant interaction in the Marquesas for such variables as the infant's and caregiver's positions, physical and visual orientation, vocalizations, and closeness to one another. The data they describe are in marked contrast to mainstream American patterns, where the mother-infant dyad tends toward exclusiveness and emphasizes reciprocal face-to-face play. Marquesan infants are encouraged from the very beginning to orient toward the broader social scene.

Comparable interaction patterns have been described for Samoa by Ochs (1982b; see also Ochs and Schieffelin 1983, 1984), who focuses on sociolinguistic data. Again contrasting Samoan patterns with white middle-class tendencies, in this instance to accomodate situations to the child, Ochs reports that "the Samoans encourage the child to meet the needs of the situation, that is, to notice others, listen to them, and adapt one's own speech to their particular status and needs" (Ochs and Schieffelin 1984:298). Whereas American middle-class children are socialized to engage in primarily dyadic verbal interactions, Samoan children are "immersed in multiparty verbal interactions" (Schieffelin and Ochs 1986:176). Ochs' (1986) investigations also shed light on the ways in which status considerations are translated into socializing speech patterns, the relationship between sociolinguistic and emotional patterns (see also Gerber 1985), and the impact of literacy instruction on socialization in Samoa (Duranti and Ochs 1986).

Sociolinguistic research among Hawaiians has also yielded rich results. The focus of much of this work has been on the contrast between verbal patterns in the home and those required in formal schoolrooms. Boggs and Watson-Gegeo (1985), for example, found a dual structure in the homes of Hawaiian children, hierarchically patterned with adults and caretakers, disputing and storytelling with agemates (see also Watson 1972, 1975; Watson-Gegeo and Boggs 1977). Studies in Hawaiian school contexts are also helping to illuminate the thorny issue of cooperation and competition among Polynesian children (and by extension among adults). A recent dissertation by D'Amato (1987), using research conducted among second graders, goes a long way toward unraveling the complexities of the intra-peer group dynamics that lie at the heart of the matter. D'Amato builds upon the earlier work of Boggs (1978), who focuses on the development of disputing routines.

But despite the heartening continuance of interest in Polynesian socialization and psychological development, much remains to be done. The need for comparative work is particularly conspicuous in its absence. Contrasts between Polynesian and Western patterns are less and less revealing; that lode has been well-mined and turns up fewer and fewer insightful nuggets. What is needed are studies of contrasts within Polynesia, and between Polynesians and other island societies. We still have no clear understanding of the impact of societal scale on socialization and psychological development within Polynesia. Nor have such key dimensions as degree of hierarchy, settlement pattern, household structure, and ecological variability been explored comparatively. As the experiential world of Polynesian peoples expands to incorporate more and more cosmopolitan modalities, systematic comparisons between rural and urban settings, between families with differing socioeconomic characteristics, and differing degrees of separation from their island roots become increasingly relevant (see, e.g., T. Baker 1986). Only through such comparisons will we eventually come to understand the full significance of what it means to be Polynesian in the modern world.

NOTES

1. An exception to this statement were slaves, usually individuals captured in warfare, who were deprived of status precisely because they were wrenched out of the lattice of their kinship network.

2. As with all Polynesian status displays, such significations were contextual-

ized. That is, there were instances in which chiefs were expected to display humility, others in which they were expected to take command, and indeed, to appear god-like in their demeanor (see Marcus, chapter 6, this volume).

3. Multiple parenting has the effect of freeing women from the full-time child care role that Jessie Bernard (1974) has found so damaging for Western women and children, making it possible for them to pursue economic, political, or other outside interests.

4. By Western standards, rates remain high among Polynesians even in urbanized areas. For example Howard et al. (1970:31) found 25.5 percent of Hawaiian households in central Honolulu (Papakolea) to contain one or more adopted children.

5. Kamehameha Schools were established in the latter part of the nineteenth century for the education of children of Hawaiian or part-Hawaiian ancestry.

5

Mana
and
Tapu

BRADD SHORE

It is not by chance that Western observers have so often sought the soul of Polynesia in the concept[1] of *mana*.[2] Nor is it coincidental that the term is one of the few Austronesian loanwords (along with taboo and tattoo) to make their way into Indo-European tongues. For without an understanding of *mana* and its related concepts, there is no path into Polynesian worldview. An even cursory glance at the literature on *mana* suggests how difficult that understanding has been to come by.[3]

Several thorny and subtle issues of definition are pervasive:

1. Is *mana* better described as substance or process (R. Keesing 1984; Valeri 1985a:99)?
2. Is *mana* better understood as cause (force, power) or effect (luck, efficacy) (Hocart 1927; Firth 1940; Hubert and Mauss 1978; Hogbin 1936)?
3. In its authentic Polynesian context, is *mana* an abstract and ubiquitous force (E. S. C. Handy 1927:26), or concrete, localized, and particular powers (Oliver 1974:55)?
4. What is the relation of *mana* to generative potency and thereby its links to women?
5. What is the relation of *mana* to the important Polynesian concepts of *tapu* and *noa?*

The Nature of *Mana*

In a paper analyzing the uses of *mana* throughout the Austronesian-speaking populations of the western Pacific, Keesing has argued that Austronesian speakers treat power as a stative verb. "Things and human enterprises and efforts are *mana*" (R. Keesing 1984:138).

Admitting that this pattern is clearer in Melanesia than Polynesia, where nominalized forms of *mana* are common, Keesing nonetheless suggests something important about Polynesian concepts of *mana*. Whatever form *mana* may take in the abstract, in use *mana* is understood through its active manifestations in the world, not as a kind of thing. "Whereas we do not metaphorically substantivize 'success' or 'sanctity' we pervasively render 'power' as if it were a quantifiable entity, a 'thing' people have more or less of. Someone who has 'it' is powerful, 'full' of 'it'. Yet 'having power', cut loose from this metaphysical substantivation, is a relationship always contextual and two-sided" (R. Keesing 1984:150).

This is another manifestation of the more general Polynesian episte-mological bias that things be known in their specific contexts and through their perceptual effects in the world rather than in terms of essential, intrinsic features (see, for example, R. Keesing 1984:148). This was the thrust of Hocart's important early analysis of the concept *mana* (Hocart 1927) and of Firth's seminal explication of the Tikopian version of the term (Firth 1940). Firth discovered that Tikopians were unable or unwilling to provide any general (i.e., decontextualized) defi-nition of their term *manu,* stressing instead an 'activity principle in nature in concrete situations' such as the "falling of rain, growth of food, advent of calms, relief of sickness" (Firth 1940:185). Thus, although Western analysts have chosen to view *mana* as some kind of general and abstract force, Polynesians seem to emphasize a variety of particular powers, or at the very least specific manifestations of a gen-eral concept.[4] This is why observers have sometimes translated *mana* as 'luck' or 'success'—focusing on the effects of power rather than on its intrinsic qualities (Firth 1940; Sahlins 1981a:31; Hanson 1987:426; Levy 1973:156). This aspect of power as understood by Polynesians underlies much of the dynamics of political history in the region and makes sense of the apparent political pragmatism characteristic of Polynesia (see especially Goldman 1970). Hanson says that in Polynesia "a primary mark of *mana* is outstanding effectiveness in action" (Han-son 1987:426). It is impossible, even in this most aristocratic of cultural areas, to completely separate rank from considerations of practical effi-cacy. In even the most rigidly ascriptive of Polynesian polities, genea-logical rank and practical success are dialectically linked and not catego-rically opposed (see, for example, Marcus 1980a; Kaeppler 1971c; and Bott 1982 on Tonga).

It is probably this characteristic Polynesian evaluation of intrinsic power in relation to its perceptible effects that underlies the associations of nobility and status with crude visibility. Whether through height or girth, brightness or generosity, chiefly *mana* in Polynesia is expressed through images of abundance. Distinctions in quality manifest themselves in distinctions in quantity, but always as indications of spiritual luster. "[T]he divine *mana* of chiefs is manifest in their brilliance, their shining. This, as much as corpulence, was the 'beauty' that marked chiefly status" (Sahlins 1981a:31).

Without an understanding of this pragmatic aspect of *mana* it is hard to comprehend the rapid conversion of many Polynesians to Christianity, or the relative speed with which a Kamehameha, or a Pomare could consolidate an empire and become acknowledged as supreme. Sahlins argues convincingly that the "apotheosis of Captain Cook" in Hawaii and his murder at the hands of disappointed Hawaiians is yet another historical rendering of a culturally distinctive understanding of power (Sahlins 1981a). Though rooted in a conception of continuity of potency through authentic descent, *mana* is ultimately understood as mobile and sometimes fickle, fluctuating according to a person's success or failure, or according to his success in maintaining good social relations (Metge 1976:64). In Samoan myth, for instance, the failure of a great chief, Tinilau, to provide materially for his people, is interpreted as a failure of his *mana*, a failure answered by the removal of his descent line and the transfer of his authority to another chief (Good 1980:34).

Sources of Mana

The Polynesian concept of *mana*, though often used with reference to chiefs, is always tied to the powers of the gods. The hierarchical Polynesian cosmos generally distinguished categorically between divine and human agency, locating the former in the heavens and the latter on the earth. Yet Polynesians were far more interested in the possibilities of exchange between such domains than in static categories. More often then not, the chiefly genealogies in Polynesia suggest divine origins for the greatest chiefs. As Goldman (1970:9) reminds us: "In Polynesia, all powers are from the gods and, in principle, are transmitted genealogically, which is to say authentically along established lines." Goldman also distinguishes between those primary powers that are direct manifestations of divine influence, and the more indirect secondary powers.

E. S. C. Handy's classic analysis of Polynesian religion also derives human *mana* from the influences of gods or spirits (E. S. C. Handy 1927:28). As noted, Handy (1927:26) interprets *mana* in the most abstract and general terms, referring to it as "a psychic dynamism manifesting itself physically." Williamson follows Handy's emphasis on divine agency as underlying *mana* when he interprets Polynesian conceptions of political succession.

If I am right . . . what the father breathed into or transmitted to his son who was to succeed him was divine power, given to him by the gods, this being done to qualify the son for holding of the family name or title. If this was so, we are getting very near to the idea that the general sanctity of say, a chief, passed to his successor; and seeing that the god could, if he liked, withhold this sanctity from the person who had been recognized as the successor . . . we reach the point that divine sanction was necessary for the selection of a successor, not only for transmitting to him the sanctity, but for endowing him with *mana;* if the god had not "taken up his abode" in the presumed successor, and had not endowed him with the *mana,* someone else would have to be chosen in and for whom the god was believed to have done so (Williamson 1924, 3:224).

Hanson suggests that the primary aim of religious ritual in traditional Polynesia was to channel the influence of the gods into areas of life where it would be useful and away from those areas where it might be harmful (Hanson 1987:426).[5]

Mana *as Fecundity*

This tracing of *mana* to its divine sources in Polynesian thought is an important clue to one aspect of the *mana* concept: either directly or indirectly *mana* is linked to generative potency, to the sources of organic creation. Handy (1927:27) made this insight the centerpiece of his analysis of *mana*. "[P]rimal *mana* was not merely power or efficacy, but procreative power, derived from an ultimate source and diffused, transmitted, and manifested throughout the universe."

The connection between procreative power, the gods, and chiefs is suggested by the importance of the term *tupu* (or its cognates) throughout Polynesia. The term means 'to grow' or 'to unfold'.[6] Derivatives of tupu are common in Polynesia, and have an interesting range of meanings. Gifford places the authentic source of Tongan *mana* with *tupui otua* —the original generator gods—rather than with any impersonal supernatural power or with lesser spirits (Gifford 1929:326). In Samoa, *tupu* means 'king'.[7] *Tupua* in Samoan is used nowadays to signify an idol or image of a god, but in older usage could also refer to deified chiefs in the form of some natural phenomenon, like stars (E. S. C. Handy 1927:2). In Hawaii, *kupua* were spirits embodied in various phenomena of nature, while the equivalent term in Niuean referred to supernatural powers, both protective and mischievous (E. S. C. Handy 1927:2).

Johansen defines the Maori term *tupu* as 'to unfold one's nature'. In Maori legend the primal deity Io creates the world by planting his words. Thus this world 'unfolded its nature as the world' *(ka tupu te ao ki te ao).* Part by part, the Maori world grew, each element in its own way, according to its nature. The opposite of *tupu* is *mate* 'to die', "indicating any kind of lack, want, insufficiency of potency." The concept of *tupu* lies behind Maori conceptions of honor, name, and revenge, and consti-

tutes an assertion of the generative powers of life against depletion, dis-
honor, and death. Johansen links *tupu* directly with *mana* but claims that
the former labels the concept of an internal unfolding of something's
own nature, while *mana* connotes "something participated, an active
fellowship" that affects vitality (Johansen 1954:40, 48, 65, 85).

The evidence throughout Polynesia for the link between fecundity
and *mana* is ubiquitous. Gifford (1929:326) reports for Tonga that "if a
man's yams grow well and his pigs multiply, it is said that he has *mana.*"
Tikopians traditionally regarded their chiefs as controlling, through
links with ancestors and gods, all forms of natural fertility in the world:
crops, rain, health, and general economic well-being (Firth 1940:179).
Firth quotes an informant who attributes such power directly to the
land: "When we look at the land to which food comes constantly then
we say 'the land is *manu.*' But when we see that no food comes that is
mara" (Firth 1940:180). He notes a further association between the ability of a chief to heal the sick *(mairo)* with this generative quality of *mana*
(Firth 1940:183).

Traditional Rotumans apparently had many of these same associations with political power. "[T]he concern [in Rotuman myth] is with
the continual regenesis of life—with the fertility of the land and the people. The fundamental issue is one of harnessing the *mana* of the gods in
the service of this goal" (Howard 1985b:47).

This concern with the fecundity of chiefs, in the more cosmic sense of
the term, was institutionalized in traditional Rotuma in the office of the
sou, a kind of a sacred chief, "an object of veneration" (Howard 1985b:
41) associated with annual rituals of increase. These rituals involved
considerable feasting and emphasized images of gustatory abundance.
In one of these rituals, a libation of kava was dedicated to the dead *sou.*
Then, atop the hill where these ancestral chiefs were buried, the living
sou was required to eat of all the grasses on the hill (Williamson 1924,
3:336). Both the *sou* and his spiritual alter ego, the *mua,* held only indirect control over fertility, as representatives of the generative powers of
the gods. Thus pigs and bananas were used in these rituals as sacrificial
gifts to feed the gods "in exchange for which the gods [were] expected to
provide prosperity, including fertility of land and people" (Howard
1985b:49). The *sou,* it seems, simultaneously contained the powers of
regeneration, and symbolized their consequences. "The *sou* was stuffed
out with mats to as large a size as possible, and dressed in the official
garments of his office. I must say as to this that it was a special duty of a
sou to get fat, as indeed it was with great chiefs of some of the other
islands" (Williamson 1924, 3:336).

In Polynesia, as elsewhere, sexual fecundity and agricultural abundance are linked in various ways. In Samoa important chiefs have traditionally signified their power by ostentatious food distributions and by

distributing various offspring throughout Samoa. Paramount chiefs are even today called *tama'āiga* 'children of [many] families', suggesting the depth and breadth of their kinship connections. The size of one's family, like that of one's body, indexes the presence of the gods, and hence both rank and *mana*.[8] Firth notes that the Tikopian classification of coconut cream as a chiefly food has to do with its links with semen, both metaphorically (in appearance) and metonymically (in its alleged capacity to produce semen in a male who eats it). "Food and sex are the two principal media of growth and prosperity, and the chiefs, as elsewhere, are honored in each. Precedence in eating and the receipt of first fruits *(muakai)* are . . . the counterpoint to the chief's religious position as the terrestrial agent for the god—bestowing food, and hence as 'owner' of all resources" (Firth 1936b:482).

Howard suggests that Rotuman chiefs are "symbolic inseminations of the land, bringing fertility and prosperity to the people" (Howard 1985b:60), a clear echo of Firth's Tikopian analysis. It is not surprising that Polynesians paid special attention to the reproductive capacities and histories of their chiefs, whose potency encompassed that of their people. This concern explains the symbolic importance of the chief's genitals in traditional Polynesia. For Maori, it was said that the chief's penis could inspire courage and renewed vigor in his people, accounting for the practice of warriors crawling through their chief's legs (E. S. C. Handy 1927:143).[9] Linton comments that in traditional Marquesan culture: "[T]here was constant mention of the genital organs of the chief, which were given names indicating their vigor and size" (Linton 1939:159).

Mangaia traditionally had three distinct chiefly offices, among which was a "Ruler of the Food" whose duties, both sacred and secular, had to do with guaranteeing the continuing fertility of the land (Williamson 1924, 3:252). Marquesans had a class of deified mortals, *atua,* who claimed the titles and attributes of gods by virtue of both their alleged powers to "impart fruitfulness to the productions of the earth, or smiting them with blasting and sterility" (Williamson 1924, 3:331).[10]

Mana *Transformed:* Tapu *and* Noa

The concept of *mana* is central to Polynesian worldview. Though common in its general features throughout Polynesia, *mana* can also provide us with a way to understand some of the major regional differences within Polynesia. Traced back to divine transmission, the potency defined by *mana* is necessarily unstable and mobile. Simply put, mana is not simply possessed; it is appropriated, and at times even wrested from its divine sources. To better understand *mana* then, we need to look at the various transformations Polynesians conceive of as possible for *mana,* and examine their institutional manifestations.

What is called Polynesian religion might be aptly described as a kind of vitalism. Its focus was on appropriating, harnessing, and sometimes dissociating generative and ordering powers from gods in the service of human needs: biological reproduction, fecundity of the land and sea, and the reproduction of the social forms that gave shape to human relations. Implicitly, then, precontact Polynesian religion was an economy of *mana* in which generative powers were appropriated, channeled, transformed, and bound. Because such potency was constructive only when properly channeled, Polynesians characteristically lived in a very dangerous world. Breaches of etiquette or chiefly protocol did not merely have social repercussions, but cosmic consequences as well. In the wrong hands, or when uncontained and disorganized, every vital power could diminish rather than enlarge human life. The set of beliefs and practices in Polynesia associated with the transformations in *mana* are virtually coextensive with Polynesian religion and much of what we call politics as well. Yet nowhere were these Polynesian concerns so clearly set out as in the complex system of beliefs associated with the terms *tapu* and *noa*.

Tapu: A Confusing Term

Though one of the most familiar Polynesian words to Western ears, *tapu* has nonetheless proven to be particularly difficult for Western observers to understand. This is probably because the meaning of a taboo seems intuitively obvious to most of us. We tend to impose our meanings uncritically on the Polynesian term.

We have voluminous ethnographic evidence for the importance of *tapu*, particularly in eastern Polynesia. Yet the range of its referents in various Polynesian locales has frustrated attempts at a synthetic general understanding of the concept. *Tapu*[11] and its negation or antithesis *noa* (*me'ie* in Marquesan) have been interpreted as suggesting the distinction between significant and insignificant aspects of life. Dening (1980:53) argues that in traditional Marquesan society "to know the *tapu* was to know a social map of Te Henua [the landscape]," and he goes on to define that landscape in the following terms. "[Marquesans] saw their people divided between *tapu* and *me'ie*. *Me'ie* they also knew as *kikino, vai noa* (common water), *tupe noa* (insignificant), *maunoa* (dark people). *Kikino* were servants: they fetched wood and water, collected breadfruit and coconuts, lived on the estates of landowners and guarded their trees against theft" (Dening 1980:73).

In this reading of the concept, *tapu* distinguishes the noble from the common. In his discussion of the Maori concept, Best noted "the condition of *tapu* pertaining to a superior chief would have considerable effect in producing a feeling of deference and respect toward him" (Best

1924a:97). Valeri, following Johansen (1954:186), glosses the Hawaiian term *kapu* as 'marked' or 'set apart', implying a need to 'pay attention'. "The divine, pure or impure, is *kapu* to persons or things that are not divine. This means that the latter have to pay attention and relate to the former in a prescribed way. Inversely, things or persons that are not divine are *noa*, because the divine beings are not supposed to be careful with them. Moreover, persons or things that are closer to the divine are *kapu* to those that are less close to it. Vice versa, the latter are *noa* to the former" (Valeri 1985a:90).

Gifford associates with an attitude of respect the most important of the Tongan social *tapus*, those linked with one's father, his brothers, a male's sister and especially his *mehikitanga* 'father's sister'. The appropriate attitude towards these relations is what Tongans call *fakaapaapa*, a combination of love, honor, reverence, and fear (Gifford 1929:17).

Though *tapu* often implies respect, it can also connote danger, fear, and even dread. This is *tapu* as 'dangerous'. Best provides a description of a Maori reception accorded a great *ariki* 'chief' of the Ngaitahu tribe, which gives a powerful image of this aspect of *tapu*. "His visits were always dreaded, and his movements, whenever he entered a *pa*, were watched with great anxiety by the inhabitants, for if his shadow happened to fall upon a *whata* (stage) or *rua* (pit for food) while he was passing through the crowded lanes of a town it was immediately destroyed, with all its contents, because the sacred shadow of the ariki (lord) having fallen upon it, the food became *tapu*, and fatal to those who partook of it" (from White, J. *The Ancient History of the Maori,* 1887–1890, quoted in Best 1924a:188).[12] This is a clear example of the negative capacity of *mana* when disordered or misappropriated.

Without multiplying examples gratuitously, we can begin to understand how *tapu* has eluded a clear definition. First, the term has two quite distinct usages, one active, the other passive. As an active quality, *tapu* suggests a contained potency of some thing, place, or person. In its passive usage, it means forbidden or dangerous for someone who is *noa*.[13] Moreover, it seems to combine contradictory properties, suggesting on the one hand sacredness, reverence, and distinctiveness and, on the other, danger, dread, and pollution.[14] Nowhere is this conceptual knot more thoroughly tangled than in the explication of the relation between *tapu* and the feminine.

Tapu *and Female Status*

In examining the relations between gender and *mana*, the differences between eastern/central Polynesia (e.g., Hawaii, Marquesas, New Zealand, Easter Island, Society Islands) and western Polynesia (e.g., Samoa, Tonga, Tokelau, Pukapuka, Tuvalu, and, to a limited extent,

Tikopia) emerge with dramatic contrast. At first glance, the ethno-graphic record would seem to support the generalization that whereas the *mana* concept devalued the feminine in the eastern islands, it exalted the feminine in the western islands. Yet a closer look should permit us to understand these differences as less categorical than this, and as trans-formations of a common notion of *tapu*.

Throughout the ethnography of eastern Polynesia, references are made to the fact that women were considered common, polluting, dan-gerous, or *noa*. Valeri accounts for the exclusion of women from sacri-fices in Hawaii by the belief in their intrinsic impurity. The feminine was linked to the passive in Hawaiian thought and with sexual as opposed to cosmic and social reproduction that is the province of male ritual activity. Sexual reproduction, which necessarily conjoins the sexes, produces the loss of boundaries between pure and impure. Here, purity is associated with autonomy and categorical integrity, while pol-lution is a product of mixtures (Valeri, 1985a:113, 123–124).

Johansen's account of the common *(noa)* status of Maori women touches on the same theme. According to Johansen, "woman is the great representative of everyday life" among Maori (Johansen 1954: 215), and is by nature *noa* just as the man is by nature *tapu*. In contrast to Hindu dogma, it is precisely this common status of women that makes them appropriate cooks: "Life in her is not as the life in the man so strong and pure that it can either damage others or be damaged itself by cooking" (Johansen 1954:214). The exclusion of men from cook houses is linked to the concept of organic and conceptual purity of men and to the belief that "woman is a representative of everyday life, *or, more accurately, that of the 'mixture' of lives*" (Johansen 1954:216, emphasis added).[15]

Goldman provides an eloquent summary of the Maori view of gender relations.

> By associating women with childbirth—a passive sexual role—and with darkness and misfortune, the Maori inevitably stigmatized descent through females. Masculine-feminine was viewed religiously as complementary and antagonistic. The masculine represented the sky, light, and divine descent; the feminine, darkness, the earth, the underworld. In myth they are in eter-nal conflict—in broadest terms that of life against death. Thus what is purely masculine, is life triumphant, so to speak; the feminine "mix" is a compro-mise (Goldman 1970:37).

In traditional Marquesan culture, female activities were rigidly cir-cumscribed by a system of *tapu* (N. Thomas 1987:124).[16] As was true elsewhere in eastern Polynesia, explanations of women's apparently degraded status focused on women's reproductive activities, reproductive organs and most particularly on the fact of menstruation. Dening states categorically:

> There is no doubt that among [Marquesans] women were thought in some sense to be dangerous and threatening. Their menstrual flow was defiling. Women owed a carefulness to the group with the use of their own personal space. Their clothes, their property, their presence could be polluting in ways that men's never were. They could lay a curse on an object by naming it for their genitals or by placing it beneath their buttocks, just as a *tapu* could be placed on an object by naming it for its head or by placing it over one's head (Dening 1980:89–90).

Identical associations are made for Hawaiians (Valeri 1985a:85), Tahitians, (Levy 1973:106), and most definitively for the Maori, for whom the vagina was sometimes called *te whare o te aitu* 'the house of calamity' or *te whare o te mate* 'the house of death' (Best 1914:132; Hanson 1982c:89; Hanson and Hanson 1983:90). Menstruating women were thought by Maori to be capable of depleting gardens, forests, or beaches of *tapu* and thus of life.

A closer look at the ethnographic record complicates the matter considerably. It has frequently been pointed out that despite the general low status of women, noble birth and primogenitural status could sometimes override gender considerations in eastern Polynesia (N. Thomas 1987; Best 1924a, 1:407; Goldman 1970:180). More important, there is a good deal of contradictory evidence about the evaluation of women's reproductive status in this region, particularly in regard to the status of menstrual blood. Best tells us that the Maori sometimes termed menses *atua* (god) viewing it "as a sort of human embryo, an immature or underdeveloped human being, *hence the tapu*" (Best "The Lore of the Whare Kohanga" quoted in E. S. C. Handy 1927:47, emphasis added). Johansen does not clarify the situation much when he muses about the status of Maori women. "It is natural to ask: why is she *noa?* Sometimes reference is made to her menstruation. *In the period of menstruation she is tapu, but of course with a very specific content of life.* Is this what makes her *noa* at other times?" (Johansen 1954:216, emphasis added).

The Marquesan evidence is equally equivocal. Handy (1923:71) informs us that all matters associated with women's reproductive processes were regarded as polluting in association with anything *tapu,* and on the same page describes a number of *tapu* marshalled to protect a mother and her unborn child against detrimental spiritual influences. Furthermore, the onset of menarche was marked ritually by a rite called *ko'ina putoto,* during which the girl was placed at the head of her *pahu-pahu* 'maternal uncles/paternal aunts' and a roasted pig was set in turn at their heads. The pig was then cut up and eaten by these relatives.

E. S. C. Handy's interpretation of this rite gives us pause for reflection. "The *tapu* of the menstrual fluid would appear to be transferred to the pigs flesh, through the medium of the sacred heads of the *pahupahu*. These relatives then ate the flesh sacramentally, thus absorbing this influence and identifying themselves with it, in order to insulate, as it were, their *i'amutu* (cross-niece) against any evil that might come through this influence" (E. S. C. Handy 1923:94).

On Nuku Hiva, ranking girls were taken to special *tapu* places at the time of their first menstruation. Here the menstrual blood would be collected and left. Handy adds that "the occasion would be regarded as very sacred for the girl and for the family." Conveniently, Handy provides a summary statement that nicely illustrates the conceptual muddle that has surrounded the analysis of *tapu*. "A woman's head was sacred *(tapu)* but her private parts and all connected with them were defiling. The *tapu* apparently arises somewhat out of the sacredness of blood— the menstrual blood and blood at delivery. . . . [P]articularly unclean was a woman at the time of her menstrual flow" (E. S. C. Handy 1923:261).

F. Allan Hanson has made a significant breakthrough in sorting out these confused strands of association. In a set of important papers reanalyzing Polynesian gender concepts, Hanson has made a bold attempt to revise the familiar ethnographic characterization of women in eastern Polynesia as antithetical to *tapu* (Hanson 1982b, 1982c, 1987; Hanson and Hanson 1983). He finds the usual characterizations of female status in this part of Polynesia to be unconvincing, and asserts instead that women were viewed not so much as repelling the gods as attracting them.

> The usual interpretation is that the gods found women to be repugnant, particularly because of their connection with menstrual blood. . . . Hence the gods would withdraw upon the appearance of a woman, taking their *tapu* with them. An alternative view is that the gods were attracted to women rather than repelled by them, and that women therefore terminated *tapu* by absorbing the godly influence into themselves. On this interpretation the female is understood . . . to represent a passageway between the godly and human realms of existence (Hanson 1987:430).

From this perspective menstruation is not understood as simply polluting, but as inherently dangerous because it represents a heightened time of female activity as the conduit between the worlds of gods and humans (Hanson and Hanson 1983:93). Human orifices were important in Polynesian thought because they played a central role in the channeling of *mana* between the realms of *ao* and *po*. N. Thomas (1987: 128) adds, "the vagina was clearly the most potent of these channels, because it was through the vagina that children emerged from the *po*."[17] This potency of the female organs of generation means that under varying conditions, the vagina could be either a source of pollution or a source of vitalizing potency, that is, *mana*. Thomas alludes to a Maori belief that certain illnesses could be cured by women pressing their genitals against the afflicted part of the body, and the similar Marquesan practice of *hakatahetahe* 'splashing' by which someone believed to have been polluted by contact with a woman, and thereby subject to leprosy, could be cured by being placed seaward of the offending woman, and being splashed by water that had come into contact with her genitals (N. Thomas 1987:128–129).

Making Sense of Tapu *and* Noa

Although a number of writers have commented on the relativity of *tapu* and *noa*—defined in relation to each other rather than in relation to some intrinsic meanings—the implications of this insight have not been fully appreciated. Although these terms suggest a categorical opposition between distinct kinds of things, such binary oppositions usually had only context-specific significance. *Tapu* and *noa*, in other words, index a relationship between things and more specifically point to alternative conditions of *mana*.

Life-giving power is not only the energy of organic increase.[18] It is not life-giving powers alone that constitute the work of the Polynesian gods, but also the imparting of order, organic design won out of chaos and without which life-forces become destructive and polluting. Thus we understand the words of the Maori elder Te Matahoro, reflecting on the coming of the new order, and the end of the traditional Maori *tapu*s. "The *tapu*s are over; the eternal traditions are lost; the *karakias* (ritual words) are lost and are not understood any more today. For the *tapu* is the first; if there is no *tapu*, then all the acts of the gods become without force *(mana)*, and if there are no gods, everything becomes insipid. The way of people, actions, and thoughts, is now one whirling around; they are confused and desperate in this country now" (from "The Lore of the Whare-Wananga," quoted in Johansen 1954:55).

In Maori worldview, the orderliness of the cosmos was linked to the notion of *tika* or *tikanga*, the proper form, unique to each phenomenon in the world. "The *tikanga* of human beings is their nature, i.e., appearance, conduct, habits, etc. It is said about Whakatau: 'There is nobody like him; he has no man-*tikanga*.' The grey hairs originate from Tura; they belong to the *tikanga* of elderly people. Tikanga is also the way in which one acts, but still the natural way" (Johansen 1954:174). Johansen cites a Maori proverb "A dog, an itinerant man, they have no *tikanga*, they have nothing" and concludes "[T]ikanga is an inner form of life which manifests itself in a definite conduct" (Johansen 1954:174).[19]

This Maori notion of a kind of Platonic form appropriate to each thing or activity is remarkably similar to the Samoan concept of *aga* (Shore 1982, 1984, 1985; see also Freeman 1983, 1984, 1985). In relation to humans, *aga* signifies social conduct appropriate to each type of person, office, or situation. It suggests the fit between a prescribed style and an individual existence, and indexes proper socialization. As Freeman (1983, 1984) has pointed out, all natural phenomena also have their *aga,* those forms of being and action that are characteristic of each natural species. The contrasting concept for Samoans is *āmio,* unbound human behavior proceeding from personal will and drive rather than from a fit with a more general, transcendent pattern. We shall return to these concepts once again when we examine the ideas behind *tapu* and *noa.*

It is the association of *tapu* with form and order that underlies the Polynesian concern with chiefly ritual and etiquette. The kava ceremony in Samoa, for example, seals any encounter among chiefs or other important persons in an envelope of pure form, encompassing and infusing with *aga* whatever follows in the way of debate or discussion.

In traditional Polynesian cosmology, the gods epitomize such perfection of form.[20] Valeri notes that in Hawaii the gods "personify to the highest degree the accepted types of human action" (Valeri 1985a:86). Each god represents a perfect model for human action, such that the pantheon constitutes a template for a full spectrum of human life. For humans, however, the perfection of the highest Hawaiian gods is accessible only through elaborate rituals in which the fixity of the ritual forms ensures the formalization of the god.[21] "[T]he mobile and immobile images of Kū index the two stages of his transformation. The first is characterized by a power that makes possible the passage from desire to plenitude, that is from movement to immobility; the second is characterized by the final state of perfection marked by immobility and the encompassment of totality" (Valeri 1985a:272).

Margaret Mead (1930b:10) alluded to the Samoans love of form, "their flair for schematization," and Valeri has suggested the association for Hawaiians between completeness, or perfection, and the love of circular movement in ritual, or in the form of royal incest (Valeri 1985a: 88). *Tapu* implies purity as a kind of potency. The power of purity is its completeness (Valeri 1985a:133) as perfected form, and its attendant capacities to organize whatever it subsumes. It is in this sense that *tapu* represents generative power *(mana)* in its contained form.

Knowledge and skill have frequently been pointed to as exemplifying *mana.* Those with specialized skill and knowledge, who Polynesians variously call *tohunga* (Maori), *tufuga* (Samoan), *kahuna* (Hawaiian), and *tahuʻa* (Tahitian), among others exhibit *mana*. In Samoa, the term refers to a craft specialist, while the Tahitian version suggests any specialist, and specifically a spirit medium and curer. The Hawaiian *kahuna* was a full-time priest. What all these specialists share is the capacity to externalize intellectual power (knowledge) as concrete, coherent products such as boats, houses, victory in warfare, and healed bodies. Knowledge embodied in organized, generative activity, whether words or deeds, replicates the work of the gods for Polynesians, and is thus *tapu* activity.

The term *noa* does not mean "polluted," but rather "free," "nothing," "unmarked," and "unconstrained." It suggests action that is unguided, without purpose or destination. "The profane, *noa*, thus characterizes everyday life, in which everything happens more informally and freely, but also more casually and haphazardly" (Johansen 1954:204).[22] We can now understand the concept of *noa* involved in the lament of the old Maori chief for the ending of the old *tapus*. "The way of people actions, and thoughts, is now one whirling around; they are confused and desperate in the country now" (Johansen 1954:198).

The Marquesan equivalent to *noa*, *meʻie* literally means 'clear skies'. In Samoan, after the death of a chief, the skies are declared *sa* or *tapu* for a time, after which they are once again ritually 'opened' *(tatala)* and declared 'clean' *(mamā)*—a Samoan idiom for *noa* that is virtually identical with the Marquesan phrasing, and certainly quite different from any concept of pollution. If these associations are accurate, then *tapu* conversely means 'contained' or 'bound', suggesting the creative (and hence sacred) containment of *mana*, and the concommitant subordination of humans to its divine wellspring. The idea that *tapu* is a state in which *mana* is ritually tied-up through the imposition of sacred form makes sense of the pervasive symbolism throughout Polynesia of containment, stasis and binding associated with the sacred.

Throughout Polynesia, chiefly behavior is normatively highly refined, constrained, and linked to images of stillness. I have documented at great length these attributes of formal power in Samoa, manifest in a great variety of Samoan institutions and symbolic productions (Shore 1976b, 1982). The phrase "formal power" is particularly appropriate, since it implies the notion of *tapu* as symbolically formalized and thereby focused *mana*. Johansen characterizes the behavior of Maori nobles as reserved, kind, and taciturn. In dress, speech, and while eating, the nobleman maintains a refined reserve, distinguishing himself from the unconstrained behavior of the commoner who, having no strong *tikanga*, manifests in his demeanor his inner dissolution (Johansen 1954:183).

Valeri says of Hawaiian chiefs that they, like gods, are conceived of as perfect unto themselves, and are thus free from desire. For this reason, they are characterized by immobility and inactivity, the highest among them being carried by retainers rather than walking on their own (Valeri 1985a:100). This ideal of divine immobility is the "passive, embodied power" of Polynesian chiefs that separated the most sacred among them from direct political activity (see Marcus chapter 6, this volume).

Rites of Sanctification: Binding

Images of binding of persons or objects pervade Polynesian symbolism. Most common, perhaps, are the ubiquitous restrictions imposed as a matter of chiefly prerogative on the harvesting of productive crops. These bans (*kahui* or *'ahui* [Marquesan], *rahui* [Maori], *fakatapu* [Tiko-pian], *tapui* [Samoan]) were often accomplished by marking (sometimes by literally encircling with a marker) the resource whose productivity was being tied up.[23] N. Thomas (1987) tries to dissociate these prohibitions from real *tapu*, but it seems clear that they derive from a common understanding about the channeling of generative power, whether in the land, the sea or in people.

In Hawaiian, *ho'okapu* is the movement from a *noa* state to a *kapu* state. Common Hawaiian metaphors for this process involve binding or tying up the focal object, while the reverse process is called *huikala*, literally 'to untie': "Huikala unties the 'tangles' of that consecration and its sign the *kapu* have tied around someone or something" (Valeri 1985a: 95). Valeri notes that the *kapu* state of an initiate was symbolized by his tangled hair.[24] For Maori a *tapu*-removing rite for an infant just after birth is called *tuuaa*, which means both 'to name' and 'to remove a *tapu*'. The link between these two concepts is perhaps made clearer by an alternate gloss for the rite, *tohi*, 'to cut' or 'to separate' (J. Smith 1974:9). Naming, untying, and cutting are three equivalent Polynesian modes of desanctifying, of freeing an object or a being from direct contact with the divine.

The tangling or binding idiom associated with the *tapu* concept turns up in modern Samoa as the concept of *fa'alavelave*, literally 'to tangle' or 'to make complicated'. By this term Samoans mean any weighty occasion or event, such as a funeral, a title-dispute or the arrival of a distinguished visitor. Samoan life is shaped by these events, such that it alternates normal or unmarked time and space with periodic entanglements —heavy times and places. The central village *malae*, normally the scene of casual encounters and children's play, is transformed into a center of social gravity, bound by the elaborate etiquette that weighty occasions require. Although these modern Samoan notions have largely lost their explicit traditional religious grounding in *tapu* and *noa,* these notions are deeply implicated in modern Samoan life.[25]

Rites of binding, and thereby sanctifying objects and persons, are found throughout Polynesia. We have noted that ritual action constitutes an imposition of form on an otherwise free entity, and can render it *tapu*. This insight underlies Firth's observation for Tikopia that "the mystical quality of *tapu* with which a chief was endowed came to him in the very act of his creation as chief" (Firth 1970b:27).

The Hawaiian word *aha*[26] (E. S. C. Handy 1927:206) means literally sennit, a twine made from coconut husk fibers and used to bind together the beams of a house, to lash together boats and in the making of certain garments. According to Pukui and Elbert, *'afa* also refers to any prayer whose effectiveness requires that it be carried out under taboo and without interruption (Pukui and Elbert 1971:5). Kaeppler cites a Hawaiian belief that to accompany the singing of a chant by the braiding of sennit fiber "caught the chant and objectified it" (Kaeppler 1982:94), so that the braided cord made in connection with the chant could function as a prayer.[27] An extension of this logic is the encasing of a sacred wooden image from Hawaii in a braided skirt, woven while a prayer is sung (p. 96). In this case the binding theme operates on two distinct levels: the original objectification of the prayer in the sennit fiber, and the subsequent wrapping of the wooden image in the skirt. Kaeppler speculates that "encasing the image in the skirt may have symbolically enveloped it in a perpetual prayer" (Kaeppler 1982:96).

Handy refers to a class of recitations called *aha* that were important in various Hawaiian temple rites. He characterizes these recitations as binding prayers whose purpose was to tie the temple and its congregation to the divine source of power. These prayers were marked by rigidly enforced silence and stillness—or more aptly, a ritualized withdrawal of all motion. An actual ceremonial cord, made for the occasion, was hung up in the temple (E. S. C. Handy 1927:206; Valeri 1985a: 294). David Malo provides an example of one of these verbal *aha* that quite vividly conveys the power of the binding symbolism for Hawaiians, and its connections with the binding of *mana:*

O Ku in the heavens.
Behold the cord done into the all-including knot.
O Ku of the wonderful, mystic ridgepole of Hanalei.
Bind, tie with the knotted *oloa.*
It is the *oloa* that shall overturn the power.
[*Mana*] is wrapped up in the *oloa* cord.
Let [*mana*] go forth to the god image.
Cut now the navel-cord of the house *mana.*
[*Mana, mana*] resides in the knotted *oloa* cord
That decorates the house of the great god Kane.

Cut now the navel-string!
Done! It is done!
(E. S. C. Handy 1927:206)

Divine benevolence is not simply requested passively in Polynesia. It is ritually harnessed by the symbolic containment and organization of unbound potency. This is nicely illustrated in ancient Hawaiian practice. Valeri, suggests that the cutting down of a tree in the wild bush for the carving of an image of a god was not by itself enough to tame the darker forces of the gods. "The gods became a positive and productive power only after having been 'bound' in the *'aha* 'binding rite' inside the temple" (Valeri 1982:13). Such binding up of dangerous energies was also the model, Valeri argues, by which the powers of the sacred Hawaiian kings were domesticated.

> Like the god, the king was conceived as an initially uncontrolled and external power which penetrated the society and conquered it by violence. . . . The ritual metaphorically posited force and conquest as its first and necessary moment. But it also set the stage for their transcendence, and so for the passage of the king from a state in which his power was not controlled by society to one in which it was identified with the society as a whole and therefore with its reproduction and its life. This passage, encompassed by the passage of the god from an uncontrolled to a controlled state, legitimized the king every time the temple ritual was performed (Valeri 1982:13).

Throughout eastern Polynesia, the chief's *mana* was (literally) tied up with his *malo* (girdle) that bound his genitals, the direct source of his generative potency. For the Maori, "The chief was the firstborn earthly representative of the gods, whose procreative powers or generative activities were evidenced in all nature. That which girt the seat of generation and procreation of the priest-chief was therefore sacred and symbolic of his power" (E. S. C. Handy 1927:145). Handy reproduces several Maori war chants that specifically associate the girding of the warrior's loins by his warbelt with the welling up of courage and energy.[28]

An important aspect of the major temple rites in Hawaii was the binding of the loins of the statues of deities just before warfare or during the annual *makahiki* harvest festival. In a *luakini* war rite, Handy reports that a new image of Lono was carved and set up in the midst of other god-images.

> The figure was at this time ungirt, standing, as the native expression puts it, "with its nakedness pendant." Some days later, after a number of preparatory rites, came the ceremony of girding the god. The king and his priests being assembled for the rite, the whole body of the priests recited in unison the "prayer of the girdle":

Gird on, gird on the malo oh Lono!
Declare war, declare it definitely,
proclaim it by messengers!
(E. S. C. Handy 1927:148; see also, Valeri 1985a).

Finally, there is the wrapping of people or statues in cloth—often
mats, as a way of redirecting and binding their potency. The wrapping
of sacred persons in great quantities of *tapa* cloth has been recorded
throughout Polynesia (E. S. C. Handy 1927:149). Mariner's account
of the marriage of the eldest daughter of Finau to the Tui Tonga suggests the desired symbolic value of this wrapping.

> The young lady, having been profusely anointed with coco-nut oil, scented
> with sandal-wood, was dressed in the choicest mats of the Navigator's islands
> [Samoa], of the finest texture, and as soft as silk; so many of these costly mats
> were wrapped around her, perhaps more than forty yards, that her arms
> stuck out from her body in a ludicrous manner; and she could not strictly
> speaking, sit down, but was obliged to bend in a sort of half-sitting posture,
> leaning upon her female attendants, who were under the necessity of again
> raising her when she required it (Mariner 1827, 1:121).

Kaeppler proposes that the importance of the beautiful feather cloaks
of Hawaiian chiefs included both protection from missiles hurled in
wartime, and a more supernatural sort of protection to the wearer, who
was wrapped in feathers arranged in designs "metaphorically linked to
genealogical and sacred concepts" (Kaeppler 1985a:119). According to
Kaeppler's hypothesis, the protection afforded by the wrapping of a
Hawaiian chief in a feather cloak was linked to the way in which the
garment was made. The underlying foundation of the cloak was a finely
meshed fibre net, *nae,* the weaving of which contributed to its protective
powers. Kaeppler (1985a:119) speculates: "if the netting was fabricated
while chanting prayers, it could *ho'oheihei* 'entangle' and capture them,
the product having the ability to serve as perpetual prayer and protect
its wearer."

The fact that *tapu* states were associated with both protection and
binding deprive us of any illusion that the distinction between *tapu* and
noa was anything so simple as sacred versus profane. As Hooper points
out, the concept of *tapu* was fraught with considerable ambivalence for
most Polynesians (Hooper 1981:1). To be *tapu* was to be empowered,
but it was also to be immobilized—literally and figuratively tied up. To
be *tapu* was to be bound to divine potency and was therefore a considerable burden. To be rendered common was to be relieved of this burden.

Using Maori evidence, Jean Smith (1974) makes an elaborate case
for the distastefulness of the *tapu* state. Consistent with the binding

imagery associated with *tapu* states, Smith argues that to be *tapu* is to be subordinated to the power of the gods, and thus to have one's own individual potency diminished. This, says Smith, was a source of considerable ambivalence among Maori. For without the *tapu*s, one was deprived of access to the powers of the gods, while with them, one's own personal potency was encompassed and contained. Thus we understand the dual significance of the Maori term *whakanoa,* which meant both to liberate something or someone from *tapu* and to bring something under one's own power. Propitiation for Maori appears thus to have involved a kind of war with the gods, and an attempt to empower oneself at their expense. According to Smith, this extraordinary tug-of-war between gods and men explains the frequent Maori practices of transferring *tapu* from god to man by ritually polluting the gods. To make men like gods, gods must be made like men (J. Smith 1974:25, 33).

To summarize and simplify somewhat Smith's complex vision of Maori worldview, the conflict between divine and human sources of potency were also manifest in the struggle between a person's power as an individual and "his divinely sanctioned social personality" (J. Smith 1974:62). I have stressed the same ambivalence for modern Samoans, whose persona reveals deep conflicts between socially sanctioned sources of conduct *(aga)* and private, individual drives *(āmio)* (Shore 1977, 1979, 1982).

Smith identifies for Maori two authentic but competing sources of prestige and power. One type of power is linked with ascribed status (and eldest brothers), direct contact with the gods and the consequent maintenance of *tapu*s. The other fountain of authority is associated with violence, achieved status (and thereby with the power of junior brothers), and personal power achieved by *tapu*-breaking (J. Smith 1974: chap. 5).

The basic ambiguity of the *tapu* concept is that it always involves an economy of potency: to empower gods is to debilitate men; to empower man is to enfeeble the gods. Thus it is not surprising that we find in Polynesia the apparent paradox that ritual acts associated with gods rendering objects and persons *tapu* might also be used by humans to free themselves from the gods. Smith describes for Maori *tapu* removal rites of fixation that mimic other Polynesian rites of *tapu*-creation. The Maori rite desanctifying a new house upon its creation was called *ruruku o te whare,* and was a ritual binding of the house, thereby separating it from divine influence and fixing it for human habitation (J. Smith 1974:40). *Tapu*-removal in these practices is not simply the opposite of *tapu*-bestowal. It merely reverses the directions of the effect, just as for Maori, the vagina, depending on the direction of movement, is understood as both the passage to life, and the conduit to death. Smith (1974: 52) argues that this tendency for Maori to identify concepts that appear to be polar opposites is not evidence of a fundamental confusion of things that are naturally opposed, but, more profoundly, a recognition of the tragic proximity of the basic sources of human life and death.

Smith argues that in Maori thought aggression is closely tied to oral experience. Eating is a life-giving activity that is also inextricably tied to the destruction of life. Not only do we see this in the famous Maori greeting, in which guests are ritually attacked by a line of warriors and tongues drawn, but also in the Maori associations between eating and cooking, on the one hand, and aggression on the other. It is in this light that we understand the significance of Karahere's description of Maori *tapu*s as the gods feeding on men (cited in J. Smith 1974:36).

Generative potency, when ritually bound, could be channeled from the gods for the work of men. Such bound potency is always implicit in states of *tapu*. That same generative potential, when uncontained—that is, when *noa*—was a pollutant and a source of considerable anxiety for pre-Christian Polynesians. Conversely, that which polluted the gods, might also thereby empower humans (J. Smith 1974:32).

This elementary insight into the logic of *tapu* makes sense of the apparently contradictory observations made about women's status by generations of observers of Polynesia. In eastern Polynesia, women's reproductive organs and processes were a source of pollution danger to men, but only because they were also a potential source of *tapu*.[29] It is the inherent uncontrollability of the sources of women's fecundity by men that rendered women so dangerous in these societies. Menstruation is the natural focus of these anxieties, being intractable to ritual manipulation. We have already noted that whenever women's reproductive processes were ritually bound (as in rites connected with the onset of menarche in the Marquesas, and the containing of menstrual blood in a ritual menstrual hut) these processes were characterized as extremely *tapu*, and not *noa*. My impression is that what men feared most in eastern Polynesia was accidental, casual, and unplanned contact with the direct sources of human generation. The same vagina that could casually pollute if it accidentally passed over anything *tapu* could be ritually redirected in the service of healing.

The Sacred Maiden

It is no coincidence that the reputation of Polynesians for sexual license comes mainly from eastern Polynesian societies such as Tahiti, Hawaii, and the Marquesas. In this part of Polynesia gender relations were emphatically sexual relations, and the dominant model for male-female relations was the conjugal pair. Given the cultural emphasis here on sexualized relations between males and females, and in light of the dan-

ger that female sexuality represented to *tapu* males, the powerful ambivalence evident in this region towards women's status is hardly surprising. What sexual relations brought together, the tapu system set apart.
The eastern Polynesian "way out" of this bind was to dissociate two
forms of reproduction—through eating and through sex. The two
activities are in complementary distribution. Men and women are relatively free *(noa)* in sex, and therefore ritually segregated and bound in
eating. The sexual freedom in eastern Polynesia had its limitations, of
course. In Hawaii, the highest chiefs and their mates were expected to
remain pure until their marriage, but were then permitted extraordinary license (Valeri 1985a:149). Though cross-cousin marriage was
considered desirable in the Marquesas, only Hawaiian sacred chiefs
were permitted (indeed enjoined to) the symbolic autonomy of brother-
sister marriage. Nonetheless, it is important to distinguish the relative
sexualization of male-female relations here from the quite different
complex of ideas associated with western Polynesia.

The so-called sacred maiden institution is reported throughout western Polynesia (and in several eastern Polynesian societies as well). It has
recently been reanalyzed in specific cultural settings in light of more
general Polynesian gender concepts (Ortner 1981; Shore 1981; Schoeffel 1978, 1979; Rogers 1976, 1977; Hecht 1977). This institution represents an important variation on the more general Polynesian treatment
of female potency, and is an important manifestation of the Polynesian
concern with binding *mana* in the interest of global regeneration.

The most famous of the sacred maids in Polynesia is the Samoan
tāupou, a titled girl whose office is linked to that of an important *ali'i*.
The term also signifies a virgin, suggesting the chastity associated with
the office (Margaret Mead 1928a, 1930b; Shore 1981, 1982; Freeman
1983). Although there is considerable disagreement in the literature
about how rigidly this requirement of chastity is enforced, the link
between sexual control and the status of the *tāupou* are, for Samoa,
indisputable (Freeman 1983; Shore 1984; Wendt 1983b). Traditional
Samoan norms of female beauty are idealized in the prototypical *tāupou*:
fatness, light complexion, and shiny, well-oiled skin. In formal address,
the *tāupou* is referred to as *'o le tāupou fa'anofonofo*—the sitting maiden—
underscoring the associations between her imposing form and her relative lack of activity. As titular head of a village girls' association
(aualuma) her functions are, for the most part, ceremonial or even decorative. She makes kava in formal gatherings and is the last to dance
when guests are entertained. Her mat girdle and elegant headdress,
made from the clipped tresses of a "redhead," link her symbolically
with the *ali'i* and suggest the feminine associations of both (Shore 1982;
Milner, personal communication).

There is, interestingly, no equivalent status in Tonga to the Samoan

tāupou. As we shall see, however, high-ranking women and girls, particularly in their roles as sisters, share the same special status as the
Samoan *tāupou*. The term *tāupou*, a Samoan borrowing, is used for all
the daughters of a Tongan chief. A high-ranking girl symbolizes her status by her physical size, well-oiled skin, and associations with stasis. A
stylized sitting posture is intended to convey a powerful image of immobility, as are the stylized movements of her dance (Gifford 1929:129–
130; Goldman 1970:307; Ortner 1981:376). Moreover, this immobility
was symbolically highlighted at royal weddings, as we have seen, by the
immobilization of the bride, who was bound in layers of mats.

A sacred-maid institution is reported for traditional Manahiki-Raka-
hanga where "[t]he symbol of food abundance was not the full storehouse as in New Zealand, but the well-fed and fattened pubescent
daughter of families of rank" (Goldman 1970:60). Buck describes the
ceremonial seclusion of this girl, removing her from all productive and
reproductive activities, and deliberately stuffing her with food contributions from her entire subtribe (Buck 1932:40). The same pattern is
found in Pukapuka (a western Polynesian society now part of the Cook
Islands). Here, the *mayakitanga* was removed from all secular activities
and withdrawn from normal reproductive activities for life (Hecht 1976,
1977; Beaglehole and Beaglehole 1938).

It is suggestive to consider the associations between corpulence, virginity, and the general fecundity of nature. For example, the Beagleholes describe the induction of the *mayakitanga* as a kind of sacrifice or
dedication of a maid to lineage gods. This sacrifice was, according to
one informant, accompanied by a prayer alluding to the impending
increase in all organic life—fish, food, and even feces (Beaglehole and
Beaglehole 1938:238).

Hecht makes the interesting observation that Pukapukans appear to
honor the status of sister by denying her any legitimate offspring. Thus
a man's sister's child becomes an honored *ilamutu* only upon being
adopted into his or her maternal uncle's family. Hecht points out that
here, as in the case of the sacred maid, the sister is rendered childless. In
the case of the *mayakitanga*, it is through enforcing virginity; in the case
of the sister who has given birth, it is through redirecting her offspring
to her brothers. Hecht's explanation for these Pukapukan practices is
political: "If the sister's line were viewed as 'superior', the institution of
the sacred maid or the adoption of the sister's issue would prevent any
line from being superior to that of the chief" (Hecht 1977:111). There is
another possibility. These practices are consistent with a concept of
sacred power, associated with sisters, that derives spiritual potency from
the redirection and binding up of generative capacities.

The Matatua tribes near the Bay of Plenty in New Zealand had the
institution of the *puhi*, a sacred maiden, usually the eldest daughter of a

ranking chief. Like the Samoan *tāupou* she was expected to remain a virgin until her marriage. Her mates were carefully selected. The *puhi* had largely ceremonial significance, but could sometimes attain considerable political power as a female chief later in life (Best 1924a, 1:450–453; Ortner 1981:372).

The Tikopian variation on the sacred-maid institution is the *fafine ariki* of the Kafika and Tafua clans. In each of these groups this special status is accorded to one woman in each generation, usually a sister or eldest daughter of the chief. This female chief, while sharing to a degree the powers of other Tikopian chiefs, appears to derive her eminence in a distinctive way. She neither marries nor takes lovers. " 'She lives properly.' And when she gets older, it is the custom for her to swim out to sea and commit suicide. . . . This is the basis of it. When she goes to the world of spirits and dwells there, she will live among the *kau kura* . . . she will live as a chief among the spirits. But if she marries, then when she tries to take her seat among the assembly as a chieftainess, she is spurned to one side" (Firth 1967:86).

These examples are sufficient to elucidate interesting associations in the sacred-maid complex among (a) withdrawal of all productive energies from normal use, (b) consumption of large quantities of food, (c) corpulence, (d) light, shiny skin, and (e) the binding of a selected individual's reproductive capacities in the interest of more abstract and general forms of societal and cosmic regeneration.[30]

In eastern Polynesia, the most sacred figure around whom *tapu* is focused is the chief, firstborn and usually male. In western Polynesia, there is a tendency for supreme honor to be accorded not to the chief but to his sister or his sister's offspring, a fact to which we shall return. The important point here is that in both cases, *tapu* suggests the ritualized canalization of the reproductive capacities of this sacred person (the chief's genitals; the sister's fecundity). The symbolic emphasis in western Polynesia on these sacred women suggests not the general importance of females over males, but the status of the sister rather than the wife as the generic meaning of female. This fact points towards a need to examine more closely the ways in which Polynesians constructed gender relations, since it is gender, understood abstractly, that underlies much of the dualistic thinking encountered in Polynesia.

At first glance, gender relations in eastern Polynesia present a vivid contrast to the western pattern. In his classic delineation of culture areas within Polynesia, Burrows (1940) distinguished central/marginal (i.e., eastern) Polynesia from western Polynesia by (among other things) a shift in kin terminologies. Western Polynesian terminologies emphasize a dualistic distinction between brothers and sisters and between their offspring. Eastern terminologies, by contrast, betray a marked simplification, a generational rather than a lineal bias, more characteristic of so-called Hawaiian kinship terminologies (Burrows 1938:125). More-over, Burrows notes for eastern Polynesia a greater terminological emphasis on affinal terms as opposed to the brother-sister emphasis in the west.

Goldman summarizes nicely the implications of these differences. "[T]he simplification of taxonomy [in eastern Polynesia] implies a reduction in the significance of the domestic status system. In eastern Polynesia, the etiquette of kinship behavior is also reduced. There are no brother-sister respects and no significant etiquettes in the cross-rela-tionships. Seniority offers a single quantitative distinction in place of the variety of qualitative kinship polarities. . . . We can see . . . a step-by-step extinction of those categories expressing duality" (Goldman 1970:472–473).

There is certainly strong evidence for this general distinction between the complementary dualisms of western Polynesia and the monolithic and quantitative gradient of power and status in the east. Thus, for instance, the (unstable) complementarity between sacred and utilitarian power in western Polynesian cultures was replaced in the east by a ten-dency towards a single rank continuum from sacred to common. Hawaiians had a dual conception of powers inherent in the rites of king-ship surrounding the taming of the powers of the god Kū. Furthermore Kamakau describes how, in the course of Hawaiian history, sacred power gradually split off from secular authority (Kamakau 1964:4, quoted in Goldman 1970:219). Yet Goldman insists, convincingly it seems, that we not mistake this split for the complementary duality of western Polynesia. "The Hawaiian concern was for the inviolable unity of pedigree and sanctity, and not with the relegation of the ali'i kapu to a specialized religious realm. Kamehameha and his son Liholiho were both kapu chiefs, emphasizing the Hawaiian preference for associating political hegemony with the highest degree of sanctity. Considered exclusively from a political standpoint the recurrent separations of power and sanctity are possible to be understood as respect for efficacy, that is, realpolitik" (Goldman 1970:219). Goldman's important point is that the separation of powers in Hawaii lacked the religious or cosmo-logical basis that it had in the west of Polynesia, and in fact was a prag-matic compromise in the face of the dominant Hawaiian stress on a uni-lateral source of political and religious power.

These differences have an important bearing on concept of gender relations. Perhaps the best documented example of this eastern Polyne-sian pattern is Maori culture. Two features of the Maori gender system stand out. First is the striking sexualization of gender relations, empha-sizing sexual conjunction of the sexes rather than their ceremonial sepa-ration. Second is the apparent devaluation of feminine status, such that the opposition between male and female becomes strongly associated

with that between sacred *(tapu)* and profane *(noa)*. In both of these features we have what would seem to be an inversion of dominant western
Polynesian patterns.

The Hansons document in considerable detail the centrality of the
conjugal dyad in Maori cosmology. Maori used the complementary
structure of sexual union, followed by the production of offspring, to
conceptualize the origin of things as diverse as gods, insects, plants,
fire, humanity, and flat rocks (and even, in other lines of descent,
rounded rocks) (Hanson and Hanson 1983:25).

Maori origin myths present the physical world as various unions of
complementary qualities, male and female. The sky (male) unites with
the earth (female) and they conceive six sons, gods associated with distinct natural elements. These myths suggest the impotence of any
power when separated from its natural mate (Hanson and Hanson
1983:23). Though various kinship relations are used to model these natural pairings, by far the most common is husband-wife, and the implicit
relationship is sexual. The Hansons have set out the most important of
these Maori pairings (Table 1) (Hanson and Hanson 1983:20).

Table 1. Maori gender pairings

Male	Female
right side	left side
east	west
sky	earth
light/day/life	darkness/night/death
activity	passivity
bellicose	reticent
war	domesticity

Several of the associations in Table 1 seem, at first glance, consistent
with the western Polynesian pattern, especially the connections between
the feminine and the static or passive. Yet the valuation of these qualities is strikingly different from those found in Samoa, Tonga, or Tokelau. Far from attributing sacredness and honor to the feminine, Maori
worldview seems to assign it negative value. The source of the dangerous and degraded status of women seems to have been the relative
uncontrollability of their generative potency. Whereas Pukapukan symbolism associates the vagina *(wu)* with matrilineage and regeneration,
Maori myth often portrays it either as a source of death—*te whare o aituā*
(house of calamity)—or, when under ritual control, as life-bestowing.
Similarly, the erect penis symbolizes vitality and martial victory, while
detumescence following sexual intercourse is associated with weakness
and with the withdrawal of the vitalizing influence of the gods (Hanson
and Hanson 1983:90).[31]

The profane status of women was equally evident in traditional Tahiti. Here, as in Hawaii, male fears of female pollution focused on the production and consumption of food. Levy quotes the report of the first missionary voyage to Tahiti. "If a man eats in a house with a woman, he takes one end and she the other, and they sleep in the middle. If a woman has a child, the provisions for it must not come in at the same door with the mother's, but there is an opening like a window through which they are received, and it would be reckoned beastly in the highest degree for her to eat while she is suckling a child" (Wilson 1799:351).

Most rigid in ancient Tahiti were prohibitions on commensality between men and women. Women were also feared for their ability to curse those with whom they had intense personal relations (Levy 1973:158). At major propitiatory rites, women were usually excluded for fear that their very presence would cause the gods to depart (Hanson 1987:430).

The distinctions between eastern and western Polynesian handling of gender relations are easy to overstate. Perhaps most obvious is the thoroughgoing conceptual dualism in the western societies based upon the complementary relations between brother and sister. Whatever gender-based dualism we find in eastern Polynesia, it rests more clearly on images of connubial sexuality, that is on the relations of husband and wife. Moreover, there is a strong tendency for monolithic conceptions of rank based on genealogical seniority to override the male-female distinction, with its bilineal tendencies. And finally, the sacred and honored status of female-as-sister in western Polynesia appears to be replaced by the polluting and profane status of female-as-wife in eastern Polynesia.

Although it would be misleading to deny altogether the obvious regional differences in gender organization throughout Polynesia, it is possible to demonstrate that the two patterns are, in fact, transformations of a single overriding Polynesian view of the relation between men and women, and between the masculine and the feminine aspects of experience. The transmutability of *mana* in Polynesian thought makes it possible to link the apparently opposed valuations of women in the two major cultural areas of the region.

We know that *mana* in Polynesian thought is linked, directly or indirectly, to generative powers, and thus at least implicitly with the most obvious source of this generativity in everyday life—the reproductive capacities of women. The association of the honored status of woman-as-sister in western Polynesia with artificial restriction of reproduction (virginity, arranged marriage, adoption of offspring by her brother) constitutes a social and cosmological redirection of her fertility and an implicit recognition of its power and potential danger. To the degree that these societies symbolically emphasize this restriction, they view the failure ritually to channel women's sexuality as dangerous (Shore 1981). The much discussed fate of the Samoan *tāupou* whose presumed virginity cannot be publicly demonstrated upon her marriage is the underside of the honor and power she represents should she be proven to have remained intact (Margaret Mead 1928a; Freeman 1983). The danger and the glory are all of one piece.

The eastern Polynesian pattern portrays the same themes, only in a different key. These societies do not appear to map the generic relation between the sexes onto the sibling-set, as is the case throughout western Polynesia. Male and female are linked not by their mutual respect and avoidance, but by their mutual attraction and necessary conjunction. The shadow of incestuous union between brother and sister falls across much of the mythology of western Polynesia. In eastern Polynesia the dominant concerns suggested by the elaborate pollution taboos associated with women seem to involve fears of excessive female sexuality, and particularly fears of male debilitation or engulfment by seductive women. It may not be overstating the case to suggest that it is such images of consuming female sexuality that underlie the Tahitian and Hawaiian prohibitions of commensality between potential sexual partners. Commensality and sex, two forms of reproduction, are linked. As Goldman has written: "Food and sex were conceptually related in Polynesia. . . . The varying combinations of these basic elements gave to each society its distinctive versions of food and sex separations" (Goldman 1970:538). Perhaps most convincing in this vein are the complex associations throughout Polynesia between the containment of the reproductive powers of women and the capacity of chiefs to guarantee the natural fertility of the land and sea.

Polynesian worldview reveals a complex economy of powers, male and female, and provides for their interchangeability. In the western islands, the separation of brother and sister makes possible a fully dualistic ideology of power in which the feminine is linked to notions of stability, order, and spiritual potency. In the eastern societies, no such stabilized dualities are possible based on gender distinctions alone. Rather than empowering women, symbolic passivity takes on a more negative or at least ambivalent value than in western Polynesia, and a pervasive competition between male and female powers replaces the balanced complementarities characteristic of western Polynesian societies. The transformability of women's death-dealing powers into life-giving powers is recognized in eastern Polynesia. But it is a subtext here, evident in the esoteric rituals through which the vagina is linked to the gods. What is submerged and subtle in the eastern islands is fully developed and symbolically rich in the western.

Summary

In this essay, I have tried to make a number of important generalizations about Polynesian conceptions of power in such a way as to underscore the obvious unity of Polynesia as a culture area, yet without doing excessive violence to local Polynesian variations. This is no simple job, and it involves risks both of overgeneralization and excessive particularism of ethnographic detail. Yet no comparative work on a culture area can evade completely the dual responsibilities to both the general and the particular. Indeed, no coherent vision of local variation in Polynesia is possible without a prior clarification of what common characteristics make it a real culture area.

The vision of power explicated in this essay constitutes a single, though rather extensive thread of argument. Its shape can be summarized as follows:

1. For Polynesians, *mana* manifests the power of the gods in the human world.

2. In Polynesian thinking, relations between humans and gods are both ambiguous and ambivalent. Gods and men are polar rather than categorical opposites, and Polynesians represented an elaborate gradient of possible relations between them.

3. Controlling these relations between divinity and humanity is a prime focus of Polynesian ritual activity. Control, primarily a godly capacity, is open to human appropriation under special conditions.

4. *Mana* is always linked to organic generativity and thus to all forces of growth and vitality.

5. Life-giving and death-dealing powers are transformations of each other, and thus *mana* has both generative and destructive poles.

6. Polynesian religions thus constitute a set of practices and beliefs concerned with ritual transformations of *mana*.

7. The arc through which power can be ritually transformed in Polynesian religions is defined by the polar states of *tapu* and *noa*. *Tapu* and *noa* states represent the relations possible between the divine and the human, but are not adequately glossed as sacred and profane.

8. *Tapu* is a state of contact with the divine by which the particular is encompassed and bound by the general, and thereby rendered intelligible. *Noa*, by contrast, represents an unbounded state of separation from the divine, and thereby represents the particular, the idiosyncratic, and the free.

9. Polynesians ritually rendered people and objects *tapu* by rites characterized by binding, tying, and containing. Such rites channeled divine potency for human ends and rendered phenomena intelligible by providing an encompassing and transcendent form, but also were acts of human submission to the divine.

10. The essential ambiguity between *tapu* as empowering humans and *tapu* as tying up or constraining them was manifest in considerable human ambivalence about *tapus* and, at least in Maori society, in elaborate rites of *tapu*-removal and deliberate *tapu*-violation.

11. Because it is linked to generative potency, the notion of *mana* bears a special relationship to the two primary sources of human life: food and sex.

12. In western Polynesia (Samoa, Tonga, Tokelau, Pukapuka, Rotuma) the bipolar qualities of power were mapped onto the brother-sister relationship, or a diarchic kingship, and thereby desexualized. The fecundity of the earth and sea were linked symbolically to the containment and redirection of a sister's capacity to reproduce. The sacred-maiden complex associated with virginity, stasis, and consumption without production thrived on those islands.

13. In eastern Polynesia (Hawaii, Tahiti, Marquesas, New Zealand) the polarities of power were mapped onto the sexualized relationship of husband and wife rather than sister and brother. Yet the complementarity of sex and food production were maintained by elaborate *tapu* systems, by which those who slept together were forbidden to eat together. Moreover the mutual transformability of *tapu* and *noa* states is vividly underscored by the extreme ambivalence accorded female sexuality. The vagina is both a path to life and to death, and under different conditions of ritual control can be a source of either *tapu* or *noa* states. The relations between *tapu* and *noa* states, and between male and female, present no simple categorical opposition between sacred and profane, but rather a set of dialectical transformations.

14. The sexualization of the male-female relationship in eastern Polynesia precludes using that relationship as the basis of any categorical dual organization. Here duality resolves itself in propagation and thereby overcomes its duality. Cross-cousin marriage in the Marquesas and brother-sister unions among Hawaiian royalty are the most dramatic manifestations of these tendencies. Elaborate dual organizations are common, however, in western Polynesia, where the more static brother-sister dyad is emphasized. Brother-sister relations produce categories, not offspring.

Research Implications

There are two broad research areas opened up by this kind of analysis. The first area is what Marcus calls reconstructionist in emphasis (Marcus, chapter 6, this volume). The general conclusions in this essay about Polynesian worldview are useful only so long as they illuminate the cultural patterns implicit in ethnographic details. The viability of this vision of Polynesian worldview rests, therefore, on a careful evaluation of the appropriateness of its conclusions for as many traditional Polynesian societies as possible. Obvious limitations in space and competence meant that only a restricted number of cases could be considered in any detail in this essay.

Genuine ethnological insights have a way of transforming bits of ethnographic data into significant patterns. The conception of *mana,* and its subsidiary notions of *tapu* and *noa,* as developed in these pages, are useful to the extent that they illuminate heretofore obscure corners of Polynesian ethnology. The characteristic Polynesian conception of ritually binding potency in the interest of social and cosmic regeneration may well make sense of practices that until now have eluded our understanding. Thus, for example, a reanalysis of tattooing practices so widespread in Polynesia may reveal cosmological significances linked to this notion of binding.[32] Similarly, traditional practices of tying together houses or canoes may be more significant than just effective construction techniques. Certainly the familiar Polynesian practice of conquering chiefs or sacred maidens making a circuit of an island is closely linked to the notions of making-*tapu* through binding. How far these notions will take our understanding of traditional Polynesia can only be determined by further careful ethnographic reconstruction and comparison.

I am especially interested to learn how far the western/eastern differences described in the preceding pages will take us. Moreover, these generalizations need to be refined for specific cases, and in relation to local differences throughout Polynesia. If broad generalizations have any usefulness, it is in laying the groundwork for a better grasp of such differences as variations on common themes. Subtle but important distinctions in worldview clearly obtain between societies as similar as Tonga and Samoa, or Hawaii and Tahiti, and these need to be worked out in detail by specialists, it is hoped with reference to the common links suggested here.

The second project that follows from this study involves the evaluation of cultural change or continuity in Polynesia. This is an important, but hardly a simple matter. It is all too easy to generalize from obvious changes in material culture to underlying shifts in worldview, but direct associations are not inevitable. Impressionistic statements about continuity or change in basic values are not very helpful either. Only a carefully formulated set of propositions, used as a baseline for traditional worldview, permits an assessment of what has remained constant in Polynesian thought, and what has changed.

The bulk of the work on this problem remains to be done. Yet it is already possible to make several tentative generalizations. First, it should be apparent from my use of verb tenses in this paper, that many institutions premised on the traditional worldview are no longer extant in eastern Polynesia. At the most obvious level, western Polynesian societies like Tonga, Western Samoa, Tokelau, and Pukapuka appear to have retained their Polynesian shape to a much greater extent than Hawaiian and Maori societies, Tahiti, the Marquesas, Easter Island, or Rarotonga. This is not to deny that all modern Polynesian societies have undergone profound historical changes. But it does suggest a regional difference in the ability of Polynesian societies to absorb Western influence and evolve into what Marcus calls a compromise culture (chapter 6, this volume). Two possible lines of explanation are apparent for this distinction between eastern and western Polynesia. One lies in the differences in contact history between those societies that have remained institutionally more traditional and those that have not. Historical factors may well account for many of these differences. The other possible explanation has to do with structural tendencies based on different kinds of worldview. Specifically, we can hypothesize that those Polynesian societies that most clearly segregated powers into institutional dual organizations were more resilient than those whose polities were based on a more monolithic theory of power. The task of pursuing such explanations is daunting. Most likely, a satisfactory understanding of change and continuity in Polynesia will involve the kind of analysis that Sahlins has undertaken for Hawaii and New Zealand, examining the relations between exogenous historical contingencies and endogenous structures (Sahlins 1981a, 1983a).

Although traditional Hawaiian and Tahitian cosmologies have apparently collapsed, recent reports suggest the extent to which aspects of the traditional worldview have been retained. For example, Ito concludes that for modern Hawaiians: "[d]espite cultural commercialization, socioeconomic hardships, and a lack of any formal enculturation system, urban Hawaiians today, fifty years [after the Beaglehole's pessimistic prediction of cultural disintegration], still maintain a shared system of values, morals, and etiological theories—a distinct worldview that indicates tough cultural resiliency" (Ito 1985a:304).

Ito's analysis of modern Hawaiian concepts of person and knowledge do indeed show parallels to traditional aspects of Polynesian worldview as outlined in these pages. Most intriguing is her discussion of Hawaiian concepts of interpersonal problems, especially those defined as entangling or binding and in need of opening up. These concepts demonstrate continuities with classic Polynesian notions of *tapu* as well as changes in the application of such concepts when deprived of their traditional cosmological underpinnings.

Alan Howard (1974) cites in detail the work of Robert Heighton, demonstrating the degree to which modern urban Hawaiians are indeed Polynesian. Especially interesting are Heighton's descriptions of pervasive dualisms in modern Hawaiian thinking, which emphasize notions very similar to *tapu* and *noa* and are associated with gender differences (Howard 1974:157). This is not to understate the degree to which traditional Hawaiian institutions and worldview has indeed changed, but only to suggest that any characterization of modern Polynesia will have to be sensitive to both what is obvious and what is not.

We should not lose sight of the interdependence of historical and structural analyses when trying to understand contemporary cultures in Polynesia. Sahlins' (1981a) recent seminal work on Hawaii and Dening's (1980) on the Marquesas demonstrate clearly what anthropologists have perhaps always known. To comprehend history is, in the end, to understand structure.

NOTES

Preliminary versions of this chapter were read at seminars at the University of Chicago and at the University of Hawaii. I gratefully acknowledge helpful comments and suggestions made on earlier drafts by the following individuals: Irving Goldman, Sherry Ortner, Bruce Knauft, George Marcus, Alan Howard, Robert Borofsky, Robert Franco, John Kirkpatrick, F. Allan Hanson, Nicholas Thomas, Robert Levy, Judith Huntsman, Roger Keesing, Sherry Errington, and Marshall Sahlins.

1. It is important to distinguish between attention to the term *mana* and an examination of its concept. As with other important concepts examined in this study, the issue is not how frequently a particular term appears in discourse (though this may provide important and convenient evidence) but rather the implication of a shared conception in Polynesian institutions, actions, and symbolic production. Thus, even in societies like Hawaii, Tahiti, or Samoa where the term *mana* appears relatively infrequently in texts, or else is used more commonly in compound forms than alone, the concept of *mana* can be shown to be of central importance in worldview.

2. There is an extensive literature on the concept of *mana,* the most important works of which are Codrington 1891, Durkheim 1947:229, Frazer 1922, Williamson 1933, E. S. C. Handy 1927, Hocart 1927, Hogbin 1936, Johansen 1954, Firth 1940, Hubert and Mauss 1978. More recent interpretations are to be found in Goldman 1970, Valeri 1985a, and R. Keesing 1984.

3. The basic insight that our common-sense notions of power might serve us poorly in understanding political traditions other than our own has been a pervasive theme in the literature of insular Southeast Asian kingdoms (B. Anderson 1972; Errington 1975, n.d.; Geertz 1980) as well as in studies of political culture in South Asia (Hocart 1927; Dumont 1970). This analysis has been inspired by that critical tradition.

4. Jean Smith (1974:6) criticizes many of the attempts to explicate in general terms the meanings of Maori terms like *wairua, mana,* and *tapu* as falling into "an unwarranted metaphysical vacuum" by reducing these rich concepts to

their lowest common denominators and thereby trivializing them. Echoing Firth's observation of Tikopians, Smith argues that Maori showed no particular interest in the general meaning of *tapu*, stressing instead "the many different fields of practical concern" exemplified in the host of specific Maori *tapu*s. Yet surely an observer as astute as Smith cannot fail to recognize a different sort of trivialization in her denial "that there was something significant in common between (sic) all the different uses of the [*tapu*] concept apart from the ultrahuman sanction which was ultimately involved" (J. Smith 1974:6). It is hard to understand why one would assume for Maori *tapu* removal a general significance in Maori thought, without the prior assumption of a similarly generic significance for that which was being removed. What Smith seems to disallow for the concepts of *tapu* and *mana*, she explicitly advocates for an understanding of Maori ritual. "Because of the inadequacies of the source material, not only is it more reliable to study what rituals have in common rather than the nature of individual rituals, but it also contributes to a greater degree of certainty if one can study themes and ideas which run through both ritual and myth" (J. Smith 1974:7).

5. If, in ancient Polynesia, human powers were inevitably borrowed from the gods, it is perhaps fitting that in parts of Christian Polynesia the term *mana* has been returned to its source. Thus, in Samoa, at least, *mana* is normally reserved in use for the power of God and is rarely heard in relation to mortals. Human political authority or domestic authority in Samoa is normally referred to as *pule* (Shore 1982:248).

6. In Samoan, *tupu* also means 'to happen' and along with terms like *māfua* 'to cause' (derived from *fua*, 'to blossom') suggest an organic emphasis on the connections between events rather than a mechanistic one.

7. This use of *tupu* for king may also be associated with a conquering warlord as opposed to a chief whose powers are based largely on pedigree. In this case, *tupu* would link semantically with the Tongan *hau* (Rotuman *sau*).

8. "Ranking of individuals within the Tongan family, termed *lahi* (abundance, plenty, greatness), is the key to the organization of Tongan society in every stratum" (Gifford 1929:19).

9. Compare this practice to the Maori aversion to women walking over anything that was *tapu*.

10. The power to produce or control fecundity implies also the power to withhold it. Thus in Samoan the converse of *mana* is *mala* 'to curse', which normally entails enfeebling sickness to an individual and loss of fertility to a family or a descent line. In Samoan *manuia* 'to be fortunate or blessed' is the antithesis of *malaia* 'accursed'.

11. In Samoan *tapu* is generally realized as *sa*, though the more familiar Polynesian term appears in Samoan in several compound or derived words, for example, *tapua'i* 'to worship, to sit still in worshipful sympathy for another's undertaking'. *Sātaputapu* means 'extremely sacred, forbidden'. According to John Mayer (personal communication, 1985), two other Samoan terms, *tapui* 'a restriction placed on resources' and *tapuni* 'to close, cover', are derived not from *tapu* but from *puni* [Samoan], which, in an interesting semantic convergence, means 'to cover up'.

12. The danger to the source and recipient of the misdirected *mana* in situa-

tions of *tapu* 'pollution' is equal. Johansen quotes a Maori chief's lament, conveying how the rigors of *tapu* status looked from on high. "It is not easy to be a great chief; he must always be on his guard that his life shall not become diluted to become an everyday life and moreover fill the whole village so that nobody else can live there except a few, namely those that have the same life as himself, not only in quality—for the whole kinship group has that—but in strength as well" (Johansen 1954:202).

13. "In countless cases 'inviolable' will be an excellent translation [of *tapu*] but still we cannot stop at that; for there are two aspects of the matter. Something may be *tapu* either for its own sake, thus being 'inviolable', or for the sake of others, because it is dangerous. This is not, however, to be understood as if these two aspects preclude one another, indeed they will very often be connected" (Johansen 1954:186).

"In the Marquesas, *tapu* meant primarily restricted or forbidden because sacred, not to be profaned, and secondly, defiled, spiritually dangerous. *Tapu* had as its fundamental meaning, sacred; thus, a first-born's head was *tapu*. The secondary meaning applied to rules to protect sacredness: thus a woman's menstrual cloth was not *tapu*, but it was *tapu* to touch it" (E. S. C. Handy 1923:257).

14. " *'Tapu'* (often rendered in English as 'taboo') has such a broad range of applicability that the term has proven difficult to define. In some contexts it might be glossed as 'forbidden', in others as 'sacred'. The source of its greatest intransigence is that some of its usages seem literally anonymous, especially the fact that the word has been rendered as both 'polluted' and 'sacred' " (Hanson 1987).

15. "The man, the highest gods, and the distant inaccessible heaven with the unchanging stars—all these contain life purely and strongly, because they are *tapu* and isolated. The man is also the person who represents the kinship group most purely.

Woman, on the other hand, often comes from another kinship group. She cooks the food which is eaten by many different persons. Different life is mixed in her. Thus also, on the earth, on which everybody treads" (Johansen 1954:222).

16. "Almost all things have *tapu* about them: such as the building of a house: the learning of a song or tradition, the getting of a body *tatooid* [*sic*] or marked with the *tatau* &c. The fire that cooks the mens [*sic*] food must not be taken to light the fire for cooking the woman's food: the men may eat the womens [*sic*] but the women must not eat that which belongs to the men; the [men] may smoke tobacco that is got by the women, but the women may not smoke that which belongs to the men or is got by them. the [*sic*] women must not wear any of the cloth that has been worn as undergarments by the Man, the Men never wear any belonging to the women: the men are so particular in this respect that they always burn all their old rags in case the women should get hold of them and wear them, they think that they would be overtaken by disease" (Darling, quoted in N. Thomas 1987:126).

17. Thomas alludes to a metaphorical expression in Tahitian that refers to the birth canal as *te ara atua* 'the path of the gods'. Stillborn children were called "the excrement of the gods" suggesting the status of the vagina as merely the

proximate source of human life, and the birth canal as the passage between the human world and the ultimate wellspring of *ora* or life.

18. I am grateful to Robert Levy for suggestions made on an early draft of this chapter that led to this section of the essay.

19. The sense in which *tikanga,* in its manifestation as tradition or custom represented a model for orderly existence for Maori is suggested by this passage from an early colonial history of New Zealand. "When war broke out between Heke and the colonists the other tribes were very generally in a state of anxiety and uncertainty how they would be affected by it. They remarked that they had no *tikanga* to guide them in this case. In any quarrel among themselves, it could at once be determined by reference to ancient usage how it became any particular tribe to act" (Edward Shortland *Traditions and Superstitions of the New Zealanders,* 2d ed., 1856:232).

20. The association among *mana,* purity, and perfection are exemplified, if in a grisly way, by the ancient Hawaiian practice of selecting only perfect physical specimens of humanity as sacrificial victims to important gods. Being a perfect instance of humanity, these unfortunates were appropriate representatives of the chiefs who were the sacrifiers, and fitting intermediaries between men and gods (Valeri 1985a).

21. For Polynesians the word, especially in ritual, constitutes a force. Handy has put it especially well. "The principle of rapport is the basis of most of the rules of *tapu,* the use of verbal spells in which words endowed with power were uttered rhythmically and forcibly, chanting, posture and gesture dancing, service of objects, places and persons as mediums and instruments, the transference of influence into or through offerings and sacrifices, and the use of physical mediums in black magic" (Handy 1927:7). As Valeri has written in relation to Hawaii, "[the word] bears a 'fruit' and can, if properly spoken become an actual entity, and operative agent that can bring about events" (Valeri 1985a: 55). For Tikopia, *manu (mana)* is believed to reside in the chief's lips, and in his capacity to control fertility through ritual knowledge made manifest in ritual language (Firth 1970b:46).

22. These qualities associated with *noa* are vividly reflected in Teuira Henry's description of the concluding episode of a major marae rite in pre-Christian Tahiti. The spirits are addressed directly by the presiding priests.

> Dismissal! Grand dismissal to make ordinary [*noa*]!
> Let sacredness remain here [in the temple] that we become ordinary [*noa*].
>
> Let holiness [*ra'a*] be thine, O god, let the priesthood hold the sanctification [*mo'a*] of the sovereign and congregation. We are now retiring to use our hands and become vile [*ha'aha'a*]: we shall do domestic work, wear flowers, paint ourselves yellow with *mati,* blow fire, curse, give each other blows, practice black art [sorcery], caress [make love], put on unconsecrated clothes [*ahu, noa*], eat pork, cavella fish, shark, bananas; and drink *ava;* look not upon us in anger for this, O god!
>
> Remain thou here, in this holy place [*vahi mo'a*], turn thy face to *pō,* look not upon the deeds of men (Henry 1928:172).

Anyone who has been (as I have) a long-time guest in a Samoan household recognizes in Henry's account the sense of confinement or restricted access to casual encounters that has been in Polynesia the sacred burden of gods, chiefs and newly arrived anthropologists.

23. Handy (1923:61) uses a quote from Melville's *Typee* to illustrate the connections between binding and the symbolic redirection of generative potency implicit in Marquesan *kahui:*

> Frequently, in walking through the groves I observed breadfruit and coconut trees, with a wreath of leaves twined in a peculiar fashion about their trunks. This was the mark of the taboo. The trees themselves, their fruit, and even the shadows they cast upon the ground were consecrated by its presence. In the same way a pipe, which the king has bestowed upon me, was rendered sacred in the eyes of the natives, none of whom I could ever prevail upon to smoke from it. *The bowl was encircled by a woven braid of grass. . . . A similar badge was once braided about my wrist by the royal hand of Mehevi himself, who, as soon as he had concluded the operation, pronounced me "Taboo"* (Melville 1876:252, emphasis added).

24. See Ito's (1985a:309) discussion of modern Hawaiian concepts of *hihia*—emotional entanglements that envelop people in "a network of resentment, hostility, guilt, depression, or vague discomfort" (Pukui, Haertig, and Lee 1972: 71–72).

25. Similarly, the Samoan concepts of *aga* and *āmio* (Shore 1978, 1982, 1984, 1985) are Samoan versions of the more general Polynesian distinction between human action bound by transpersonal forms and personal behavior that is free of these constraints. The elaborate symbolic analysis summarized in Appendix B of Shore (1982) reflects the pervasiveness of the distinction between *tapu* and *noa* in modern Samoan culture despite the relative unimportance of these terms in modern Samoan.

26. Valeri renders the term as *'aha* (Valeri 1985a:294).

27. Kaeppler cites a similar practice from the Tuamotu Islands, reported by Kenneth Emory (Kaeppler 1982:95, n. 6).

28. For example:

> Let the fountain gush forth
> from the spring and from within . . .
> and you, put your warbelt on
> Double the fringe of your *maro* (war belt) up.
> Let your *maro* provoke your enemy
> (From John White, *Ancient History of the Maori,* 1887–1890, 2:108).

> Give me my girdle, to pass between the legs,
> Give me my girdle, to pass around the waist
> Fasten to the left, fasten to the right
> (From Elsdon Best, "Notes on the Art of War," 1902:69–70).

From the Moriori of Chatham Island comes the following chant:

> Whose is the *maro* [loin cloth] which is outspread? . . .
> The *maro* of the Lord, the *maro* of Waiorangi . . .
> Fight to the east, fight to the west, fight to the distant east!
> Rise! Stand up!

Gird it that it may encircle!
Whose is the *maro* [loin cloth] which is outspread?
(From H. D. Skinner, *The Moriois of Chatham Island,* 1923:110–111).

29. Not surprisingly, what is true for sexuality is equally true for eating. Jean Smith provides an exact parallel to the dual valence of female sexuality in Polynesian thought and the Maori attitude toward special foods. "Thus while ritual eating of *tapu* food was an act of subjugation, wrongful eating of *tapu* food resulted in subjugation by the food. To eat food could result in life or death" (Smith 1974:39). Once again, the distinction between purity and pollution in eating as in sex has to do not with two discrete categories of objects or persons, but with issues of control and containment. Like purity and pollution, *tapu* and *noa* are alternate states of the same thing and not distinct things.

30. Ortner has proposed that the effect of these beliefs is that "[t]he girl . . . is almost wholly turned into a symbolic object by her kin." In this view, the aim of such institutions is not cosmological but rather secular and political, women being used as "sexual bait to 'pull in' (desirable) men" (Ortner 1981:376). Yet it is important to recognize that these Polynesian associations of status with images of limiting or binding have a far more general distribution than in relation to women, and are suggested by many Polynesian institutions associated with *mana.* There is, whatever the political implication of these beliefs in relation to women, a conception of power that is authentically linked to cosmological issues.

31. Though Maori women in general were devalued in relation to men, seniority of descent could in fact outweigh the gender distinction. Primogeniture was sufficiently important for the Maori to guarantee that the firstborn of a senior line would be ritually honored—whatever the sex (Best 1924a, 1:407). High-ranking women were considered *tapu* and important titled women such as *puhi* and *tapairu* could attain considerable political power.

Nor were Tahitian women totally excluded from power or status. As among Maori, the firstborn of either sex was accorded special honor in noble families. Furthermore, late in Tahitian history we see the emergence of female chiefs, and there is reason to suspect that ranking women played an important role behind the scenes (Goldman 1970:180). Descent through a high-ranking mother was critical in distinguishing relative status for half-siblings, a pattern common throughout Polynesia.

32. I am grateful to Robert Franco for suggesting the possible links between the conception of binding developed here and tatooing practices.

6

Chieftainship

GEORGE E. MARCUS

Pa Fenuatara's position was difficult. He acted in many ways as the
head of the Kafika clan, making decisions for both his clan and the
community as a whole. Yet he was not the chief and his father alone
could perform the most sacred rites. In the last resort it was only his
word which had final validity. To say that Pa Fenuatara had great
influence but no authority is hardly a correct way of putting it,
because a legitimacy was accorded to his decisions by virtue of his
unchallenged right to be his father's successor. Yet, he had to move
carefully. Unlike his father who could give arbitrary decisions because
he was the chief and who had all the aura of his ritual powers as sanctions, Pa Fenuatara had no chiefly taboo, no command over gods, no
title of *ariki* (chief). His decisions, therefore, had to have some measure of public support to be effective. He was concerned accordingly
not to appear in any way to be arrogating to himself privileges that
were his father's, and he took at times what seemed to be a line of
almost excessive humility. . . .

The essence of the matter was that to the Tikopia people at large
the old chief had held on to life far too long. They saw him decrepit
and doddering, barely able to perform his ritual functions, and
though still entitled to all the respect and awe which a Tikopia chief
inspires, not contributing anything of value to the body politic. Even
in ritual matters it was a question whether his survival was of advantage to the community. There was an idea that the ills from which
Tikopia suffered in 1952 were in some part due to a correlation
between lack of health and prosperity in the land, and the waning
physical powers of the chief.

> RAYMOND FIRTH
> "A Polynesian Aristocrat"

THE figure of the chief has pervaded anthropological writing on Polynesia, more so in the predominant effort at reconstructing Polynesian
societies before and at the time of European contact than in the ongoing
ethnography of contemporary conditions. First as the early travelers',
and then as the scholars' synecdoche for Polynesian culture, chieftain-

ship mirrors in turn the salient idiom of indigenous discourse—expressed in myth, everyday talk, and explanations to the ethnographer—about their own societies. Consequently, in this essay, we are not dealing so much with a discrete literature specifically focused on chiefs (in fact, this literature is ironically quite small) as with an integral frame of reference in terms of which Polynesian societies have been more generally and historically described. To talk about precontact Polynesia is inevitably to talk about chiefs.

In the anthropological treatment of chieftainship, which has followed the lead of early contact accounts, there are two recurring images of chiefs. One is of the chief as sacred being, separate from his people, and generally mystified in status. The other is of the chief as an exemplary being, respected and admired by his people for embodying the ideals of personhood that they all share and approximate in varying degrees. It is not that in some island groups chieftainship conformed solely to the first image, and that in other groups it conformed to the second image, or that even in a single society some chiefs were mystified and others were men of the people. Rather, to different degrees there have always been these two simultaneous sides to chieftainship—the kingly side and the populist side.

The following examples manifest a range of ways in which the two images have combined. In Tonga, mystified chieftainship attaches to a special quality or substance of being, while mere title-holding alone is associated with the populist side of chieftainship.

> In Tonga being a great aristocrat *(sino'i 'eiki)* is considered an end in itself. It means that one is given universal recognition and deference, accorded the special language of respect, given gifts of food, and sought after in marriage. 'To be known' is the synonym for high rank; to be 'not known' is to be of low rank. In the traditional system, titles involved ruling and responsibility. Being an aristocrat means pure privilege, so much so that many of the great aristocrats of the 18th and 19th centuries, even though they ruled political *Kāinga* 'kindreds' and had titles, did not bother to use their titles or even to get themselves appointed, and were known by their personal names instead. Nor were they particularly interested in personal power. The title was and still is spoken of as a 'garland' *(kakala),* meaning that it can be taken away whereas the 'blood' *(toto)* is one's own forever (Bott 1981:38).

In Samoa and Tikopia, by contrast, sanctity accrues to the title-holder, who is a kingly chief with it, but merely an exemplary person without it. In Samoa,

> Margaret Mead (1930b) relates a revealing story from Manu'a, the site of her famous early fieldwork. The story recounts a legendary rivalry between the two half-brothers, Alia-Tama, the younger, and Alia-Matua, the elder, for political power in Manu'a. The two men, the legend goes, were walking

along a path on a particularly hot afternoon. Suddenly seized by thirst—for power, it turns out—the younger Alia begs his older brother to climb a coconut tree to pluck a green drinking coconut. The older brother demurs, complaining that the dignity and mana of his chiefly status prevents him from performing menial services. Alia-Tama then suggests that his brother simply remove his tapa crown, which was the symbol and repository of his chiefly power. The suggestion appearing logical enough to Alia-Matua, he takes off his headpiece, places it on the ground, and climbs the tree. Wasting no time, the younger brother snatches the tapa crown, places it on his own head, and runs off to Fitiuta in Manu'a, where he is proclaimed Tui Manu'a.

Personal qualities may certainly enhance political power in Samoa, but power per se is clearly separable from any particular person who may wield it. Political power lies primarily in a title and is conceived of as external to the person who might happen to bear it. Without a title, as many talented and otherwise distinguished Samoans have discovered, one is—in an important sense—nobody. With it, even the most unprepossessing person is imbued with the dignity and distinction of this office (Shore 1982:69).

Firth's portrait (see chapter epigraph) of the Tikopian aristocrat, Pa Fenuatara, is particularly revealing of how both images of chieftainship are combined in a single institution. While his father reigns as the mystified chief in office, separate from his people, Pa Fenuatara lives in his shadow as a popular hero, a man of the people. He is supposed to succeed to the title but in fact never does, as Firth tells us, since his father lived too long. In so doing the old chief transgressed the ritual function of kingship, which is to ensure the well-being of the community.

Polynesian systems of hierarchy rest on an understanding of chieftainship as the core of a system of status attribution that encompasses entire populations. The central argument of this essay is that after a long period in Polynesian scholarship of not very interesting, highly stereotypic views of chiefs, there is now an emergent revitalization of perspective based on two different trends of research. These converge in posing the notion that Polynesian chieftainship everywhere combines kingly and populist characteristics.

Whether viewed as a status that orients and defines Polynesian hierarchy, as a quality of personhood, or as an institution of political economy, chieftainship must be seen in fundamentally relational terms. The dichotomy between chief and commoner can be conceived either in an absolute hierarchy emanating from kingship, where the power and character of a chief are parallel to those of a king, or in a floating system of rank distinctions at the base of society, where the power and performance of the chief are understood as the work of the people. In the latter instance, a chief's personal status is socially defined in terms normally applied to common people. Figure 1 presents a summary of dimensions that define the two qualities of chieftainship that combine in different ways in different Polynesian societies.

The Kingly Side	The Populist Side
Exclusivity as a value	Inclusivity as a value
Absolute criteria of rank	Contextual criteria of rank
Socially distant, mystified in status	Heroic figure, but approachable
Different order of being, not accountable by ordinary standards of behavior	Accountable as an ordinary person
Definer of ritualized context for others by his presence; the passive embodiment of power	Active embodiment of power, in the shadow of kingly status to which it is variantly related

1. The two sides are continuously or discontinuously related, depending on the society. They may appear in different persons or offices, or as two sides of the same chiefly person. In some societies they are always integrated, in others they are separated by situational context or stage of life cycle.

2. The two sides are culturally expressed in systems of status attribution. They are anchored in title-holding, concepts of sacred personal substance, and standards of heroic or exemplary behavior.

Figure 1. Kingly and populist sides of chieftainship

Two kinds of recent research on Polynesia have shaped this composite view of chieftainship. One involves a commitment to reconstruction and the sophisticated reclamation of an older tradition of scholarship that preceded the functionalist revolution in anthropology (Jarvie 1964). The other involves a commitment to contributing to the ongoing ethnographic record in the wake of the social transformation of Polynesian societies. Although a sophisticated exploration of ideas about kingship in the context of the reconstructionist project has opened afresh the question of the meanings of chieftainship in Polynesia, and especially the sacredness of chiefs, it has been from the perspective of seeing chiefs against the ordinariness and commonality of Polynesian life provided by recent fieldwork that the clearest insights into chiefs as popular heroes have come. The reconstructive project is largely an armchair enterprise that aims to retrieve Polynesian ideology, more alive in the past than at present, while the other is largely a fieldwork enterprise based upon observations of contemporary Polynesian practices. Together they suggest an intimate synthesis of the two images of chieftainship, with continuities between past and present. Reintroducing ideas of kingship into Polynesian ethnology gives substance to the indispensable conceptualization of chiefs as sacred; contemporary fieldwork on the everyday life of Polynesians, including chiefs, allows the popular, everyday aspects of chieftainship to be examined.

These recent trends in research that are modifying our understanding of chieftainship arise from two deeper, more enduring sets of orientations that have long shaped Polynesian anthropology. These are (1) the dialectic relationship between the ethnography of particular societies, carried out by individual, independent investigators, along with the salient urge toward comparative synthesis of Polynesia as a culture area; and (2) the tension between, on the one hand, a reconstructionist goal that conflates, often in the timeless language of the ethnographic present, historical materials and contemporary ethnographic fieldwork, and on the other, the inclination to take modern Polynesians for what they are in the context of long-term Euro-American contact.

Long after the culture-area approach waned in cultural and social anthropology generally, it has remained strong in Polynesia, partially as a consequence of overlapping histories of origin and differentiation of island societies. The study of any particular island group is thus often reflected against a backdrop of controlled comparison that periodically surfaces in someone's effort to tie the results of research together in a single panoramic view. Understanding chieftainship has always been a key focus for such synthetic efforts, but this is even more the case with recent efforts at structuralist syntheses, in which Polynesian cultural codes are systematically expressed as ideas about kingship and chiefly power. At the same time, ethnographies of particular island societies provide continual challenges to and qualifications of such syntheses, which then stand or fall by their capacity to accommodate and account for variation.

The dialectic between efforts at synthesis and studies of specific societies has in turn been dominated by the attempt to reconstruct the precontact past of Polynesian societies. One seminal exception has been Firth's ethnographic project on Tikopia, which was also a pioneering instantiation of functionalism as ethnographic practice. Although in recent years Firth's continuing ethnography of the Tikopia has been interesting for its documentation of change, its long-term interest has been its concern with a people who have been a living survival of Polynesia's past, and are thus an invaluable ethnographic aid to the reconstructionist project.

The task of representing contemporary Polynesian cultures has been pioneered less in western Polynesian societies such as Tonga and Samoa where it has been easier to emphasize continuities with the precontact record, than in eastern Polynesian societies such as Tahiti, Hawaii, and the Marquesas, where contemporary ethnography has required a novel approach. This is the focus on personhood, which has the potential for both gaining insight into contemporary Polynesian cultures generally, and contributing to the emerging structuralist syntheses of traditional chieftainship. The personhood perspective suggests ways in which the kingly and populist sides of chieftainship can still be observed as interpersonal process in some contemporary Polynesian societies.

These broader orientations of Polynesian studies thus significantly affect how the perspective on chieftainship has been changing, and dictate a way of organizing this chapter. In the next section I treat the emerging attempt to synthesize Polynesian ethnology by reintroducing long-dormant notions of kingship into the concept of chieftainship, thus providing a richer way to view both the sacredness and ordinariness of chiefs. In the following section I discuss the perspective on chiefs that emerges from contemporary ethnography, where ideas of personhood and symbols of collective identity in change are more salient than residual notions of sacredness. The point is not to see earlier chiefs as sacred beings and current ones as populist heroes, but to understand how these sides of life fit together in particular times and places. In the third, and longest, section I consider the role of chieftainship in the context of contemporary Polynesian political economy, where its meanings are quite different from those prior to contact, but in which the contrast between kingly and populist remains an important guide to explaining the place of chiefs in contemporary stratification systems. By giving special attention to current ethnographic accounts of chieftainship, I mean to emphasize the worth of research into contemporary Polynesian societies. Such research considers what chieftainship has become, while recognizing both continuities and discontinuities with the past.

There are two further caveats. First, I have made no attempt to develop a comprehensive review of ethnographic materials on chiefs, island group by island group. Rather, I have written this essay with the view that the synthetic stress in Polynesian studies has a solid empirical foundation. Thus, the narrow base of examples in this essay (mainly from my own work in Tonga, and from other societies of western Polynesia—Fiji and Samoa—where chieftainship has survived most saliently and on a large scale) should have a resonance amid variation, similarity, and contrast, for all other Polynesian island groups.

Second, the kingly/populist continuum developed in this paper effectively collapses the chief/bigman distinction used by Sahlins, in his now classic 1963 paper contrasting Polynesia and Melanesia emblematically by type of political leadership and organization. It suggests not only that chiefs who share much in common with Melanesian big men are to be found in Polynesia, but that big men who share much in common with chiefs, and in fact are chiefs, are to be found in Melanesia. In other

words, the broader field of comparative synthesis for phenomena discussed in this paper could cross-cut the conventionally defined geographic divisions of Melanesia and Polynesia and, if recent work is any
indication (e.g., Petersen 1982), of Micronesia also.[1] Nonetheless, the
Polynesian boundary is retained in the anchoring of notions of chieftainship in the institution of kingship throughout the region, and, if
Sahlins is correct, a distinctive pan-Polynesian form of it. From a cultural rather than a social structural emphasis, then, it is a more interesting move to isolate the Polynesian culture area for an internal comparative synthesis.

Reconstruction Synthesis: On the Sacredness of Chiefs

Area-wide reconstruction syntheses of recent decades (Sahlins 1958;
Goldman 1970) have been informed by functionalist theory in anthropology, which has meant a preponderant attention to social structure
rather than to cultural systems. They have been guided by a desire to
unfold the evolutionary development of Polynesian societies, from the
perspective of ecological adaptation in Sahlins' case, and the competition for status in Goldman's. Ambitious reconstructions of individual
societies have been much less common. Most notable are Douglas
Oliver's (1974) unparalleled three-volume reconstruction of Tahitian
society and Elizabeth Bott's (1982) account of Tongan society at the
time of Captain Cook's visits, written in the late 1950s but long-delayed
in publication. Valerio Valeri's recent work on Hawaii (1985a) is the
only one of those works to embrace a post-functionalist, structuralist
framework, an approach being pioneered in Anglo-American research
by Marshall Sahlins.

Discussions of chieftainship were at the center of the major function-
alist/evolutionary syntheses. For Sahlins' earlier synthesis, the levels
and forms of chieftainship were measures of social stratification among
populations adapted to particular kinds of ecosystems. This experiment
in the then burgeoning field of cultural ecology is of less relevance here
than the ethnographically richer synthesis of Goldman, which focused
on variant forms of chieftainship and political roles across Polynesian
societies. The central concept was status rivalry, which Goldman
viewed as inherent in Polynesian cultures. Goldman's work effectively
synthesizes an immense amount of functionalist research, and in social
structural terms it provides excellent discussions of the principles of
rank, exchange relations, and politics. What is missing in the function-
alist/evolutionary accounts is an understanding of precontact Polynesia
in cultural terms, and it is such a restatement and deepening of the early

social structural work that is promised by the current effort at synthesis, guided by structuralist theory, and by a return to older styles of textual research.

The recent thrust toward a cultural synthesis centers on chieftainship, which is, after all, the focal concern of most indigenous texts. Furthermore, in any discussion of chieftainship, the sacredness of chiefs is the crucial analytic pivot on which a cultural perspective depends. Yet this is precisely the sort of issue that functionalist scholarship tended to elide. Functional analysis was strong on conceptualizing systems of action, but was weak on treatments of ideology. There were attempts to classify and categorize behavioral indicators of sacredness, but they leave one with a lingering sense of being on the outside looking in, of talking about sacredness in a way that misses its coherent indigenous formulation.

As long as the emphasis was on social structure, the sacredness of chiefs had to be inferred from social action and its explication came to rest on the formal exegesis of terms like *mana* and *tapu,* isolated from their meanings in myths and oral texts. The nature of chiefly power must certainly be understood with reference to such concepts, and their exegesis remains a fertile subject for interpretation (R. Bowden 1979; R. Keesing 1984; see Shore, chapter 5, this volume), but to isolate key symbols or concepts, free form, so to speak, misses completely the narrative coherence in indigenous texts about chiefs.

In the functionalist tradition, Firth's research is the paramount work on the ideological context of chieftainship, if only because his ethnography is so detailed. In a recent article on the sacredness of Tikopian chiefs, the intent of which is to suggest what sacredness means in the contemporary transformation of Tikopian society, Firth (1979:154–155) specifies the sociological sense in which Tikopian (and Polynesian) chiefs are sacred. Firth lists alternative ways in which a chief or king can be sacred. These consist of internalized possibilities (being in his own person a god; being believed to have an infusion of divine personality, that is, an extended spirit possession; or being a vehicle of the divine, as in spirit mediumship) and externalized possibilities (the chief as a subject of divine inspiration, but not habitation; or as having divine legitimation—chiefly office as authorized by divine fiat, by descent from the divine or from an ancestor with divine sanction). Firth then points to the last of these possibilities—divine legitimation—as the most common form of sacredness of Polynesian chiefs. In the functionalist program, it is difficult to go much further than typing the sociological form of chiefly sacredness and discussing its content in terms of an exegesis of the *mana/tapu* complex, which is articulated in the everyday speech of contemporary Polynesians in a vague shadowy way, if at all.

A different turn has been taken by Sahlins. Having assimilated French structuralist techniques of analysis, which traditionally have operated not so much on the observation of social action as on texts (myths, stories, folklore, ritual performance), he has turned back to interests in Polynesian materials that pre-date or have remained outside the predominant functionalist orientation. This is the work of comparative mythology, folklore, and literature, which were domains of Continental scholars such as Bakhtin, Dumézil, and Lévi-Strauss, and of some English researchers including Frazer and, most notably, Hocart (who, like Sahlins, had first-hand ethnographic knowledge of Fiji, but also like Sahlins, made his major contribution in broad comparative syntheses). The style of this classic work is universalist and globally comparative. Sahlins' recent essays have these qualities, but their main interest for the study of Polynesian chieftainship is that they move this subject to absolute center place, and they do so by introducing to it systematic ideas about kingship. The influence of classical ideas of kingship was present in earlier work on Polynesia, which did not have the theoretical sophistication or the aid of experience from fieldwork that characterizes contemporary research. Sahlins' recent work reintroduces dormant notions with the benefit of a powerful technique of analysis and a feel for the area derived from intensive modern fieldwork.

Attention to mythical expressions of kingship thus gives substance to the study of chieftainship in Polynesia, without which it has a rather headless character. Sahlins is applying these revived ideas about kingship to available textual materials, and most importantly to contact accounts, which give a full-bodied narrative to earlier, much vaguer notions about the sacredness of chiefs. Polynesian chieftainship in its various forms appears to be a set of ideas rooted in stories (theories?) of kingship that provide a framework for observing chiefs as actors in social life.

Thus far Sahlins' work is only in the form of essays (1981a, 1981b, 1983c) and, by the application of a set of ideas about kingship to examples drawn at will, is merely suggestive of synthesis. How these ideas might work for the whole Polynesian area depends on subsequent applications by Sahlins and others. This project is clearly different from past attempts at synthesis in two respects. It is incremental and explicitly dependent on testing by others. It has therefore been suggestive rather than comprehensive. Furthermore, it brackets the compelling evolutionary frame of past syntheses. Although the evolutionary character of synthesis is important, avoiding it is an expectable move in the approach that Sahlins takes. Structuralist accounts of transformation describe variation, but do not presuppose historical connections along an evolutionary continuum. Regardless, the current movement toward

cultural synthesis will remain incomplete until it links up with sociological constructions, for which the evolutionary frame has seemed compelling.

The following sections briefly describe Sahlins' view of kingship and
an important application by Alan Howard to a society where kingship
might not be thought to apply, but which more fully evokes the kingly/
populist poles that define Polynesian chieftainship.

The Stranger-King in Fiji

Sahlins' essay, "The Stranger-King: Dumézil among the Fijians"
(1981b), sets out notions about Polynesian kingship that resonate
through his other recent essays (Sahlins 1981a, 1983c). A Polynesian
theory of kingship (and by extension, of chieftainship), when culled
from structuralist analyses of indigenous texts, is the form of a Polynesian theory of society. It corresponds to Western ideas about what such a
theory should concern—the basis of social order, the conditions of
inequality, and the nature of power immanent in human relations.
Sahlins' style is very much that of Hocart and Dumézil, who, among
others, are his inspirations in this enterprise. Their conceptualizations
of kingship draw universally from the myths that concern the origins of
great civilizations, East and West, for which kingship has always been
the central figure.

Sahlins begins with the connection that Dumézil drew between
themes about political sovereignty common in both Polynesian and
Indo-European civilizations: the advent of a foreign ruler and his
absorption by indigenous people. In myth, power and its embodiment
in chieftainship originate outside society, erupt upon an indigenous
scene of peace and equality, and become domesticated or absorbed in an
atmosphere of popular resentment (here Sahlins relies on Pierre Clastres 1977). The Polynesian (if not universal) idea of kingship thus
originates as an alien in the act of usurpation. The king becomes incorporated both through ritual and intermarriage, symbolically and bio-
logically appropriating the reproductive powers of the land while insti-
tutionalizing the power of alien (and divine) origin.

Chiefs in any Polynesian society are thus part of a status system that
in ideology and practice gravitates between the kingly and populist
characterizations discussed in the introduction. Giving a rich narrative
content to the long-observed separation and mystification of Polynesian
chiefs is the main contribution of Sahlins' essay. There is one dimension
to chieftainship—the foundational one of origin—that makes them
powerful aliens in their own society. Yet however much this is recognized on ritual occasions, chiefs are also of the people—their collective
product, so to speak—and while this dimension is also present in

Sahlins' essay, it is perhaps more readily expressed in the myths and practices of those Polynesian societies where the kingly pole of chieftainship was never, or only weakly, expressed in the actual sociological institutionalization of kingship.

The Kingly/Populist Parameters of Chieftainship in Rotuma

In the first important application of the stranger-king perspective on Polynesian chieftainship, "History, Myth and Polynesian Chieftainship: The Case of Rotuman Kings" (1985b), Alan Howard demonstrates that although indeed Rotuman chieftainship is a completely indigenous practice, its meanings can be understood in the general framework that Sahlins has reintroduced into Polynesian studies—the autonomous stranger-king versus the domesticated populist leader. Particularly important in Howard's rich analysis of Rotuman chieftainship, as expressed in myth, is the antagonism between the claims of the people of the land (whose primary value is as food producers) to empower the chief through their collective efforts, and the autonomous power of chiefs themselves, derived from an alien and divinely conceived source. The uneasy resolution in myths and ritual of this Rotuman (and more generally Polynesian) problem lies in some form of complementarity between the two sources of power, which nonetheless remain in opposition. The Rotuman case illustrates well the strength, both of populist ideas and of divine kingship, in Polynesian political thought as expressed in the ideology and practice of a local system of chieftainship (see also Howard 1986b).

The final section of Howard's paper suggests a translation of these ideologically expressed tensions that define chieftainship into the practice of chiefs as social actors. He seeks to explain status indicators in terms of rank (elevation in status) and social distance (mystified demeanor in interpersonal behavior) as a working out in practice of the ideas of Rotuman chieftainship. If the study of chiefs is to be more than an armchair exercise, this move toward viewing ideas in practice is essential. Those involved in reconstructionist projects who are analyzing texts must also consider sociological elements, and this is most easily accomplished in those contemporary Polynesian societies where, allowing for historical transformations, chieftainship is still a salient institution.

Howard's application of the kingly/populist perspective on chieftainship is important precisely because Rotuma (where kingship as an institution is weakly developed) might otherwise be considered a counter case in which the parameters of this perspective are weakly defined. Because the populist side of Rotuman chiefs is so pronounced in their definition, the problem of the alien power of the paramount chief or king is keenly reflected in myth. Only by working through less well-known cases in Polynesian studies, like that of Rotuma, will the synthetic value of the kingly/populist perspective be fully tested.

The Reconstruction of Ancient Polynesian Society

It is appropriate to end this section by noting the continuing possibilities for the sociological reconstruction of Polynesian cultures. Although these are not as obvious or as central as the above work which is based on structuralist analyses of myths and rituals, the latter must ultimately be reintegrated with social-structural syntheses such as that of Goldman. Sahlins' essay on Hawaii (1981a) is an interesting partial fulfillment of this reintegration of his structuralist analysis with Polynesian practice and historical events (but see Marcus 1982 for a discussion of some problems with structuralist accounts of history.)

Perhaps the most interesting work that relates to the reconstruction of precontact Polynesian political economy comes not from research on Polynesia at all, but from the study of Southeast Asian polities. In their works on the pre-twentieth-century Balinese "theater state," Clifford Geertz (1980) and James Boon (1977) have suggested that Bali resembled a Polynesian socio-political order with an Indic overlay. Shelly Errington (n.d.), in her yet unpublished work on the polity of Luwu in Sulawesi, has also suggested this Polynesian character of Southeast Asian states.

In suggesting this idea, these scholars have referred to the applicability to their case of Goldman's key notion of the status lineage, which poses the problem of understanding how a political organization based on descent among an elite of chiefs meshes with the local organization of commoners in kindreds. The top-to-bottom organization of chieftainship that is kingly and exclusive at the top, grading continuously into a populist and inclusive variant of chieftainship at the bottom, suggests a substantive cultural perspective on the status lineage. In Polynesian studies, this cultural perspective, now being worked out in the essays of Sahlins and others, has yet to be integrated with existing social structural reconstructions, such as the status lineage. By contrast, such an integrated view characterizes the work of the above mentioned Southeast Asianists. They have offered cultural accounts of core structures of political economy, which also depend on notions of kingly/populist chieftainship not that different from Hocart's. We thus have available for Bali a vivid picture of a theater state *(Negara)* in a world of status lineages *(dadia)* that suggests an eventual extension of the field of comparison which we have been considering, from a Polynesian world to a more broadly encompassing Malayo-Polynesian one.

The Ongoing Ethnographic Enterprise: On Chiefs as Persons

The recent interest among ethnographers in focusing cultural analysis at the level of the person is, in a sense, an overcoming of historic circumstances that have made present Polynesian societies relatively unattractive for fieldwork investigations in cultural anthropology. At the level of social and cultural institutions, the break with the past was sufficiently dramatic to undermine assumptions about the superficiality of westernization that have generally underlain much modern ethnography. A culturally distinctive subject in contemporary Polynesia could only be reclaimed by more subtle means, and this has been achieved by focusing on the most enduring level of cultural distinctiveness for any society, that of indigenous conceptions of personal agency.

This interest seems to have developed most strongly in eastern Polynesia (see A. Howard 1974; Kirkpatrick 1983; Levy 1973; and especially White and Kirkpatrick 1985), where it has been assumed in past scholarship that the historic destruction of culture was greatest. But it is also being pursued in western Polynesia (see, in particular, Marcus 1978b, 1980b; Shore 1982), where the institutional continuities with the past are stronger and where systems of chieftainship remain elaborate.[2] Although the ethnography of personhood in eastern Polynesia has implications for the study of chieftainship, it is in western Polynesia that this line of research most directly converges with the perspective on chieftainship emerging in the reconstructionist project.

Contextualizing the study of chieftainship in the framework of personhood leads to an emphasis on the populist side of chiefs, since their sacred (or kingly) side has been considerably demystified during the course of the twentieth century. Chiefliness as an idiom for evaluating persons and things is common in everyday talk in a number of Polynesian societies, but especially in those such as Tonga and Samoa where chiefly systems have remained so pervasive. In Tonga, the distinction between chief and commoner is a prevalent manner of speaking among the population, particularly in assigning rank in gender relations within the categories of kinship. The core of Tongan kinship is the brother/sister relation, in which the superior rank of the sister and her descendants to her brother and his descendants is expressed as her *'eiki* 'chiefly' position in relation to his *tu'a* 'commoner' position. Chiefly attribution is also common in the characterizations of routine events that define the pace of daily life, including funerals, feasts, and food exchanges. Depending upon degree of elaboration, any event can be classed as *me'a faka 'eiki* 'chiefly or chief-like matters'.

In Samoa, as in Tonga, chiefliness is an idiom for characterizing virtuous behavior and a formally correct presentation of self. One often hears contemporary Tongans and Samoans talk of the aristocentric bases of their cultures. For example, as Albert Wendt said in his defense of Derek Freeman's recent book about Margaret Mead and Samoa:

> Our public face is nearly always placid, obedient, courtly, orderly, generous, hospitable, considerate, impassive. Freeman knows this face well; it is the *tu-faatamalii,* the way of the true aristocrat, the ideal on which all human behavior must be modelled; it is a very severe and demanding way which is enforced by our elders and our churches on everyone, including our children. That was as true in the 1920s as it is today.
>
> There is also the opposite way, the way of the *tu-fanua,* he who transgresses, who does not behave like a *tamalii,* and brings shame to his *aiga,* village, country. Extreme anti-*faatamalii* behavior is described as *tu-faamanu,* the ways of the beast (Wendt 1983b:14).

Interestingly, the core of Shore's (1982) recent analysis of the Samoan person turns on the contrast between *aga* 'social conduct' and *āmio* 'personal impulse', of which the above distinction that Wendt draws between aristocratic, cultured behavior, and out-of-control, animalistic behavior is an elaboration. Thus, the idiom of the chief is used conventionally to evaluate the manner and bearing of Samoan persons.

Although it is true that chieftainship is a phenomenon of much wider participation in Samoa than in Tonga, during the modern period chiefly ideals have been synonymous with popular ideals in both cases. Far from being extraordinary behavior, these ideals represent standards of personal behavior that any Tongan or Samoan is encouraged to approximate.

Thus, in the framework of personhood, chiefs are seen by their people as fundamentally collective creations or products. The chief defines honor for his people just by his holding the status of chief, but his people participate decisively in the successful outcome of all his actions and managed performances.

This complementarity, with an emphasis on the dynamism of the collectivity riveted on the chiefly person, is a theme that runs deep in Polynesian history. But only in the modern era, with the decline of the sacred, is this lopsided complementarity between chief and people, with the accent on the efficacy of the latter, unobscured. Partly as a result of the reporting bias of accounts on which they depend, reconstructionist efforts tend to place undue emphasis on chiefs in the kingly domain, or on the auratic, licentious quality of chiefs who, by excessive displays of personal power, put themselves above and outside normal society. Dramatic and attention-focusing as these chiefly figures of special aura or violent character were, they only defined a part of what chieftainship was about. Particularly as it extended to the base of society, chieftainship was not only a position of local leadership and collective symbolic focus, but also a generally employed idiom for evaluating and controlling common behavior.

As a sliding scale, chieftainship evoked simultaneously both the discontinuity of the stranger-king or the warrior of extraordinary power—alienating himself from common humanity in his rebellion and usurpation—and the continuity of middle-range or routine chieftainship —completely encompassed by evaluations of appropriate behavior in daily, settled life. It is the more routine side of chieftainship rather than chiefly excess (which is outside society and thus defines its limits) that embodies the tension relating the chief simultaneously to title (kingly glory) and to exemplary personhood—a tension that can be explored in the ongoing ethnography of a number of contemporary Polynesian societies.

The obverse and no less important way of considering the popular side of chieftainship is to ask what has become of the sacredness of chiefs in contemporary Polynesian societies. In his recent paper on the sacredness of Tikopia chiefs, Firth (1979) has addressed this question. Although there remain mystified ritual contexts of chiefly participation in the traditional sense, chiefs in Tikopian society have become important symbols of cultural survival. Tikopians now have a pervasive self-consciousness about their place in a much larger and more complex political and economic order. The aristocentric focus of Tikopian culture has become an expression of ethnic identity, a bulwark with which to stabilize the forces of change. Even though they may become skeptical of chiefly authority the Tikopia still find chieftainship very much worth the fiction of mystification. As Firth says:

> The dogged persistence of ascription of *tapu* to their chiefs by the Tikopia, in the face of modern skeptical attitudes, is to my mind part of their struggle to preserve their community through its traditional values. . . . There is threat to Tikopia society—through dispersion into colonies elsewhere in the Solomon Islands, through the disruptive forces of the job market, and through the pressures of external economic and political control. . . . By focusing external recognition of the society on the chiefs as major symbols of Tikopia, and by continuing to endow them with sacredness, the Tikopia have concentrated their survival stakes. If the chiefs go, then Tikopia society goes. . . . So, in effect, the Tikopia impose restrictions upon their chiefs. By keeping them sacred, the Tikopia make it harder for anyone to get rid of them—and for the chiefs themselves to abdicate their responsibility, to slip out of the symbolic role into that of ordinary citizens (Firth 1979:164).

The sacredness of chiefs as a self-consciously preserved orthodoxy that sustains cultural identity, no matter how much assimilation there may be, constitutes a de facto strategy in a number of contemporary

Polynesian societies—especially those similar to Tonga and Samoa—
that have preserved large-scale chiefly hierarchies. Tonga is perhaps
most interesting in this regard. It retains an ancient kingship from
whose auratic source still emanates official hierarchies and standards of
chieftainship, in the shadow of which derivative chiefly statuses abound
among the population. Perhaps nowhere else in contemporary Polynesia does chieftainship pull so strongly in both directions—toward a populist embodiment on the one hand, and an official edifice of kingly glory
on the other.

In Tonga, the sacredness of chiefs has become a popular and self-conscious emblem of Tongan culture sustained in a complex world of
change. It is an important anchor for Tongans as they travel interna-
tionally, go abroad for long periods as migrant workers, and as they
become consumers of Western goods and imitators of Western lifestyles
to an unprecedented degree at home. The king, and those great aristocrats who are the products of strategic dynastic marriages of past generations, oblige by preserving their character as strangers in their own
society. Legitimated by the mystique of bloodline and their special, if
not divine descent, they are alienated from ordinary standards of personhood by virtue of their quasi-divine status.

Few of these great aristocrats, known by their pedigrees rather than
by formal titles, remain alive in Tonga, however, and the present king is
far less concerned with cultivating the auratic side of kingship through
the arranging of marriages than was his mother. Consequently, now
more than ever, Tongans of chiefly status, by title, blood, or some combination of the two, have ambiguous personal orientations to everyday
interactions. They live in a changing society, where a heightened cultural self-consciousness, reinforced by a long-standing populist valuing
of smooth integration into everyday life, has eroded chiefly exemption
from common standards, save for a few great aristocrats.

One might argue that the great aristocrats were like an ethnic group
in an otherwise homogeneous culture. Characteristic of ethnically
marked actors elsewhere, they were distinguished as separate, or even
as alien, beings. Nowadays the aristocrats are more assimilated as persons, but associations with a highly auratic form of surviving kingship
—seen as the domesticated stranger-king of myth—are still present.
Such chiefs, who range so ambivalently between kingly glory through
blood ties and a secular idiom of heroic populism, embody in practice
the latter-day counterpart of mythical stranger-kings.

As a condensation of collective ethnicity, chieftainship also gives specific content to values and personal styles of which Polynesians have
become proud. These include interdependence, service, the honor of
humility, and the willing assumption of obligations and burdens. All of
these are positive orientations to social life that emphasize subordina-

tion, and must therefore be keyed to some higher source of authority (for an interpretation of how status rivalry arises amidst such values, see Marcus 1978b). Although in contemporary life many of these values are expressed in the context of church participation, chiefly positions also define a focus of authority in relation to which Polynesians enact the values of subordination. These values establish specific cultural boundaries in the face of an ever greater penetration of Euro-American worlds.

The question of whether the forms of chieftainship were always so populist, even in the traditionally most stratified societies, or whether they became that way in the course of post-contact history is moot, if only because so little is known about the daily life of commoners from contact accounts. One version of an answer is that Polynesian cultures following contact became more homogenized through the diffusion of chiefly culture as a form of mass culture. As old forms of stratification broke down, chiefs who survived this decline cultivated European lifestyles as new sources of exclusivity and association with the alien, divine-like power of Europeans. But even this stopgap to a decline in sacredness has waned in the twentieth century. Most modern chiefs could not pass as other than persons who are dependent on their people for their positions, and this is clearly recognized by both parties. Chiefly distinctions of prestige have come to be applied flexibly and situationally to mark relative status differentials among ordinary people. Finally, the chiefly ideal of proper behavior has become synonymous with a populist one; it is a way of talking about exemplary personhood that anyone can approximate, but which actual chiefs are supposed to embody.

The other version of an answer to the question about the populist side of chieftainship is that not much has changed at all, that chieftainship as a status attribution was always diffused through the thoroughly hierarchical structures of Polynesian societies (in the image of Louis Dumont's Homo Hierarchicus). Although there may have been elaborate, official, kingly mystification of chieftainship at the top, variants of the same institution were widely shared as popular culture among commoners at the bottom. In this version, the current personhood ethnography merely captures the fundamental populist dimensions of chieftainship that were always there, but tended to be underplayed in reconstructionist efforts.

The truth is somewhere between the two versions, but it seems clear that there never was a purely non-chiefly sector of Polynesian societies. Rather chieftainship, as diffused status categories and as persons with graded chiefly status, pervaded society. How historical transformation from society to society affected the existing situations is an issue that depends in turn on how much the populist side of chieftainship, emphasized in contemporary ethnography, is a register of change and how much it is an artifact from the time when Polynesian societies were not so closely observed.

We can appropriately conclude this section with a brief discussion of how populist and kingly sides of chiefs as persons (special human beings) interact in the two societies of contemporary Polynesia, where society-wide systems of chiefly offices survive most elaborately, and where the sacred (kingly) side of chieftainship is most sharply differentiated: Tonga and Samoa. Such an enterprise fully carried out would show how the theory of chieftainship in Polynesia, retrieved by a structuralist project of reconstruction such as that of Sahlins, can be articulated at the level of social action and negotiation in the everyday life of contemporary Polynesia, and with careful qualification and extrapolation, in Polynesia at the time of early contact.

The Chief's Two Bodies in Tonga and Samoa

The observation of contexts, in which persons who hold chiefly status by whatever criteria try to integrate themselves into the flow of routine and ceremonial social occasions, would offer a set of loci to study the expression in social action of the kingly-populist dimensions of chieftainship. I have characterized such contexts in terms of the social drama of role distance, a concept borrowed from Erving Goffman, which conveys the dual social identities of contemporary Polynesian chiefs that operate simultaneously in any situation (Marcus 1980b).[3] From a Euro-American perspective, a reserved, dignified orientation to the public exposure of self is characteristic of Polynesians (see Levy 1973), but biographically, specific persons in community contexts are expected to be thoroughly known and predictable beings, whose integration into social life is to be immediate, natural, and trouble-free. Most of what constitutes the social control dimensions of everyday discourse concerns an evaluation of the social competency of specific others, with a well-developed vocabulary of critique for the awkward.

Easy integration into social relations as normal persons is usually problematic for chiefs, because they are among the few specialized role-players and are thus always to some degree strangers in their own society. Great aristocrats by title and/or blood descent, who are recognized as such society-wide, are walking context-markers, separated from society, and are only like ordinary persons within a narrow, close, circle of kin. Most other chiefs also passively define contexts in which they move, reorienting the behavior of others present in a weaker version of the context-defining function inherent in great aristocrats. Yet, without mystified personhood, they must situationally stand apart from their chiefliness and be accepted as persons among their constituencies.

Their status is thus dualistic and always ambiguous. It must be negotiated situationally and depends on a trade-off between recognition of
the chief's identity within the official system of chiefly status attribution
and his standing as an exemplary and powerful person among the particular collectivities who see themselves as the source of a chief's capacity to be effective or powerful. How persons acquire chiefly status or
office; what strategies of self-presentation they use, given the predicament of their simultaneously alienated and domesticated selves; and
how possessing chiefly status maps onto the culturally constructed
phases of life of any person, are all important questions for developing
fully this line of micro-focused ethnographic research on contemporary
chiefs within the personhood framework (see Brenneis and Myers 1984;
Duranti 1981a).

With its kingship intact, Tonga has perhaps a classic chiefly system in
which principles of sacred embodiment by descent from rarefied ancestors are at the heart of chiefly status attribution, with mere title-holding
marking ordinary chieftainship. Titles are an ornament for blood aristocrats, but they are the core of chiefly status for those who by blood and
substance are ordinary persons. Moreover, the distribution of recognized chiefly status is tightly controlled from above, although there are
shadowy, officially unrecognized, claims to chiefly status among the
population at-large. These folk attributions of chiefly status escaped
assimilation or eradication in the powerful centralization of the Tongan
polity by the founder of the present Tupou dynasty during the late nineteenth century.

In its surviving chiefly structure, Tonga is thus much more the land
of the stranger-king than the populist hero. Consequently, most chiefs
who as persons cannot relate to one of the aristocratic bloodlines, or
only do so distantly or ambiguously, have a difficult experience in the
continuing social drama of role distance. Different outcomes of this process are possible from chief to chief, and a chiefly structure that appears
tightly controlled and defined from the top turns out to be highly contingent in the negotiation of ambiguities at the bottom. Chiefs prove themselves to be more or less persons, more or less strangers among the people of their estates, over whom they have legally very restricted
prerogatives and privileges. What they can in fact realize substantively
from their titles depends on their ability to distance themselves from
their formal chiefly roles on some occasions, while fulfilling their roles
as representatives of their people on others (especially in ceremonials
that celebrate kingship).

The less a chief confronts his people face-to-face on non-ritual occasions, the better it is for his self-esteem. Relations over time are more
comfortably mediated by the institution of the *matāpule,* who are ceremonial attendants appointed by titleholders from among their estate

populations to represent and speak for them on ritual occasions, and to serve as general go-betweens. In contrast to their Samoan counterpart, the *tulāfale, matāpule* traditionally and at present have not been major political figures, and do not derive considerable independent power from their intermediary roles. Rather, they have played fully subordinated political roles. This is primarily because the chiefly system in Tonga has been based on the hegemony of great aristocrats and the control of chiefly status attribution from above.

The Tupou centralization of Tonga was just the last and most successful of recurrent centralizing efforts by high chiefs. Thus even ordinary chiefs in Tonga, dependent on title-holding in the centralized official system for their status, are ill at ease in their populist environments as they try to fit in as persons. However, they are able to make use of their titles as resources in the urban environment of the Tongan capital and in wealthy overseas Tongan communities, they are alienated by degrees from everyday life as ordinary chiefs, and in the few cases of great aristocrats, they are alienated as stranger-king facsimiles.

In Samoa, by contrast, chieftainship permeates the grass-roots of the society in the form of the *matai* system. As an institution, it rises up hierarchically into an arena of uncertain kingship at the top. In place of a kingly office is a group of paramount titles established by historical political struggles inherent in the *matai* system. Although genealogical priority is certainly part of Samoan chieftainship, particularly in the process of evaluating individuals for succession to titles, succession to *matai* titles is fundamentally populist and elective, and title-holding takes precedence over blood descent as the defining criterion of chiefly status. Thus Samoa is more a land of the populist hero than of the stranger-king. Chiefs at all levels are the products of their constituencies from whom their authority derives. Less mediators than power-brokers in this chiefly system, *tulāfale*, unlike Tongan *matāpule*, often have been the major political actors, overshadowing the *ali'i* they formally serve.

Samoan chiefs variantly do have personal aura and do experience alienation from their *'aiga,* but they are persons first, and accountable as such. The characterizations of chiefs in the novels of Albert Wendt, and particularly that of the old *matai,* a Lear-like figure, in *Pouliuli* (1977), portray better than any contemporary ethnography the Samoan version of the kingly/populist bind that defines the experience of chiefs as persons. Wendt's old *matai* experiences a traumatic sense of role distance as the novel opens.

> Early on a drizzly Saturday morning Faleasa Osovae—the seventy-six-year-old titled head of the Aiga Faleasa, faithful husband of a devoted Felefele, stern but generous father of seven sons and five obedient daughters, and the most respected alii in the village of Malaelua—woke with a strange bitter

taste in his mouth to find, as he looked out to the rain and his village, and then at his wife snoring softly beside him in the mosquito net, and the rest of his aiga (about sixty bodies wrapped in sleeping sheets) who filled the spacious fale, that everything and everybody that he was used to and had enjoyed, and that till then had given meaning to his existence, now filled him with an almost unbearable feeling of revulsion—yes, that was the only word for it, revulsion. He despised everything he had been, had become, had achieved (Wendt 1977:1).

In viewing the psychocultural integration of chiefs as persons into contemporary Polynesian life, Fiji, for example, is more like Tonga, Tikopia more like Samoa, and some family of resemblances could be established for all Polynesian societies where chieftainship as a personal status survives with some salience. Assessing the way in which the idea of the sacred persists in the definition of chieftainship and framing this issue in the context of the ethnography of personhood, would be a productive way to proceed with ongoing fieldwork projects that focus on chiefs in contemporary settings. What is missing and is essential, however, is some macroscopic understanding of the institutional existence of such chiefly structures as part of the political economy of development and dependency in late-twentieth-century Polynesian societies.

Chieftainship in Contemporary Political Economy: Submerged Aristocracies and Ossified Hierarchies

The role of chieftainship in contemporary Polynesian societies is puzzling: it persists as an institution of political economy even though much of the transformation of twentieth-century Polynesian societies has challenged chieftainships on all levels. This I term the neo-Hocartian question, because it relates to the central emphasis Hocart (1927) gave to symbolic aspects of kingship in the evolution of contemporary forms of government. Especially in the late twentieth century, alternative paths for mass socioeconomic mobility have grown up rapidly around ossified chiefly hierarchies, which still involve the repetitive production of ceremonial events that costs the general population much in services, goods, and cash, but to which they apparently remain committed nonetheless. There are now constant international flows of population to and from the islands. Education, and particularly overseas education, is subversive to chiefly systems. Yet in Tonga, Fiji, and Samoa popular commitment to chiefly establishments remains strong, however much grumbling and complaining in sotto voce about the excessive cost of chieftainship one can hear in these societies. This attitude to chieftainship can also be observed to varying degrees in other societies where it persists less elaborately (such as the Cooks, Tikopia, Tahiti, the Marquesas, and the Tokelaus, among others).

It would be naive to think that some of the old aura of chiefs does not survive in Polynesia, but it would be equally naive to depend too much upon the mystified character of chiefs and chiefly prestige to explain their secure, but not unchallenged, hold on contemporary populations. For example, Shore provides an excellent, sensitive discussion of the fate of the *mana* concept in contemporary Samoa (1982:248–249; see also Shore, chapter 5, this volume) as it has shifted from an attribute of sacred, passive power associated with the *ali'i* to an attribute of God. The sacred/secular split in chieftainship, one institutional expression of which is the division of labor between *ali'i* and *tulāfale* in Samoa (and *'eiki* and *matāpule* in Tonga), has shifted in favor of the secular, active form of power, with some residual, often vague connotations of embodied, passive power.

In essence, then, chieftainship has been considerably demystified for the knowing populations of contemporary Polynesia, who nonetheless consistently obey their chiefs, share in chiefly status, and accept extraordinary obligations of expenditure in chiefly orchestrated rituals. This they do even though very little flows down the hierarchy in redistribution relative to what moves up (contrary to conclusions drawn by anthropologists from accounts of precontact life). Since chieftainship was and remains a thoroughly grass-roots phenomenon in Samoa, its persistence there is less of a puzzle than in Tonga and Fiji, where in the political consolidation of these states, the already predominant stranger-king character of chieftainship became even more amplified. By no means is chieftainship an egalitarian institution in Samoa, but it involves mass participation in the competition for chiefly office at every level of *fono* organization (see Duranti 1981a). This is not the case in Tonga with its centrally controlled establishment of specially privileged nobles, which only selectively recognizes claims to chiefly status that surface among the population.

In Tonga, Fiji, and Samoa, the strength of the official establishment is manifested in the occasional mobilization of large segments of the population, or the entire population, to celebrate chieftainship. Such events, replicated on a smaller but more frequent scale throughout the society, require extravagant contributions from people at a time when they are pulled by other institutions, particularly local churches, for their participation and service. Under circumstances of demystifying, secularizing change, the notion that the everyday politics and economics of Polynesians are underlain by a vision of society, symbolized in chiefly rituals, is certainly inadequate to explain these activities. Yet, one can still hold that a neo-Hocartian questioning of the survival of elaborate chieftainship (and in Tonga, of kingship) is an interesting way to begin an investigation of modern political economy in Polynesia.

The background and baseline for investigating contemporary chieftainship is the recent spate of very sophisticated studies on early contact (for examples see Dening 1980 and Sahlins 1981a), and the excellent literature on Pacific history, particularly concerning the colonial period of the late nineteenth and early twentieth centuries (for example, France 1969; Lātūkefu 1974; Kuykendall 1938, 1953, 1967; Newbury 1980; and Rutherford 1971). The latter literature is especially important for the study of contemporary Polynesia because it concerns the formation of what I have called (for Tonga) compromise cultures. By this term I refer to the first long-term adjustments of Polynesian cultures to Euro-American contact, in which Polynesian versions of Western institutions were created and older institutions and customs were censored, reorganized, and retraditionalized. These compromise cultures—earlier Polynesian versions of Western culture—now represent, in indigenous perception, the traditions being subjected to rapid change.

In its treatment of chieftainship, the historical literature has had the virtue of not mystifying chiefs, treating them instead as historical actors in events, essentially like European actors. Unlike the anthropological literature, historical accounts provide a detailed and forthright view of chiefs as individuals and personalities (see the portraits in Davidson and Scarr 1970). But this virtue is also a flaw in that the historical literature is not sufficiently sensitive to the distinctively indigenous worlds inhabited by these chiefly personalities. Although focusing on indigenous actions and interests, this is still history from the European point of view. Because of the subtle ways in which Polynesian cultural distinctiveness has survived, however, historians cannot be too severely charged with neglect.

For Tonga, Fiji, and Samoa, the three societies in which chieftainship survives most elaborately, the key issues are to define ethnographically the operation of status attribution systems and to state their significance for political economy. The ethnographer observes status attribution systems as a set of practices in relation to institutional frameworks, and wants answers to the following questions: Who holds chiefly status? How is it acquired, asserted situationally, passed on, and lost? What does chiefly status mean instrumentally and symbolically for those who possess it and for those who control its definition and conferral? The latter question, as will be seen, is the critical one for discussing chieftainship as an issue of contemporary political economy.

Modern Polynesian sociopolitical entities came into being with the introduction of Western-modeled state organization and church organizations that either replaced chiefly functions or share their popular allegiance. Economically, modernity has involved the transformation of island populations into small-holding peasantries tied to restricted commercial market sectors (e.g., see Marcus 1978a). Chiefly structures survived in the midst of these new institutions as official hierarchies with

well-defined status positions, but also with unofficial, only partially controlled, status distinctions and associations in their shadow.

The official hierarchies have a mass social expression in the periodic
performance of ritual events, which, as noted, require great expenditure of effort and material resources by large segments of the population. The timing and scale of these events evolved as a function of the
politics that shaped compromise-culture traditions and conventions.
More ambiguous are the residual claims to chiefly status floating among
the population outside the official systems. They are derived partly
from indirect associations with those holding chiefly status in the official
systems, but they are also a reaction to leftover commitments to chiefly
office that have officially disappeared, yet are remembered in local traditions. These are the loose ends of consolidation processes that defined
new orders in these societies, which were built on the freezing or restriction of active chiefly politics and culture. The apparent purpose of surviving chiefly establishments is to attribute authoritative chiefly status
among the population and to celebrate a culture of chieftainship according to stabilized compromise-culture visions of society. Both the motivation for and consequences of investing in such chiefly systems in
contemporary Polynesian societies are complex issues raised by the neo-
Hocartian question.

It is indeed worth thinking of such systems of chiefly status attribution as the modern form of the kingly/populist tension, rooted in the
mystical conception of Polynesian chieftainship. The official system
emanates from and celebrates kingship (in the case of Tonga) or kingly
ideas (in the case of Fiji and Samoa), whereas the shadow system of
chiefly status attribution—what I have called submerged aristocracy—
is the de facto populist side of surviving chiefly culture. The critical
issue is how the official kingly system articulates with the submerged,
populist one. As discussed in the last section, one important manifestation of this articulation is the chief's two bodies, how the personality of
any particular chief is negotiated biographically and situationally in
contemporary society. The other important issue of articulation is that
of political economy, which concerns a competition for control of prestige valuation over things and people against the background of changes
brought about by processes of urbanization, migration, and the increasing commercialization of exchange relationships. Being challenged is
not so much the value of chiefly status as the authority of the official system to monopolize its recognition and conferral.

Among competing systems of status attribution (through education,
church participation, and business enterprise), the chiefly system still
remains hegemonic. This is manifested by willing investment at the village level in chiefly events and by the fact that, except for those few who
opt out of an interest in chiefly status altogether, a claim to status in any

arena usually is enhanced by a claim to chiefly status. In Samoa, acquiring a *matai* title is a requisite basis of status achieved by any other means. In Tonga, a successful man, in a much more complex way, usually acquires a chiefly association that whatever its origin becomes recognized officially, popularly, or both. Nevertheless, the prominence of chiefly systems of status attribution over alternative criteria, which was clearly the case in ancient Polynesia (see Goldman 1970) and during the compromise-culture periods, was never so fragile as it is now. A major task of contemporary fieldwork is to judge how far this prominence has in fact been eroded from society to society.

Much depends on perceptions of the ways in which managers and members put the official chiefly system to political use. Some uses are seen as quite legitimate expressions of power, others as unjust. From a Western perspective, there is an immense tolerance of privilege abuse by subordinates of particular chiefly figures or chiefly establishments in Polynesian societies. But what constitutes excess in Polynesian terms? In Polynesia, there is always an undomesticated dimension to power which when wielded is recognized as abusive, but is nonetheless tolerable. The weakening of chieftainship by the promotion of restricted official chiefly systems of legal privilege has undoubtedly reduced the tolerable limits of chiefly excess in modern Polynesia, especially now that many chiefs within official systems have lost their personal aura. This, added to a diminished hold of chiefly establishments over channels of elite formation in their societies, has resulted in a general lessening of popular forbearance of chiefly power abuse, despite the enhanced symbolic significance of these establishments in cultural survival (see Marcus 1981 for a discussion of Tongan elite formation against a background of global political economy).

I will illustrate this general perspective on the contemporary political economy of chiefly culture with a discussion of Tonga, where kingship survives in an overt form. Before so doing, it is worth presenting a portrait of how Tonga compares with its neighbors Fiji and Samoa in the adaptation of chiefly structures to Western-modeled state organizations and social strata.

Contemporary Tonga is a monarchy in which the king rules as well as reigns under a constitution, with a parliament consisting of nobles' representatives and people's representatives (see Marcus 1980a). The new dynasty selected a group of noble titles from among the array of pre-Tupou chiefly distinctions, and made it the core of a societal chiefly establishment emanating from the kingship. Each hereditary noble owns estates, although there are legal restrictions on his control over land tenure and estate populations. At the village level, a folk culture rich in chiefly associations has remained, but it is only partially and selectively recognized by the official chiefly establishment. Thus, Tonga is a case of extreme consolidation and centralization, under indigenous direction, superimposed from the top on the mass of society. This left unrecognized loose ends that have nonetheless been important as sources of local reputation to Tongans as they have moved through alternative channels of mobility available to them: education, church participation, government service, and to a lesser extent, business.

Fiji preserved strong concepts of chieftainship at both the top and bottom of society. Yet, though chiefly rituals occur frequently at all levels of society, the instrumental functions of chieftainship are covertly exercised through the holding of positions in the state apparatus. There is a much clearer official articulation of chieftainship from top to bottom of society than in Tonga, largely because of the self-conscious reinvention of the indigenous system, not by indigenous rules but by colonial overseers. Although this move may have clarified land tenure claims for administrative purposes in the new order (see France 1969), it left an official system (much more diffused throughout the society than in Tonga) along with a submerged body of folk chiefly distinctions (see Walter 1978b).

Without an overt kingship, Fiji nonetheless has a much more pervasive and lively chiefly system than does Tonga, ironically because of the penetration of a European-designed, lineage-based administrative structure with regular positions for chiefs that, over time, has shaped indigenous opinion about what is traditional. Also, the plural nature of Fijian society and the quite explicit atmosphere of ethnic politics cannot be underestimated as factors accounting for the greater vitality of chieftainship, top to bottom, in Fiji than in Tonga. Cultural boundary maintenance is thus an immediate concern among Fijians for whom, as elsewhere, the chief is a central figure.

In Samoa, chieftainship in the form of the *matai* system builds in strength from the bottom to a more amorphous factionalism among high chiefs at the top. This factionalism has been contained in the modern period by the orderly sharing of power among great chiefs in the administration of government. As in Fiji, the chiefly system in Samoa permeates the society and is thinly masked by the institution of Western political economy. Unlike Fiji or Tonga, the strength of Samoa's chiefly system is foremost in its populism—the embeddedness of chiefly status and office in basic units of social organization—and in the fact that it never underwent directed change, either by colonial overseers (as in Fiji) or by indigenous rulers (as in Tonga). Although certainly not completely unchanged in its character, the *matai* system has a certain continuity and authenticity that the surviving chiefly official systems in Tonga and Fiji lack.

Nonetheless, there is an official chiefly hierarchy at work in Samoa (see Keesing and Keesing 1956), with ramifying unofficial associations and claims to status deriving from it. Its central social arena, particularly visible to the public and accessible to foreign researchers, is the Land and Titles Court. This creates the same kind of kingly/official-submerged/populist tension as in the chiefly systems of the other two societies, except that the decidedly populist official system in Samoa perhaps has a more solid legitimacy to it, relative to possible submerged challenges.

Chiefly Status Attribution in Contemporary Tonga

From the perspective of kingship and modern statecraft, the persistence of a superimposed, society-wide chiefly establishment serves a number of practical purposes. It has functioned for monarchs and their advisors like a systems framework has for the Western bureaucratic state and corporation. The system gives the rulers a holistic grasp, or operating model, of their domain. Exclusive knowledge, and particularly special genealogical knowledge, has always been a source of chiefly power in Polynesia. In the transformation of Tongan society an even greater premium was placed on those who continued to cultivate it. Although genealogical knowledge has been quite variably preserved among the contemporary population, it was cultivated and comprehensively developed, in line with the dynasty's version of history, by Queen Sālote (Tupou III) during her long reign (1918–1965). She selected particular nobles for training in traditions and genealogy. Placing all persons and groups in a grid of historic chiefly genealogies, as well as monitoring the assignment of clergy in Tongan churches to congregations throughout the Kingdom, enabled Sālote to identify all of her subjects (a population of about 40,000 by the middle of her reign). She was in fact famous for this capacity and astounded her subjects by her intimate personal knowledge of them.

Sālote's reign is now generally seen in retrospect as a sort of cultural golden age. Strictly limiting outside influences through British protection, the queen relied on the two distinct organizations of mass participation in the new order—the largely elitist chiefly system and the largely populist churches—to personalize her relationship with her subjects.[4] Clearly seen as a great aristocrat and a special being by Tongans, she appealed directly to the underdeveloped populist side of her office, which, because of her ability to know everyone, ironically increased the awe in which she was held.

Sālote also cultivated a politics of kinship and arranged marriages through which she upgraded the status of selected titleholders by linking them to the royal line or one of its collaterals. During her reign there still survived several great aristocrats, the products of strategic unions of past generations. As contemporary, absolute measures of aura or kingly glory, they were standards by which any person's path of prestigious descent could be compared. Thus, under Sālote, the official chiefly system reached a pinnacle of mystification during recent times.

In the period since the succession of her son, Tupou IV, in 1965, the official chiefly establishment has lost much of this aura. Tupou IV has been a modernizer, opening Tonga to diffuse influences of the world economy. Although the genealogical map has also served him as a sort of systems model of his realm, he has shown little enthusiasm for the politics of kinship as it relates to the maintenance of the chiefly establishment.

In addition to providing a cognitive aid to rule, the official system constitutes an organization that is mobilized on regular occasions to celebrate and legitimate the kingship. Like *Negara* in Bali, lesser versions of kingly rituals are practiced by and for nobles among their own constituencies. Funerals, feasts, and kava drinking ceremonies compose the cultural repertoire for such celebrations when nobles visit their estates or are visited by their people. In turn, nobles occupy ritual offices around which the population is mobilized on a regional or societal scale to perform ceremonies focused on the king. Royal births, deaths, and coronations are all occasions for this mobilization of the official chiefly establishment. More routinely, the king makes an annual tour of his realm, when, region by region, elaborate homage is paid him. In the tradition of his mother and the ancient kings, he establishes a personal rapport with his people and takes the opportunity during these tours to settle disputes that may have arisen within the official chiefly system.

The official chiefly system is also useful as a deflection of social criticism for which the king might otherwise be the target at a time of rising expectations and social consciousness among the population. The nobility is an exposed status group of formal privilege from whom the present monarch, a modernizer, has distanced himself, though without repudiating them as an institution. The popular evaluation of the king and his nobles is thus not synonymous, the latter being more than ever exposed as ordinary persons behind their titles. The nobles are highly vulnerable to criticism from a population that is moving away from the old compromise-culture adaptations of which the official chiefly system was a part. They are dependent on the king for their chiefly legitimacy, but the king is by no means as dependent on them, because there is still an auratic, stranger-king character to his person.

Finally, the official chiefly establishment can be seen as a tightly controlled status attribution system, which in turn controls recognition of claims to chiefly status. Aside from the control of the apparatus of government, this is the most subtle form of power held by the Tupou monarchs, exercised, as noted, with much more interest formerly than at present.[5] This function of the official chiefly system derives precisely from conventions limiting the self-expression or display of being chiefly. To glorify or assert one's own status as a chief is extremely bad form in Tonga (as well as in several other Polynesian societies), and is only tolerated without ridicule by those who are unambiguously and manifestly aristocrats by their known blood descent. For all others, in the preferred humble style of honor, one's chiefliness must be recognized rather than self-proclaimed. The highest form of chieftainship is essentially passive, embodied power that requires a kind of division of labor for its social construction. Thus in Tonga, Fiji, and Samoa, ceremonial attendants are key figures who represent the active side of chiefly power. Thus, also, the common notion exists in Polynesia that chiefs depend on their people, that the latter are essential complements to the chief and are the real actors. For middle-range chiefs with titles or for those with more ambiguous claims to chiefliness outside the official system, there is a total dependence on a recognition of their status, usually from above, but also on occasion from below. The latter constitutes a populist recognition independent of the official system, about which those in the official system tend to be very sensitive.

In Tonga, with its still sacralized kingship, the official chiefly establishment maintains a virtual monopoly on such recognition. Any explicit, independently motivated recognition of chiefly status approaches subversion, alluding to a chiefly world before the Tupou consolidation. When very occasionally there is a popular recognition of someone's status, without a preceding official one, the kingly establishment is clearly uneasy. Most often, no matter how valid any idiosyncratic claim to chiefly status may appear by genealogical argument, any attempt to assert it without appeal to official recognition (on a ceremonial occasion, by king or noble) is apt to be ridiculed as playing uppity.

The mass of putative commoners in contemporary Tonga remain remarkably committed to this chiefly attribution system rather than defect from it. This is not because of coercion; the kingship influences, but does not dominate, the contemporary diverse channels of mobility. In fact, its control of the population is severely challenged by centrifugal forces such as migration. Nor is chiefly culture so vital to cultural survival, as it was in the past formation of Tonga's compromise culture. Rather, the creation of the official chiefly system has left most latter-day Tongans with unresolved, but compelling personal affiliations to chiefly status, in both present definition and collective historical memory. This situation has created the variegated, ambiguous folk system of submerged aristocracy that exists in the shadow of the official chiefly establishment.

Submerged claims to chiefly status among the populace take several forms. The most sensitive for the official chiefly establishment, and especially for the kingship, are those based on descent from the now-defunct sacred Tu'i Tonga kingship, once the pinnacle and source of kingly glory in Tonga. Major Tu'i Tonga genealogical connections were absorbed by the present Tupou dynasty, which originated in a line of high chiefs, collateral to the Tu'i Tonga line. Remembered associations of particular individuals and groups with the Tu'i Tonga, kept alive in local traditions, and deviant from the genealogical interpretation of the Tupous, are one potentially powerful source of challenge to the kingship. Then there are those persons, putative commoners, who clearly descend from lines that held chiefly positions in the pre-Tupou period, but who were excluded from the official noble establishment, for whatever reasons. These are known as 'eiki si'i 'petty chiefs' in contemporary Tonga, but sentiments of lost status are expressed occasionally in local talk. For example, X would be a noble today if only he had been included in the official system, or X would be a particular noble today if only, by accident, some junior line had not been holding the office when it was selected by the Tupous for ennoblement. Finally, there are persons who bask in the light of someone else's title-holding, and who enjoy informal associations with chiefly status without its responsibilities or official recognition.

These kinds of association actually account for real or potential chiefly status claims among a great number of commoner families in contemporary Tonga. Whether or not they get recognized is one of the key issues for fieldwork investigations of surviving chieftainship in Tonga. It is this sense of possessing valid claims to chiefly status despite being left out of the official system that keeps interest alive in chieftainship on a mass basis in Tonga—a kind of "every man a chief" populism.

Interestingly, each of these forms of unofficial, unrecognized, and subtly articulated forms of chiefly status reflects the well-established priority of the criterion of blood or substance over title in the attribution of chiefly status. This translates into a preferred style of embodying chiefly status rather than holding it as an office. It constitutes, at the same time, an ambivalent expression of resentment about status decline in the new order, an implicit challenge to the consolidation that the Tupou dynasty brought about, and a popular sharing in chiefly honor as the bulwark of collective Tongan identity in change.

Particularly in the case of the historic Tu'i Tonga affiliations, demonstrable disdain for title-holding while having one's chiefly "being" known (that is, prominently gossiped about) by others is a way that many Tongans hope to share in chiefly status. Thus the official, kingly side of chieftainship glides into the unofficial, populist side, which retains its credibility precisely because historically a higher place has been given to passive, unmarked embodiments of chieftainship than to its active, self-proclaiming expression. The widespread appropriation of the loose ends of chieftainship outside official kingly glory—the phenomenon of submerged aristocracy—remains one of the most subtle and ironic populist expressions of chieftainship in contemporary Tonga.

I would argue that wherever chieftainship has survived institutionally in contemporary Polynesia, some version of the Tongan situation holds: a streamlining or freezing of official chiefly statuses has left a residue of chiefly identifications among the population, who, as they maintain their cultural identity in an impinging Euro-American world by generalizing the virtues of chiefs, try to sort out their own chiefly status affiliations. Tonga is perhaps only the most politically interesting version of this more general survival of chieftainship.

For ethnographic research specifically on chieftainship in contemporary Polynesia (as noted, such focused research has been rare), the main innovative task is to examine the practices by which chiefly status gets attributed contextually and over time. Only in this way can ethnographers distinguish official and folk versions of a chiefly system, how they articulate, and what they mean in the now rapidly changing institutions of the compromise-culture periods of Polynesian societies.

"Falling Low:" Status Degradation as a Reverse Image

The larger social process that contextualizes specific events is that of status rivalry, which as the substance of chiefly relations has been emblematic of Polynesian culture in both past and present Western accounts. Nowadays, status rivalry spills over into all arenas of hierarchy in Polynesian life. The specifically Polynesian cultural marking of this activity is not so much on social climbing or status acquisition, as on conserving status against a long-term or dramatic decline (see Marcus 1978b).

In the West, the image of status rivalry is often weighted toward the winning rather than the losing of status. Although this can also be a way to look at status rivalry in Polynesia, it misses the distinctive themes of humility as honor, the psychocultural restraint on the expression of anger and aggression, and the importance of interdependence. It also fails to appreciate the conception of lower status as a desirable, if not the desirable position in a hierarchy, where the highest position is often one of context-making passivity that would be immobilizing to political actors. In an important recent paper interpreting the symbolism of Hawaiian religious images, Kaeppler (1982) suggests that the aim of status rivalry, and particularly, warfare—its major earlier medium—was not so much to kill the opponent as to humiliate him. Degradation as the satisfying end to competition, or immobilizing one's opponent, leaving him so low as to be without social virtue while leaving oneself in place with freedom of action preserved, seems to be the emphasis in status rivalry. In modern Tongan society, status games still seem weighted toward achieving someone else's decline of status or salvaging one's own status on the slide downward (noble succession disputes are an exemplary arena for illustrating the peculiarly Tongan tone of such status rivalry; see Marcus 1977). This emphasis on a politics of status decline may be a function of the limits placed on active chiefly politics in the new order, but it seems to have older roots.

So, in research on contemporary status attribution systems, the accent on losers rather than winners, on securing status in the shadow of someone else's glory or authority, on aggressively asserting pride in humility, and on suffering nobly are all suggestions about what to look for stylistically in Polynesian status rivalry. Now as before, chieftainship is about status rivalry, but it is by no means transparent as simply agonistic behavior.

Directions

Recent advances in the study of chieftainship within the frame of the reconstructionist project demonstrate that research progresses in Polynesian ethnology by fresh rememberings of past perspectives forgotten. Their redemption is stimulated by changing theoretical undercurrents that more generally affect anthropology. It is probably true that in the project of reconstruction, there is nothing new to be said in an absolute sense; there is only the innovative and more sophisticated reinterpretation of materials in the face of dominant, but exhausted avenues of inquiry. Sahlins' structuralist assessment of Polynesian texts, after his conversion from functionalist practice, is such a case. The result is a contemporary framework for synthesizing reconstructionist efforts that proceeds by radically juxtaposing examples to support certain broad themes, thus stimulating integrative efforts by researchers of particular island groups, who revise or challenge the emerging synthesis.

An essential test of textual analysis is the adequacy with which it can be meshed with the analysis of historical events, at least up to and including the period of early contact with Euro-American worlds. Sahlins' recent Hawaiian essay (1981a) is a promising move in this direction that could be profitably explored in every other Polynesian group.

A greater research challenge is to make sense of chieftainship in the contemporary social and political orders of Polynesia. Although I have noted and emphasized continuities, this enterprise should operate on a very deliberate premise of radical breaks with the past so as not to feed facile assumptions concerning the persistence of cultural forms.[6] I have done so by drawing attention to research issues concerning personhood on the one hand and political economy on the other.

At stake here is a synthesis of contemporary Polynesian societies that would depend heavily on excellent historical work as well as on ongoing ethnography, and would be sensitive to the existence of compromise cultures and their rapid transformations in modern Polynesia. Such ethnography would focus on a cultural analysis of the person as a means of describing distinctively Polynesian institutions and ideologies, and on modern versions of (mostly self-conscious) traditional complexes based on chieftainship and status attribution systems. The latter are indigenously regulated mechanisms for interpreting and accommodating change in a post-colonial world order. Self-consciously traditional matters in Polynesia are as contemporary as migration, urbanization, and commercial markets; they are most appropriately viewed as parts of the same sociocultural whole.

What I am referring to might be called the emerging modernist synthesis in Polynesian ethnology (combining compromise culture and political economy of development themes), which parallels, interweaves with, but for its own vitality, is a separate project from the reconstructionist one. Just as concerns with chieftainship have been at the heart of the latter, so they continue to be central to the former. Chieftainship may eventually be displaced as a synecdoche for Polynesia in the modernist project. But puzzling about the form, content, and diverse local meanings of chieftainship in societies where it remains unambiguously salient is as indispensable a focus for the modernist project as it has always been for the reconstructionist one.

NOTES

I am deeply grateful for the very intelligent readings of a first draft of this chapter by the editors, Rob Borofsky and Alan Howard, as well as by Aletta Biersack, John Kirkpatrick, Michael M. J. Fischer, and Jim Wooten. I, of course, remain solely responsible for this final version.

1. In an important paper, Douglas (1979) attempts just this sort of synthesis in outline. Unlike mine, her perspective is social structural, deals with sociological categories of ascribed/achieved status, and seems to be oriented toward extending and interrelating early Sahlins' ecological focus and Goldman's status rivalry motif with leadership in the Pacific. The difficulty with a sociological synthesis is that, for the sake of a systematic frame on which to map similarities and differences, it elides cultural distinctions and more sensitive comparisons. Finally, it is interesting to note that because of the way in which the issue was influentially framed by Sahlins, much more explicit attention has been paid to the chief/leadership question in Melanesia than in Polynesia. Thus, ironically, there is a much larger focused literature on chiefs for Melanesia than for Polynesia. In Sahlins' formulation, the chief was the unquestionably salient institution in Polynesia, but in Melanesia, the big man was less than a chief.

There was thus an active debate about the distinction between big man and chief in Melanesia—the usual ethnographic debate over the fuzziness of analytic categories when imposed on reality. This chapter is a further twist on such qualifications, since it suggests finally the integral presence of the big man–like criterion for chieftainship in Polynesia, in cases where chiefs are more populist than kingly. This does not diminish the importance of the distinction, but it does encourage viewing the phenomenon of chieftainship in a broader conceptual and areal way, as well as encourages a more focused literature on chiefs for Polynesia (as already exists for Melanesia).

2. The current interest in personhood is not limited to Polynesia, or to Oceania for that matter. In fashion more globally, it seems to be one means, among others, of redeeming the culturally distinctive subject of ethnography in a world more thoroughly penetrated by superficially homogeneous styles of modernity, which have originated historically in the West. Within Oceanic ethnography, the study of the person grades easily into well-established concerns with systems of exchange and gender relations. This suggests a kind of synthesis, different from the reconstructionist one, which would encompass societies in all three of the traditional ethnographic areas of Oceania—Micronesia, Melanesia, and Polynesia. It would depend primarily on the modern fieldwork enterprise and would focus on the intersections of interests in gender, exchange, and personhood (see especially White and Kirkpatrick 1985). Chieftainship would be relevant to such an ambitious areal synthesis, but it would by no means be as central a concern as it is in any variety of specifically Polynesian area syntheses.

3. My reference to the chief's two bodies is to Ernst Kantorowicz's classic study of medieval European kingship (1957), which has been influential in both recent structuralist reconstruction (cited by Sahlins 1981b, amid multiple references linking Polynesian kingship to a more global context) and contemporary ethnographic analyses of chiefs (Shore 1982). The two body idea (king as mystified symbol and king as person) and the legal/political problems this posed in the medieval world capture approximately the kingly/populist tension at the heart of the emerging interpretation of Polynesian chieftainship in both the reconstructionist and ongoing ethnographic projects.

4. In the use by the monarch of a genealogical grid for statecraft, and in the emphasis on a personal relationship between king and every subject, Tonga bears interesting comparison with modern Saudi Arabia. There, following the consolidation of the kingdom, the ramifying princely lineages of the House of Saud became the infrastructure of effective political control (the princes number in the thousands) as well as a cognitive map of his realm for the king. The late King Faisal, like Queen Sālote, was also known for his face-to-face meetings with his subjects and for his uncanny ability to identify them.

5. The modern sultanate of Brunei is a monarchical state, similar to Tonga, in that it makes various political uses of an official system of honors. In Brunei, however, the system of honors expands and becomes more baroque. Considerable public funds are spent annually on decorations, and there is a very complex set of distinctions of noble rank by which the regime can enhance a person's status. The chiefly system in Tonga is, by contrast, spare. It was built on the salvaging of a very few titles from the decline of the chiefly order, and few have

been added since. Moreover, except for the royal family, there are few emblems of office or status, such as decorations or uniforms. Aside from the historic choice by the ruling dynasty to restrict the chiefly system, the relative modesty of Tongan chieftainship follows from traditional styles of holding chiefly status: the priority of blood over title and of passive over active expression of chiefly status. The signs of chieftainship are never self-proclaimed, but are, as noted, expressed in the recognition by others, from the kingly source above, or from the populist source of one's constituency below. "Disdaining the title" is the pose of Tongan aristocrats that makes status recognition a much more subtle game in Tonga than in monarchical states such as Brunei, which invest in elaborate, visible, if not ostentatious, systems of status recognition.

6. For example, it is tempting to see the figure of the traditional chief in the local leaders of church and government organization in the postcontact period, rather than to presume that the surviving vitality of chieftainship resides in the ossified frameworks of rituals and status distinction in which chiefly systems have been explicitly preserved. There is much to recommend this, especially where chieftainship has not survived in any other way (as in much of eastern Polynesia) and given that churches and government were, after all, built on the decline of chiefly hierarchies. It is only reasonable to suppose that leaders in the former took the substantive place of those in the latter. Discerning subdued chiefly styles of leadership in the present becomes even more complicated when there are lively parallel systems of leadership that survive to the present, with many cross-connections among them. But my inclination here is to not be too quick to see chiefly styles in the new forms of leadership, simply because such a perspective undercuts awareness of the profundity of change—what was chiefly became thoroughly common in some cases. The cognitive redefinition of chiefly styles has to be taken fully into account among those stressing the continuity of chiefly status.

7

 Art
and
Aesthetics

ADRIENNE L. KAEPPLER

But the famous spheres of exchange, what are they but the functional
moment of a system of objects? And the system of objects? The transposition on another plane of the scheme of society.

MARSHALL SAHLINS
Culture and Practical Reason

THE study of Polynesian art and aesthetics has been largely a recitation
of objects of material culture, a listing and analysis of song and dance
types, the analysis of myth and poetry, descriptions of architecture, and
the imposition of Western aesthetic judgments.[1] It is time to move on: it
is time to illuminate how objects, architecture, songs, dances, poetry,
and oratory are parts of society and the structure of social reality; how
they provide a basis for understanding the nature of society; how artistic
and aesthetic structures are social structures; how art and aesthetics
communicate meanings on different planes; how symbolic action is
social action. Although the study of Polynesian art has traditionally
ignored such holistic concerns—separate individuals have studied artifacts, music, poetry, houses, or social structure—there has recently been
some movement toward more integrated studies. In most Western
academies, however, art, music, dance, and literature are still studied
by art historians, musicologists, dance historians, and literary critics
respectively, while social scientists concentrate on other aspects of
sociocultural systems.

But life does not take place in separate categories, not even in the
Western world. Activities, contexts, and categories include social interaction, objects, spaces, movements, words and sounds; and each individual understands how these all fit together even if he or she is not particularly interested in them. How can we as outsiders understand
Polynesian worlds if we rigidly separate categories? Can we comprehend social and cultural patterns without understanding the layout of
space, how one moves in it, what one wears while moving, and how all
of these elements change according to contexts and activities? Can we

understand exchange systems without noting what is exchanged and the production that went into making it, including such "things" as dances? The determination of categories and contexts applies not just to social categories or social interaction, but also to those things categorized by Westerners as the arts, and relegated in recent years away from the mainstream of what is "really important" in anthropology.

As studies have repeatedly demonstrated, Polynesian society has an important dimension of inequality (Sahlins 1958; Goldman 1970; chapters 3, 5, 6, this volume). Inequality is present in kin groups, societal groups, and the arts. Polynesian societies treat inequality in a way that distinguishes them from other societal types, but the specifics of hierarchy and submission within each island group strongly contribute to the definition of its individual character. The arts are embedded so deeply into Polynesian social forms that they help to define the dimensions of inequality, as well as what is Polynesian. Indeed, the pervasiveness of inequality in Polynesian categories of thought gives rise to what we might call an aesthetic of inequality, to which I will return near the end of this chapter.

Of what does this aesthetic consist? What do we mean by aesthetic? Which arts are characteristic of Polynesia and what can we learn about Polynesia by studying them? This chapter suggests answers in the context of a review of past and present studies.

Approaches of the Past

During the late nineteenth and much of the twentieth century, a number of museum-based anthropologists in New Zealand and Hawaii studied Polynesian material culture. Among them were Gilbert Archey, Elsdon Best, W. T. Brigham, Peter Buck (Te Rangi Hiroa), Edwin Burrows, Roger Duff, Kenneth Emory, E. S. C. Handy, Augustus Hamilton, Ralph Linton, and H. D. Skinner. A few American art-historians, such as J. Halley Cox and Paul Wingert, worked on aspects of Polynesian art, while European artists such as Paul Gauguin and Picasso drew inspiration from Polynesian objects and themes. Most anthropologists who worked in Polynesia, however (with a few exceptions, including Augustin Krämer [1902–1903], Alfred Métraux [e.g., 1937], and K. von den Steinen [1925–1928]), showed little scholarly interest in Polynesian art. A few armchair analysts such as Baessler, Balfour, Bastian, and Beasley included Polynesian materials in their wide-ranging writings about art.

Implicit in much of this early work are the assumptions that (1) we know what art is and therefore do not have to define it, and (2) that art is universal. But such assumptions cannot serve as the basis for an ade-

quate cross-cultural analysis. Polynesian languages do not have indigenous words or concepts for art (nor has such a word been reconstructed
for Proto-Polynesian). How then can we talk of Polynesian art? What
have scholars included in this nonexistent category? Is the fabrication of
ordinary useful objects to be considered art? Is clothing art? or ritual
objects? Is ritual itself art? And what about houses, interior decoration,
the use of space, petroglyphs, tattoo, hair-styles, scent, or the characters
used in Easter Island script? Because the study of ethnology includes
everything that shapes human experience—social organization, economic exchange, ritual, myth, religion, magic, literature, movement,
music, language—ethnographers should investigate each of these modeling systems to illuminate the underlying presuppositions that structure them all.

In order to include all those topics that are traditionally dealt with in
studies of Polynesian art and exclude what other chapters of this book
cover, my conception of art is very broad. I define as art any cultural
form that results from creative processes that use or manipulate words,
sounds, movements, materials, or spaces in such a way that they for-
malize the nonformal. I use the term aesthetics to refer to evaluative
ways of thinking about these cultural forms. My emphasis here will not
be on artistic or aesthetic content (see Kaeppler 1979a for a review), but
rather on concepts relevant to the study of Polynesian art and aesthetics.

Although the arts might be considered cultural as opposed to social,
such a distinction is artificial. In my view the arts can best be understood as cultural forms embedded in social action. Sahlins'notion that
objects are the transposition on another plane of the scheme of society
might be extended to the more basic notion that both the arts and society are transpositions on other planes of the deep structures or schemes
of particular Polynesian worlds.

Much of the early study of Polynesian art was tied to nineteenth century anthropological theory. Among the earliest persons to deal with art
were New Zealanders with ties to Britain. Sir George Grey, Governor of
New Zealand, collected numerous artifacts (which are now located in
the Auckland Museum and the British Museum) and manuscripts
(which are now located in the South Africa Public Library, Capetown,
and the Auckland Public Library), but published primarily on mythology (Grey 1855). Horatio Robley, who fought with the British Army in
New Zealand from 1864 to 1866, was interested in Maori *moko* 'tattoo';
he illustrated and published a remarkable number of contemporary
examples (Robley 1896). Many of Robley's artifacts are now in Dres-
den, Germany, while his collection of preserved, tattooed heads is now
in the American Museum of Natural History, New York. It was Augustus Hamilton and Elsdon Best, however, who wrote the important

works of their time on Maori art (Hamilton 1901; Best 1923, 1924b).
Influenced by W. H. R. Rivers, Percy Smith, and other British anthropologists, Hamilton and Best often combined empirical evidence with
uncritical acceptance of the theoretical leanings of others. Nevertheless,
their early fieldwork and publications are still basic for understanding
the history of the study of Maori art.[2]

H. D. Skinner, after spending time in Cambridge studying with
A. C. Haddon,[3] became a new bright light of Maori studies, and especially of art and material culture. Skinner's morphological approach
incorporated the evolutionary orientation of Haddon. He challenged
the diffusionist hypotheses of Percy Smith and others with diffusionist
theories of his own, tracing Polynesians to Cambodia and certain art
motifs to the Sepik River area of New Guinea (Skinner 1924a:234–
239). He in turn was challenged by Gilbert Archey (1933), particularly
over the origin and evolution of *manaia* (an enigmatic carving motif
resembling a human/bird figure in profile, see fig. 1). This argument
was later joined by Terence Barrow (1956:317–318), Douglas Fraser
(1962:143), J. M. McEwen (1966), Michael Jackson (1972), and Peter
Gathercole (1979a).

A Maori view was represented by Te Rangi Hiroa (Peter Buck), who
supported Archey in the *manaia* controversy and held to a theory of local
evolution, while criticizing the diffusionism of Rivers (Sorrenson 1982:
13). Buck cared little for theory, however, and produced voluminous
descriptions of material culture without regard for its relationship to
social institutions, even when he studied his own ancestral Maori. Buck
maintained this narrow perspective after going to the Bishop Museum
in Honolulu in 1927.

The Bishop Museum had been a major center for the study of Polynesian societies since its inception in 1889, but Buck was preceded there
by scholars who similarly emphasized the study of material culture for
its own sake. William T. Brigham, the first curator and director, was a
geologist who brought an anthropological naiveté to the Bishop Mu-

Figure 1. Maori lintel *(pare)* probably from a small storehouse. The central
head is flanked by *manaia* figures in profile. National Museum of New Zealand,
Wellington (ME 13972).

seum that he never overcame, in spite of extensive travel and contact with anthropologists. In 1899, John Stokes, who held a similar view of material culture, joined him at the museum. Kenneth Emory joined the staff in 1920, but, although he wrote competently on such topics as Hawaiian tattoo (1946) and the association of material culture with traditions (1975), his studies of stone remains and historical linguistics overshadowed his contributions in these areas. The Bayard Dominick Expedition in the 1920s attracted some of the premier talents of American anthropology to the Bishop Museum and to Polynesian ethnology generally: E. S. C. and Willowdean Handy, Ralph Linton, W. C. McKern, Edward Gifford, and Edwin Burrows wrote baseline ethnographies that included detailed descriptions of material culture in the Marquesas, Tonga, Uvea, and Futuna.

Burrows was particularly interested in the arts of music and dance. His contributions, especially on music, laid the groundwork for all future studies of Polynesian music. His monographs on the music of the Tuamotus (1933) and Futuna and Uvea (1945) remain the authoritative works on the music of these areas, and his study of Polynesian part-singing (1934) has stood the test of time equally well. E. S. C. Handy, in collaboration with Jane Winne, a music teacher at Punahou School in Honolulu, contributed a monograph concerning music in the Marquesas (1925). Meanwhile, Helen H. Roberts was invited to Hawaii to record and analyze traditional Hawaiian music in 1923 and 1924, and her work (1926) remains one of the few important publications on this topic. The only other noteworthy early studies of Polynesian music, musical instruments, and dance were a monograph on the traditions and genres of Hawaiian dance by Nathaniel B. Emerson (1909), and Johannes C. Anderson's compilation of material from written sources (including the journals from Cook's and other explorers' voyages), as well as from information obtained from residents in Polynesia up to about 1930 (J. Anderson 1933). Except for Hans Fischer's (1958) study of musical instruments there were few other serious studies of Polynesian music or dance until the 1960s. Apparently most researchers shared Roberts' view that "the subject is extremely technical, involving as well a knowledge of physics, music history, dancing, and art form in general, psychology, languages, ethnology, to mention only the most vital. Great difficulties lie in the way of bringing a knowledge of any exotic music to even those readers who should be most interested— musicians, and ethnologists whose knowledge of music is often limited" (Roberts 1932:101).

One of the earliest comparative studies of Polynesian art forms was Ruth H. Greiner's discussion of decorative design. A Bishop Museum fellow from Yale University in 1921–1922, she undertook the study "with a view of obtaining evidence of migratory movements of Pacific races" (Greiner 1923:3). Her work included a careful examination of museum objects and a listing in narrative and tabular form of the many motifs found in the Marquesas, Hawaii, Samoa, Tonga, New Zealand, and other areas. Skinner's view of Greiner's work—that she "has produced a work of great importance in Polynesian studies, and she has clarified the problem of the origin of Polynesian decorative design" (Skinner 1924b:141)—has not stood the test of time. For example, Greiner's study of Hawaiian bark cloth was based entirely on examples at Bishop Museum that were collected during the nineteenth and twentieth centuries. I have shown elsewhere (Kaeppler 1975) that eighteenth-century Hawaiian bark cloth is extremely different, in both the "watermark" impressed designs and the painted and stamped upper layer of designs, along with their arrangements. Thus nineteenth-century Hawaiian bark cloth can tell us little about the migration of Pacific peoples, or of the diffusion of designs in prehistoric times. The Marquesan section of Greiner's work is the most interesting, but her examples here, too, were nineteenth- and twentieth-century objects, many of which had been collected only a few years before by Linton and Handy. She concluded that "the fact that most of the angular geometric designs of Polynesia are also present in Melanesian art, leads to the supposition that Polynesian art is not a thing apart from all other art but that it is a part of an underlying Oceanic art or culture which is characterized by this same angular geometric feature *and that this art was carried by the Polynesian people to the farthest outposts of Oceania*" (Greiner 1923:00; emphasis added).

Could Skinner, who usually argued for diffusion into Polynesia from elsewhere, really have been paying attention to what she wrote? Her motif analysis, however, is detailed enough to be used in other ways. It would be more useful today, however, if she had analyzed European influence on design or the evolution of design, rather than theorizing about migration and diffusion.

Despite conducting field research in Samoa in the 1920s, when the arts and the aesthetic system were relatively intact, and despite her position in a major museum, Margaret Mead published little on Samoan art forms except for a note on the "Samoan kilt" (1929).[4] She did, however, write a short paper on New Zealand Maori art (1928b) and made some observations on tattooing in Polynesia (1928d). Willowdean Handy (1922) wrote an important monograph on Marquesan tattooing, which included design content and social context. Haddon and Hornell published their work on canoes in 1936. With the exception of a recent book on Hawaiian canoes (T. Holmes 1981) it has not been superseded. Likewise, Churchill's (1917) work on club types of nuclear Polynesia has only recently been superseded in its Fijian section (Clunie 1977).

Whereas most of the scholars mentioned above used art as a handmaiden to theories about migration and diffusion, Ralph Linton[5] studied art and material culture as a topic in its own right. As far as I am aware, he was the first anthropologist to explore indigenous views of art and aesthetics in Polynesia. His article, "Primitive Art," published in the *Kenyon Review* in 1941 was widely read,[6] as was the book he co-authored with Ralph Wingert, *Arts of the South Seas* (1946). The latter accompanied one of the few comprehensive Pacific Art exhibitions ever held in the United States.[7]

Linton also seems to have been one of the few anthropologists interested in separating art and aesthetics from material culture in general. He not only questioned Marquesans about their own concepts, but showed them pictures of European sculpture in order to explore their ideas about naturalism and abstraction. Although his definition of aesthetics specifically relates to the creation of beauty, which he considers a universal urge (Linton 1941:36), his work is in many ways a precursor of modern approaches. For example, he acknowledges the close relationship between the carving of images and associated chants "in which the genealogies of [the artist's] tools and materials were traced from the beginning of the world so that their offspring, the image, would have its proper place in the scheme of things" (Linton 1941:38).

Although Linton (1941:38) wrote that "the maker of images accompanied his work by chants," it is equally likely that in the Marquesan view a chanter accompanied his chant by making images. Linton thus gives primacy to making the image while I would give primacy to the chant, even though the perceived necessity for making the image may have occasioned the chant. The fabrication of a stone image while chanting a curing prayer and then placing the image into a *me'ae* 'temple' gives permanence to the prayer and substance to the chant. An integral association of visual and verbal modes of expression was found in many parts of Polynesia and is, I believe, a fundamental characteristic of Polynesian art and aesthetics. Perhaps this association could be considered a criterion for traditional authenticity.

Because Linton was unable to elicit aesthetic or evaluative terms from wood carvers in the Marquesas (and from others in similar situations in other parts of the world), he concluded that "the processes of both creation and appreciation go on among primitive peoples with little or no manipulation of verbal symbols" (Linton 1941:40). Had he looked at other ways of making chants visible (such as dance or the making of string figures), he might have found terms or verbal expressions related to value and meaning comparable to *kaona* in Hawaiian, *taonga* and *whakahurihuri* in Maori, *heliaki* in Tongan, and *hesingihaki* in Bellonese. These terms relate to aesthetic principles, including the importance of layers of meaning that one apprehends by skirting a subject and approaching it from different points of view, rather than by getting directly to the point.

Linton (1941:49) may have had such concepts in mind when he wrote that "the aim of the primitive artist is to present his subject as he and his society think of it, not as he sees it." Indeed, that which goes into the process of artistic production, including mental images of a product as well as its fabrication, is often more important than the product itself, which can be considered a byproduct. The artistic product is important only to the degree that it assists the aesthetic process and stimulates thinking about cultural forms.

Linton's (1924) attempt to separate aesthetic from religious uses of human figures is less successful in that he takes an evolutionary view of the degeneration of the human figure to account for certain Polynesian designs. The interpretation of designs is always a dangerous undertaking—whether by outsiders, or by indigenous scholars separated in time from when the designs were culturally and socially meaningful.

Paul Wingert was an art historian who was considerably ahead of his time in that he considered primitive art as equal in artistic merit to Western art. He essentially replaced the science of art (represented in the Pacific by such individuals as Haddon and Skinner) with an appreciation of art from an outsider's point of view. He attempted to distinguish the arts by area and culture, discussing them in terms of formal elements in order to aid understanding and appreciation. His detailed descriptions of individual works, from which he abstracted statements about style, draw attention to similarities and differences of design elements and sculptural forms within Polynesia. His lack of fieldwork and anthropological perspective, however, is evident in that the Polynesians themselves have little place in his analysis and that works of art seem to exist independent of people.

J. Halley Cox, primarily a watercolorist, was an intellectual descendant of Wingert. Cox (1974) described and categorized Hawaiian sculpture from the perspective of art history, naming and popularizing the so-called "Kona style." Unfortunately, others have begun to use this term as if it were an indigenous Hawaiian categorization. Although there were localized carving styles within the Hawaiian Islands, the "Kona style" as defined by Cox is not a local one, but a style of carving wooden images associated with the war god Kūkā'ilimoku during the time in which chief Kamehameha was in power.

The interpretation of present-day Tongans of the carvings on incised clubs made in the eighteenth and nineteenth centuries illustrates the difficulty of attempting to interpret artistic or cultural forms that are divorced in time from their social and cultural context. Tongans in the 1960s and 1970s suggested to me that human figures carved on a club were indications of the warriors slain by it. This, however, contradicts the Tongan aesthetic principle of *heliaki,* as well as historical knowledge about the designs. Whereas carving a slain warrior after a battle would be to come directly to the point, carving a warrior image before a battle

Figure 2. Incised head of a Tongan club.
Vertical and horizontal lines form the
space definers for geometric designs that
are "decorated" with human and animal
figures. Pitt Rivers Museum, Oxford.

might give potency to the club, and by *heliaki* refer metaphorically to
important people, places or events. And surely the carvings of figures
with high-ranking headdresses found on these clubs (fig. 2) do not indicate that one has slain a Tuʻi Tonga (the only person who could wear
such headdresses).

Linton held that the human figures carved on Tongan clubs have no
religious significance and that they, along with the incised animals, are
of secondary importance to the more pervasive angular geometric carvings that fill the spaces. Placed in the context that I have explored elsewhere (Kaeppler 1978c) of "melody, drone, and decoration" (a Tongan
aesthetic paradigm that is part of the sociocultural deep structure), the
incised human and animal figures can be seen as decoration, while the
geometric designs are the melody, or essential feature, of the carving.
The drone, or space-definer, consists of lines that frame or outline the
spaces in which the geometric designs and figures are carved (fig. 2). A
further layer of decoration consists of carved ivory inlays that were
added to some clubs after the rest of the carving was finished, and
intruded on the carved design. The presence or absence of figures might
be considered to correspond to contexts that vary with the rank and
prestige of their owners or users. This is analogous to the way that *ngatu*
or *fuatanga* bark cloth differentiates context. *Ngatu* (in which the primary
lines run crosswise and intersect with a set of long lines that run the
entire length of the piece) is used by commoners. *Fuatanga* (in which the
primary lines run lengthwise and intersect with a series of crosswise
lines that measure its size) is used by chiefs and aspiring commoners on

ritual or ceremonial occasions. *Ngatu* and *fuatanga* are also differentiated by design and color.

Modern Approaches

Underlying Structures and Aesthetics

Such aesthetic ramifications are only interpretable in relation to the structural principles that underly society. Indeed, only complete immersion in the traditions of a society and its variety of cultural forms can elicit the aesthetic principles embedded in its deep structure. It is, in turn, the inclination for such immersion that differentiates anthropology from conventional art history or musicology. Thus the anthropological study of art and aesthetics cannot simply focus on objects or artistic products per se; rather, such studies must be part of competent ethnography. Nor can the study of Polynesian art and aesthetics deal simply with two- or three-dimensional visual forms. Instead, such studies must try to show how visual and verbal modes of expression are embedded in social structure and cultural philosophy, as well as how ritual and belief systems are integrally related to artistic and aesthetic systems.

It is this problem that I attempted to solve in my study "Melody, Drone, and Decoration: Underlying Structures and Surface Manifestations in Tongan Art and Society" (Kaeppler 1978c). I characterized my theoretical position at the time as ethnoscientific structuralism.

> Structural relationships among the arts and society are seen in terms of homology, that is, as consistency relationships between various cultural and social manifestations and the underlying structures that they express. . . . Structuralism here is given the requirement that the structure derived is recognized by members of the society as a set of principles with which they helped to organize their lives—not necessarily verbalized as such, but derived from ethnographic data in several domains in which the structure consistently repeats itself (Kaeppler 1978c:261).

In that paper, I attempted to demonstrate how various artistic domains in Tonga partake of an underlying structure, and how they are, in effect, the transformation of the scheme of society on another plane—that "the various artistic and social domains are surface manifestations of underlying structures of the society" (Kaeppler 1978c: 262). Because no words in either Tongan or English apply to the structural elements within the several domains, I used an analogy derived from Tongan music—*fasi,* the melody or leading part, which consists of essential features; *laulalo,* or the drone, which defines or outlines the space in which the essential features operate; and *teuteu,* or decoration, which elaborates specific features that are not otherwise necessary. The domains used for analysis were vocal music, dance, musical instruments, overall performance, bark cloth manufacture, bark cloth design, material culture, societal structure, and kin groups. The analysis suggested that:

> artistic works in Tonga have conceptual similarities in their underlying structure. Design space and design elements can only be combined in certain ways according to certain rules which are culturally understood by artist, performer and spectator. Areas are nearly always rectangular, divided into square compartments by lengthwise and crosswise lines. Squares are usually divided again by diagonal or straight lines forming triangles, squares, and rectangles. Only at the last stage are curved lines added (if they are added at all) and such curves are always in relation to a straight line or a line that has crossed the square or rectangle. This is most apparent in bark cloth designs, but can also be seen in incised clubs, basketry, tattooing, prehistoric pottery, and even in a *lakalaka* dance where the dance space is a long rectangle divided in half (men on one half, women on the other half) and each performer having a sense of a square for himself. For the most part, leg movements are side to side and forward and back within this square. Curved lines come only in the *haka* arm movements giving to the surface structure a graceful curving appearance, especially in the women's movements. Polyphony, too, can be considered rectangular—the drone underscores the design space, while the *fasi* moves above it and decorative parts curve among them. The convergence of rectangles, squares and curves in varied artistic media create works of art and carry with them the possibility of aesthetic combinations and potential aesthetic experiences. I propose that aesthetic experiences, at least in Tonga, are realised when fundamental cultural principles are made specific in works of art (that is, when the deep structure is manifested in a cultural form resulting from creative processes which manipulate movement, sound, words or materials) and are comprehended as such by individuals (Kaeppler 1978c:273–274).

From this analysis several tentative conclusions were drawn:

1. Some underlying structural features have revealed themselves in an analysis of the ethnographic data, or if you will, in an analysis of the surface manifestations of various domains of Tongan art and society. These underlying features may be some of the unconscious, or at least unstated, principles by which individuals help to order their lives.
2. What the artisan does during creation may be essentially a series of transformational processes by which he converts the underlying principles or conceptualizations of these principles into a work of art which has potential for aesthetic experiences for those who comprehend (consciously or unconsciously) the underlying structure. I would further venture that it may be because the underlying structure is not comprehended by outsiders that they do not react to the surface stimuli of works of art in the same way as members of the society for which they were made.

3. I hesitate to propose rules or a grammar that will transform the underlying structure to generate works of art in Tonga, although Tongans continually demonstrated the processes to me (they seldom verbalised them, however, and never stated them as rules). Simply stated, they usually began with what I have called the drones, long lines, or space definers, and used these as a reference for placement of the leading part (motif/*fasi*/ *haka*/ etc.) and in some ways the leading part can be considered as a decoration of the drone. Only when the drone and leading part were satisfactorily arranged were the more creative parts added. Thus, in effect, the leading part decorates the drone and the "decoration" decorates the leading part.

4. How and why a specific arrangement is chosen is preeminently context-sensitive. For example, which direction the lines run in a bark cloth depends on its ultimate use, and which *lakalaka* will be chosen for performance depends on the occasion. This context-sensitivity is often apparent throughout the entire choice and arrangement of the movements, sounds, words, or materials.

5. It appears that the traditional function of the arts in Tonga has been to reflect and reinforce in a positive manner the sociopolitical system based on social status and societal rank. Although this is relatively easy to discern in material culture, other domains can now be seen to partake of the same underlying conceptual structure, in addition to what their surface manifestations tell us, and the more general statement can now be proposed with more credibility (Kaeppler 1978c:273–274).

Spatial Arrangements of Social Events and House Forms

An understanding of the deep structure or underlying principles of Tongan aesthetics and society also helps us to understand the conceptualization of space in other cultural forms such as the kava ceremony or house shape. Although Elizabeth Bott (1972) sees the Tongan *taumafa kava* layout as a circle, and Edmund Leach (1972) sees the layout as two opposing semi-circles of chief and kava mixer, I interpret it as "rectangular" with two complementary ends. The chief and his *matāpule* 'ceremonial attendants' occupy one end, the kava mixer and his helpers, who are known collectively as *tou 'a,* occupy the other end, and two lines of specified individuals are spaced in between. Neither end is more important than the other. The chief must have a kava mixer (of the prescribed genealogical group) in order to carry out the ritual, whereas the kava mixer can only carry out the ritual on the instruction of the *matāpule* on an occasion designated by the chief. In between sit those to whom the ceremony is relevant, for without them there would be no need for the ceremony.

Barbara Ritchie (1983:32a) has applied the "melody, drone, and decoration" paradigm to Tongan house forms. She treats the basic rectangle between the house posts as the "drone, or space definer," the *fata* arrangement (superstructure above the house posts or lack of *fata*) as the "melody or essential feature" corresponding to its use for chiefly or non-chiefly purposes or aspirations, and the curved apse ends and roof curves as the "decoration or elaboration of specific features." The placement of people in the house and its other functions can ultimately be related to the rectangle. The *tamai* 'father' or in this case 'chief of the house', sits at one end of the rectangle within which all socially relevant action (for example the drinking of kava) occurs. Behind him, in the decorative curved apse end, is his sleeping place and the place for the storage of important *koloa* 'valuables'.

Carrying the analysis further, I suggest that the structuring of space in Tongan houses and villages, as well as in kava ceremonies, is related to context and to the placement of space definers (drone) in the same way that *ngatu/fuatanga* bark cloth define context and space. Important ceremonies (such as *taumafa kava*) are held outside the house, with the *'eiki* 'chief' of the occasion at one end of the rectangle. That is, the *mala'e* 'village green' is a rectangle with a chief's house at one end forming the curved decoration in which the chief may sit during the ceremony. Informal occasions take place inside the house, transforming the short side of the rectangle on formal occasions (held on the *mala'e*) to the long side of the rectangle on informal occasions (fig. 3). The chief moves to the (new) short side of the rectangle and the decorative apse end of the house is now behind him. In the aesthetics of Tongan ritual, no one can walk behind the chief. The apse end of the house or the house itself, depending on the context, marks the boundary of the ritual space (taking the symbolic place of the stone back rest of the Tu'i Tonga

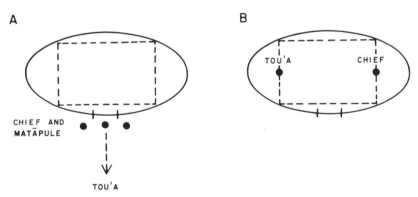

Figure 3. Schematic representation of placement of chief and *tou'a* for formal and informal kava drinking in Tonga. *A*. Formal. Chief sits in doorway of the house at one end of *mala'e*; *tou'a* prepares kava at the far end of the *mala'e*. *B*. Informal. Chief sits at one end inside the house; *tou'a* prepares kava at the opposite end of the house.

at Heketa). Like *ngatu* and *fuatanga* bark cloth, context and status in kava ritual are indicated by changes in orientation of long lines as space definers.

An interesting analysis in a similar vein was done by Bradd Shore (1982) in his chapter on the aesthetics of social context in *Sala'ilua*. He applies the Samoan distinction between center and periphery to the context of the dance floor, and relates the two styles of social life (one involving restraint of, the other expression of, impulses) to contrastive styles of movement in dance. Restraint is expected both in social interaction and on the dance floor from the most dignified person present, while lack of restraint and clowning are expected of the less dignified. Who is regarded as dignified changes with the actors and the occasion. Shore concludes that the contrasting patterns expressed in the dance

> are highly conventional for Samoans, and reflect a set of symbolized associations opposing on the one hand center, focus, grace, inhibition, and control, and on the other periphery, aggression, power, expansiveness, and disorder. The dance floor, mediating between these two aspects of the dance, is a kind of microcosm of the larger village arena, where an almost identical set of associations is made between village center (*'a'ai* or *malae*) and periphery (bush or the 'back' of the village). These geographical associations were seen to have important implications for the village legal and moral system. On the dance floor, the periphery is associated with the orator or those representing the orator, the males, the untitled, and those showing respect. The center is left for the *ali'i*, the *taupou*, or, more generally, for anyone commanding respect and deference (Shore 1982:260).

Shore's analysis suggests significant contrasts between Samoa and Tonga. Whereas Tongans appear to order space in relation to rectangles with the chiefly person on one end, Samoans appear to order space in relation to circles with the chiefly person in the center. This ordering is also found in the form of important houses. In Tongan houses social action occurs within the rectangle formed by the main posts (even though there may be curved apse ends) while in Samoan houses the operational space is circular (Shore 1982:80).

In Tikopia, Raymond Firth notes that circularity is given by nature and rectangularity is provided by culture; thus the Tikopia house (being a cultural feature) is rectangular, and space within it divides rectangularly. The seaward side of the house, *mata paito*, is not only higher ranking—being associated with canoes, fish, ancestors, men, and chiefs— but sacred, in contrast to the landward, profane side of the house, *tuaumu*, which is associated with ovens, vegetable food, social activity, the living, women, and those of lesser rank. Movement and social action within the Tikopia house are governed by these spatial regularities as well as by proximity, precedence, and orientation, both in direction and elevation (Firth 1970a:191–198).

In his analysis of the Moalan house, Sahlins (1976:36) shows how space is a model of and for society, and how "the house functions as the medium by which a system of culture is realized as an order of action." The Moalan house "is divided down the long axis into a 'chiefly side', traditionally set parallel to the sea, and a 'common side' toward the inland" (Sahlins 1976:32). In addition, each end is associated with a side, so that the chief of the house is associated with one end and one side. Sahlins analyzes the house as a modeling system for dual organization, tripartite organization, and the four-class system of the Moalan social order. He concludes that

> the house functions as the medium by which a system of culture is realized as an order of action. What is in analysis a set of parallel classifications, or a single structure operating on different planes, is in experience an undivided totality. The four-class code is practice as well as form. Unfolding in a habitation so structured, the relationships between persons are themselves inhabited by the same structure.
>
> These relationships necessarily extend to the objects of family life. Cultural categories and economic goods are here defined in terms of one another: the quality of the mat signifies the virtue of the cultural space; conversely, the collection of different objects in the one space represents a commonality of cultural virtue. . . . It is a process of mutual valuation. What it implies is that economic value is Saussurean, it is the differential standing of a given object in a system of meaningful relationships. (This would only be fair, since Saussure understood linguistic value by the economic.) The effect of the process is to establish structures of differentiation between goods which are isomorphic with, as they substantialize, the categorical distinctions among men (Sahlins 1976:36).

In exploring the structuring of space we are thus faced with a conjunction of artistic and aesthetic considerations on the one hand, and social and philosophical considerations on the other. As the above comparison of Tonga, Samoa, Tikopia, and Moala suggests, an in-depth study of spatial patterning in various Polynesian societies would almost certainly illuminate the underlying structures of those societies,[8] and might even provide insight into the question of what makes Polynesian societies Polynesian.

The Performing Arts

Surprisingly few studies of dance or human movement have been conducted in Polynesia (see Shennan 1981 for a review). With few exceptions, those that do exist are only faintly anthropological. Worthy of note, however, are Moulin's (1979) study of Tahitian dance and Shennan's (1984) study of Maori action songs. My own studies of Tongan dance have been done from an anthropological perspective. Also noteworthy are ethnographic commentaries, such as Shore's, that relate dancing to other features of the Samoan social order.

In addition to his observations regarding spatial ordering and dance, cited above, Shore (1982:258) notes that "in pre-contact Samoa, dancing was contextually differentiated into *pōula* (night dancing), and *ao siva* (day dancing)." Stylistically, he asserts, it was differentiated into "*siva* (dancing proper) and *'aiuli* (clowning)" (Shore 1982:259). I suspect that *ao siva/pōula* and *siva/'aiuli* are not really contrastive pairs, but rather that *siva* and *ula* were two genres of human movement, each of which could be performed either formally, during the day *(ao)*, or informally, during the night *(pō)*,[9] and that *'aiuli* referred to a style of performance (i.e., without restraint). It is likely that in Samoa *ula*[10] was usually performed at night while *siva* was usually performed during the day, giving reason for the terms entering the early literature most often as *ao siva* and *pōula*. Thus, the second differentiation (in my view) should not be *siva/'aiuli* but *sa'o/'aiuli*, which could operate for both *siva* and *ula*.

The next essential step is an analysis of all structured movement in Samoa which might include the ritual parading, presentation, and counting of fine mats and food, as well as dance genres not mentioned by Shore, such as *sāsā*, *fa'ataupati*, and *mā'ulu'ulu*. These carefully choreographed dances contrast with the primarily improvised genres mentioned by Shore. The choreographed group dances underscore Shore's (1982:258) characterization that "the dance in Samoa may be profitably understood as an important arena where those feelings and impulses are structured and where appropriation of style to context is learned and reinforced."

Margaret Mead (1968:273) and Lemert (1972) argue that dance is a reversal of the stratified social order in which personal expression is allowed in an egalitarian arena, but as Shore (1982:258) has noted, "a focus on this [show-off] function masks the equally important part that dance plays in directly confirming and reinforcing certain distinctive cultural patterns rather than compensating for them."

One of the problems with studies of dance (including my own) is that they do not really address the abstract conceptualization of what dance is to the people of the societies we study, or whether the varied manifestations described as dance by outsiders are grouped together by the people themselves in a way that separates them from non-dance. In 1980, building on my previous work, I concentrated on the Tongan aesthetic principle *heliaki* as found in dance and other structured movement systems in Tonga, in order to discover if Tongans had a concept that is comparable to the Western concept of dance, and how Tongan dance might be distinguished from ritual movement (Kaeppler 1985b). Structured movement systems considered were the ceremonial presentation of pigs; the ceremonial enumeration of pigs, kava roots, and baskets of

food; the ceremonial mixing of kava; group speeches with choreographed movements; and spontaneous choreography performed in conjunction with *hiva kakala* 'sweet songs'. An examination of each of these
activities illustrated some of the important characteristics of contexts
and movements, and considered such elements as public and non-pub-
lic venues, formalization of movements (including the role of the side
head-tilt), and the speech-making importance of some movement
genres. The elemental notion of *heliaki* 'to say one thing and mean
another' was explored in its many forms and to see how its presence or
absence helped define and categorize ritual movement, dance, and their
overlap. The study also examined the ways such forms function as
social metaphors to express on a different plane the underlying principles and cultural philosophy of hierarchical rank and prestige.

It is this element of categorical distinctions, found so pervasively in
social action and the arts, that forms "a symbolic scheme of practical
activity—not just the practical scheme in symbolic activity" (Sahlins
1976:37). The arts and aesthetic concepts are inseparable from social
action. Who is to say which is the modeling system for the other?

Work is progressing on a comparative ethnomusicology of western
Polynesia and the outliers by Dorothy Lee (Fiji), Jacob Love (Samoa),
Adrienne Kaeppler (Tonga), Raymond Mayer (Uvea), Richard Feinberg and Jacob Love (Anuta), Jane Rossen (Bellona), Dieter Christensen (Tuvalu), and Allan Thomas (Tokelau), with the aim of exploring
the ideological role of music in these socially stratified societies. Native
categories are being examined, but rather than compare empirical
details of content, an attempt will be made to extract comparable conceptualizations about music and its place in social action. Ultimately
the goal is to illuminate sociological as well as sound differences
between the musical traditions of western and eastern Polynesia.

Except for that of Burrows, most early studies of Polynesian music
were oriented toward musicology rather than anthropology. Examples
of the modern musicological orientation are Mervyn McLean's analysis
of 651 Maori scales (1969a) and song types of the New Zealand Maori
(1969b; McLean and Orbell 1975) and Richard Moyle's musicological
research in Samoa, Tonga, and Lau (1971, 1972, 1978, 1987). These
studies by McLean and Moyle, however, are much like Wingert's visual arts studies of the 1940s, in that Polynesians themselves have little
place in the analyses, and music appears to exist independently of the
people. Most early studies of music did not acknowledge the importance
of dance as part of music, nor did they place proper emphasis on the significance of poetic text. More modern, anthropologically relevant,
studies of Polynesian music (in addition to those currently being conducted in western Polynesia and the outliers), include the work of Chris
Thompson (1971) and Dorothy Sara Lee (1984) in Fiji; Jacob Love

(1979) in Samoa; Norma McLeod's (1957, 1972) analysis of Firth's sound recordings and other data on music and dance in Tikopia; and Elizabeth Tatar's (1982) description of Hawaiian music, which attempts to reconstruct an emic classification by style, function, and voice quality. Tatar's musical analysis, which is based upon spectrograms of wax cylinder recordings, also reveals a pattern of stratified sound organization that can be related to stratified social organization. A study of the music and movement of *hula ku'i* 'dance that combines old and new' by Amy Stillman (1982) relates this important genre to late-nineteenth-century Hawaiian society.

A great deal remains to be done. For example, what is the relationship between improvisation and set pieces, and how do these concepts relate to social action and societal organization? The relation of improvisation to formal oratory is an issue discussed by Judith Huntsman (1981a), who proposes that oral narratives be studied as creative art. With his examination of Samoan oratory, Alessandro Duranti (1981b) has made a start in that direction. Oratory—not just what is said, but how it is said—is surely one of the most important arts of Polynesia, with recognized classes of orators and poets. Except for the early work of Katharine Luomala (1955), there are few studies of storytelling as an art form. Although there are studies of the mythological importance of poetry and stories, there are few studies of performance practice, their relationship to the other arts, and their place in social action.

The making of string figures (cat's cradle) was traditionally one of the important performing genres in Polynesia, yet published studies about them are primarily "how to" monographs that tell us little about the aesthetics of performance, how chant is made visible through the figure, if there are hidden meanings, or what importance string figures have sociologically or as artistic forms in their own right.

Where, too, are studies or even mention of the arts aimed at the olfactory sense? The symbolic and metaphorical importance of smell can be noted for Tonga, where, for example, a musical genre is known as *hiva kakala* 'sweet songs'. *Kakala,* however, does not simply mean 'sweet', but 'sweet smelling' and implies that the smell comes from flowers. In poetry, sweet-smelling flowers refer metaphorically to chiefs or to a beloved, and references to a mixture of sweet smells refers to a mixing of genealogical lines. In Tonga, flowers are admired and ranked primarily according to smell, rather than according to their visual appearance.

The Visual Arts

Important work has been done on the visual arts of the New Zealand Maori during the last two decades, particularly on tattoo and wood carving, but also in other areas, such as Neich's (1977:35–55) examination of how art was talked about in traditional oral literature. After an early study by Robley in 1896, the study of Maori *moko* 'tattoo' languished until the recent studies by Michael King (1972), David Simmons (1983), and Peter Gathercole (1988). Each of these studies is done from a different perspective, but each relates the study of *moko* as an art form to its social and historical background.

The study of Maori carving has, in the past, often been marred by guesswork (based on objects that lack documentation on when or where they were made, used or collected) about area styles and chronology. Although such guesswork is on its way out, many of the "authoritative" works on Maori art can best be characterized as "guessalogs" in these respects. Still working in this tradition is David Simmons, whose statements on area style are often undocumented, except by his own intuitive knowledge and by claims of a few modern-day Maoris that are impossible to substantiate. Simmons' pronouncements on date of collection are also unrewarding; he states, for example, when questioned about his evidence for a Cook-voyage provenance, that if the objects were "not brought back by Cook himself [they] were brought back by his shadow" (Willett 1983:11). Indeed, Simmons' attributions to time period and tribe of nearly every object in the *Te Maori* catalog indicate his dependence on educated guesswork rather than documentation (Simmons 1984).[11] In contrast, however, other New Zealand researchers, such as J. M. McEwen (1966), Sidney Mead (1971b), Peter Gathercole (1976, 1979a, 1979b), Roger Neich (1977, 1983), and Kernot (1983), have concentrated on documented examples in order to explicate chronological, stylistic, and contextual foundations for the study of Maori carving, as well as how carvings change along with Maori society. The recent travelling exhibition "Te Maori" and the associated exhibition catalog (S. M. Mead, ed., 1984) provide new, important insights into Maori art, and illustrate how both the art and its analyzers have changed.

Using as a basis the sound empirical study by Buck (1924–1926) on the evolution of Maori clothing, Sidney Mead (who like Buck represents an indigenous Maori point of view) has further examined this subject. Although he does not take the analysis to its logical conclusions, Mead has made considerable progress toward demonstrating that clothing transposes on another plane the scheme of society.

Other modern work on Maori art is also compelling. Michael Jackson (1972) has done a structural analysis of the symbolic meanings of Maori door lintels and related the designs to canoes, feather boxes, and tattooing, as well as to kinship and societal structure. Salmond (1978) finds links between meeting house structure and categories that structure the Maori cosmos. Annette Weiner (1985) has examined cloaks and greenstone ornaments as inalienable wealth. Gathercole has emphasized the adaptive elements of certain Maori motifs, especially the *manaia* and many curvilinear motifs. These "had the ability to form and reform together as designs on a very wide variety of objects, in the flat and the round. In the case of nineteenth-century examples, this eclecticism is sometimes seen as evidence for the collapse of the tradition. . . . I prefer to regard eclecticism as evidence of the ability of Maoris to come to terms with new situations and, as part of their general artistic tradition, to express their reactions to these situations in carving" (Gathercole 1979a:225). He then goes on to suggest that it "might be possible to use a lintel design as an ideal formula, expressing human, ancestor, and god relationships in a particularly comprehensive yet succinct way. This lintel formula could then be used to analyze details of design on a range of other objects where it was not expressed so completely" (Gathercole 1979a:225).

These ideas, in addition to Sidney Mead's (1975:178) view on opposition and complementarity have recently been expanded by Allan Hanson, who suggests that in Maori art, "subject matter is less significant than formal organization," that the underlying bilateral symmetry should be broken in some way, and that this artistic convention communicates "messages about ambivalent tension between union and separation" (Hanson 1983:213, 223). Although one might accept Hanson's ideas on symmetry, the argument that content is less relevant to Maori art is unconvincing. Nevertheless, Hanson's contributions, along with the recent efforts of Gathercole, Kernot, Mead, Neich, and Salmond have placed the understanding of Maori art on a more sophisticated level than elsewhere in Polynesia.

An important catalog of Hawaiian sculpture was published by Cox and Davenport (1974) and a study of Hawaiian petroglyphs was published by Cox and Stasack (1970). Although these studies are rather art-historical in their analysis, they furnish important baseline descriptions for all future work.

In my studies of Hawaiian art, I have attempted to show how featherwork constitutes a transposition of the scheme of society to another plane by suggesting that objects are part of socially given categories that were an important part of "the changing social relationships between people, the gods, and the environment and were used in the service of prestige, power, authority, and status (Kaeppler 1985a:109).

This study, along with its companion studies on wooden images (Kaeppler 1982) and tattoo (Kaeppler 1988), illustrate how the arts were involved in social action. Such investigations also help to clarify the relationships between the prestige and power of chiefs and relationships among the gods. With regard to wooden images, for example, I noted that "the bodily forms of the images, the stance, and especially the exaggerations and stylisations of certain features can be related to the importance in Hawaiian culture of genealogy, respect and disrespect, and *kaona,* or veiled meaning, also found in poetry and dance" (Kaeppler 1982:83).

In addition to recent work on Maori and Hawaiian art and aesthetics, research is progressing on the art of Easter Island, the third important area that used to be known as Marginal East Polynesia. Once the center of ethnological speculation and popular theorizing, archaeological and ethnohistoric research on Easter Island has dispelled much of the previous mystery. Still, only a few studies of the island's rich artistic tradition have emerged. Much of the early literature focused on the pictographic script on *rongorongo* boards, often with disappointing results, and the huge volume by Thor Heyerdahl (1976), *The Art of Easter Island,* is distinguished by its lack of analysis. In its stead, Heyerdahl presents further evidence to support his view that Easter Island had direct contact from South America, and that Polynesians came to Easter Island only late in the island's prehistory. Filled with exciting adventure stories of finding in caves the small stone sculptures that Heyerdahl considers a major art form, the book is a throwback to the nineteenth-century use of art objects for justifying theories of migration. Other, more recent, archaeological work has furnished the much needed background for ongoing and future studies of Easter Island's art and aesthetics.

A little-known article by Katharine Luomala (1973) on moveable images from Easter Island refutes some early questionable work on the prehistoric existence of a sacred puppet theater. Also of interest is a set of papers on art and symbolic systems presented at an interdisciplinary symposium on Easter Island in September 1984, during which the latest research concerning the island was presented. Joan Seaver's symposium paper, which focused on contemporary religious sculptures, elaborated on an earlier article (1984) that provided a historical summary and view of contemporary Easter Island art. Kaeppler examined bark cloth images and their symbolic continuities with wood and stone carving. Extensive work on rock art was reported on by Georgia Lee, and Jo Anne van Tilburg presented an analysis of the large stone images. Lee (1986) and van Tilburg (1986) have recently finished dissertations on these subjects.

An overview of Tahitian material culture by Roger Rose (1971) has recently been supplemented by Karen Stevenson and Alain Babadzan. Stevenson (1981) conducted a specialized study of the artifacts associated with her ancestral Pomare family, and is preparing her dissertation on Tahitian body ornamentation. Babadzan investigated the symbolism of Tahitian *to'o* 'images of coconut fiber and red feathers' (1981) and *ti'i* 'stone images' (1982). But the lack of modern studies from the Cook Islands (except for Borofsky's unpublished study of ethno-identification of material culture), Austral Islands, Mangareva, Tuamotus, and the Marquesas probably makes central eastern Polynesia the least studied area in the world in the visual and performing arts.

Building upon the basic work of A. M. Hocart (1929, 1952), George Roth (1934), Alan Tippett (1968), Laura Thompson (1940), and Karl Larsson (1960), the study of Fijian material culture has recently been advanced by S. J. P. Hooper (1982), who focused on valuables; Simon Kooijiman (1977), who focused on bark cloth; Rod Ewins (1982a, 1982b) who has worked with mats, bark cloth and other artifacts; and Fergus Clunie, who in numerous studies (e.g., Clunie 1977, 1986; Clunie and Ligairi 1983) has attempted to reconstruct material culture and its changes over time.

In contrast to the investigation by multiple individuals into the arts of New Zealand and Fiji, Raymond Firth stands as the only major source for understanding Tikopian art, aesthetics, and social life. It is significant that Firth's delvings into aesthetics and the arts reflect the work of a mature anthropologist who has spent many years analyzing Tikopia social life. Although he had written earlier on tattoo (Firth 1936a) and material culture (e.g., Firth 1947, 1959a), his later articles on the aesthetics of social space (Firth 1970a) and on Tikopia headrests as an art form (Firth 1973) illustrate how an understanding of a social system can be furthered by a study of the arts. Firth is the supreme example one might cite of the necessity of studying art and aesthetics in their social contexts. Yet even Firth has not yet exhausted the range of possible directions suggested by the arts.

Considerable work has been done or is underway on the visual and performing arts of Tonga; some work has been done on Tokelau, Samoa, and Tuvalu; little has been done on Rotuma or Niue. Cross-cultural studies have been done on Polynesian bark cloth (Kooijiman 1972) and basketry (Conner 1983), which give some indication of the importance of these material objects in the social life of traditional Polynesia.

Linguistic Analogies

Sidney Mead (1971a) has used linguistic analogies in his study of the form and decoration of Polynesian adzes. In association with others Mead (Mead et al. 1973) has analyzed the decorative system of the Lapita potters of Sigatoka and the relationships of decorative systems within Fiji. Green applied the Lapita rules developed by Mead et al. (1973) to an analysis of Polynesian bark cloth and tattoo designs. Although Green's purpose was to add "art to the empirical base supporting a hypothesis that the Lapita cultural complex was ancestral to

Polynesian culture" (Green 1979a:31), he has also illustrated the possibility of examining continuity and change in Polynesian art from the
prehistoric past into historic times. These are the only attempts of which
I am aware to derive grammars for the visual arts in Polynesia.

A similar type of analysis, however, was my study of the structure of
Tongan dance (Kaeppler 1967b, 1972), which was based on etic and
emic distinctions derived from structural linguistics. Starting with the
assumption that only a small segment of all possible movements are significant in any single dance or movement tradition, and that these significant units could be discovered, I attempted to isolate minimal units
(i.e., movement emes which I termed kinemes) using the process of
contrastive analysis (i.e., whether kinetically different movements were
considered the same or different). The result was an inventory of the
significant movements of Tongan dance. Just as speech can be committed to paper in a phonetic notation and the allophonic variations noted
for each phoneme, human movement can be recorded using a kinetic
notation, such as Labanotation, and the allokine variations noted for
each kineme.

Kinemes are minimal units of movement recognized as contrastive
by people of a given dance tradition. Although they have no meaning in
themselves, kinemes constitute the basic units from which dance of a
given tradition is built. The next level of structural organization I
termed morphokinemic. A morphokine is the smallest meaningful unit
in the structure of a movement system,[12] but only certain combinations
of kinemes are meaningful. In contrast to spoken language, in which
linear sequences of contrastive sounds (phonemes) form meaningful
units (morphemes), a number of kinemes often occur simultaneously to
form a meaningful movement. I did not find further analogies with language based on lexemes or sememes to be useful in this analysis of
dance structure. Instead, Tongans organize morphokines (which have
meaning as movement but do not have lexical meaning) into a relatively
small number of motifs, which, when ordered (i.e., choreographed)
simultaneously and chronologically form dances.

My method of analysis involved two processes, both based on observation and interviewing. The first process involved derivation of emic
units by observing movements and asking informants which they considered the same and which different. The second process, which proceeded contemporaneously, aimed at derivation of the system by discovering the relationship between emic units as they occurred in
performance and in people's conceptions of performance.

Grammar is a term usually reserved for the principles by which
morphemes or words are strung together to form correct or appropriate
utterances within a given speech community. Although generally used
in the singular, as if each language has but one grammar, different con-

texts may require different grammars. Thus, in Tonga as in many other cultures, delivering an oration at a formal ceremony requires different speech patterns than when conversing with intimates. Like language, movement is structured by a set of principles into recognizably correct and appropriate forms, and therefore may be thought of as grammatical. Also like language, different contexts may require different forms, with each dance genre employing different grammars. And just as two languages may contain identical inventories of phonemes, yet be mutually unintelligible because their grammars differ, so it is with dance. The kinemes of Tongan and Samoan dance, for example, are very similar, but their grammars differ. As a result, the dances are mutually unintelligible. A Samoan would have to learn the grammar and motif vocabulary of Tongan dance to make cultural sense of it, and vice versa (see also Kaeppler 1967b, 1972, 1986).

Oratory, poetry, music, dance, sculpture, barkcloth, mats, decorative design, architecture, spatial arrangements, and exposure to olfactory sensations all structure human experience and embody the deep structure, or presuppositions, of a specific society. Within Polynesia, research on ethnoaesthetics and artistic grammars has just begun. Such studies are important to the future of Polynesian studies, not just because of what we have to learn about art and aesthetics, but for what they can teach us about the nature of Polynesian societies and the ways they have changed and are changing.

Traditional, Evolved, and Nontraditional Art

So far this chapter has focused on traditional art and its evolved forms. Many of the traditional arts have persisted, although they have changed through time. Others have been reconstructed after decades (or in some instances, centuries) of non-performance, and in some instances modern adaptations of traditional forms have been created. Art forms that have changed along indigenous lines, while retaining their traditional structure and sentiment, I have called "evolved traditional" (Kaeppler 1979c:185). For example, Maori meeting houses are still carved along traditional lines, and certain contemporary Hawaiian dances are choreographed with traditional structure and sentiment. But a recent trend, led by Samoan novelist Albert Wendt (1983a), emphasizes the study and importance of innovation and creativity among contemporary Polynesian artists. He complains that outsiders place too much value on purity, tradition, and authenticity, and have encouraged the islanders to follow suit. It seems to me, however, that many artistic products (particularly in the visual arts) fabricated in Polynesia today are essentially nontraditional—what I have called "folk art" and "airport art" elsewhere (Kaeppler 1979c:185),[13] even if made by traditional techniques. As noted above, the integral association of visual and verbal modes of expression might be considered a criterion for traditional authenticity. The carving of an image, for example, was inextricably a part of religious ritual, and was accompanied by chants. That contemporary Polynesian carvers of such images are usually Christian makes the process nontraditional, even though the resulting product might be identical in form to one that is traditional or authentic.

Many Polynesian artists with whom I am familiar have no desire to copy slavishly old processes or products; rather, they wish to create new forms based on their own individual background and experience. For example, Rocky Ka'iouliokahihikolo'ehu Jensen and the other members of the Hale Nauā III society of Hawaiian artists (Rose 1980:154–156) consider their products to be fine art that have made Hawaiian themes understandable in today's world. Similarly, some contemporary Maori carvers, although they may carve in the style of their ancestors, do not use the same processes or aspire to produce the same kinds of products as their traditional ancestors. Thus Reverend Hapai Winiata developed his own artistic style, which links the present to the past, Christianity to traditional religion, and Western art to Maori art. His incorporation of Western stylistic elements into Maori tradition reflects an ideological commitment to the bicultural, biracial reality of contemporary Maori society (Kernot 1981). The works of other contemporary Maori artists are discussed by Katerina Mataira (1984). Even further along this continuum is the work of Kuai Maueha, the late wood carver from Bellona, who eschewed his Bellonese artistic background and created an art style of his own. Although there is some question about Solomon Island or Maori influence, as well as uneven critical acclaim from Bellonese, other Polynesians, and outsiders as to the quality of Kuai's work, there is no disagreement about its creativity and non-traditionality. His work was exhibited in 1983–1984 at the East-West Center in Honolulu, the Australian High Commission in Suva, and in other Pacific centers.

Acculturated music has also been given serious consideration by Allan Thomas (1981:185) whose discussion of European source tunes illustrates that in Polynesia "the tune is merely a vehicle for vocal performance, unlike the European ideal where the rendition of the tune is the essence of music." Thomas goes on to show the folly of studying music by simply analyzing sound recordings of single performances, emphasizing instead the importance of improvization, ornamentation, and context, noting that what might have been harmonic music in the Western mode is better understood in a Pacific context if viewed as layered contrapuntal music around a generative melody. Although acculturated music involves borrowing, it is the incorporating music system that shapes the product into its final form. It is therefore necessary to study all aspects of that system, including traditional and contemporary components, if one is to understand fully the artistic process and its resulting products. The acculturative processes that transform European concepts into Polynesian ones must also be seen from this perspective to be properly understood.

"Precontact fabrication" is a concept of limited value in the study of Polynesian art and aesthetics, except perhaps for old-fashioned museum curators and private collectors. In my view, whether or not an object was made prior to European contact is irrelevant to its aesthetic merit. Simply because an image or bark cloth beater was carved with metal tools does not make it less Polynesian, or less authentic. The introduction of metal tools to Polynesia made possible an artistic efflorescence that probably would not have occurred without it. A more appropriate basis for assessing authenticity would be to relate visual to verbal modes of expression. But how can we ever know, for example, which Hawaiian wooden images were carved in accompaniment to traditional prayers? Some wooden images collected on the visit of HMS *Blonde* to Hawai'i in 1824 were carved for sale. They probably were carved by the same artists who produced images prior to the overthrow of the *kapu* in 1819. The products were virtually the same, but it is likely that the process differed, with the later fabrication of images omitting the chanted prayers that were so central to earlier image production.

Although a simple dichotomy between traditional and nontraditional is commonly used in the study of art and aesthetics, I believe this leads to a distorted perspective, and that the concept of evolved traditional is needed to understand changes in Polynesian art. Art forms are produced within specific time and sociocultural frames, and we, as anthropologists, cannot properly study them out of phase with the particular systems within which they are embedded. Studies of art and aesthetics must therefore be tied to time frames that are more specific than precontact or postcontact, pre-Christian or post-Christian. Traditional art and its evolved forms need to be examined ethnohistorically, while studies of nontraditional art must be related to knowledge about the functioning societies that produced it. Exploring the relationship between artistic and societal change may help us to better comprehend the nature of both art and society, as well as the processes of sociocultural change. As I have noted elsewhere, for instance, the use of art "in the acceptance of change was especially useful in Hawai'i, where the general populace was not well versed in the intricacies of genealogy. Unlike Tonga . . . where the components of genealogy and their association with prestige were more widely known and material culture was a conservative force for recognising prestige as separate from power, in Hawai'i material culture assisted in modifying attitudes that would ultimately equate prestige with power" (Kaeppler 1985a:105).

Aesthetics and Social Stratification

One of the most significant changes between traditional and contemporary Polynesian art is a shift from an aesthetic of inequality to an aesthetic of equality. Although this change is more marked in some Polynesian societies than in others, it provides a useful framework for exploring the nature of artistic change within the region. The following seven dimensions of inequality can be identified as relevant to both ethnohistorical and contemporary studies; in traditional Polynesian society these were tied either to genealogy or to achieved positions that tended to become genealogical.

1. Unequal access to clothing and ornamentation. Here one might investigate who wears works of art as clothing or ornamentation (such as jewelry or tattoo). How do wearers obtain these works of art? Who makes them? Who inherits them? Who can appropriate them? What does access to works of art imply socially and culturally, especially with regard to *mana* and *tabu?*
2. Unequal distribution of valuables during ceremonial exchanges. What valuables or other gifts are given on ceremonial or ritual occasions? There is a significant differentiation here between western and eastern Polynesia; one might ask how wealth is intertwined with social categories in each of these sub-areas.
3. Unequal elaboration of rites of passage. For whom are rites of passage publicly celebrated? What kinds of artistic objects and performances are associated with the rites, and how are the rites themselves commemorated?
4. Inequality of celebrity status as reflected in artistic performances. For whom is poetry (and its attendant music and dance) composed? Who can recite, sing, or dance for whom? Is there anything special about the placement of the performers?
5. Inequality of living conditions. Who has more grandiose houses than others? How are the various buildings placed in a homestead and how are homesteads arranged within villages? Who designs and builds houses? What is the layout of space within a house?
6. Unequal access to sacred places. Such places were often marked by sacred objects, or works of art, to protect the sacred power of the place. They also protected some individuals from the sacred power of their competitors, and others from having their sacred power infringed upon. Who could use these sacred places? Who designed and built them? Who protected the places and people who used them? What did access to sacred places imply socially and culturally?
7. Unequal or special status given to artists. How do individuals become artists? Is the status of artist hereditary? Who evaluates the

arts or the processes by which they are produced? Are there recognized critics and if so, how do they attain their position?

These dimensions of inequality are essentially contextual and reflect the position of individuals within the social order, but one must also investigate possible stratification or complementarity of the content. Such investigations should relate to specific time frames; no doubt answers will differ dramatically between ethnohistoric and contemporary studies. Inequality is intertwined with prestige, power, authority, and status, and studies of artistic manifestations can help to illuminate these aspects of society. In Polynesia, the arts traditionally sustained inequality and enhanced the position of male and female chiefs. As social concepts were transformed so were artistic concepts. In the transformations of inequality lie a fruitful prospect for future studies of Polynesian art and aesthetics. In addition, studies of art in the context of tourism (e.g., see Te Awekotuku 1981) should help to reveal the nature of economic restructuring as Polynesians approach the twenty-first century.

Conclusion

Traditional Polynesian aesthetic traditions were concerned with appropriate materials, form, and use. Objects and performances conforming to Polynesian aesthetic ideas preserved in visual and verbal forms the cultural concern with hierarchical ranking, status, and power. They gave pleasure to Polynesians if used in appropriate ways on appropriate occasions. And through their use they acquired a kind of historical and aesthetic power and became objectified representations of social relationships among gods and people.

Contemporary Polynesian aesthetic traditions are more diffuse, with island groups becoming distinct from each other as a result of differing internal histories and external influences. Inequality[14] has become less central to artistic production and performance, especially in areas such as Hawaii and New Zealand; being an artist and acquiring works of art are socially now within the means of everyone. With increasing social equality have come new art forms and new aesthetic concepts. The old and new in art and aesthetics have yet to be systematically studied for many parts of Polynesia, but they offer fertile ground to those who would search on another level for the scheme of society.

NOTES

1. Art and aesthetics are probably the least studied components of Polynesian ethnology, and Polynesia is probably the least studied area of world art history.

Within the Pacific Arts Association and in specialist groups that deal with music, dance, or oral literature only a few are Polynesianists. Thus, the writing of this paper has been a lonely pursuit. It is unlikely that there will be rapid advance in this area, however, until more anthropologists take the subject seriously and investigate how the arts are part of the social action that makes Polynesian societies Polynesian. I would like to thank Roger Neich, Jacob Love, Peter Gathercole, and Alan Howard for helpful comments on the manuscript.

2. Although much of Best's work was not published until the 1920s, his fieldwork was carried out at the beginning of the century.

3. Haddon (1901:68) had previously written a note on Maori scroll design suggesting that the *manaia* might be "degraded and conventionalized representations of birds," which argued "in favor of a Melanesian element in the population of New Zealand."

4. Margaret Mead (1928a, 1930b) did include some information on poetry, oratory, and dance in her major monographs on Samoa.

5. Ralph Linton was Curator of Ethnology at the Field Museum, Chicago, and Professor of Anthropology at the University of Wisconsin and Yale University for many years. He was a member of the Bayard Dominick Expedition of the Bishop Museum to the Marquesas, and the collections he made are now at the Bishop Museum in Honolulu, the Field Museum in Chicago, and the American Museum of Natural History in New York.

6. This article was for many years assigned reading in courses in the philosophy of aesthetics at the University of Hawaii.

7. This exhibition, held in 1946 at the Museum of Modern Art, New York, was not superseded until the exhibition of 1979 at the National Gallery of Art, Washington, D.C., which was organized by Douglas Newton, Peter Gathercole, and Adrienne Kaeppler (see Gathercole, Kaeppler, and Newton 1979; and Davenport 1981 for a review of the exhibition). Other public showings that emphasized aspects of Polynesian art include an exhibition on Polynesian sculpture at the Art Institute of Chicago and the Museum of Primitive Art, New York, in 1967–1968 (Wardwell 1967); exhibitions of Polynesian objects collected on Cook's voyages in Honolulu (Kaeppler 1978a) and Vancouver; exhibitions of Polynesian objects in honor of Cook's voyages in New Zealand (Duff 1969) and London (Cobbe 1979) (some objects had been collected on Cook's voyages while others had not); an exhibition of Polynesian objects in honor of Cook and Bougainville in Paris (Museé de l'Homme 1972) (which also included objects collected on their voyages and others that were not); an exhibition on Hawaii that traveled the United States for two years (Rose 1980); and the recent *Te Maori* exhibition that brought treasures from New Zealand collections to several venues in the United States (S. Mead 1984).

8. Anne Salmond (1978) and Roger Neich (1977) have examined Maori social space and the house as a model of the cosmos.

9. A similar distinction existed in Tonga where there was *'aho me'e* 'day dance' and *pō me'e* 'night dance'.

10. According to Limasene Neich, *ula* implies daring and "the idea of two groups challenging each other to be more daring with acrobatic tricks and erotic displays." (Roger Neich, personal communication, March 1, 1984).

11. A case in point is Simmons' entry in the *Te Maori* catalog for the lintel illustrated here as Figure 1. Simmons' entry attributes this object to "North-

land, Doubtless Bay, Ngati Kahu tribe." He further elaborates that it dates from the eighteenth century, "is one of the two extant pieces in this carving style," and inexplicably calls it a threshold, *paepae,* rather than a lintel (Simmons 1984:183). This object was formerly in the Hooper collection and had no such documentation (Phelps 1976:411). Without explanation Simmons has given it a complete provenance and a new function. Also unexplained is how two examples can form a style.

12. This is not to deny, of course, that lesser movements can communicate meaning in other than a structural sense. I explicitly use an analogy to structural linguistics, in which morphemes are considered minimal units of meaning.

13. It is difficult to consider much "airport art" as art. In my view such things as fake Hawaiian god figures carved by Tongans for sale to tourists are no more Polynesian art than plastic tikis made in Japan and sold in Hawaiian airport shops as souvenirs.

14. I am referring here to inequality based on genealogical (and quasi-genealogical) precedence rather than economic inequality.

8

 The Early
Contact
Period

ROBERT BOROFSKY
ALAN HOWARD

"ONE of the . . . beauties of Pacific history," Scarr notes, "is the richness of the documentary material" (Daws 1979:126). Even a cursory examination suggests the vast literature that exists on the subject. Dening's (1980) study of the Marquesas, for example, contains more than 950 references; Gunson's (1978) study of South Sea missionaries over 750.[1]

This rich, historical documentation is not simply happenstance; it results from the interaction of several factors. In respect to Western literature concerning the contact period, for instance, at least three factors played a prominent role. "The second half of the eighteenth century," Frost observes, "saw the beginnings of scientific exploration and survey of, and collection in, vast regions of the globe" (Frost 1979:5). In addition, advances in navigation meant that sea travel was safer during this period, encouraging scientists and artists to accompany the explorers. "A vessel like Cook's *Resolution* . . . combined the values of a fortress and a travelling laboratory" (B. Smith 1960:2). The rate of literacy also rose considerably at this time among certain groups. In England it doubled among men. "Literary ambition and disposition to authorship" (Burney in J. C. Beaglehole 1967:lxxxix) led numerous people to keep records of their voyages. On Cook's third voyage alone, at least 27 individuals kept accounts.

Other factors—missionary concerns with literacy and Polynesian concerns with tradition—encouraged the production of an indigenous literature. Koskinen (1953:21) notes, "the missionaries began to create a literary form for the native languages at the same time that they themselves learnt to master them. It was considered necessary to teach the heathen the Gospel by means of the written word, as well as by preaching." A desire to record past memories supposedly motivated 'I'i, a

Hawaiian historian, to write on the Hawaiian past. Another Hawaiian historian, Malo (1951:1–2), began his manuscript on *Hawaiian Antiquities*—written around 1840—by observing, "when traditions are carried in the memory [alone] it leads to contradictory versions . . . [they are] made worthless."

But this richness of historical documentation is a mixed blessing. Its very vastness has proved intimidating at times to scholars. Few have developed broad, comparative analyses that integrate materials from diverse island groups. In contrast to Scarr's above quote, John Ward (1966:198) observes: "A major obstacle to writing the history of the British islands in the Pacific is the complexity and extent of the sources that have to be studied."

The material, moreover, contains definite biases. The literature is weighted far more toward Western perspectives than toward Polynesian ones. (The main exception to this trend is in Hawaii, where a good collection of indigenous literature exists for the nineteenth century.) Although one can appreciate the reasons for the differential production in written materials between the two groups, the result is an unfortunate one. Indigenous perspectives are often underrepresented in scholarly studies. This constitutes a significant problem since data suggest Polynesians perceived certain historical events in rather different terms from Europeans. European and Hawaiian accounts disagree, for instance, as to whether Cook had a sexual liaison at Kaua'i.

Also, writings by Hawaiian historians such as Malo, 'I'i, and Kamakau frequently involved retrospective data collected years after contact. People's recollections were open to a variety of distortions. Regarding the assertion that Cook was murdered for his *tabu* violations—a statement recorded by Lt. Peter Puget of Vancouver's squadron—Sahlins (1981a:26) comments that "if the interpretation was historically inaccurate as of 1 February 1779, it had become true as of 1793," a result of Cook's changed status in Hawaiian eyes.

There are other difficulties as well. Various retrospective accounts portray Polynesian traditions in uniform or static terms, thereby missing their varied and dynamic nature. Indicative of this problem is the procedure the missionary Dibble followed in his research on Hawaiian traditions: "At the time of [our] meeting each scholar read what he had written—discrepancies were reconciled and corrections made by each other, and then all the compositions were handed to me, out of which I endeavored to make one connected and true account" (Dibble 1843:iv). We must be careful not to fall into this trap today. Much of Malo's book apparently derives from information accumulated on the island of Hawai'i, and from Malo's association with the chief Auwai. One must be careful, as a result, in generalizing Malo's account to the archipelago as a whole. Significant cultural difference existed within the group.

Nuances of language may also lead scholars astray. Westerners often termed Polynesian attempts to appropriate their goods theft, implying a set of legal associations that were often inappropriate for the situation.

A valuable way of perceiving the complexities involved in analyzing this literature is to review the ways historians and anthropologists have examined the material to date. Both groups have encountered similar problems.

Historical Approaches

Understanding how historians have approached Pacific history involves grasping what modern historians usually regard as two different perspectives.[2] The first is called imperial, or Eurocentric, history. It dominated the field into the 1950s. As the name implies, it focuses on the imperial expansion of the European powers. According to Davidson (1966:6) the perspective emphasizes the Western "acquisition of sovereignty or of political control; the establishment of law and administration; emigration from the mother country to the colonies; commerce within the empire; and, behind all these and giving unity to the whole, the notion of a 'civilizing mission.' " Of particular concern is the formal role played by Western explorers, administrators, and missionaries in this expansion. "Before the late 1940s," Ralston (1985:156) asserts, Pacific history "focused almost exclusively on the exploits and ambitions of Western imperial and missionary agents."

Today, imperialistic accounts are often viewed as reflecting certain biases. One that is frequently cited concerns Pacific islanders' limited influence on historical events. In imperialistic works Pacific island populations were depicted as "the passive victims of alien exploitative trading and labor recruiting practices" (Ralston 1985:157). Another frequently cited bias involves an overemphasis on the West's fatal impact. According to Howe (1984:350), certain imperialist writers suggested that Europeans "have caused nothing but disruption and dislocation of the [Pacific] Islanders' lifestyles."

The second historical approach to Polynesian-Western interactions is termed island-oriented history, or the new historiography. It has dominated Pacific history since the 1960s. In contrast to imperialistic history, island-oriented history emphasizes the less formal agents of European expansion: beachcombers, traders, and whaling crews. Building on C. R. Fay's concept of informal empire, Davidson, the approach's reputed founder, stressed "the importance of looking at the activities of private Europeans who were not representatives of their nations nor agents of their governments but simply people following their own interests and careers outside the political boundaries of empire as well as within them" (West 1973:115). Howe, an island-centered historian, asserts it is "not sufficient to concentrate on explorers, missionaries, and government agents. A lowly beachcomber, an impoverished sandalwood trader, a ragged whaling crew in search of rest and recreation might perform activities or make observations as significant as those of any top-hatted evangelist or ostrich-plumed governor" (Howe 1984: xiii).[3]

Island-oriented history, in Maude's (1971:20) phrasing, emphasizes the perspectives of the governed more than that of the governors. It examines European expansion from the perspectives of those who resided on the Pacific islands. The emphasis is on the ways European policies and approaches were shaped by local conditions. Cultural interaction, not cultural domination, is the focus of concern. The fatal nature of Western impact is questioned, and the active role that indigenous populations played in determining their own fates is stressed. Howe (1984:348) asserts that "recent historical research suggests that the processes of cultural contact were not always . . . one-sided, that Islanders were quite capable of taking their own initiative and, rather than passively accepting Europeans and their ways, either rejected or deliberately exploited the newcomers for their own reasons."[4]

Although the island-oriented perspective dominates the modern literature and has gained widespread acceptance, it must be treated with a degree of caution. Accounts involving this perspective often contain biases that readers should be aware of in order to understand the state of Pacific history today. First, they tend to stereotype imperial history as emphasizing the fatal impact when that was not the sole, or even primary, concern of many works within this category. Moreover, in asserting the active role of Pacific islanders in the contact process, there has been a tendency among island-centered historians to pass over the fact that serious disruptions and dislocations did occur on many islands. As Oliver comments in his review of Howe's book *Where the Waves Fall* (1984): "to assert that any sizeable percentage of island cultures has escaped 'disruption and dislocation' during those early decades of contact . . . is to ignore a huge mass of credible, first-hand accounts" (Oliver 1984:C12). Finally, despite assertions to the contrary, modern historical accounts have continued to remain mostly Eurocentric in character. They still focus on European actions. Ralston (1985:151), an island-centered historian, admits that although "a move from agents of the imperial metropolitan powers to small-time operators on the periphery has . . . been effected, . . . [Pacific history] was and still is organized through foreign factors."

Two historical circumstances helped shape the biases modern Pacific historians often manifest in describing their field. Just as many imperial histories were written during the colonial era—and reflect the influences of that period—island-centered history has developed during the recent post-colonial period and reflects its influences. Modern Pacific history, Maude (1971:24) asserts: "has a very practical and therapeutic role to enact in assisting the rehabilitation of the Pacific peoples at the end of a traumatic era of European political, economic and technological ascendancy by renewing their self-respect and providing them with a secure historical base from which to play their part as responsible citizens of independent or self-governing communities in a new world."

Island-centered history developed during Davidson's tenure as chair of the Pacific History Department at the Research School of Pacific Studies in the Australian National University. In formulating a new approach to Pacific history, scholars associated with the Department at times overstated the biases of earlier writers. As these historians came to dominate the field, their perspectives became embedded in the literature. The department's influence is quite impressive.[5] Even as early as 1971, Maude was able to observe that scholarly publications associated with the Department of Pacific History outnumbered all other works in the field added together.

Now into its third decade, various Pacific historians have begun reflecting on what has (and has not) been accomplished by the island-centered approach. On the strong side, it has led to the re-evaluation of the nature of European-islander contacts. As Ralston notes: "Davidson's dictum that the . . . subdiscipline of Pacific history should be island-oriented led to the reconsideration of many highly eurocentric interpretations of past interactions between Islander and white. Long-held beliefs that Islanders were the passive victims of alien exploitative trading and labor recruiting practices were convincingly exposed as false or only partial truths" (Ralston 1985:156–157).

For Polynesia, the island-centered approach has produced a series of outstanding monographs, including France (1969), Gilson (1970), Gunson (1978), Maude (1968, 1981), Newbury (1980), and Ralston (1978). These publications provide a foundation on which to build general, comparative analyses.

Still, problems remain to be solved. First, a major difficulty exists regarding how to move beyond Eurocentric accounts. Maude has suggested collecting indigenous oral materials. But as Borofsky (1987) notes, such accounts often have their own biases and inaccuracies.

Second, beyond its concern with less Eurocentric views and less formal agents of European expansion, island-centered history has yet to develop a theoretical perspective to draw its empirical studies together. Discussing Spate's (1979, 1983) and Howe's (1984) recent attempts at synthesis, Ralston (1985:158) comments, "their works are most important additions to the field, but neither, despite the scope of their endeavors, has offered encompassing generalizations or theoretical insights into what are basically empirical studies."

Third, deriving from its restricted theoretical vision, and very much tied to it, has been the approach's limited concern with comparative analysis. Howe states the point well.

> Researchers have been so diligently ferreting out and publishing their detailed findings that a good many of them have lost any basic sense of direction. They have become too immersed in the internal complexities to see the general background. Pacific islands history is a breeding ground for more and more highly specialized articles, monographs, and symposia. . . . Few writers seem able to pull back from the microcosm to consider the implications, if any, for a broader or macrocosmic view of [Pacific] islands' history (Howe 1979:83).

Ralston's (1978) account of beachcomber communities is one of the best comparisons. Yet as Campbell indicates, she "fails to take full advantage of the [comparative] method. Comparison should produce more than just a new set of generalizations; it should alert one to explanations, ramifications, and strands of causality which one might otherwise miss because of their obscurity, or because they are too obvious" (Campbell 1978:190).

As a result of these recent reflections, a sense of uncertainty or caution, depending on whom one reads, has developed regarding the direction of Pacific history. Routledge (1985:81) suggests that a certain "pertinacity of doubts" exists today regarding the field's goals.

Anthropological Approaches

Although anthropologists have approached Polynesian-Western interactions from a different perspective, they have, like Pacific historians, faced difficulties in enunciating details of their perspective within a broad, comparative framework. Here again it is helpful to examine two different, but related, approaches.[6]

The first aims at reconstructing Polynesian cultures prior to Western contact. Although it does not, strictly speaking, address issues of Polynesian-Western interaction, its value lies in establishing a baseline from which to explore changes in the post-contact period. The problems inherent in this endeavor can best be illustrated by examining two recent efforts: Oliver's (1974) account of ancient Tahitian society and Valeri's (1985a) account of Hawaiian religion.

Oliver's *Ancient Tahitian Society* (1974) has been well received in reviews. Firth (1976:565) describes the three-volume work as "amply documented, carefully annotated . . . sensitively analyzed, . . . [allowing] us for the first time to base our reflections, comparisons—and speculations—about ancient Tahitian society on a firm foundation of clearly sifted evidence." The reason for such praise is Oliver's judicious interpretation of the data. To quote Newbury (1976:244), "the care and circumspection with which [the recorded evidence] is treated sets a very high standard in ethnohistorical 'reconstruction'. The temptation to indulge in new theories about social and political change is avoided . . . the lasting impression is a healthy scepticism about the limits to our knowledge."

Though not always specified in print, a hesitancy is sometimes voiced among scholars regarding what is referred to as Oliver's limited theoretical vision. It is relevant therefore for readers to understand Oliver's position in this respect. When Dening (1985b:103), commenting on Oliver's later book, *Two Tahitian Villages*, gently chides Oliver for refusing "to say what he thinks [his study] means in relationship to wider issues," Oliver replies that he is concerned with ethnographies per se: "first, with making them fuller, more faithful representations of various distinctive ways of life; and secondly, doing so objectively and in language that will permit them to be compared one with another." He considers this "to be a sufficient goal in itself, one that does not require any other justification" (Oliver 1985:111–112).

Valeri's *Kingship and Sacrifice* (1985a) has received a more ambivalent reaction. Sahlins praised the book on the dust jacket of *Kingship and Sacrifice,* but Charlot (1987:111) comments that Valeri "often announces his interpretation . . . rather than offering arguments in support of it." And Alan Howard (1986a:531–532), while acknowledging the insightfulness of Valeri's analysis, asserts that his desire to impose coherence on the data leads him to underplay the diversity and fluidity of Hawaiian culture. The reason for this ambivalent reaction, we believe, lies in Valeri's strong interpretative program: he orders the data in accordance with a set of axiomatic propositions. Although this allows him to tie together seemingly disparate information in an insightful manner, it also leads to questionable interpretations.

Scholars disposed toward reconstruction are thus often caught in a bind. When they move beyond simply trying to present the data in a coherent manner—not an easy task given their fragmented and ambiguous character—authors open themselves to charges of misinterpretation. But to take the more cautious route means that critical issues of theoretical and comparative importance may never be addressed by those most sensitive to the material's significance.

A second anthropological approach focuses on the processes of cultural change. Recent works by Dening and Sahlins are prime examples. Examining their publications, we perceive some of the problems now facing anthropologists studying cultural change.

Dening (1980) presents an in-depth narrative of Marquesan history from 1774 to 1880, interspersed with a set of reflections regarding the processes at work. Overall, the book has been well received. Boutilier (1982–1983:755) calls it "a brilliant piece of ethnohistorical and historical research," and Spate (1980:22) describes Dening's reflections as "penetrating essays on the human condition." Still, despite its generally warm reception, a problem exists. There is a gap between Dening's astute reflections and the details of his historical narrative. Both are of high quality. But we never see precisely how one fits into the other. To give Dening his due, he is sensitive—more than most scholars—as to how we impose our meanings on the past. Rather than provide an artificial order to events, he prefers leaving the relation between narrative and reflections ambiguous. Writing history, Dening (n.d.:42) observes, "is inevitably an exegesis of an exegesis."

Sahlins' work (1981a, 1985) appears to be better integrated. The dynamic interplay between structure and process, culture and history, are explored through details of early Hawaiian-European contact. His work, too, has been well received. Leach (1985:220) terms *Historical Metaphors and Mythical Realities* brilliant, and Gathercole (1986:24) asserts "Sahlins has a formidable ability to take ideas . . . and give them new cutting edges . . . [*Islands of History* is a] highly stimulating discussion of the relationship between history and structure." But Sahlins ultimately faces the same problem as Dening. Although his broad generalizations are embedded in a historical narrative, at times he is selective concerning the evidence marshaled to support his points, and some reviewers have questioned his analyses on this account. Thus, like the formulation of cultural reconstructions, the study of social change is confronted with a tension between broad generalization and supporting details. Rarely are the two fully integrated within a single analysis.

A Suggested Approach

As other authors in this volume have done, we would like to suggest some possible directions for future research. What follows is an attempt to reframe certain issues in a way that may make them more amenable to resolution.

First, we believe there is value in maintaining a dialogue between modern ethnographic and reconstructionist perspectives. Little direct evidence exists to illuminate Polynesian perspectives at the time of contact, but we can use modern anthropological interpretations to gain insight into the cultural logics formerly at work in Polynesian societies. Present-day ethnographic writings can suggest the contexts that framed Polynesians' actions, that gave their behaviors meaning, in the past. The model we have in mind is somewhat akin to Braudel's structures of the *longue durée*—the enduring structures of a society that persist through centuries. For instance, in the following analysis we emphasize Polynesian concerns with status, on the assumption that status rivalries have constituted a persistent theme in Polynesian societies over the long term.

Obviously there are limits to such a procedure. One must be cautious about interpreting the past in terms of the present. But if we are clear about our assumptions and the limitations they impose on our analyses, there is value in maintaining a dialogue between modernist and reconstructionist perspectives.

Second, it is important to move beyond the examination of individual cases, individual exchanges, to the flow of Polynesian-Western interaction at specific locales over time. There is no doubt that Europeans misconstrued Polynesian motives and vice versa. Still we can gain a sense of each party's perspective by examining sequences of interactions at particular sites. Noting how event B followed event A and how this, in turn, seemingly led to event C, we can begin to understand the meaning each party's actions had for the other. We can begin to see Polynesian and Western cultures in process, adjusting to and negotiating a relationship with the other over time.

Third, we feel there is much value in developing controlled comparisons across a number of island groups. Such comparisons offer a valuable framework within which to analyze individual case studies. We will suggest, for example, that violent conflicts tended to represent a stage within a broader pattern of early Polynesian-Western relations. We then use this perspective to make sense of events on specific islands; exploring when and how violence occurred at Samoa in contrast to Tahiti, at Hawaii in contrast to the Marquesas.

Fourth, it is important to be aware of the limitations of the data. We believe Dening and Oliver are correct in emphasizing the tentative nature of broad generalizations. Given the problems already noted, a sense of caution is not only helpful, it is crucial to sound analysis. An awareness of the limitations should not simply be admitted and then indirectly dismissed. As Dening illustrates in his Marquesan study, the data's limitations need to frame the very analysis.[7]

In the remainder of this chapter we compare Polynesian-Western interaction on four Polynesian archipelagoes. Utilizing the fact that early explorers often visited the same locales (because of their known anchorages), we follow Polynesian-Western interaction at specific sites, observing the processual nature of relations over time. In the Marquesas, we explore the first five Western visits to Vaitahu Bay on Tahuata: Mendaña in 1595, Cook in 1774, Ingraham in 1791, Marchand later in 1791, and Hergest in 1792. For the Society Islands, we study the first four visits to Tahiti: Wallis at Matavai in 1767, Bougainville at Hitia'a in 1768, Cook at Matavai in 1769, and Boenechea off Tai'arapu in 1772. For Hawaii, we examine the first five visits to the island group (focusing on Hawai'i and Kaua'i, where visitors stopped the longest): Cook at Kaua'i and Ni'ihau in 1778; Cook (and Clerke) at Hawai'i, Kaua'i, and Ni'ihau in 1778–1779; Portlock and Dixon at Hawai'i, O'ahu, and Ni'ihau in 1786; La Pérouse at Maui in 1786; and Portlock and Dixon again at Hawai'i, O'ahu, Kaua'i, and Ni'ihau in 1786–1787. Finally, for Samoa we focus on the first five visits listed by Gilson (1970:65–67) focusing on Tutuila: Roggeveen in 1722, Bougainville in 1768, La Pérouse in 1787, the HMS *Pandora* with its tender in 1791, and Bass in 1802.[8]

Trade Negotiations and the Issue of Theft

The nature of Polynesian actions during early encounters remains somewhat enigmatic. Direct data are too few and too ambiguous to shed light on what lay behind various Polynesian actions. We might add that the intentions of Europeans have not always been clear either, despite a seeming wealth of documentation regarding their viewpoints. Our task in this section is to explore avenues for improving our understanding of the perspectives Europeans and Polynesians brought to their encounters with one another. To illustrate our approach, we will focus on the issue of theft during the early days of contact.[9]

Numerous accounts indicate that European explorers were upset by unsanctioned appropriation of their property. "Thieving by Polynesians," Dening (1966:40) notes, "almost drove the sea-captains to distraction." The most common explanation is that Polynesians did not recognize Western conceptions of private property. "It was no more possible for the islanders to keep their hands off the Europeans' belongings," Moorehead (1966:21) asserts, "than it was for the Europeans to abandon their rule that private property was sacred." Dodge (1976:34) adds: "the Tahitians . . . had no idea of personal property as understood by Europeans." Pearson (1969) develops this theme by suggesting that Europeans misunderstood the protocol surrounding the arrival of drift voyages. The vessel and its entire contents were given over to the host who then, in turn, was obliged to provide voyagers with new items on their departure. "Whatever the islanders might have considered to be their rights over the property of their visitors," Pearson (1970:140) remarks, "it is certain that the Europeans recognized no such understanding."

Despite the frequency with which scholars cite these explanations, we should be cautious about accepting them. European sea captains were not all equally upset by Polynesian actions in this regard. Although every explorer expressed concern about the problem of theft, Wallis, Cook, Portlock, and Dixon seemed significantly more disturbed by it than Bougainville and Marchand. The same explorer, moreover, responded in different ways on different occasions. Although Cook reacted rather sharply to some incidents, he seemed far more tolerant of others. Polynesian chiefs likewise projected variable attitudes. Many chiefs participated, directly or indirectly, in the unsanctioned appropriation of shipboard property. Banks commented that during Cook's first voyage to Tahiti, "the chiefs were employd in stealing what they could in the Cabbin while their dependents took every thing that was loose about the ship, even the glass ports" (J. C. Beaglehole 1962, 1:263). Yet some chiefs prevented their subordinates from taking things and even helped Europeans regain lost items. Banks appreciatively records the assistance of Tubourai (Tupura'a i Tamaiti) in this respect. Waxing poetic, Banks calls him Lycurgus after the Greek law giver (J. C. Beaglehole 1962, 1:258). What we have, in other words, is a range of reactions on both sides to Polynesian appropriation of European possessions.

European Perspectives

To properly understand the nature of such incidents it is not sufficient to limit our investigation to specific attitudes of particular individuals. It is also essential to comprehend the broader contexts that framed the interactions. Both the explorers' journals and modern histories indicate that certain medical, technological, and social factors shaped the actions of the Western explorers during this period. Scurvy, for example, was a problem that seriously affected many ships' crews. Medical science had still not accurately diagnosed the causes of the disease, with the result that various folk theories prevailed. Thus de Langle regarded fresh water as a palliative, and Cook advocated the use of malt. The one measure explorers usually agreed upon in treating scurvy was the value of island visits, on time spent ashore.

Western ships, moreover, faced storage problems. As Oliver noted (1961:86), the "small ships had neither space nor facilities for carrying the right quantities and kinds of food and water and fuel required on long voyages." European explorers usually arrived at Polynesian islands short, at times even destitute, of provisions. Visiting the islands was not simply a pleasant change of pace; it was often a dire necessity if the ships were to complete their missions.

The Europeans' technological edge in weaponry also shaped early interactions with Polynesians. Numerous journal entries underscored the widespread observation that the latter were intimidated by shipboard firepower. Boenechea wrote about "the terror and dread in which they hold our weapons" (in Corney 1913:333). And Banks noted that Tahitians "often described to us the terrour which [Wallis' guns] put them into" (in J. C. Beaglehole 1962, 1:307). European weapons had their limitations, however. Gunpowder was ineffective when wet (which, in part, is why the French failed to defend themselves effectively at Samoa), and Polynesians could overwhelm musket-firing soldiers if they attacked en masse at close quarters, preventing the soldiers from reloading (as happened at Hawai'i).

Dependent on sailpower, and possessing boats that drew several feet of water, European ship captains sought protected bays with safe anchorages for their stays. That Western ships repeatedly visited Matavai at Tahiti, and Vaitahu in the Marquesas, had to do with the nature of the harbors these locations afforded. The requirements of European shipping thus facilitated certain Polynesian groups' developing long-term relations with Europeans, though—and this is important—the relations did not usually involve the same European individuals. Nonetheless each group was able to build a set of understandings regarding the other. Bougainville's positive reception at Tahiti, Pearson (1969) asserts, derived from Wallis' earlier use of force there. By Bougainville's visit, Tahitians had come to appreciate the lethal qualities of Western weaponry. Westerners learned from each other's journals effective ways for resolving problems at particular anchorages. Commenting on the regulations Cook drew up for his visit to Tahiti in 1769, J. C. Beaglehole (1974:176) observes "obviously Cook had . . . paid attention to Wallis' journal." And when La Pérouse successfully placed his ship under *tapu* at Maui, to keep Hawaiians off it, he noted he "had learned [about the word *tapu*] from the English accounts" (La Pérouse 1799, 1:342–343).

If we are to believe the explorers' journals (and biographies about them), many of the sea captains used force only with reluctance. Beaglehole notes that Cook "as a humane man . . . took Lord Morton['s reminder] seriously" to "restrain the wanton use of Fire Arms" and to view the shedding of blood among the people visited as "a crime of the highest nature" (Beaglehole 1974:187, 150). We can see this concern to avoid violence in Wallis' initial encounter with Tahitians. When Tahitians "cheated" the British in trade and struck several of the sailors (on June 21), Wallis gave "strict orders that no man should hurt or molest" them (Robertson 1973:28). And when the Tahitians took some of the water casks (on June 23), Gore tried to demonstrate, without actually wounding anyone, the effective range of Western firearms by firing a musquetoon in front of them. (The Tahitians were startled by the gun's noise, but failed to realize they were supposed to watch where the shot landed, making Gore's lesson a failure.) Obviously this humane perspective did not always dominate, and it is questionable whether it was shared by many ordinary seamen. But the journals do suggest that a sense of restraint shaped many sea captains' initial encounters because they wanted to view themselves (and have readers of their journals view them) as "civilized," as being able to use reason rather than brute force in their interactions with non-Western groups.

It is within this context that one can make sense of European concerns for the unsanctioned appropriation of their shipboard property. What upset the explorers more than the violation of their sacred property rights, we believe, was the way Polynesian actions affected trade, especially how it undermined the Europeans' ability to assign high valuations to their goods. To allow goods to disappear overboard, without getting needed supplies in return, meant the ships had less to trade with, less to exchange for provisions, after the initial overtures of hospitality had passed. It is critical here to remember a point previously made: because of limitations in Western technology, many of the explorers were in considerable need of fresh supplies. When troubles arose at Tahiti, for example, Wallis did not leave because, to quote Robertson (1973:34), his "water was now very short and not near sufficiency to carry [him] to any known place." Polynesian appropriations could also undermine a ship's sailing capabilities. The taking of a quadrant at Tahiti, the attempted appropriation of a kedge anchor in the Marquesas, and the seizure of a cutter at Hawai'i all raised questions regarding Cook's ability to carry out his missions of exploration. Dening states the point well. (He makes it in regard to Cook, but we would extend it more broadly to other explorers.) "On a voyage his property was his limited capital. A sextant stolen was an irretrievable loss. His things—his nails, his beads, his handkerchiefs—had a present, monetary value. They were bartered for food and water. . . . He was transient. . . . His wealth lay in what he possessed, not in his distribution against tomorrow's needs and moral bonds" (Dening 1980:18).

Against this background it is easier to understand differential responses by explorers to Polynesian actions. Bougainville and Marchand were more tolerant of unsanctioned appropriations and displayed more restrained reactions to it. Both visited for relatively short periods: Bougainville stayed approximately twelve days at Tahiti; and Marchand nine at the Marquesas. In contrast, Wallis, Cook, and Dixon and Portlock stayed considerably longer and, correspondingly, were more distressed by the unsanctioned removal of goods. Staying briefly and replenishing supplies quickly, the former explorers were not as involved in long-term trade relations. The loss of goods was thus of less concern. The latter group, in contrast, needed to be concerned. The reason Cook impounded twenty-two canoes for the stealing of an iron rake at Tahiti —a case frequently cited as a Western overreaction to the loss of private property—was to set an example. Tahitians "were daily either committing or attempting to commit one theft or other" (Cook in Beaglehole 1955:101). With plans for a still longer stay, Cook perceived he might well lose far more if some action were not taken.

The explorers had a limited number of options available to them in coping with Polynesian attempts to appropriate their property. One option, chosen by several sea captains, was simply to tolerate the loss of material. During an exchange of presents between Marchand and a high status Marquesan, for example, the former's handkerchief and snuff-box were taken. Marchand downplayed the incident "as he did not wish to disturb the joy of [the] day" (Fleurieu 1801:38). At Tahiti, Banks notes that he and Cook "had resolvd . . . rather to put up with our losses than . . . frighten the Indians the consequences of which we knew to be scarcity of provisions" (Beaglehole 1962, 1:287). But this alternative was a limited one at best. Followed to any great extent, it meant the loss of valued goods and a reduced ability to trade.

A second option was to leave after a short stay. This is the alternative Bougainville chose at Tahiti. Cook, Ingraham, Hergest, and Marchand chose it at the Marquesas. Portlock and Dixon did the same at the island of Hawai'i. Regarding his stay in the Marquesas, Cook observed that even with the killing of a thief, the Marquesans "would very often exercize their tallant of thieving upon us, which I thought necessary to put up with as our stay was likely to be short among them" (Beaglehole 1961:366). The obvious problem with this option was that it limited the ability to reprovision ships, to obtain the diet of fresh fruits, vegetables, and water thought necessary as antiscorbutics. It also raised problems of crew morale, since sailors frequently desired rest and recreation ashore. And it left open the question of where else they might go for reprovisioning. The problem of appropriation was common throughout the Pacific. Avoiding it at one island meant facing it at another.

A third option was violent retribution. But the blatant killing of Polynesians was, if we are to believe their journals, morally reprehensible to many sea captains of the period. They preferred less drastic steps, such as shooting off cannons (without shot) or killing birds—demonstrations of their weaponry that did not lead to the loss of human life. But since European weaponry was foreign in nature, the implications of such demonstrations were often missed by Polynesians. When La Pérouse attempted to show a Samoan chief the effectiveness of French firearms by killing some birds, we are told the chief concluded the weapons were mainly used for that purpose. Usually someone had to be killed before Polynesians understood the deadly implications of European weaponry.

We can infer a second, and equally important problem with the use of violence. It threatened to upset trade relations. Bougainville (1772: 236), hearing some of his men had killed a Tahitian, stated: "I immediately went ashore with an assortment of silk stuffs, and tools . . .

[which] I distributed . . . among the chiefs, expressing my concern to them on account of the disaster which happened the day before, and assuring them that I would punish the perpetrators." And following the killing of a Tahitian for taking a musket, Cook wrote "we prevail'd on about 20 of them to come to the Tent and their sit down with us and endeavour'd by every means in our power to convence them that . . . we still would be friends with them" (Beaglehole 1955:80).

Complicating the problems generated by violence was the fact that it usually required repeated application to be effective. Even after Polynesians had grasped the lethal character of Western weapons, they often continued their attempts to obtain shipboard property without permission. Threats of violence were sometimes effective, but they did not always solve the problem. Quoting Ingraham (1971:48), "a motion with a musket was sufficient to make [the Marquesans] all jump overboard. Yet in a little time they grew bolder, seeing we did not hurt them." Europeans thus confronted a dilemma. Violence, as a sole strategy for controlling the actions of Polynesians, required repeated displays. Yet violence was perceived as having definite moral and economic costs. Having to repeatedly kill the very people with whom they wished to trade was not a very practical solution to their problem.

The option that often proved most effective in controlling Polynesian appropriation over the long term was reliance on indigenous authorities. Chiefs not only supervised the orderliness of particular exchanges, but were also able to get missing property back. They often assumed such responsibilities unasked. A Mr. Boutin informed La Pérouse at Samoa that "since the chief had come on board, the islanders . . . were . . . much quieter and less insolent" (La Pérouse 1799, 2:132). During Cook's stay at Tahiti, Tupura'a i Tamaiti assisted in the return of stolen objects; Ereti (Reti) did the same for Bougainville during his visit (Bougainville 1772:223). And at Hawaii, particular chiefs were "of great use to us in preventing the Indians from thieving" (Samwell in Beaglehole 1967:1161).

But there was a problem here too. A variety of data suggest chiefs were often involved in the taking of Western property. Kalaniopu'u's chiefs, King asserted at Hawai'i, "have the vice of thieving . . . if they are not allway[s] the principals they are suspect'd to be the aides & abettors" (Beaglehole 1967:515). At Tahiti, both Cook and Banks suspected Purea and Tutahah as "principals" in certain incidents. Boenechea commented that "thievishness . . . was observed even in those of the highest ranks" (Corney 1913:333). No matter who took the items, moreover, they might well end up in the chiefs' hands. Tahitian chiefs had a standing levy on various luxury items, Oliver (1974:1159) notes, including "most items of European origin, however incomprehensible or useless."

The example of the Hawaiian chief Palea illustrates the problem.
During Cook's first visit to Kealakekua Bay, Palea was instrumental in
keeping order on board ship. "We should have found it difficult to have
kept [the Hawaiians] in order," Cook noted, "had not a chief . . .
named Parea [Palea] now and then [exerted] his authority" (in Beaglehole 1967:491). Law described one incident: "About 10 AM [on January
21] a Man Stole something out of the Ship which by some means or
other was made known to Parea—who went in search of him when he
found him the Man jumped into the Water & Parea after him they both
stayed under Water for a Long time when Parea . . . came up & said
. . . the thief was Dead" (in Beaglehole 1967:509; see also Samwell in
Beaglehole 1967:1161). But according to Samwell and others, Palea was
also involved in the unsanctioned appropriation of British property. "It
is pretty clear that [Palea] had set the Man to steal the Armourers
Tongues & Chizel & not improbable but that he was the Man who stole
the Cutter" (Samwell in Beaglehole 1967:1207). What is intriguing
about the theft of the armorer's tongs is that soon after they were stolen,
Palea "sett off . . . for the shore promising to bring the things back."
Still Samwell felt: "circumstances make it probable that this whole
affair was occasioned by [Palea] . . . the whole Scheme had been con-
certed between him and his people" (in Beaglehole 1967:1193).

Why should the chiefs encourage the taking of shipboard property
while protecting against it? To answer this question we must turn to
Polynesian perspectives on these early encounters.[10]

Polynesian Perspectives

A number of anthropologists have asserted that the themes of status and
status rivalry are pervasive in Polynesian society. Quoting Goldman:
"In Polynesia, it is the status system—specifically, the principles of aristocracy—that gives direction to the social structure as a whole. Principles of status dominate all other principles of social organization"
(Goldman 1970:7). And "rivalry is inherent . . . in Polynesian status
rules. From the standpoint of the status system, rivalry may be understood as a necessary response to ambiguity of rank" (Goldman
1970:24).

Data suggest that these themes pervaded Polynesian social relations
in the past. Kirch (1985:307) asserts that: "the political history [of the
Hawaiian archipelago] during the final two centuries prior to European
intrusion, was one of constant attempts by ruling chiefs to extend their
domains through conquest and annexation of lands." Oliver (1974:
1076–1077) suggests that an important goal for Tahitians was "command over the services of as many other persons as feasible." A com-

mon cause of inter-district warfare in Samoa "was competition for the various supreme titles . . . the ascendancy of . . . one family necessarily meant the military conquest and humiliation of the other" (Howe 1984:233–234). Even in the less hierarchical Marquesas, Dening (1980: 234) records "there were many instances of domination."

It is relevant to add that conflicts for power were often rather brutal affairs, even by European standards. Many wars, Ellis (1829, 2:494) observed, were "most merciless and destructive." In Tahiti,

> the victors swept through the communities of the defeated—burning, pillaging, destroying gardens and groves and slaughtering everyone they could find. To illustrate the mood of the conquerors, infants were sometimes transfixed to their mothers, or pierced through the head and strung on cords; or, women were treated with various 'indignities' after which they were disemboweled and derisively displayed. And men were sometimes beaten flat with clubs and left to dogs and pigs, or lined up to serve as rollers for beaching or launching the victor's canoes (Oliver 1974:398).

It is important to note that several accounts written by Europeans in the early postcontact period suggest that Polynesian concepts of appropriation were closely aligned to issues of status. These accounts leave little doubt that Hawaii, Tahiti, Samoa, and the Marquesas had concepts akin to the English term theft, and some meted out rather severe punishment for property violations. Our best information in this regard derives from Tahiti. Ellis stated that among Tahitians, "if detected, the thief experienced no mercy, but was often murdered on the spot. If detected afterwards, he was sometimes dreadfully wounded or killed" (Ellis 1829, 2:371). Banks commented that Tupia (Tupaia) "always insisted . . . that Theft was punished with death and smaller crimes in proportion" (Beaglehole 1962, 1:386).

But it is important to stress the ambiguities regarding the application of these abstract pronouncements to specific cases. "By conventional Western standards," Oliver notes, "the [Tahitian] attitude toward theft was somewhat ambivalent. On the one hand, a proven thief could usually be killed with impunity. Notwithstanding which, there appears to have existed a widely shared admiration for clever thievery, including some emulous veneration of Hiro, god of thievery" (Oliver 1974:1054). Whether a thief was ever punished, and if so how severely, seems to have depended on the statuses of the individuals involved, the items stolen, and the circumstances under which the thief was caught. The ultimate determinant of what punishment, if any, would be invoked for theft depended on the offended party's ability to enforce a punishment. As Moerenhout (1837, 2:16–17) phrased it for Tahiti: "it was a case of

might makes right." Or, according to Ellis (1829, 2:369), "the administration of justice . . . was regulated more by the relative power and
influence of the parties, than by the merits of their cause."[11]

If one accepts these data and the conclusions drawn from them, we
can make considerable headway in understanding chiefly perspectives
regarding the appropriation of shipboard property. Two interrelated
factors seemingly were at work. First, the whole process of controlling
theft played into the chiefs' hands. It not only allowed them to display
their authority to Western sea captains but to draw forth gifts of gratitude from them as well. With it, chiefs were rather important; sea captains found them invaluable aids in limiting the loss of goods. It thus
appears that Western weaponry and Polynesian appropriation acted as
counterweights to one another. The weapons affirmed Western technological superiority, and once aware of their destructive potential, Polynesians generally traded on terms favorable to Europeans. But Polynesian appropriations drew the explorers into reinforcing the status claims
of local chiefs. Western sea captains paid Polynesian chiefs considerable
attention and presented them with many gifts to gain their assistance.

Second, from a Polynesian perspective, the social status of the European visitors was ambiguous. As Pearson states, Europeans could be
categorized as castaways, dependent on their Polynesian hosts for suste-
nance. Alternatively, they could be classed as "stranger-kings"—for-
eigners who had come to usurp chiefly power, as Sahlins (1985) insight-
fully notes. From this latter viewpoint, the visitors were not dependent
on their hosts but were possible conquerors of them. Even if one does
not accept Pearson's and Sahlins' speculations, one can reasonably conclude that Europeans initially held ambiguous positions in Polynesian
hierarchies, if for no other reason than they lacked preassigned places.

Confronted with this ambiguity in rank, the literature suggests that
many Polynesians at first took a cautious attitude toward Europeans,
treating them with deference. But such hospitality did not necessarily
signify that Polynesian chiefs actually acknowledged the Europeans as
being of high status. Polynesian status principles, based on notions of
efficacy (see Shore, chapter 5), required Westerners to demonstrate
their potency through concrete actions. To achieve full recognition of
high rank required, among other things, resisting the challenges of
chiefs. Despite initial appearances to the contrary then, the status of
Europeans was probably very much open to negotiation. The attempted
seizure of shipboard goods can be seen as part of this negotiation process. It challenged the sea captains' ability to command respect, to
enforce behavior appropriate to individuals of high rank. In such circumstances, "might makes right" not only referred to issues of appropriation but to issues of status. Modern ethnographic accounts make

clear that property rights in Polynesia constitute a subset of rules governing interpersonal relations.

In this regard it is intriguing to observe Polynesian reactions to European violence during early encounters. The explorers' journals indicate that violent episodes rarely disturbed Polynesian interest in trade. On June 24, 1767, Wallis' cannonfire "struck such terror amongst the poor unhappy crowd [of Tahitians] that it would require the pen of Milton to describe" (Robertson 1973:41). Yet trade resumed the next day. At Vaitahu, Cook's men killed a Marquesan trying to appropriate an iron stanchion. But within two hours, Wales indicates, the Marquesans "had returned and trafficked as before" (Beaglehole 1961:829). Within two days of de Langle's death and the melee at Tutuila, Samoans came out to trade with La Pérouse. And within six days of the retribution meted out by the British after Cook's death, Hawaiian canoes were coming out to the ships "in great numbers" (Samwell in Beaglehole 1967:1216). That Polynesians seemed willing to trade under such conditions suggests that European violence fit within the cultural parameters of their own expectations. According to Oliver (1974:1059), in Tahiti, "offenses against the position [or] property . . . of a tribal chief . . . resulted invariably in severe penalties, from temporary exile to death." It does not seem unreasonable to conclude that Europeans, like chiefs, were expected to respond with violence to provocations and status challenges.

To state that issues of status and power were involved in these events is not to suggest that they were the exclusive concerns of Polynesians. Other factors were at work as well. As Turnbull (1813:282) phrased it, seizing goods was also "the cheapest and easiest method of purchase." Particularly for commoners, who lacked a chief's ability to mobilize goods, appropriation constituted an alternative to trade. Still, to acknowledge that multiple factors were involved in Polynesian actions in regard to shipboard property is not to diminish the central role the negotiation of status probably played in the process, especially for chiefs.

If our analysis of Polynesian perspectives on the appropriation of European property is correct, we need to look again at explanations that attribute Polynesian "thievery" to differing conceptions of property. Such explanations place too much emphasis on the items taken, on Western property per se. It might be closer to the mark to view the tensions surrounding the appropriation of shipboard property as stemming from differing perceptions of what was being negotiated. Europeans saw goods as items of trade. They were negotiating for supplies. High status Polynesians may have been interested in Western goods, but equally important was the negotiation of status. Polynesians, and particularly Polynesian chiefs, had an interest in evaluating the potency of the newcomers, in placing them within a graded hierarchical structure according to indigenous principles. (Consistent with this perspective, many Western goods were valued as status symbols; chiefs used them to signify high position.)

Toward a More Comparative Perspective: Patterns of Violence

The value of comparative analysis in Polynesian ethnology is well established, as the works of Burrows (1939b), Goldman (1970), Kirch (1984a), Williamson (1924, 1933), and Sahlins (1958) illustrate. And yet, despite their recognized value, comparative studies are rare in the analysis of Polynesian-Western interaction. As noted above, Pacific historians have tended to narrow their focus to specialized topics on particular islands or, at best, to single archipelagoes. What we want to suggest in this section is the value of casting a broader net of analysis. We want to stress the importance of comparison for illuminating the general processes that patterned interaction, processes that gave form to specific events on particular islands. We do so by exploring the violent encounters that erupted between Polynesians and Europeans during the early period of contact.[12]

Various explanations have been offered for the violence that erupted between these two groups. Aggression on the part of Polynesians, Pearson (1970:121) suggests, could be precipitated by "the need to protect the population and resources of each island from the threat of depredations and diseases and from the inevitable drain on food supply that must accompany [a European] visit." It could also derive from "European breaches of [Polynesian] protocol or of the terms on which their hosts understood [Europeans] to have been welcomed" (Pearson 1970: 144). Explanations for European aggression often emphasize the attitudes held toward indigenous populations. Campbell asserts, for instance that "sailors' attitudes to Polynesians during this time were fearful. . . . These attitudes, allied to the callousness of the age, when applied to Polynesians amounted to an almost total disregard for local life and interests" (Campbell 1982:73).

Such explanations, while not without merit, raise as many questions as they answer. Take, for instance, Campbell's claim that Europeans had a callous disregard for the lives of Polynesians. Enough evidence can be found in the explorers' journals to require a clear qualification to the effect that many sea captains consciously exercised restraint over their men's actions. Such blanket explanations also fail to account for why conflicts arose at certain times and places and not at others. And although Pearson is probably correct in suggesting that European crews created problems for indigenous inhabitants of the islands, his analysis skims over the dynamics by which certain of those problems led to violence.

Approaching this issue within a comparative framework, one can perceive a general pattern to the violence at Tahiti, Samoa, and Hawaii. Following first contact, Europeans initiated trade with Polynesians. During the exchanges that followed, Polynesians attempted to appropriate a number of articles from aboard ship. Initial European reactions were restrained; the attempts at appropriation were met with threats and harmless displays of weaponry. When Polynesians failed to grasp the implied threats, a Polynesian might be killed. (At Hawaii a chief was slain, at Tahiti a person of unknown status; no one was killed during this stage at Samoa.) Following this initial European assault, within hours in some instances, days in others, the Polynesians attacked in force. Such attacks brought forth large-scale European violence, resulting in the deaths of numerous Polynesians. Violence then subsided and trade resumed.

To do a detailed analysis of each case is beyond the scope of this chapter, especially given the voluminous nature of the literature. But let us outline the main points, beginning with Tahiti.

Tahiti

As the fog cleared on June 19, 1768, the British ship *Dolphin,* commanded by Wallis, was approached by "upwards of a hundred and fifty canoes" (Robertson 1973:21; see also Hawkesworth 1775:39). The British, sick (presumably from scurvy) and seriously short of water, drew Tahitians into trading. When some Tahitians refused to leave the ship without obtaining iron, and others in canoes became "a Little surly," the British fired a nine-pound shot over their heads. This seems to have had "the desired Effect" of frightening them (Robertson 1973: 22). It is worth describing the first recorded seizure of shipboard property. "One of the [Tahitians] was standing close by one of our young Gentlemen, Henry Ibbot, who wore a Gold Laced Hat. This Glaring Hat attracted the fellow's fancy, and he snatched it off and Jumped overboard with it in his hand. When he got about twenty yards from the ship, he held up the Hat and wore it round his Head. We called to him and pointed muskets at him, but he took no notice of the muskets not knowing their use" (Robertson 1973:22; cf. Hawkesworth 1775:40).

In the face of (what the British viewed as) provocations, including, of course, the unsanctioned appropriation of their property, the British displayed restraint. An event on June 21 is typical. Tahitians in canoes tried to board a British barge and "run aboard" of the cutter, carrying "away her boomkin and [tearing] the mizen" (Robertson 1973:30). Robertson "then ordered the Marines to point the muskets at them, but they Laughed at us" he noted, "and one struck [the prow of his canoe] into [the] Boat's stern." Robertson, finding "them so very resolute" and believing himself "under the necessity of using violent means," ordered two of the crew to wound the "most resolute . . . fellows" (Robertson 1973:30–31). But the crew were imperfect in their aim, killing one Tahitian and wounding another. Trading (and Polynesian appropriation of European property) continued on a regular basis over the next two days. On June 24, about 300 canoes with approximately 4,000 men—under the guise of trading—attacked the *Dolphin,* throwing stones on her deck (Robertson 1973:40–41). Initially British sentries responded by firing among the canoes. But this had little effect. When the British "found lenity would not do," grapeshot from the ship's cannons were fired into the midst of the Tahitians, causing considerable destruction and terror. The Tahitians returned to trade on the following day. On June 26 the British, fearing that the massing of Tahitians on shore presaged another attack, fired a "few round and Grape shot" among them (Robertson 1973:52). Trade was reestablished on June 27. Relations between the two groups during the rest of Wallis' stay were quite amicable. Although there were occasional incidents of violence during the subsequent visits of Bougainville, Cook, and Boenechea, where Europeans killed a small number of Tahitians, there was none of the formally organized violence of June 24, 1768, by either side. Friendly relations prevailed between the two groups.

Samoa

The first direct European contact with Samoans at Tutuila occurred on December 8, 1787, when La Pérouse met canoes about three leagues out at sea. Trading began immediately. It continued over the next two days as La Pérouse sailed near shore and finally anchored off the island. On December 10, "a hundred canoes" came round La Pérouse's two ships and bartered various provisions for glass beads (La Pérouse 1799, 2:128). Confusion over trading ashore on December 10 was set right by "some Indians, whom [the French] took for chiefs" (La Pérouse 1799, 2:129). On board LaPérouse's ship a "chief" likewise seemed to keep order. La Pérouse commented (1799, 2:132), "I made this chief many presents."

When a Samoan in "an absolute act of hostility" attacked a French sailor with a mallet, La Pérouse, to avoid shedding blood, had four strong sailors take the Samoan and throw him in the water. La Pérouse added: "Perhaps a little severity would have been proper by way of example, to awe these people, and render them sensible of the superiority our arms gave us over their personal strength; for their stature being about five feet ten inches high, their muscular limbs, and Herculean form, gave them such an idea of their superiority, as rendered us little formidable in their eyes" (La Pérouse 1799, 2:129–130). Later, "wishing . . . to impress [a Samoan chief] with a high opinion of our strength," La Pérouse "ordered different trials of the use of our arms to be exhibited before him: but their effect made little impression on him; and he appeared to me, to think them fit only for killing birds" (La Pérouse 1799, 2:132).

It was in this context that de Langle went ashore for additional supplies of fresh water on December 11 in order to treat the scurvy afflicting his crew. Following a misunderstanding, the nature of which is not clear, de Langle and eleven other Frenchmen were killed by the Samoans.

Differing explanations of the massacre have been offered by Samoan and French commentators. The Samoan explanation—at least the one we have on record—focuses on "the indignity offered to one of [the Samoan] chiefs" (Oceanus 1814:381), in other words a matter of status. The French explanation focuses on de Langle's humane character. La Pérouse commented: de Langle's "humanity . . . occasioned his death. Had he but allowed himself to fire on the first Indians who entered into the water to surround the boats, he would have prevented his own death" as well as that of the others (La Pérouse 1799, 2:140).

To La Pérouse's astonishment, the next day five or six Samoan canoes came out to trade with the French. Full of supplies, La Pérouse brushed them off, firing a cannon near the canoes to splash but not actually harm the occupants. (He considered it unfair to kill them when he had no proof they had participated in the previous killings.) La Pérouse then left.

The next vessel to stop at Tutuila appears to have been the *Pandora* (Gilson 1970:67). The *Pandora*'s tender repulsed a Samoan night attack on June 22, 1791, causing "terrible havoc" and the death of several Samoans (Edwards and Hamilton 1915:12). Following this conflict and, we presume, a much better appreciation among Samoans of the lethal capabilities of Western weaponry, trade relations took on a more positive tone. George Bass, the next European to trade at the island, described the Samoans as "friendly and receptive" (Gilson 1970:67; see also Bowden 1952:112).

Hawaii

During Cook's second visit to the Hawaiian Islands, he became the first known European to make contact with the inhabitants dwelling in the southern portion of the archipelago.[13] The British learned that their earlier visit to Kaua'i, and their killing of a Hawaiian there, were known to the inhabitants. On November 27 trade flourished. A paramount chief, Kahekili, visited Cook on board ship and Cook commented, "I did not hear they attempted to steal any one thing" (in Beaglehole 1967:475). Even a black cat that fell overboard was returned. On November 30, Kalaniopu'u, another paramount chief and Kahekili's opponent, visited Cook off the eastern side of Maui. Circumnavigating the island of Hawai'i from December 1 to January 15, Cook quite successfully traded for food. Again, there were few problems with Hawaiians taking shipboard property.

As Cook approached Kealakekua Bay on Hawai'i on January 16, 1779, an estimated thousand canoes came out to the British ships. Trade flourished, but the appropriation of shipboard property became a problem. To quote Law, "they began today to make use of their fingers too freely" (in Beaglehole 1967:490). A boat's rudder and even Cook's keys were taken. Cook's response was to have a few muskets and "Great guns" fired off "in order to shew the Chiefs the effect of them & to what distance they would carry." Samwell stated that the Hawaiians were "much astonished" (Samwell in Beaglehole 1967:1158). But Cook commented that they seemed "more surprised than frightened" (in Beaglehole 1967:490).

On anchoring at Kealakekua Bay, unsanctioned appropriation by Hawaiians was brought under control by various Hawaiian chiefs, including Palea. One of the chiefs even retrieved Cook's keys. Cook went ashore on January 17. Hawaiians prostrated themselves before him (Samwell in Beaglehole 1967:1159). Called Lono, a Hawaiian deity, Cook participated two days later in a religious ceremony at a Hawaiian *heiau* 'shrine'. Samwell stated that Cook "was invested . . . with the Title and Dignity of Orono [Lono] . . . a Character that is looked upon by [the Hawaiians] as partaking something of divinity" (in Beaglehole 1967:1161–1162). Though some items continued to disappear from aboard ship the British were not disturbed. Matters were well in hand, controlled as they were by the chiefs. The British, moreover, found themselves well supplied with gifts of food.

The British left Kealakekua Bay on February 4. Following damage to the *Resolution* in a gale off Maui, however, they returned on February 10 for repairs. On February 13, when "a great number of large canoes arrived in the Bay" (Samwell in Beaglehole 1967:1191) the British began effective reprovisioning of their ships, though this time food was mostly obtained through trade rather than gifts. Unsanctioned appropriation by Hawaiians of shipboard property became a serious problem. Clerke noted that "every day produc'd more numerous and more audacious depredations" (in Beaglehole 1967:531–532). On February 14, following the loss of a British cutter (to Palea?) the previous night, the British blockaded the bay and Cook went ashore to take Kalaniopu'u, the paramount chief of the island, hostage, pending the safe return of the cutter. Cook's plan proved unsuccessful. A large Hawaiian crowd gathered as Cook, Kalaniopu'u, and some British marines stood on the beach. News arrived that a chief trying to leave the bay had been killed by the British. In response to a threatening gesture, Cook fired a round of small shot at an individual. The Hawaiian escaped unharmed, being protected by a mat. Still, the crowd was aroused. Violence followed on both sides. The Hawaiians made a "general attack" (Phillips in Beaglehole 1967:535) that the British were unable to fend off effectively, and Cook was killed. As Samwell later commented, the Hawaiians "were totally unacquainted with the Effect of fire arms, they thought their Matts would defend them . . . & in the heat & fury of Action they were not immediately convinced of the contrary" (in Beaglehole 1967:1202). In retaliation for the Hawaiian attack and especially Cook's death, the British killed a number of Hawaiians. After a four-day hiatus, trade was reestablished. By February 20, Hawaiians were coming out to the ships in great numbers. Samwell commented: "They tell us that they are all sorry for what has happened" and wished to reestablish ties of friendship (in Beaglehole 1967:1217). According to Clerke, in the final days before the British departure on February 23, the Hawaiians acted "with the utmost justice and honesty" (Beaglehole 1967:549). This was the extent of Hawaiian-European conflict during the early contact period in Hawaii. There was no further violence during the three subsequent European visits to the area by Portlock and Dixon in 1786 and 1786–1787, and La Pérouse in 1786.

Obviously one must be cautious about forcing these data into a formal structure. One perceives more of a trend than a fixed sequence of stages. But a pattern emerges nonetheless, despite differences in detail. It can be expressed as trading, with, over time, increasing unsanctioned Polynesian appropriation of shipboard property, followed by violence, followed by renewed trading (with, over the short term at least, diminished violence). Seen from a comparative perspective, violence was thus not a random event. It was a regular step in the development of trade relations. It tended to occur at certain times and not at others.

Why Did Violence Occur?

Assigning responsibility for the violence was, and still is, a Western preoccupation. Were the Europeans culpable by using firearms too vigorously to protect their property? It does seem clear that in many instances they initiated the violence. Or were Polynesian actions sufficiently provocative and life-threatening to warrant extreme measures? There certainly seem to be indications that in many instances they were, or at least appeared so from a European perspective.

The question of Cook's death has been a particular focus for speculation. Did he cause his own death by overreacting to the loss of property? La Pérouse assigns responsibility to the English for initiating hostilities, and suggests that Cook's imprudence "compelled the inhabitants of Owyhee [Hawai'i] to have recourse to a just and necessary defence" (La Pérouse 1799, 1:346). Or was Cook's death the result of his own humane values, his unwillingness to use violence except as a last resort? Williamson, one of Cook's officers, implies as much in his comment that, "these barbarians must first be quelled by force, as they afterwards readily believe that whatever kindness is then shewn them proceeds from love, whereas otherwise they attribute it to weakness, or cowardice, & presents only increase their insolence" (in Beaglehole 1967:1349). Samwell stated the matter more simply: "for after all that may be said in favour of these or any other Indians, it is still certain that their good behaviour to us proceeds in great measure from fear" (in Beaglehole 1967:1219).

The issue so put is unresolvable. Too much is unknowable, including the intentions and attitudes of the main actors involved. And even if precise data were available, such events are too complex to assign simple notions of causality. But we can come to understand the dynamics that repeatedly precipitated violence in those early encounters between Europeans and Polynesians.

Given the character of the cultures involved, and the nature of the encounters, we ought not be surprised by the frequency of violence. The meetings were of a political nature for both parties, and both sides were familiar with violence as a political instrument. There is little doubt that, despite a commitment to civilized action, most sea captains were prepared to use force to achieve their ends when necessary. European sea captains presumably saw themselves as so vastly superior technologically that they possessed the luxury of restraint. They did not anticipate being seriously challenged. But on the high islands of Polynesia, notwithstanding the tradition of hospitality shown to guests, political challenge was a way of life, and warfare was endemic. From this perspective violence was almost an inevitable part of the developing relations between the two groups.

The Marquesas

One of the great values of comparative studies is that they help pinpoint anomalies. Exceptions to patterns often raise critical questions otherwise ignored. We take as an example the encounters between Europeans and Marquesans at Vaitahu Bay on Tahuata. The process of establishing stable relations there appears to have been at variance with the pattern described above.

Cook arrived on April 8, 1774, and soon began trading. The next day, when Marquesan attempts to appropriate shipboard property became a problem, a "thief" was "accidentally" killed by musket fire. (Cook commanded the officer to fire over the culprit's canoe but the officer misinterpreted Cook's order.) When the British demonstrated to other Marquesans, who were trying to appropriate the kedge anchor, how far musket balls traveled by shooting over their heads, the islanders immediately seem to have grasped the point and left the anchor alone. No other violence occurred during Cook's visit, nor did any erupt during the subsequent visits of Ingraham, Marchand, and Hergest. That one killing constituted the total violence between the Marquesans and the Europeans is suspicious; so is the fact that Marquesans so readily perceived the lethal implications of Western weaponry. The behavior of Marquesans toward Ingraham, Marchand, and Hergest parallels that of Tahitians toward Bougainville, Cook, and Boenechea: there was apparent recognition of Western superiority in weaponry and few audacious attempts to seize goods from aboard ship. Why was violence so muted in this instance? The reason, we suspect, derives from Mendaña's earlier visit to the bay in 1595. Though Mendaña's visit took place several generations earlier, one wonders if Marquesans retained some knowledge of European weaponry, and of the perhaps 200 people killed by the Spaniards.

The violence at Vaitahu in 1595 raises a related question. Why was there so much Spanish violence when there appears, from Quiros' journal, to have been so little Marquesan provocation? The data suggest that at least two factors were at variance with the pattern at Tahiti, Hawaii, and Samoa. First, Mendaña was not short of supplies on his arrival at Vaitahu. He had left Peru little more than a month before with four modestly supplied ships. It was only Quirós' concern with the uncertainties of the voyage ahead that caused Mendaña to take on water there. Having little need for trade, the Spaniards apparently were less concerned with remaining on good terms with the indigenous inhabitants. When eleven Marquesans approached the ship, rather than trade, the Spaniards fired on them, killing five.

Second, Mendaña either did not share the Enlightenment concern for restraint displayed by later sea captains, or he was unable to control his soldiers, who lacked such ideals. Quirós (1904:2C) states in his journal: "It may be held as certain that two hundred natives were killed in these islands . . . [by the] impious and inconsiderate soldiers." Given this background, the small amount of violence during Cook's visit may have acted more as a reminder than a first lesson about the deadly nature of European weaponry.

The general point we want to stress is that comparative analysis is an important, indeed crucial, tool for understanding the dynamics of Polynesian-Western interactions. The myopic view of focusing on only one island or one point in time misses much of the context that framed the encounters. Comparative analysis not only illuminates these broader contexts, it allows us to see specific cases in perspective.

Summary

In this chapter we have critically reviewed historical and anthropological approaches to the study of early Polynesian-Western interactions. Although impressed by the wealth of literature on the topic, we have noted significant problems. In regard to Pacific history we commented on three: (1) the accounts remain focused on European perspectives; (2) they often reflect a limited theoretical vision; and (3) they suffer from a lack of comparative analysis. As a result, historians of the Pacific have had difficulty in charting new directions, in developing Davidson's vision of island-centered histories. Anthropologists have also had problems. They have been caught between a concern for broad syntheses and the need to support generalizations with detailed data. The cautious approach, exemplified by Oliver, focuses on the ethnographic materials, and on presenting them in a cogent, organized manner. The usual criticism voiced here is that the approach lacks theoretical vision. Valeri's work on Hawaii exemplifies the opposite perspective. He offers an interpretive program based upon strong theoretical assumptions. The problem with this approach is its tendency to overinterpret primary materials, to fit facts to predetermined forms.

Ambiguities in the documentary data exacerbate these problems, and although the sheer amount of literature is impressive, it contains significant biases. The accounts, for instance, were usually written from a European perspective; they often depict Polynesian societies in static terms, ignoring internal diversity and social dynamics.

In an effort to provide directions for future research, we have suggested three strategies for interpreting the data on early interactions between Europeans and Polynesians: (1) the development of a stronger dialogue between presentist and reconstructionist approaches, so that each informs the other (our reliance on cultural notions of status and status rivalry to account for Polynesian actions is an example of this strategy); (2) a focus on the sequence of interactions at specific localities, as opposed to treating each episode by itself; and (3) the use of controlled comparisons to highlight regularities in these sequences.

In the process of illustrating our perspective we offered new interpretations of issues that have preoccupied students of the early contact period. We were led to question the suitability of such concepts as theft to describe Polynesian actions, since they carry semantic loadings in English that are problematic. We suggested that such actions were a part of a negotiating process. European sea captains sought to optimize the conditions of trade and to affirm a particular self-image of themselves as "civilized." Polynesians focused on the interpersonal implications of property disposition. For high-ranking Polynesians, appropriating shipboard goods also involved the issue of status, especially vis-à-vis Europeans. The role of chiefs was central, we suggested, both because the Europeans saw them as a means of controlling unsanctioned appropriation, and because the chiefs found status advantages associated with the monitoring of trade. It is unlikely we will ever fully know what precisely motivated the various individuals involved to behave as they did. But what we have sought to sketch out are the contexts within which these individuals operated and which gave their actions meaning.

In exploring the value of comparative analyses we focused on the issue of violence. We observed a general pattern to the development of violence at Tahiti, Samoa, and Hawaii, and described it in terms of a sequence: trading, with, over time, increasing unsanctioned Polynesian appropriation of shipboard property, followed by violence, followed by renewed trading (with, over the short term at least, diminished violence). With this as background, we explored the case of the Marquesas, which seemingly deviated from this model, and found it to be an important case for clarifying certain points.

Our concern in this chapter has been to suggest new possibilities for examining old issues. Scholars such as Davidson, Dening, Maude, Oliver, Sahlins, and Valeri have pointed the way; they have shown the possibilities the voluminous materials present to scholars bold enough to seize the challenge. Our chapter constitutes part of this continuing discourse. It is another statement in an ongoing conversation about the patterns of early Polynesian-Western interaction. And it is another sentence in a modern conversation about how to effectively study these patterns.

NOTES

We would like to express appreciation to Gavan Daws, Greg Dening, Dave Hanlon, Allan Hanson, Kerry Howe, Judy Huntsman, Brij Lal, Jocelyn Linnekin, Doug Oliver, Karen Peacock, Caroline Ralston, and Jan Rensel who read drafts of this chapter. Their many comments proved quite helpful in formulating (and reformulating) the themes discussed here. A special debt of gratitude is owed Dave Hanlon who read and provided indepth comments on two versions.

1. For additional references on topics covered in this section regarding the nature of the source material, see in respect to (1) its voluminous nature: Dening 1966:25, Howe 1984:44, and Spate 1977:222; (2) the European governments' concern with expanding both knowledge and national commerce (as

well as the international rivalries sometimes involved): J. C. Beaglehole 1955: cclxxxii, Cook in Beaglehole 1955:134, Beaglehole 1966:194, Dening 1966:26 and 1974:16, Foster's footnote in Bougainville 1772:221, Maude 1971:14, Oliver 1961:94, Robertson 1973:98, and Spate in Gunson 1978:36-37; (3) examples of descriptions recorded and built upon for advancing knowledge: Clerke in J. C. Beaglehole 1967:591-630, Fleurieu 1801:55-142; (4) techno-logical and medical improvements in respect to sea travel: Oliver 1961:85-86; (5) the rise of literacy and the increase in recorders of information: J. C. Beaglehole 1961:cxxxi-clvii and 1967:xxiii-xxvii, Furet and Ozouf 1982: espe-cially 5-17, McKay, Hill, and Buckler 1984:865, Maude 1968:170-177, and Stone 1969; (6) missionary concerns that helped produce an indigenous Polyne-sian literature: Dibble, quoted in Finney et al. 1978:309-310, Gunson 1978: 237, 247, and Latukefu in Rutherford 1977:123; (7) Polynesian concerns with recording information: 'I'i 1959:ix, Malo 1951:1-2, Parsonson 1967:44, and Thrum 1918:42; (8) richness of Hawaiian language newspapers as a source of information on Hawaiian perspectives: Daws, cited in Morris 1975:50; (9) dif-fering perspectives in Polynesian and Western accounts of particular events: J. C. Beaglehole 1967:266, Morris 1975, Sahlins 1981a:12; (10) biases based on imperfect recall and changing times: Borofsky 1987:150-152, D'Andrade 1974, and Loftus and Loftus 1980:419; (11) Hawaiian writers' source material collected years after contact: Malo 1951:vii-viii, xiii, 'I'i 1959:vii, ix-x, Thrum 1918:45, note also Gunson 1963:416-418; (12) biases in the homogenization of culture: Obituary (for David Malo) 1853, Borofsky 1987, Charlot 1987, Feld-man 1986, A. Howard 1986a, Malo 1951:vii-xv, and Valeri 1985a:185; and (13) further comments on biases, especially Polynesian ones: Charlot 1985, e.g., p. 5, Daws 1969:228, Kelly 1967, Langdon 1969:163, Malo 1951:viii, though in relation to B. Smith 1979:161, note Samwell in J. C. Beaglehole 1967:1201.

2. For additional references on topics covered in this section regarding his-torical approaches, see in respect to (1) general comments on imperial, or Euro-centric, history: Davidson 1966:5, Hezel 1980:113, Maude 1971:16, Routledge 1985:82, and Spate 1980:22; (2) its focus on European imperial expansion: Howe 1979:81 and 1984:xiii; (3) its focus on formal, imperialistic agents: Howe 1979:81 and 1984:xiii, Langdon 1973:226, and Ralston 1985:156; for an exception to this trend, see Kuykendall 1938; (4) the supposed passivity of indigenous populations depicted in imperial history: Howe 1977:147 and 1984: 347-348, and Ralston 1979:126; (5) the supposed fatal impact perspective in imperialistic history: Fisher and Johnston 1979:4, Fisher 1979:81, and Howe 1977:145-146; (6) general comments on island-centered history (or the "new historiography"): Howe 1977:148 and 1984:xiii, 347-352, and Ralston 1985: 156-159; (7) its focus on less formal agents of imperialism: Davidson 1975, Howe 1979:82, Langdon 1973:226, Lātūkefu 1977:242, and Ralston 1978; (8) its focus on the governed rather than the governors: Davidson 1966:7, 13, 14, Howe 1979:82, Maude 1971:20, Ralston 1978, and Routledge 1985:82; note also France 1969:xii and Maude 1968:178-232; (9) fatal impact perspective questioned by island-centered history: Davidson 1970:267, Firth in Daws 1979: 127, Howe 1977:147-151, and Ralston 1985:157; (10) Howe's overstatement of fatal contact issue: Firth in Daws 1979:127, Moorehead 1966, Ogan 1985:

210, and Spate 1985:165; (11) island-centered history as still Eurocentric in character: Howe 1985:169, Routledge 1985:84, and Hezel 1980:113; (12) Davidson as father of island-centered history: Howe 1979:81–83 and Maude 1973:9; (13) biases in descriptions of historical approaches deriving from decolonization context: Howe 1977:151 and 1984:xii–xiii, 351–352, Maude 1971: 20, and Routledge 1985:84; (14) the role of ANU in the development of Pacific history: Howe 1984:xiii, Maude 1971:16, and Ralston 1985:156; (15) the need to move beyond Eurocentric accounts and biases (including problems involved in using oral traditions): Biersack 1985:170, Davidson 1966:10, Dening 1966: 36–42, Fisher 1979:84–85, Lātūkefu 1968, Lavondes 1967, Maude 1968:xx and 1971:8–12, and Mercer 1979; also note Hanlon 1984:145; it is relevant to note Dening's position in this regard 1980:42; (16) the limited theoretical scope of island-centered analyses: Howe 1979:88 and 1985:171, Routledge 1985:89, and West 1973:117; and (17) the limited comparative scope of island-centered history: S. Firth in Daws 1979:127, Howe 1984:xiv, Spate 1978:42, Laracy 1978:251, and Ralston 1985:162, fn. 19.

3. The concern with less formal agents fits into a broader trend of Western history in regard to paying increased attention to non-elites. As Sahlins (1985: 32–33, 53–54) points out, it parallels changes within our own society.

4. For an interesting parallel regarding the over-emphasized passivity of indigenous populations, see DeVoto's comments (in J. Howard 1952:8–9) regarding the role depicted for American Indians in United States history.

5. A reading of Hexter (1972:482–498) suggests interesting parallels between the island-centered approach's rise to prominence in Pacific history and the rise of the French Annales School to prominence in European history.

6. For additional references on topics covered in this section regarding anthropological approaches, see in respect to (1) the cultural reconstructionist approach and the problems involved in it: Borofsky 1987:45–59, Colson 1985, Gruber 1970, Hobsbawm and Ranger 1983, and Leaf 1979:146–149; (2) reviews of Oliver's book: Crocombe 1976, Healy 1977, Langdon 1975, and Tagupa 1973; (3) reviews of Valeri's book: Linnekin 1985a, 1986; (4) significant early studies of social change in Polynesia: E. Beaglehole 1957, Firth 1959b, and F. Keesing 1928; (5) more recent important examples of studies concerning social change in Polynesia: Firth 1970b, Hanson 1973, A. Howard 1964, 1966, Marcus 1978a, and Monberg 1967; (6) reviews of Dening: Brady 1982, Dening n.d.:41–42, Ralston, 1985:162, Strauss 1981:906, and Tagupa 1981; (7) reviews of Sahlins: Gailey 1983, A. Hanson 1982a, A. Howard 1982b, Marcus 1982, Newbury 1982, Ogan n.d., Ortner 1985, and Trask 1985; (8) Sahlins' view of the dynamic interplay between structure and process: Sahlins 1985:136–156; and (9) the limited data supporting Sahlins' analyses: Marcus 1982:597–600 and Ogan n.d.:5–7.

7. Rather than rely on secondary sources to inform our argument, we prefer to follow in the footsteps of Oliver, Dening, and Sahlins and rely on primary resources. As Oliver (1974:xi) notes in explaining how he came to write *Ancient Tahitian Society:* "many of the generalizations [previously] current about Tahitian social relations . . . were in reality scholars' inventions that had come to acquire 'authenticity' more through reassertion than through retesting with primary sources." It is because of our concern for stressing the importance of pri-

mary sources that we provide extensive footnotes regarding the material con-
sulted in our analyses. The footnotes are only partial renderings of a much
larger set of materials. Our purpose in providing these listings, cumbersome as
it may be, is to inform readers of the documentary foundations for our arguments.

8. Regarding the documentary sources on these visits, see in respect to (1)
the Marquesas: Mendaña in 1595 (Quirós 1904), Cook in 1774 (Beaglehole
1961), Ingraham in 1791 (Ingraham 1971), Marchand in 1791 (Fleurieu 1801),
and Hergest in 1792 (Vancouver 1798); (2) Tahiti: Wallis in 1767 (Robertson
1973; Hawkesworth 1775), Bougainville in 1768 (Bougainville 1772), Cook in
1769 (Beaglehole 1955, 1962), and Boenechea in 1772 (Corney 1913, 1915); (3)
Hawaii: Cook in 1778 (Beaglehole 1967; Ellis 1782), Cook (and Clerke) in
1778–1779 (Beaglehole 1967; Ellis 1782), Portlock and Dixon in 1786 (Portlock
1789; Dixon 1789; Nicol 1822), La Pérouse in 1786 (La Pérouse 1799), and
Portlock and Dixon in 1786–1787 (Portlock 1789; Dixon 1789; Nicol 1822);
and (4) Samoa: Roggeveen in 1722 (Roggeveen 1970), Bougainville in 1768
(Bougainville 1772), La Pérouse in 1787 (La Pérouse 1799; Oceanus 1814), the
HMS *Pandora*'s tender in 1791 (Edwards and Hamilton 1915), and Bass in 1802
(Bowden 1952).

9. For additional references on topics covered in this section regarding European perspectives concerning Polynesian appropriation, see in respect to (1)
Bougainville's and Marchand's relatively tolerant attitude toward theft: Bougainville 1772:222 and Fleurieu 1801:34, 38; (2) Cook's acceptance of the loss
of British property under certain circumstances: Banks in Beaglehole 1962,
1:282–283 in relation to Banks in Beaglehole 1962, 1:268–274, Cook in Beaglehole 1955:95–96 in relation to Cook in Beaglehole 1955:87–92; see also Cook in
Beaglehole 1955:103; (3) limited medical knowledge in treating scurvy: Cook in
Beaglehole 1967:479, La Pérouse 1799, 2:133, Roggeveen 1970:150, and Watt
1979:especially 144–147; (4) Cook's keeping at sea for lengthy periods: Beaglehole 1966:309, note also the condition of Cook's crew in Beaglehole 1967:503–
504 and Ellis 1782, 2:82; (5) the supply capability of Polynesian islands: Cook
in Beaglehole 1955:136, Bayly in Beaglehole 1967:484, and Robertson 1973:
103; for a contrast with Micronesia: see Ralston 1978:48 (one can make a similar point by noting how long certain explorers stayed: Cook initially stayed at
Tahiti three months and on his second visit to Hawaii three and a half months,
Portlock and Dixon on their second visit stayed four months at Hawaii); (6) the
limitations of Western firearms: Cook in Beaglehole 1955:101, Phillips in
Beaglehole 1967:536, La Pérouse 1799, 2:144, and Robertson 1973:32; (7) the
sea captains' desire for protected bays and safe anchorages: Boenechea in Corney 1913:298–303, Bougainville 1772:238–239, Fleurieu 1801:31, and Ingraham 1971:45; (8) the absence of a safe anchorage off Maui and Cook's resulting
need to return to Kealakekua Bay: King in Beaglehole 1967:527, and Samwell
in Beaglehole 1967:1189; (9) the possibility that Tahitians attacked Wallis
because of their familiarity with the earlier wreck of Roggeveen's boat, *De Afri-
caansche Galey*, in the Tuamotus: Molyneux in Beaglehole 1955:557, plus
Beaglehole's footnote on the same page, Driessen 1982:17–26, Newbury
1980:5, Oliver 1974:539, Roggeveen 1970:121–125, and Bougainville 1772:
273; (10) Western sea captains building up knowledge of locales from their own

repeated experiences and the journals of other explorers: Banks in Beaglehole 1962, 1:306–307, Cook in Beaglehole 1955:117, Wales in Beaglehole 1961:794, Fleurieu 1801:129, La Pérouse 1799, 2:121, 125, and Robertson 1973:13 in relation to Corney 1915:458–460; (11) Western efforts at restraint in using their weaponry: Cook in Beaglehole 1955:101, 117, Wales in Beaglehole 1961:829, King in Beaglehole 1967:530, Clerke in Beaglehole 1967:535, J. C. Beaglehole 1974:200, La Pérouse 1779, 2:132, 136, 138, Fleurieu 1801:40, Robertson 1973:33–34, and Vancouver 1798, 2:88, 91; (12) absence of such restraint among certain individuals: Orchiston and Horrocks 1975:524 and Horrocks 1976:12; (13) Cook issuing regulations to control the price of British goods: Cook in Beaglehole 1955:75, 1961:368–369, and 1967:474, King in Beaglehole 1967:495–496, and Samwell in Beaglehole 1967:1150; (14) theft undermining a ship's sailing capabilities or mission: Cook in Beaglehole 1955:87 and 1961:366, Clerke in Beaglehole 1967:533, King in Beaglehole 1967:549, and Samwell in Beaglehole 1967:1194; (15) Europeans' often ineffective initial display of weaponry because of Polynesian ignorance of its lethal power: Cook in Beaglehole 1967:490, Samwell in Beaglehole 1967:1158, La Pérouse 1799, 2:130, 144, and Robertson 1973:30, 33–34; (16) intimation of violence as a means to prevent theft: Beaglehole 1961:366, Bougainville 1772:227, Fleurieu 1801:34, Portlock 1789:163, and Vancouver 1798, 2:88; (17) Cook's efforts to reestablish trade relations: Beaglehole 1955:80 and 1961:366; (18) chiefly assistance in preventing theft at Tahiti: Banks in Beaglehole 1962, 1:268–269, and Bougainville 1772:223; (19) chiefly assistance at the Marquesas: Vancouver 1798, 2:90–91 and Fleurieu 1801:42–43; (20) chiefly assistance at Samoa: La Pérouse 1799, 2:132; (21) chiefly assistance at Hawaii: Law in Beaglehole 1967:490, Cook in Beaglehole 1967:491, King in Beaglehole 1967:502, 511, Clerke in Beaglehole 1967:532, and Samwell in Beaglehole 1967:1161, 1164; (22) chiefs encouraging theft at Hawaii: Clerke in Beaglehole 1967:532, Burney in Beaglehole 1967:563, Samwell in Beaglehole 1967:1193, 1207, 1218, and Ellis 1782, 2:84; (23) chiefs encouraging theft at Tahiti: Banks in Beaglehole 1962, 1:282 and Beaglehole 1955:110–111; (24) chiefs encouraging theft at Marquesas: possible case of this in Fleurieu 1801:128; and (25) chiefs' acquisition of stolen material: for Tahiti note Banks in Beaglehole 1962, 1:291, Cook in Beaglehole 1955:102, and Oliver 1974:1001; for Hawaii note King in Beaglehole 1967:518, Dixon 1789:106, and Portlock 1789:199–200.

10. For additional references on topics covered regarding Polynesian perspectives concerning appropriation, see in respect to (1) Polynesian concerns with status and status rivalry: Borofsky 1987:77–78, Goldman 1970:4–28, Gunson 1979:especially 28, A. Howard 1972:818, Kirch 1984a:14, Marcus 1978b:especially 253, 267, Ritchie and Ritchie 1979:80, and Shore 1982:especially 196–220; also chapters 3, 5, and 6, this volume; (2) Robertson's perceptions of Tahitian status: 1973:83, 100; also see Hawkesworth 1775:44–45; for an example of a mistake, see Oliver 1974:1179 and Cook in Beaglehole 1955:522; (3) supportive evidence regarding status competitions in precontact and early postcontact Polynesian societies, see Oliver 1974:1171–1350; (4) Polynesian involvement in warfare and the brutal nature of it: Bougainville 1772:253, Dening 1978 and 1980:67, 102, Kirch 1985:307–308, Oliver 1974: 375–408, 987–992, 1217ff., and Vayda 1956:147, 152–155; note also Goldman

1970:559; (5) in the abstract, strict punishments for theft in Polynesia: Banks in Beaglehole 1962, 1:386, Boenechea in Corney 1913:356, Varela in Corney 1915:259, Dening 1974:75, Kamakau 1964:37, and Oliver 1974:1056; (6) the condoning of theft in practice: Fornander 1918–1919, 5,2:284–293, esp. fn. 12 on 292, Handy 1923:276, Malo 1951:66, Dening 1980:166, and Oliver 1974:342; (7) contextual factors affecting whether or not and to what degree a thief was punished: Daws 1968b:69, Dening 1974:75, Fornander 1919, 5,2:284–293, Handy 1930:129, and Oliver 1974:1056–1059; (8) "might making right" regarding morality of theft: Oliver 1974:1062; see also Malo 1951:57–58 and Oliver 1974:1059; (9) rewards Western explorers often gave Polynesian chiefs for their assistance: Cook in Beaglehole 1955:77, 82, 86, King in Beaglehole 1967:564, Bougainville 1772:225, Corney 1913:309, 317, Hawkesworth 1775:44–45, and Robertson 1973:24; also note Sahlins 1981a:42; (10) the Polynesian focus on knowing things by their practical effectiveness and pragmatic value: Borofsky 1987:125–128, Firth 1967:179, 185, 191–193, Koskinen 1968:37, and Shore n.d.:24, 29; (11) Tahitian efforts to reestablish trade: Robertson 1973:46–47, 55ff., and Hawkesworth 1775:44ff.; (12) Samoan attempts to reestablish trade after the massacre of the Frenchmen: La Pérouse 1799, 2:139; and (13) the situation at Hawaii after Cook's death: King in Beaglehole 1967:565, Samwell in Beaglehole 1967:1215–1217; also note Samwell in Beaglehole 1967:1204.

11. One possible reason for the severe punishments surrounding theft was that chiefs also had their property stolen. According to Cook, "It is not always in the power of the chiefs to prevent robberies, they are frequently rob[b]ed themselves and complain of it as a great evil" (Beaglehole 1967:222). In an important sense, such thefts constituted challenges to the chiefs' status just as they did to that of the Western captains.

12. For additional references on topics covered in this section regarding comparative analysis and patterns of violence, see in regard to (1) the violent attitudes of Europeans: Pearson 1970:140, 142–144; (2) earlier contact with Samoa: Roggeveen 1970:151–156 (on June 15, 1722 Roggeveen passed by Tutuila) and Bougainville 1772:278–284 (on May 5, 1768 Bougainville passed by Tutuila); (3) Westerners vulnerable because of large number of Polynesians surrounding or on board ship: Cook in Beaglehole 1967:490–491, Fleurieu 1801:33, and Ingraham 1971:46, 50; (4) details regarding the massacre of the Frenchmen: La Pérouse 1799, 2:135–138, 142–148, Gilson 1970:66, and Oceanus 1814; (5) explanations for Cook's association with Lono: Sahlins 1981a:9–28 and 1985:104–135, Daws 1968a and 1968b:8–28, and Malo 1951:145; (6) accounts of Cook's death: Clerke in Beaglehole 1967:533–534, 538–539, Ellis 1782:105–112, King in Beaglehole 1967:555–558, Phillips in Beaglehole 1967:534–539, Samwell in Beaglehole 1967:1195–1201, and others in Beaglehole 1967:536–538, 569; (7) an additional perspective by Cook regarding the use of force to maintain good social relations with indigenous populations: Cook in Beaglehole 1961:292; (8) the killing of Marquesans by Mendaña's crew: Quirós 1904:20–21, 24, 26; (9) the matter of supplies in relation to Mendaña's visit: Beaglehole 1966:64–65 and Quirós 1904:21–22; and (10) the lack of humanitarian concern for indigenous populations by Mendaña

or his crew: Beaglehole 1966:64, 77, and Quirós 1904:20–21, 25; though note the exception in Quirós 1904:21, 25, 26.

13. For details regarding Cook's first visit to the Hawaiian Islands, specifically to Kaua'i and Ni'ihau, see Cook in Beaglehole 1967:263–286 and Samwell in Beaglehole 1967:1081–1086.

9

Looking Ahead

ROBERT BOROFSKY

ALAN HOWARD

THE hallmark of good research is that it generates new questions. No matter what one's concern with Polynesian ethnology, the work of the past few decades has opened the door for a wide range of new projects. For purposes of discussion, we divide our remarks into four sections, each reflecting a set of related issues: prehistory and the reconstruction of early contact sociocultural systems, historical change, contemporary Polynesian society and culture, and comparative analysis.

Prehistory and Reconstruction

Recent evidence on changing island environments has greatly altered perspectives on archaeological thinking. The old view of static environments has given way to a view of islands that have been in a state of dynamic change. Some previous shorelines, for example, have subsided while others have uplifted. This means one has to be extremely cautious in evaluating the likely location of early settlement sites. This realization suggests that we must treat with caution our data on earliest settlements and must view present scenarios of settlement sequence as tentative at best.

Furthermore, the massive increase in archaeological data has muddied the picture in several ways. In western Polynesia the once neat image of a settlement sequence from Fiji to Tonga to Samoa no longer seems quite so clear. The same is true with the outliers. The relatively early settlement dates for Tikopia, Anuta, and Taumako suggest the pattern is not as simple as previously conceived. And as Kirch (chapter 2, p. 25) notes for eastern Polynesia, in light of the similar datings of early Hawaiian and Marquesan sites, the "orthodox scenario for the dispersal of Polynesians through eastern Polynesia is in need of rethinking." Recent archaeological research has created a great deal of room for imaginative projects aimed at refining our understandings of settlement sequences and inter-island contact. There is need for more intense settlement studies in all the archipelagoes and for a clearer delineation of range and variation in settlement over time.

Kirch lists several topics that require further analysis: paleodemography; production systems; human impact on ecosystems; space, settlements, and society; and development of social complexity. In each case there is a need for greater clarification of the developmental processes occurring in specific environments. Recent research in paleodemography, for example, raises questions regarding population variation in relation to processes of sociocultural transformation. Although results have been encouraging, what is now needed is a finer-grained analysis of local demographic sequences.

Much significant work has been accomplished in the area of production systems by focusing on faunal materials as well as extractive and exploitative technology. But successes in this area have raised the need for greater clarification of the particular processes involved in development. Prehistorians have made considerable progress by widening their analyses to include topics not directly falling under the rubric of production, such as craft specialization, trade systems, and support for elaborate ceremonial structures. By analyzing intensification in terms of changing relations between labor and the means of production they have raised new and exciting analytical possibilities. In regard to ecological considerations, hierarchies of constraint, environmental opportunity, and nature-culture interaction have replaced simple determinism as models for analysis. But we still need to know more about how adapting to changing environments stimulated transformations in Polynesian societies.

The development of social complexity remains one of the continuing concerns of Polynesian prehistory. We have moved from the broad suggestions of Sahlins and Goldman to detailed analyses of particular archipelagoes at particular times. But the degree to which one factor or another played a role in an archipelago's development remains to be determined. Kirch is correct in stressing the need for multicausal analyses and reliance on a tripartite approach involving ethnography, linguistics, and archaeology.

Attempts to reconstruct traditional Polynesian systems have enjoyed a renaissance in recent years, as several of the chapters in this book make clear. Important efforts such as Oliver's (1974) work on Tahiti and Valeri's (1985a) book on Hawaiian sacrifice demonstrate what can be accomplished with patient, cautious scholarship on the one hand, and theoretical daring on the other. Along with Sahlins' stimulating theoretical forays into reconstruction (mainly on Hawaii and Fiji), Oliver and Valeri show just how rich the available sources are.

In his chapter (5) on *mana* and *tabu,* Shore suggests certain directions for exploration that arise out of his analysis. One is a testing of his synthesis against the ethnographic record. "The conception of *mana,* and its subsidiary notions of *tapu* and *noa,* as developed in these pages," he notes, "are useful to the extent that they illuminate heretofore obscure corners of Polynesian ethnology" (p. 166). The goal is to "make sense of practices that until now have eluded our understanding" (p. 166). Shore provides a clear analysis that others can take as a frame of reference both for interpreting disparate data, from tattooing to sacred maids to menstrual taboos, as well as for developing new analyses.

Kaeppler's essay (chapter 7) also suggests possibilities for exploring interrelationships that have hitherto been neglected. She points out ways that ethnoaesthetics relate to social organization, and demonstrates the potential for inferring features of social formations from both archaeological materials and museum artifacts collected during the early period of contact. There are opportunities here that have barely been exploited.

Recent research into social organization has suggested ways to reinterpret earlier texts, including myths and legends. Given what we now know about the flexible, contextual nature of Polynesian social organization, we are in a much better position than our intellectual forefathers to understand how Polynesian social systems worked and were reproduced over time.

Historical Change

Issues of historical change have also been recast by Pacific historians and historically oriented anthropologists. The island-centered historians have developed new perspectives, and anthropologists such as Greg Dening and Marshall Sahlins have reframed issues of change in illuminating, innovative ways. Several of the authors in this book pose questions for research that reflect these new orientations.

Shore (chapter 5), for example, asks to what degree differences in indigenous cultural orders, as manifested in worldviews, can explain the differential impact of Western contact on particular archipelagoes? Shore is particularly interested in whether the dual organizations of western Polynesian societies made them more resilient to change than the monolithic power structures of eastern Polynesia. A related question is how Polynesian worldviews have altered over time. It would be quite valuable to explore, for instance, changes in the conception of *mana* during the postcontact period. What, for example, was the impact of Christianity on it? As Shore notes elsewhere (1982:248), *mana* today is almost exclusively used in relation to God in Samoa. Changes in the usage of other key concepts such as *tapu, noa, ali'i,* and *alofa* might also be revealing in this regard.

One cannot help wonder how the kingly/populist tension worked itself out in various Polynesian societies over time. Marcus' analysis (chapter 6) of an ossified hierarchy is suggestive for Tonga, but how did the kingly/populist tension evolve in Tahiti, especially after French intervention, or in New Zealand following the Maori Wars? And how did chieftainship respond to European intrusion on the atolls, where hierarchy was more limited? What we need is a better sense of the continuity and change through time of chiefly institutions in Polynesian society.

We might also ask to what degree modern expressions of chieftainship are Western creations? Given the role of Western missionaries and advisors in shaping missionary kingdoms, as well as Western administrators and scholars in fostering invented traditions, one might wonder to what degree and in what ways Polynesian cultures today represent a compromise between Western and Polynesian conceptions of the Polynesian past (see, e.g., France 1969, Hanson 1989, Simmons 1976).

Kaeppler (chapter 7, p. 234) boldly states the case for studying aesthetic expression in historical perspective: "Within Polynesia, research on ethnoaesthetics and artistic grammars has just begun. Such studies are important to the future of Polynesian studies, not just because of what we have to learn about art and aesthetics, but for what they can teach us about the nature of Polynesian societies and the ways they have changed and are changing." Her chapter raises several issues concerning continuity and change in Polynesian aesthetics. For example, if we assume a traditional aesthetic of inequality in many Polynesian societies, then we need to ask how Polynesian aesthetics have altered as the structures of inequality have changed. Have aesthetic performances changed in ways that reflect new forms of inequality, or in some instances, movements toward equality? Other questions concern the ways in which the "grammar" of aesthetics is affected by changing technology (such innovations as steel tools, slack-key guitars, and videotaping).

In our chapter on early contact we stress certain issues that need further exploration. We noted that given most texts were written by and for Europeans, there is an essential bias to them (see, e.g., Dobyns 1988). Indigenous accounts have their biases as well. But the fact that European and indigenous biases were often different opens the way to a comparative dialogue, as suggested by Borofsky (1987). Comparing the two sets of biases, we can learn something about the processes that went into each's construction of events. It is important that a number of scholars of Polynesian ancestry have joined the dialogue in recent years. Prominent in this regard are the works of Trask (1983) and Dorton (1986) in Hawaii and Awatere (1984), Kawharu (1975, 1977), Marsden (1975), S. Mead (1983, 1984), and Walker (1987) in New Zealand. Although their views cannot be seen as representative of Polynesians at the time of contact, by self-consciously taking an insider's view, their work is often laden with fresh insights.

We need to explore multiple ways to mine the existing material. Sahlins' brand of structural history is one possibility, although a reading of reviews of his work suggests that rather than resolving the major issues he has momentarily set them aside with the breathtaking sweep of his vision. Another possibility is the approach stressed in chapter 8, which analyzes interactions among specific groups over time and infers meaning from each's responses to the other's actions.

Conspicuously underrepresented in the field of Polynesian history are studies from a Marxist perspective. Christine Gailey's recent publication (1987) relating changes in the status of Tongan women to infrastructural changes following European intrusion is a notable exception. Although her analysis has been criticized for distorting the evidence (see James 1988), it nevertheless suggests a number of key issues that require more attention than thus far received.

Most of the historical work in Polynesia has focused on sequences of events in particular societies. Important exceptions are Maude's (1981) work on the Peruvian labor trade and Ralston's (1978) study of beach communities in the nineteenth century, both of which take a comparative perspective. In our chapter on early contact we attempt to provide a stimulus to comparative history by constructing a model to account for patterns of violence in early Polynesian-European encounters. We grant that it may not fit all cases in all respects during the early contact period. But its aim is to be suggestive, to challenge others to develop more suitable frameworks.

There are many other topics that require comparable exploration. To what degree, for example, can the rise and decline of indigenous paramounts be attributed to internal versus external factors? Certainly Western firearms and technical expertise played a role in the rise of Kamehameha, Pomare, and Taufa'ahau. But one must be cautious in overestimating Western influence. In Tahiti and Samoa it appears that competing factions both gained access to Western weapons, thereby negating the advantage possessed by one or the other side. Much more needs to be done regarding the factors behind the indigenous consolidation of power on Polynesian islands following contact, especially once we set aside some of the more simplistic formulations and biases regarding the role of Europeans.

The reduction of the paramounts' powers and the rise of alternative power brokers in their place has not generally received the attention dedicated to the paramounts' initial consolidation of authority. Yet it is equally important. In its dynamics one can perceive the seeds of modern Polynesia's economic and political dependency. At least three factors seem to have been involved. Part of it likely can be traced to the traditional political cycle of Polynesian polities. The rise and decline of paramounts was a pattern common to many island groups. The alliance between paramounts and various Europeans, which had played a role in the rise of particular paramounts to power, also seems to have unraveled to some degree as the two groups each sought to dominate the other. Finally, there is the whole issue of indirect imperialism that framed the process (see, for example, Robinson 1972). Polynesian kingdoms were encouraged to become more Western in order to maintain their political independence. But in assuming Western political structures some weakened their traditional bases of power, making them more vulnerable to Western control. In this regard one would like to know more about how Western dominance was maintained in Polynesia through symbolic manipulation. Why was a limited degree of force sufficient to impose Western dictates in particular archipelagoes?

There is also the question of religious transitions. The overthrow of the Hawaiian *kapu* system in 1819 has been analyzed and reanalyzed. But it still remains to insert related events on many archipelagoes within "a coherent structural-historical process," as Sahlins phrased it (1981a: 75). We need a better understanding of the dynamics of Polynesian religions and the ways religious and political concerns were intertwined on many archipelagoes. "The present national religion," the missionary Davies observed for Tahiti, "is so blended with the civil concerns or the privileges and authority of the chiefs, that they have no conception the one can stand without the other" (cited in Newbury 1980:32). Religious change, especially conversion to Christianity, must be examined within this context.

In addition, there is the issue of economic transitions. Initially, Westerners were dependent on Polynesians for supplies, and Polynesians were often able to dictate the terms of trade during the early contact period. But increased contact bred increased dependency on Western traders in many archipelagoes. One of the critical issues that needs to be analyzed is the inability of Polynesians to establish themselves as economic middlemen and traders. Even more significant is the issue of land: How did indigenous tenure change during the nineteenth century? By what means did Europeans progressively increase their control over land through time? One of the more interesting considerations, given the tensions surrounding land tenure, is that land itself was often of ambiguous value to Westerners in many archipelagoes. Land often needed extra-archipelago supporting conditions, such as a world cotton shortage or special trade concessions relating to sugar, for Westerners to realize the profit they sought from controlling land. The significance of land was not simply in the economic control Westerners sought over it, but also in the political involvement in indigenous affairs they then came to desire as a result of owning it (Ralston 1978:165).

The issue of gender relations needs more careful examination as well. The nature of sexual relations between Polynesian women and European men during the early contact period, barely touched upon in our analysis, remains at a highly speculative level, and would benefit from an intensive comparative analysis. Changes in gender relations in the postcontact period have been the subject of major works by Gailey (1987) on Tonga and Linnekin (1988) on Hawaii. In addition, Ralston and Thomas (1987) have edited an issue of the *Journal of Pacific History* on gender relations. But much remains to be done to clarify the ways in which gender relations were altered by various changes during the postcontact period, and how contemporary gender relations reflect themes of continuity and change with the past.

Another topic of interest, which reverses the traditional focus of study, is the impact Polynesia made on Western societies. We know that eighteenth-century explorers' accounts of Polynesia took Europe by storm. Between 1770 and 1800, more than 100 editions or impressions were published regarding Cook's journeys. Accounts by early explorers often provided the basis for commentaries on Europe. The "noble savage" different writers depicted as residing on one or more Polynesian islands became a vehicle for criticizing shortcomings in European society as well as constituting a means for exploring Europe's ancestral roots.

Smith suggests the exploration of the Pacific stimulated the development of new intellectual perspectives in Europe. He states: "the wealth of new material which arrived . . . from the Pacific during the last two decades of the [eighteenth] century . . . was one of the factors which led to the collapse in scientific circles of the chain of being as an acceptable explanation of universal nature" (B. Smith 1960:123). Elsewhere he asserts, "the opening of the Pacific is . . . to be numbered among those factors contributing to the triumph of romanticism and science in the nineteenth-century world of values" (B. Smith 1960:1). Moreover, Polynesia had an impact on European fashions. Europeans manufactured "Tahitian" toys and jewelry. " 'Tahitian' verandas were designed for country houses; 'Polynesian' wallpaper [became] fashionable" (Daws 1980:11). Fitting with their own cultural concerns, Europeans created technological and artistic imitations of Polynesia as they perceived it.

In contrast to the powerful impact of romanticized imagery, the economic impact of Polynesia on the West was relatively minor. The ports of trade for Polynesia were mainly Valparaiso, Sydney, and San Francisco. One might cogently argue that trade with the Far East and the Americas contributed to the economic development of Europe, but one would be hard pressed to make such an argument for Polynesia. Perhaps there is a relationship here—one of Braudel's structures of the *longue durée*—between the significant cultural, and minor economic, impact Polynesia had on the West. Certainly part of the explanation for Polynesia's initial intellectual impact was timing. The first indepth contact occurred during the Enlightenment. But perhaps part of it was due to the region's limited resources and distance from Europe. European perceptions of Polynesia remained positive far longer than they did of China or North America, where European economic penetration was more extensive. We know that once-positive views of Australian aborigines and North American Indians turned negative as economic development in both regions increased (see, e.g., B. Smith 1960:202; Pearce 1988). In any case, much remains to be done to clarify the mutual impact of Polynesian and European cultures on one another.

Contemporary Polynesian Society and Culture

Following World War II the pace of change in Oceania dramatically quickened. Modern medicines brought death rates down to low levels, and since birth rates remained high, populations increased at an unprecedented pace. This encouraged outmigration to urban areas, which were seen as places of employment and educational opportunities. An increasing proportion of people took advantage of opportunities to migrate to industrialized areas in New Zealand, Australia, Hawaii, and the mainland United States, where they formed Polynesian enclaves. In an important sense Polynesian communities are no longer bounded by beaches and reefs as they once were. Samoan communities now extend beyond Apia and Pago Pago to Auckland, Honolulu, and San Francisco. Not only do goods and money circulate freely among these localities, but people do as well. To draw a social boundary around one village or one island now seems arbitrary and unrealistic.

Political changes have been equally dramatic. Prior to World War II, Tonga was the only independent state. Since then Western Samoa, Fiji, and Tuvalu have become nation-states, and the Cook Islands has become self-governing (although still associated with New Zealand). In addition, previously docile Polynesian populations in Hawaii, New Zealand, and French Polynesia have turned militant and become political forces to be reckoned with.

The processes of urbanization and modernization have touched every part of Polynesia, albeit differentially and in differing degrees. The result is that Polynesian communities are much more varied than ever before in regard to education, wealth, and diet. Life has become more complex even on the most remote atolls. No Polynesian group has remained untouched.

These changes raise a multitude of questions and have stimulated new forms of research. Much of the work now being done has, either directly or indirectly, an applied aspect to it. This is perhaps most obvious with studies of health behavior and education, but it also holds in the areas of politics and economics. It has become increasingly difficult to distinguish pure ethnological studies from applied ones, and indeed, government reports often provide excellent data. As more Polynesians have become sophisticated scholars, their observations and studies have taken an important place in the overall picture. The publications of the University of the South Pacific, mostly authored by indigenous islanders, constitute a landmark in this regard.

Although none of the chapters in this book deal directly with this applied orientation, several of the essays raise relevant issues. Howard and Kirkpatrick's discussion of social organization in chapter 3, for example, raises questions regarding the degree to which underlying structural principles have been adapted to new community contexts. How, for example, are the principles of seniority and gender expressed among Polynesians in different types of communities? To what extent have changes in education and occupation affected the application of these principles? And how are traditional kinship groupings being redefined today, with potential members residing in distant and culturally distinct locations?

In chapter 4, the Ritchies offer a number of suggestions for exploration. They point to a need for research on contemporary Polynesian conceptions of socialization. There is also a need to explore the effects of exposure to new socialization models on Polynesians and how childrearing is affected by significant changes in parental activity patterns. The Ritchies face the issue of applying anthropological insights to existing social problems head-on. It is important, they point out, to find new ways to help Polynesians cope with the stresses of urbanization. A low level of parental interaction with children may have worked well in community-oriented environments where others took up the slack, but in settings where the nuclear family constitutes the main socializing agent serious problems can arise. The Ritchies alert us to the problem of major discontinuities among expectations in Polynesian homes and Western urban communities. They suggest that although punishment is expected to be swift and harsh in the home when community standards are violated, procedures within the larger legal system of Western cities are much more protracted, capricious, and unpredictable. Problems such as these need to be better understood if we are to translate our academic insights regarding Polynesian life into effective practical advice.

Shore (chapter 5) and Marcus (chapter 6) raise questions concerning principles of status and prerogative in modern Polynesian communities. How are the legacies of *mana* and status rivalry played out in modern political contexts? And what has happened to the concept of *tapu?* Drivers along Hawaii's highways see *kapu* signs in various places. In what sense is this an elaboration or transformation of the concept discussed by Shore? Marcus' concern with political economy, especially when connected to issues relating to the invention of tradition, raises intriguing questions. To what degree, for example, are modern expressions of chieftainship an attempt to retain a symbolic identity among economically peripheral groups? And to what degree are indigenous movements, such as *Maoritanga* and the Hawaiian Renaissance, shaped by Polynesian efforts to come to terms with new economic, political, and social pressures of the past several decades (see, e.g., Linnekin 1983, Ogan 1984, Hanson 1989)? We need a better understanding of how the principles of hierarchy operate in modern Polynesian communities. It seems quite natural to focus on chieftainship in Samoa, Tonga, and Fiji, where the institution remains strong. But how do the principles of status now operate among Hawaiians, Tahitians, Rarotongans, and Maori?

Kaeppler's chapter (7) on art and aesthetics likewise raises a number of issues concerning the adaptation of traditional forms to modern contexts. Not only does she draw our attention to the development of "airport art," which is geared for the tourist industry, but her essay raises questions concerning the place of art within the modern political arena. To what extent, for example, have particular artifacts and performances become political symbols for expressing identity and mobilizing sentiment? And, more generally, what is the role of art and aesthetics within modern Polynesian contexts? The ethnographic data bearing on these issues are surprisingly thin.

On the whole, the quality of ethnographic research being done today is impressive. But although excellent studies of particular institutions exist for various archipelagoes, the record remains somewhat uneven and shows significant gaps. This makes it difficult to gain a holistic understanding of particular societies—of how various detailed studies all fit together. As a result, cross-cultural comparisons are hampered. Patchwork data on one group are compared with patchwork data on another.

Another problem concerns the dimension of time. Many fine ethnographies were done decades ago on particular communities. Their very quality calls for restudy, so we can gain a perspective on how they have changed through time, and how they have responded to intensified relations with the larger world economic system. Better yet would be long-term monitoring of societies. The project conducted by Huntsman and Hooper in the Tokelaus, which has involved ongoing contact over a period of two decades, might serve as a model in this regard. The value of longitudinal research is that it helps avoid the pitfall of perceiving Polynesian societies as static structures and provides a much better basis for grasping the nature of dynamic social processes characteristic of these societies.

We might add here that the way is open for considerable innovation in the recording of ethnographic information, given recent technological advances. The possibility now exists for doing ethnographies in hypermedia (see A. Howard 1988), allowing readers to explore the ethnographic record in innovative ways, and to add to it where appropriate. Perhaps it will become appropriate to talk about on-line data bases in the future, rather than ethnographies. Accounts may be open, rather than restricted, and people from targeted communities may have the option of adding to and correcting an accumulative account regarding themselves. What one would then have would be an ongoing, growing record of Polynesian groups, evolving out of a dialogue among indigenous as well as outside observers.

Comparative Analysis

Polynesia has often been touted as a laboratory for comparative studies, and indeed some of the best scholarly work in the region has taken advantage of this opportunity.

We believe the goals of comparisons should be three-fold: (1) they should aim at illuminating underlying structural patterns shared among Polynesian groups as well as explaining variations on common themes; (2) they should strive to illuminate key variables that have facilitated continuity and change through time; and (3) they should look for similarities and differences between Polynesia and other areas within Oceania and beyond. Within this rubric of goals two types of comparisons are needed.

The first is controlled comparisons of island groups with similar institutions. One such example is Kirch's "comparative note" regarding Hawaii and Tonga. He points out that "Hawai'i and Tonga are two of the most elaborated Polynesian chiefdoms, and convergences in their respective evolutionary pathways are of particular interest, since (given the great isolation between the two societies) these must have arisen from the commonly inherited structural base, and from similar evolutionary conditions and constraints" (Kirch 1984a:262). Hanson's (1973) comparative analysis of political change in Tahiti and Samoa illuminates similarities and differences in the ways these archipelagoes responded to European intrusion. Feinberg's (1988) analysis of differences in chieftainship on the outliers of Anuta and Nukumanu provides another example. In this instance it is the contrast between a high island (small as it may be) and an atoll that is of central interest.

Marcus uses the method of controlled comparison in the section of his chapter called "The Chief's Two Bodies in Tonga and Samoa." He sees chieftainship in the two archipelagoes as representing opposite poles of the kingly/populist continuum. One might ask how this contrast evolved. Given accounts of prehistoric relations between the two groups, might a pattern of schizmogenesis have developed? Or do these differences derive from differences in the postcontact period?

The second set of comparisons is broader in nature. They follow the pattern set by Williamson (1924, 1933), Burrows (1939b), Sahlins (1958), and Goldman 91970), and explore general patterns and processes within Polynesia as a whole.

Shore's analysis is a particularly good example of the insights that can be drawn from such an approach. As Shore states in chapter 5 (p. 164): "no coherent vision of local variation in Polynesia is possible without a prior clarification of what common characteristics make it a real culture area." Certainly one must exercise caution interpreting prehistoric and early historic Polynesian worldview, given the limited nature of the sources. But it is clear that such generalizations prove immensely valuable for interpreting individual cases. Shore's analysis of *mana* provides a framework for comprehending the concept in Pukapuka as well as Hawaii, and it reveals important possibilities for reflecting on how the concept was incorporated into Christianity. His analysis of variations between western and eastern Polynesia is particularly suggestive. It creates a framework for further exploration of variations in kinship, political organization, and responses to change within and between these subregions.

The Ritchies' (chapter 4) analysis of cultural targets for child training provides another example of the insights gained from bold pan-Polynesian comparisons. The importance of context, relatedness and kinship, status and respect, sharing and caring, and unity through consensus are important themes in every Polynesian society, though their specific manifestations may vary. Also pervasive are the importance of communities as primary contexts for socialization and of peers as socialization agents. Within this general framework, one can explore the conditions under which social reproduction occurs in different societies. Why do societies that are as different as Pukapuka and Hawaii possess so many similarities in childrearing? And how are these reproduced through time in such markedly different social environments? What specific variables might help explain the difference in social character that has developed among different groups of Polynesians? How, for example, can we account for differences in violence among Polynesian communities? Why does Samoa have high rates of violence while in Rotuma and Pukapuka violence is relatively rare? Why do some Polynesians adapt easily to the demands of an urban environment while others experience much difficulty? These are only a few of the questions one might subject to comparative analysis.

The Ritchies also raise important questions regarding styles of learning. Much has been written on the contrast between Western competitive and Polynesian cooperative learning styles. It has been "verified" with various tests and statistics. But such formulations are clearly an oversimplification. Polynesians can also be highly competitive, and it would be surprising if this fact were not reflected in their learning styles. That Western researchers should focus on cooperative aspects at the expense of competitive aspects of Polynesian learning indicates something about Western images of Polynesians. We need to move away from global distinctions toward a more sensitive appraisal of subtleties. Certainly significant variations exist among Polynesian groups. It would be valuable to know what these are and why they exist. We must, in brief, pay more attention to learning as a process and how it varies in different contexts and among different groups. The arbitrary, oversimplified analyses of us versus them will no longer do.

The possibilities for broad comparison are almost endless and crosscut all of the dimensions dealt with in this volume. We need to re-examine old issues, such as how cultural and ecological factors have interacted in different environments to generate variations upon a common cultural base (note Roscoe 1988). And we need to explore new ones, such as how notions of tradition are being used to validate and justify contemporary actions. Related to this issue is the question of how concepts of cultural identity are being reshaped to meet modern conditions. In this regard, one might compare the modern adaptations of various Polynesian groups to different urban settings, for example, to Auckland, Los Angeles, and Sydney.

We also would like to draw attention to the possibilities for broader comparisons between Polynesia and other parts of Oceania. The series sponsored by the Association for Social Anthropology in Oceania provides examples of what can be accomplished when multiple authors contribute toward a comparative understanding of important issues. Topics such as adoption (Carroll, ed. 1970; Brady, ed. 1976), land tenure (Lundsgaarde 1974; see also Crocombe 1971), resettlement (Lieber 1977), and siblingship (Marshall 1981), have all benefitted from this type of interregional comparison.

Focused comparisons between Polynesia and Melanesia, and Polynesia and Micronesia, would also be beneficial. One of the better known attempts in this direction is Sahlins' (1963) bigman/chief article. In response to Sahlins' analysis, a number of scholars have pointed out that it is not an either/or situation for either region. There are ambiguities and gradients that exist with respect to leadership in both Melanesia and Polynesia. But it might be valuable to ask again, building on Sahlins' insights and with the new ethnographic data at hand, how and why the regions differ in their political organization. The issue of trade networks would also benefit from interregional comparisons. In both Melanesia and Polynesia, exchange is often multi-stranded and constitutive of social groups. In what ways do the processes work differently in the two regions, and how do they relate to differences in political organization? And given differing conceptions of gender between the two regions, can one arrive at credible generalizations regarding the factors involved?

Another set of interesting comparisons one might draw between Melanesia and Polynesia concerns their responses to Western contact (and Western responses to them). In a seminal article, Valentine (1963) compares Western colonization of Polynesia with that of Melanesia. He suggests that differences between the two regions regarding colonization and indigenous responses to it derive from the fit (or non-fit) of indigenous institutions with European ones.

With regard to Micronesia, a natural basis for comparison would be the atolls in both regions. Although Alkire (1978) and Mason (1959) provided an important start in that direction, much remains to be done in examining the interaction of cultural factors with the ecological constraints of atoll environments. Robert Levy (1972) and Alan Howard (1979) saw fit to include Micronesia and Polynesia under the same umbrella for discussing psychological and psychiatric phenomena, but little has been done to compare and contrast social institutions between the two regions.

Moving beyond Oceania, Marcus (chapter 6) notes important similarities between certain Polynesian and Southeast Asian polities. He finds Goldman's notion of status lineage relevant to both regions. And several Japanese scholars who have read Shore's analyses on Samoa are intrigued by the parallels between the two cultures in respect to dual organization. Polynesia's cultural commitment to an ideology of hierarchy and divine chieftainship certainly makes it ripe for comparison with other regions marked by institutions of kingship, as A. M. Hocart (1927) recognized long ago. There is also much room for comparing Polynesia and other regions of the world in respect to issues of decolonization, the impact of the world economic system, and the effects of modernization on health and well-being.

To summarize, the main goal of this book has been to frame questions for exploration. To do this, each author in his or her own way provided a retrospective account of earlier work in a particular specialty. They then described new possibilities for research. What we hope readers will end with is a sense of the rich possibilities for analysis that exist in the region. The words written by the explorer Louis de Bougainville in 1772 remain as appropriate today as they were then.

> "Who can give an account of the manner in which they were conveyed hither, what communications they have with other beings, and what becomes of them when they multiply on an isle."

BIBLIOGRAPHY

Adams, Henry
   1947 *Tahiti; Memoirs of Arii Taimai E, Marama of Eimeo, Teriiere of Tooarai, Terinui of Tahiti, Tauraatua I Amo*. Robert Spiller, ed. New York: Scholars' Facsimiles and Reprints.

Alkire, William
   1978 *Coral Islanders*. Arlington Heights, Ill.: AHM.

Allen, Jim
   1984 In Search of the Lapita Homeland. *The Journal of Pacific History* 19:186–201.

Ambrose, W., and R. C. Green
   1972 First Millennium BC Transport of Obsidian from New Britain to the Solomon Islands. *Nature* 237:31.

Ammerman, A. J., L. L. Cavalli-Sforza, and D. K. Wagener
   1976 Toward the Estimation of Population Growth in Old World Prehistory. In *Demographic Anthropology*, edited by Ezra Zubrow, pp. 27–61. Albuquerque: University of New Mexico Press.

Anderson, A. J.
   1979 Prehistoric Exploitation of Marine Resources at Black Rocks Point, Palliser Bay. In *Prehistoric Man at Palliser Bay*, edited by B. F. and H. Leach, pp. 49–65. National Museum of New Zealand Bulletin no. 21. Wellington.
   1981 A Model of Collecting on the Rocky Shore. *Journal of Archaeological Science* 8:109–120.
   1982a North and Central Otago. In *The First Thousand Years: Regional Perspectives in New Zealand Archaeology*, edited by N. Prickett, pp. 112–128. Palmerston North: New Zealand Archaeological Association.
   1982b A Review of Economic Patterns During the Archaic Phase in Southern New Zealand. *New Zealand Journal of Archaeology* 4:45–75.

Anderson, Benedict
  1972   The Idea of Power in Javanese Culture. In *Culture and Politics in Indo-nesia,* edited by C. Holt, pp. 1–69. Ithaca: Cornell University Press.

Anderson, Johannes C.
  1933   *Maori Music with its Polynesian Background.* Polynesian Society Memoir no. 10. Wellington.

Archey, Gilbert
  1933   Evolution of Certain Maori Carving Patterns. *Journal of the Polynesian Society* 42:171–190.
  1965   *The Art Forms of Polynesia.* Auckland Institute and Museum Bulletin no. 4.

Ausubel, David P.
  1961   *Maori Youth.* Wellington: Price Milburn.

Awatere, Donna
  1984   *Maori Sovereignty.* Auckland: Broadsheet.

Ayres, W.
  1973   The Cultural Context of Easter Island Religious Structures. Ph.D. diss. Tulane University.
  1979   Easter Island Fishing. *Asian Perspectives* 22:61–92.

Babadzan, Alain
  1981   Les Dépouilles des Dieux. Essai sur la Symbolique de Certaines Effigies Polynésiennes. *RES* 1:8–39.
  1982   La Position Actuelle des *Ti'i* aux îles de la Société. *RES* 4:62–84.

Bach, John
  1968   The Royal Navy in the Pacific Islands. *The Journal of Pacific History* 3:3–20.

Baker, Paul, Joel M. Hanna, and Thelma Baker, eds.
  1986   *The Changing Samoans: Behavior and Health in Transition.* New York: Oxford University Press.

Baker, Thelma
  1986   Changing Socialization Patterns of Contemporary Samoans. In *The Changing Samoans: Behavior and Health in Transition,* edited by P. Baker, J. M. Hanna, and T. Baker, pp. 146–173. New York: Oxford University Press.

Bales, R. F.
  1970   *Personality and Interpersonal Behavior.* New York: Holt Rinehart and Winston.

Bargatzky, Thomas
  1980   Beachcombers and Castaways as Innovators. *The Journal of Pacific History.* 15:93–102.

Barker, R. G., and H. F. Wright
  1954   *Midwest and Its Children.* Evanston: Ron Peterson.

Barnes, J. A.
  1962   African Models in the New Guinea Highlands. *Man* 62:5–9.

Barrau, Jacques
  1961   *Subsistence Agriculture in Polynesia and Micronesia.* Bernice P. Bishop
         Museum Bulletin no. 223. Honolulu: The Museum.

Barrow, Terence
  1956   Maori Decorative Art: An Outline. *Journal of the Polynesian Society* 65
         (4): 305–331.

Bateson, Gregory
  1936   *Naven.* New York: Cambridge University Press.
  1979   *Mind and Nature: A Necessary Unity.* New York: Dutton.

Baudet, Henri
  1965   *Paradise on Earth: Some Thoughts on European Images of Non-European
         Man,* translated by Elizabeth Wentholt. New Haven: Yale University
         Press.

Bayard, D. T.
  1976   *The Cultural Relationships of the Polynesian Outliers.* University of Otago
         Studies in Prehistoric Anthropology no. 9. Otago, New Zealand.

Beaglehole, Ernest
  1937   Emotional Release in a Polynesian Community. *Journal of Abnormal
         and Social Psychology* 32:319–328.
  1944a Character Structure: Its Role in the Analysis of Interpersonal Rela-
         tions. *Psychiatry* 7:145–162.
  1944b *Islands of Danger.* Wellington: Progressive Publishing Society.
  1957   *Social Change in the South Pacific: Rarotonga and Aitutaki.* London:
         George Allen and Unwin.

Beaglehole, Ernest, and Pearl Beaglehole
  1938   *Ethnology of Pukapuka.* Bernice P. Bishop Museum Bulletin no. 150.
         Honolulu: The Museum.
  1941   *Pangai, A Village in Tonga.* Polynesian Society Memoirs, vol. 18. Wel-
         lington.
  1946   *Some Modern Maoris.* Wellington: New Zealand Council for Educa-
         tional Research.

Beaglehole, Ernest, and James Ritchie
  1960   Basic Personality in a New Zealand Maori Community. In *Studying
         Personality Cross-Culturally,* edited by Bert Kaplan, pp. 493–518. Evan-
         ston: Ron Peterson.

Beaglehole, J. C.
  1950   Review of *British Policy in the South Pacific (1796–1893),* by John Ward.
         The English Historical Review 254:122–124.
  1966   *The Exploration of the Pacific.* Stanford: Stanford University Press.
  1974   *The Life of Captain James Cook.* London: Adam and Charles Black.

Beaglehole, J. C., ed.
  1955   *The Journals of Captain James Cook on His Voyages of Discovery: The Voyage
         of the* Endeavour *1768–1771.* London: Cambridge University Press
         (for the Hakluyt Society).

1961   *The Journals of Captain James Cook on His Voyages of Discovery: The Voyage of the* Resolution *and* Adventure *1772–1775*. London: Cambridge University Press (for the Hakluyt Society).

1962   *The* Endeavour *Journal of Joseph Banks 1768–1771*. 2 vols. Sydney: Angus and Robertson.

1967   *The Journals of Captain James Cook on His Voyages of Discovery: The Voyage of the* Resolution *and* Discovery *1776–1780*. Parts 1 and 2. London: Cambridge University Press (for the Hakluyt Society).

Bekker, Konrad
1951   Historical Patterns of Cultural Contact in Southern Asia. *Far Eastern Quarterly* 11:3–15.

Bellwood, P.
1972   Settlement Pattern Survey, Hanatekua Valley, Hiva Oa, Marquesas Islands. Pacific Anthropological Records no. 17. Honolulu: Department of Anthropology, Bernice P. Bishop Museum.

1979   *Man's Conquest of the Pacific*. New York: Oxford.

Benedict, Ruth
1934   *Patterns of Culture*. Boston: Mentor.

Bennet, J. A.
1976   Immigration, "Blackbirding," Labour Recruiting? The Hawaiian Experience 1877–1887. *The Journal of Pacific History* 11:3–27.

Bernard, Jessie
1974   *The Future of Motherhood*. New York: The Dial Press.

Best, Elsdon
1902   Notes on the Art of War. *Journal of the Polynesian Society* 11:11–41, 47–75, 127–162, 219–246.

1914   Maori Beliefs Concerning the Human Organs of Generation. *Man* 14:132–134.

1923   *The Maori School of Learning*. Dominion Museum Monograph no. 6. Wellington.

1924a   *The Maori*. 2 vols. Memoirs of the Polynesian Society no. 5. Wellington.

1924b   *The Maori as He Was: A Brief Account of Maori Life as It Was in Pre-European Days*. Wellington: Dominion Museum.

Biersack, Aletta
1982   Tongan Exchange Structures: Beyond Descent and Alliance. *Journal of the Polynesian Society* 91:181–212.

1985   Review of *Where the Waves Fall*, by K. R. Howe. *American Ethnologist* 12:169–170.

Biggs, Bruce
1960   *Maori Marriage: An Essay in Reconstruction*. Wellington: Polynesian Society.

Biggs, B., D. S. Walsh, and J. Waqa
  1970   *Proto-Polynesian Reconstructions with English to Proto-Polynesian Finder List.*
          Working Papers in Linguistics, Department of Anthropology, University of Auckland.

Boggs, Stephen
  1978   The Development of Verbal Disputing in Part-Hawaiian Children.
          Language in Society 7:325–344.

Boggs, Stephen, and Karen Watson-Gegeo
  1985   *Speaking, Relating and Learning: A Study of Hawaiian Children at Home and
          at School.* Norwood, N.J.: Ablex.

Bollard, A. E.
  1981   The Financial Adventures of J. C. Godeffroy and Son in the Pacific.
          The Journal of Pacific History 16:3–19.

Boon, James A.
  1977   *The Anthropological Romance of Bali, 1597–1972: Dynamic Perspectives in
          Marriage and Caste.* Cambridge: Cambridge University Press.

Borofsky, Robert
  1982   Making History: The Creation of Traditional Knowledge on Puka-
          puka, a Polynesian Atoll. Ph.D. diss., University of Hawaii.
  1987   *Making History: Pukapukan and Anthropological Constructions of Knowledge.*
          New York: Cambridge University Press.

Bott, Elizabeth
  1972   Psychoanalysis and Ceremony. In *The Interpretation of Ritual,* edited by
          J. S. La Fontaine, pp. 277–282. London: Tavistock.

Bott, Elizabeth (with the assistance of Tavi)
  1981   Power and Rank in the Kingdom of Tonga. *Journal of the Polynesian
          Society* 90:7–81.
  1982   *Tongan Society at the Time of Captain Cook's Visits: Discussions with Her
          Majesty Queen Salote Tupou.* The Polynesian Society Memoirs no. 44.
          Wellington.

Bougainville, Louis de
  1772   *A Voyage Round the World Performed by Order of His Most Christian Majesty
          in the Years 1766, 1767, 1768, and 1769.* London: J. Nourse.
          Reprinted in 1967. Ridgewood, N.J.: Gregg Press.

Boutilier, James
  1982– Review of *Islands and Beaches,* by Greg Dening and *Early Tahiti,* by
  1983   Edwin Ferdon. *Pacific Affairs* 55 (4): 754–756.

Bowden, Keith Macrae
  1952   *George Bass 1771–1803: His Discoveries, Romantic Life, and Tragic Disap-
          pearance.* Melbourne: Oxford University Press.

Bowden, Ross
  1979   *Tapu* and *Mana:* Ritual Authority and Political Power in Traditional
          Maori Society. *The Journal of Pacific History* 14:50–61.

Bowles, J. R.
  1985   Suicide and Attempted Suicide in Contemporary Western Samoa. In
          *Culture, Youth, and Suicide in the Pacific: Papers from an East-West Center
          Conference,* edited by Francis Hezel, Don Rubinstein, and Geoffrey
          White, pp. 15–35. Honolulu: East-West Center.

Brady, Ivan
  1976a   Adaptive Engineering: An Overview of Adoption in Oceania. In
          Transactions in Kinship: Adoption and Fosterage in Oceania, edited by Ivan
          Brady, pp. 271–293. Honolulu: University of Hawaii Press.
  1976b   Socioeconomic Mobility: Adoption and Land Tenure in the Ellice
          Islands. In *Transactions in Kinship: Adoption and Fosterage in Oceania,*
          edited by Ivan Brady, pp. 120–163. Honolulu: University of Hawaii
          Press.
  1982   Review Article. Les Iles Marquises: Ethnography from Another
          Beachhead. *American Ethnologist* 9:185–190.

Brady, Ivan, ed.
  1976   *Transactions in Kinship: Adoption and Fosterage in Oceania.* Honolulu:
          University of Hawaii Press.
  1983   Symposium: Speaking in the Name of the Real: Freeman and Mead
          in Samoa. *American Anthropologist* 85:908–947.

Braudel, Fernand
  1980   *On History,* translated by Sarah Matthews. Chicago: University of
          Chicago Press.

Brenneis, Donald, and Fred Myers, eds.
  1984   *Dangerous Words: Language and Politics in the Pacific.* New York: New
          York University Press.

Brookfield, H. C.
  1972   Intensification and Disintensification in Pacific Agriculture: A Theo-
          retical Approach. *Pacific Viewpoint* 13:30–48.

Brooks, Candace C.
  1976   Adoption on Manihi Atoll, Tuamotu Archipelago. In *Transactions in
          Kinship: Adoption and Fosterage in Oceania,* edited by Ivan Brady, pp. 51–
          63. Honolulu: University of Hawaii Press.

Buck, Sir Peter
  1924–   The Evolution of Maori Clothing. *Journal of the Polynesian Society,* vols.
  1926   33, 34, 35.
  1932   *Ethnology of Manahiki and Rakahanga.* Bernice P. Bishop Museum Bul-
          letin no. 99. Honolulu: The Museum.

Burrows, Edwin G.
  1933   *Native Music of the Tuamotus.* Bernice P. Bishop Museum Bulletin no.
          109. Honolulu: The Museum.
  1934   Polynesian Part Singing. *Zeitschrift fur Vergleichende Musikwissenschaft*
          2:69–76.
  1939a   Breed and Border in Polynesia. *American Anthropologist* 41:1–21.

1939b *Western Polynesia: A Study in Cultural Differentiation.* Ethnological Studies no. 7. Gothenberg.
1940   Culture Areas in Polynesia. *Journal of the Polynesian Society* 49:349–363.
1945   *Songs of Uvea and Futuna.* Bernice P. Bishop Museum Bulletin no. 183. Honolulu: The Museum.

Campbell, I. C.
1978   Review of *Grass Huts and Warehouses,* by Caroline Ralston. *The Journal of Pacific History* 13:191–192.
1980   Savage Noble and Ignoble: The Preconceptions of Early European Voyagers in Polynesia. *Pacific Studies* 4:45–59.
1982   Polynesian Perceptions of Europeans in the Eighteenth and Nineteenth Centuries. *Pacific Studies* 5:64–80.

Carino, Socorro Babaran
1970   Eighteenth Century Voyagers to the Pacific and the South Seas and the Rise of Cultural Primitivism and the Noble Savage Idea. Ph.D. diss., University of Illinois, Urbana-Champaign.

Carroll, Vern
1970   Adoption on Nukuoro. In *Adoption in Eastern Oceania,* edited by Vern Carroll, pp. 121–157. Honolulu: University of Hawaii Press.

Carroll, Vern, ed.
1970   *Adoption in Eastern Oceania.* Honolulu: University of Hawaii Press.

Cassels, R.
1984   The Role of Prehistoric Man in the Faunal Extinctions of New Zealand and Other Pacific Islands. In *Quaternary Extinctions: A Prehistoric Revolution,* edited by Paul S. Martin and R. G. Kline, pp. 741–767. Tucson: University of Arizona Press.

Chapelle, T.
1978   Customary Land Tenure in Fiji: Old Truths and Middle-Aged Myths. *Journal of the Polynesian Society* 87:71–88.

Charlot, John
1985   *The Hawaiian Poetry of Religion and Politics: Some Religio-Political Concepts in Postcontact Literature.* Laie, Hawaii: Institute of Polynesian Studies.
1987   Review of *Kingship and Sacrifice: Ritual and Society in Ancient Hawaii,* by Valerio Valeri. *Pacific Studies* 10 (2): 107–147.

Chirot, Daniel, and Thomas Hall
1982   World-System Theory. *Annual Review of Sociology* 8:81–106.

Christensen, C. C., and P. V. Kirch
1981   Non-Marine Molluscs from Archaeological Sites on Tikopia, Solomon Islands. *Pacific Science* 35:75–88.
1986   *Nonmarine Molluscs and Ecological Change at Barbers Point, Oʻahu, Hawaiian Islands.* Bishop Museum Occasional Papers, vol. 26. Honolulu: The Museum.

Churchill, William
1917   *Club Types of Nuclear Polynesia.* Washington, D.C.: The Carnegie Institution.

Cipolla, Carlo
1965   *Guns and Sails in the Early Phase of European Expansion.* London: Collins.

Clark, J. C., and P. V. Kirch, eds.
1983   *Archaeological Investigations in the Mudlane-Waimea-Kawaihae Road Corridor, Island of Hawaii: An Interdisciplinary Study of an Environmental Transect.* Department of Anthropology Report no. 83-1. Honolulu: Bernice P. Bishop Museum.

Clastres, Pierre
1977   *Society Against the State.* New York: Urizen Books.

Clay, Marie
1976   Early Childhood and Cultural Diversity in New Zealand. *The Reading Teacher* (January): 333–342.

Cleave, Peter
1981   *Sounds, Parts of Speech and Phrases.* Working Paper: Department of Sociology, University of Waikato.

Clement, Dorothy
1982   Samoan Folk Knowledge of Mental Disorders. In *Cultural Conceptions of Mental Health and Therapy,* edited by A. Marsella and G. White, pp. 193–213. Boston: Reidel Publishing Company.

Clunie, Fergus
1977   *Fijian Weapons and Warfare.* Bulletin of the Fiji Museum, no. 2. Suva.
1986   *Yalo i Viti: Shades of Viti: A Fiji Museum Catalogue.* Suva: Fiji Museum.

Clunie, Fergus, and Walesi Ligairi
1983   Traditional Fijian Spirit Masks and Spirit Masquers. *Domodomo, Fiji Museum Quarterly* 1:46–71.

Cobbe, Hugh
1979   *Cook's Voyages and the Peoples of the Pacific.* London: British Museum.

Codrington, R. H.
1891   *The Melanesians: Studies in Their Anthropology and Their Folklore.* Oxford: The Clarendon Press.

Cole, Michael, and Sylvia Scribner
1974   *Culture and Thought.* New York: Wiley.

Colson, Elizabeth
1985   Defining American Ethnology. In *Social Contexts of American Ethnology, 1840–1984: 1984 Proceedings of the American Ethnological Society,* edited by June Helm, pp. 177–184. Washington, D.C.: American Anthropological Association.

Conner, Jane B.
1983   Polynesian Basketry. Master's thesis, University of Auckland.

Consortium for Longitudinal Studies
1983   *As the Twig Is Bent.* Hillsdale, N.J.: Erlbaum.

Cook, Thomas D.
1983   Research, Program Development, and the Education of Native Hawaiians. *American Psychologist* 38:1015–1021.

Cordy, R.
  1974a Complex Rank Cultural Systems in the Hawaiian Islands: Suggested Explanations for Their Origin. *Archaeology and Physical Anthropology in Oceania* 9:89–109.
  1974b Cultural Adaptation and Evolution in Hawaii: A Suggested New Sequence. *Journal of the Polynesian Society* 83:180–191.
  1981 *A Study of Prehistoric Social Change: The Development of Complex Societies in the Hawaiian Islands.* New York: Academic Press.

Corney, Bolton Glanvill, trans. and comp.
  1913 *The Quest and Occupation of Tahiti by Emissaries of Spain During the Years 1772–1776,* vol. 1. London: Cambridge University Press (for the Hakluyt Society).
  1915 *The Quest and Occupation of Tahiti by Emissaries of Spain During the Years 1772–1776,* vol. 2. London: Cambridge University Press (for the Hakluyt Society).
  1919 *The Quest and Occupation of Tahiti by Emissaries of Spain During the Years 1772–1776,* vol. 3. London: Cambridge University Press (for the Hakluyt Society).

Couper, Alastair Dougal
  1967 The Island Trade: An Analysis of the Environment and Operation of Seaborne Trade among Three Island Groups in the Pacific. Department of Geography, Australian National University. Manuscript.

Cox, J. Halley, with William H. Davenport
  1974 *Hawaiian Sculpture.* Honolulu: University of Hawaii Press.

Cox, J. Halley, with Edward Stasack
  1970 *Hawaiian Petroglyphs.* Honolulu: Bernice P. Bishop Museum.

Cristino, C., and P. Vargas
  1980 Prospeccion Arqueologica de Isla de Pascua. In *Estudios Sobre la Isla de Pascua,* edited by C. Cristino, pp. 193–225. Santiago: Universidad de Chile.

Cristino, C., P. Vargas, and R. Izaurieta
  1981 *Atlas Arqueologico de Isla de Pascua.* Santiago: Universidad de Chile.

Crocombe, Ron G.
  1964 *Land Tenure in the Cook Islands.* New York: Oxford University Press.
  1967 From Ascendancy to Dependency: The Politics of Atiu. *The Journal of Pacific History* 2:97–111.
  1976 Historical Ethnography of Tahiti. *Reviews of Anthropology* (May/June): 309–316.

Crocombe, Ron, ed.
  1971 *Land Tenure in the South Pacific.* New York: Oxford University Press.

Cummins, H. G.
  1977 Holy War: Peter Dillon and the 1837 Massacres in Tonga. *The Journal of Pacific History* 12:25–39.

Curtin, Philip
    1984   *Cross-Cultural Trade in World History.* New York: Cambridge University Press.

Dalton, George, and Jasper Kocke
    1983   The Work of the Polanyi Group: Past, Present, and Future. In *Economic Anthropology: Topics and Theories,* edited by Sutti Ortiz, pp. 21–50. Lanham, Md.: University Press of America.

D'Amato, John
    1987   "We Cool, Tha's Why": A Study of Personhood and Place in a Class of Hawaiian Second Graders. Ph.D. diss., University of Hawaii.

D'Andrade, Roy
    1974   Memory and the Assessment of Behavior. In *Measurement in the Social Sciences,* edited by H. Blalock, pp. 159–186. Chicago: Aldine.

Davenport, William
    1959   Nonunilinear Descent and Descent Groups. *American Anthropologist* 61:557–572.
    1969   The Hawaiian "Cultural Revolution": Some Economic and Political Considerations. *American Anthropologist* 71:1–20.
    1981   The National Gallery Presents Ethnographic Art from Oceania. *Studies in Visual Communication* 7:74–81.

Davidson, James W.
    1942   European Penetration of the South Pacific 1779–1842. Ph.D. diss., St. John's College, University of Cambridge.
    1966   Problems of Pacific History. *The Journal of Pacific History* 1:5–21.
    1970   Lauaki Namulau'ulu Mamoe: A Traditionalist in Samoan Politics. In *Pacific Island Portraits,* edited by James W. Davidson and Deryck Scarr, pp. 267–299. Canberra: Australian National University Press.
    1975   *Peter Dillon of Vanikoro: Chevalier of the South Seas,* edited by O. H. K. Spate. New York: Oxford University Press.

Davidson, James W., and Deryck Scarr, eds.
    1970   *Pacific Island Portraits.* Canberra: Australian National University Press.

Davidson, Janet
    1968   Nukuoro: Archaeology on a Polynesian Outlier in Micronesia. In *Prehistoric Culture in Oceania,* edited by I. Yawata and Y. H. Sinoto, pp. 51–66. Honolulu: Bernice P. Bishop Museum.
    1971   *Archaeology on Nukuoro Atoll: A Polynesian Outlier in the Eastern Caroline Islands.* Auckland Institute and Museum Bulletin no. 9.
    1984   *The Prehistory of New Zealand.* Auckland: Longman Paul.

Daws, Gavan
    1967   Honolulu in the 19th Century: Notes on the Emergence of Urban Society in Hawaii. *The Journal of Pacific History* 2:77–96.
    1968a   Kealakekua Bay Revisited: A Note on the Death of Captain Cook. *The Journal of Pacific History* 3:21–23.
    1968b   *Shoal of Time: A History of the Hawaiian Islands.* Honolulu: University of Hawaii Press.

1969　Review of *The Works of Ta'unga: Records of a Polynesian Traveller in the South Seas, 1833–1896,* by Ron G. Crocombe and Marjorie Crocombe. *The Journal of Pacific History* 4:227–228.

1978　"All the Horrors of the Half Known Life": Some Notes on the Writing of Biography in the Pacific. In *The Changing Pacific: Essays in Honour of H. E. Maude,* edited by Niel Gunson, pp. 297–307. New York: Oxford University Press.

1979　On Being a Historian of the Pacific. In *Historical Disciplines and Culture in Australasia,* edited by John Moses, pp. 119–132. St. Lucia: University of Queensland Press.

1980　*A Dream of Islands; Voyages of Self-Discovery in the South Seas.* New York: W. W. Norton and Company.

Dening, Greg
1966　Ethnohistory in Polynesia: The Value of Ethnohistorical Evidence. *The Journal of Pacific History* 1:23–42.

1971　Tapu and Haka'iki in the Marquesas, 1774–1813. Ph.D. diss., Harvard University.

1978　Institutions of Violence in the Marquesas. In *The Changing Pacific: Essays in Honour of H. E. Maude,* edited by Niel Gunson, pp. 134–141. New York: Oxford University Press.

1980　*Islands and Beaches: Discourse on a Silent Land Marquesas 1774–1880.* Honolulu: University of Hawaii Press.

1982　Sharks That Walk on the Land: The Death of Captain Cook. *Meanjin* 41:427–437.

1985a　Review of *The Art of Captain Cook's Voyages,* by Rudiger Jappien and Bernard Smith. *New York Times Book Review* (11 August): 1, 18–19.

1985b　Review of *Two Tahitian Villages,* by Douglas Oliver. *Pacific Studies* 8:101–103.

1986　Possessing Tahiti. *Archaeology in Oceania* 21 (1): 103–118.

n.d.　A Poetic for History: Transformations That Present the Past. Unpublished manuscript.

Dening, Greg, ed.
1974　*The Marquesan Journal of Edward Robarts 1794–1824.* Honolulu: University of Hawaii Press.

Dibble, Sheldon
1843　*History of the Sandwich Islands.* Lahainaluna, Hawaii: Press of the Mission Seminary.

Dixon, George
1789　*A Voyage Round the World; But Most Particularly to the North-West Coast of America.* . . . London: Goulding. Reprint. Bibliotheca Australiana no. 37. New York: Da Capo Press, 1968.

Dobyns, Susan
1988　Thieves, Captains, and Kings: Perceptions of Cultures in Contact. Paper presented at the 87th Annual Meeting of the American Anthropological Association.

Dodge, Ernest
    1965   *New England and the South Seas.* Cambridge: Harvard University Press.
    1976   *Islands and Empires: Western Impact on the Pacific and East Asia.* Minneapolis: University of Minnesota Press.

Dorton, Lilikala
    1986   Land and the Promise of Capitalism: A Dilemma for the Hawaiian Chiefs of the 1848 Mahele. Ph.D. diss., University of Hawaii.

Douglas, Bronwen
    1979   Rank, Power, Authority: A Reassessment of Traditional Leadership in South Pacific Societies. *The Journal of Pacific History* 14:2–27.

Driessen, H. A. H.
    1982   Outriggerless Canoes and Glorious Beings: Pre-Contact Prophecies in the Society Islands. *The Journal of Pacific History* 17:3–26.

Duff, R.
    1956   *The Moa Hunter Period of Maori Culture.* 2nd ed. Wellington: Government Printer.

Duff, Roger H.
    1969   *No Sort of Iron: Culture of Cook's Polynesians.* Christchurch: Art Galleries and Museums' Association of New Zealand.

Dumont, Louis
    1970   *Homo Hierarchicus.* Chicago: University of Chicago Press.

Duranti, Alessandro
    1981a   *The Samoan Fono: A Sociolinguistic Study.* Pacific Linguistics, Series B, no. 80. Canberra: Research School of Pacific Studies, The Australian National University.
    1981b   Speech Making and the Organization of Discourse in a Samoan *Fono.* *Journal of the Polynesian Society* 90 (3): 357–400.

Duranti, Alessandro, and Eleanor Ochs
    1986   Literacy Instruction in a Samoan Village. In *The Acquisition of Literacy: Ethnographic Perspectives,* edited by B. Schieffelin and P. Gilmore, pp. 213–232. Norwood, N.J.: Ablex.

Durkheim, Emile
    1947   *Elementary Forms of the Religious Life.* Glencoe, Ill.: Free Press.

Earle, T. K.
    1977   A Reappraisal of Redistribution: Complex Hawaiian Chiefdoms. In *Exchange Systems in Prehistory,* edited by T. K. Earle, pp. 213–229. New York: Academic Press.
    1978   *Economic and Social Organization of a Complex Chiefdom: The Halele'a District, Kaua'i, Hawaii.* University of Michigan Museum of Anthropology Anthropological Papers no. 63. Ann Arbor.
    1980   Prehistoric Irrigation in the Hawaiian Islands: An Evaluation of Evolutionary Significance. *Archaeology and Physical Anthropology in Oceania* 15:1–28.

Edwards, Edward, and George Hamilton
1915   *Voyage of the H.M.S. 'Pandora',* edited by Basil Thomson. London: Francis Edwards.

Elley, W. B., and F. Mangubhai
1981a   *The Impact of a Book Flood in Fiji Primary Schools.* Wellington: New Zealand Council for Educational Research, and Suva: Institute of Education, University of the South Pacific.
1981b   The Long-Term Effects of a Book Flood on Children's Language Growth. *Directions* 7:15–24.

Ellis, William
1782   *An Authentic Narrative of a Voyage Performed by Captain Cook and Captain Clerke in his Majesty's Ships Resolution and Discovery During the Years 1776 to 1780.* . . . 2 vols. Reprint. Bibliotheca Australiana no. 55. New York: Da Capo Press, 1969.

Ellis, William (Rev.)
1829   *Polynesian Researches.* 2 vols. London: Fisher, Son and Jackson.

Emerson, Nathaniel B.
1909   *Unwritten Literature of Hawaii: The Sacred Songs of the Hula.* Bureau of American Ethnology Bulletin no. 38. Washington, D.C.

Emory, Kenneth P.
1928   *Archaeology of Nihoa and Necker Islands.* Bernice P. Bishop Museum Bulletin no. 53. Honolulu: The Museum.
1946   *Hawaiian Tattooing.* Occasional Papers of the Bernice Pauahi Bishop Museum 18 (17): 235–270. Honolulu: The Museum.
1959   Origin of the Hawaiians. *Journal of the Polynesian Society* 68:29–35.
1975   *Material Culture of the Tuamotu Archipelago.* Pacific Anthropological Records no. 22. Honolulu: Department of Anthropology, Bernice P. Bishop Museum.

Emory, Kenneth P., W. J. Bonk, and Y. H. Sinoto
1959   *Hawaiian Archaeology: Fishhooks.* Bernice P. Bishop Museum Special Publication no. 47. Honolulu: The Museum.

Emory, Kenneth P., and Y. H. Sinoto
1965   Preliminary Report on the Archaeological Investigations in Polynesia. Mimeographed report submitted to the National Science Foundation. Honolulu: Bernice P. Bishop Museum.

Erikson, Erik H.
1959   *Ego Identity and the Life Cycle.* New York: International Universities Press.

Errington, Shelly
1975   *A Study of Genre: Meaning and Form in the Malay Hikayat Hung Tuah.* Ph.D. diss., Cornell University.
n.d.   *Meaning and Power in a Southeast Asian Realm.* Princeton: Princeton University Press. In press.

Erskine, John Elphinstone
    1853   *Journal of A Cruise Among the Islands of the Western Pacific. . . .* Reprint.
           London: Dawsons of Pall Mall, 1967.

Evans-Pritchard, E. E.
    1940   *The Nuer, A Description of the Modes of Livelihood and Political Institutions of
           a Nilotic People.* Oxford: Clarendon Press.

Ewins, Rod
    1982a *Fijian Artifacts. The Tasmanian Museum and Art Gallery Collection.*
           Hobart: Tasmanian Museum and Art Gallery.
    1982b *Mat-weaving in Gau, Fiji.* Suva: Fiji Museum.

Fabian, Johannes
    1983   *Time and the Other: How Anthropology Makes Its Object.* New York:
           Columbia University Press.

Fairchild, Hoxie Neale
    1961   *The Noble Savage: A Study in Romantic Naturalism.* New York: Russel
           and Russel.

Feinberg, Richard
    1978   Anutan Ethnoepistemology: The Roots of Knowledge on a Polyne-
           sian Outlier. Unpublished manuscript.
    1981   What is Polynesian Kinship All About? *Ethnology* 20:115–131.
    1988   Socio-Spatial Symbolism and the Logic of Rank in Two Polynesian
           Outliers. *Ethnology* 27:291–310.

Feldman, Jerome
    1986   Art Styles and Prehistory of Hawaiian Sculpture. Unpublished man-
           uscript.
    1989   The Art Styles of Hawaiian Sculpture. Unpublished manuscript.

Ferdon, Edwin N., Jr.
    1961   A Summary of the Excavated Record of Easter Island Prehistory. In
           Archaeology of Easter Island, edited by T. Heyerdahl and E. N. Ferdon,
           Jr., pp. 527–536. Monographs of the School of American Research,
           no. 24 (1). Santa Fe.

Fergusson, David M., Joan Fleming, and David P. O'Neill
    1972   *Child Abuse in New Zealand.* Wellington: Department of Social Wel-
           fare.

Finney, Ben
    1966   Resource Distribution and Social Structure in Tahiti. *Ethnology* 5:80–
           86.

Finney, Ben, Ruby Johnson, Malcolm Chun, and Edith McKinzie
    1978   Hawaiian Historians and the First Pacific Seminar. In *The Changing
           Pacific: Essays in Honour of H. E. Maude,* edited by Niel Gunson, pp.
           208–316. New York: Oxford University Press.

Firth, Raymond
    1936a Tattooing in Tikopia. *Man* 36:236.
    1936b *We, the Tikopia.* 2nd ed., 1957. London: George Allen and Unwin.

1940   The Analysis of Mana: An Empirical Approach. *Journal of the Polynesian Society* 49:483–510. Reprint. In *Tikopia Ritual and Belief,* by Raymond Firth, pp. 174–194. Boston: Beacon Press, 1967.

1947   Bark-Cloth in Tikopia, Solomon Islands. *Man* 47:69–72.

1957   A Note on Descent Groups in Polynesia. *Man* 57:4–8.

1959a   Ritual Adzes in Tikopia. In *Anthropology in the South Seas: Essays presented to H. D. Skinner,* edited by J. D. Freeman and W. R. Geddes, pp. 149–159. New Plymouth, New Zealand: Thomas Avery and Sons.

1959b   *Social Change in Tikopia: Restudy of a Polynesian Community After a Generation.* London: George Allen and Unwin.

1960   A Polynesian Aristocrat. In *In the Company of Man,* edited by Joseph B. Casegrande, pp. 1–40. New York: Harper and Row.

1961a   *Elements of Social Organization.* London: C. A. Watts.

1961b   *History and Traditions of Tikopia.* Wellington: The Polynesian Society.

1963   Bilateral Descent Groups: An Operational Viewpoint. In *Studies in Kinship and Marriage,* edited by I. Schapera, pp. 22–37. Royal Anthropological Institute of Great Britain and Ireland, Occasional Paper no. 16. London.

1964   *Essays on Social Organization and Values.* London School of Enonomics Monographs in Social Anthropology no. 28. London: Athlone.

1967   *Tikopia Ritual and Belief.* Boston: Beacon Press.

1970a   Postures and Gestures of Respect. In *Échanges et Communications: Mélanges Offerts à Claude Lévi-Strauss à l'Occasion de son 60ème anniversaire,* edited by Jean Pouillon and Pierre Maranda, pp. 188–209. The Hague: Mouton.

1970b   *Rank and Religion: A Study of Polynesian Paganism and Conversion to Christianity.* Boston: Beacon Press.

1970c   Sibling Terms in Polynesia. *Journal of the Polynesian Society* 79:272–287.

1973   Tikopia Art and Society. In *Primitive Art and Society,* edited by Anthony Forge, pp. 25–48. New York: Oxford University Press.

1976   Review of *Ancient Tahitian Society,* by Douglas Oliver. *Journal of the Polynesian Society* 85:553–565.

1979   The Sacredness of Tikopia Chiefs. In *Politics in Leadership: A Comparative Perspective,* edited by William A. Shack and Percy S. Cohen, pp. 139–168. Oxford: Clarendon Press.

Fischer, Hans

1958   *Schallgerate in Ozeanien; Bau und Spieltechnik: Verbreitung und Funktion.* Strasbourg: P. H. Heitz. Translated as *Sound-Producing Instruments in Oceania.* Boroko: Institute of Papua New Guinea Studies. 1983.

Fischer, J. L.

1970   Political Factors in the Overthrow of the Hawaiian Taboo System. *Acta Ethnographica Academiae Scientiarum Hungaricae* 19:161–167.

Fisher, Robin

1979   Cook and the Nootka. In *Captain James Cook and His Times,* edited by Robin Fisher and Hugh Johnston, pp. 81–98. Seattle: University of Washington Press.

Fisher, Robin, and Hugh Johnston, eds.
  1979   *Captain James Cook and His Times.* Seattle: University of Washington
         Press.

Flannery, K. V.
  1983   Archaeology and Ethnology in the Context of Divergent Evolution.
         In *The Cloud People: Divergent Evolution of the Zapotec and Mixtec Civiliza-
         tions,* edited by K. V. Flannery and J. Marcus, pp. 361–362. New
         York: Academic Press.

Flenley, J. P., and S. M. King
  1984   Late Quaternary Pollen Records from Easter Island. *Nature* 307:47–
         50.

Fleurieu, Charles
  1801   *A Voyage Round the World 1790–1792 Performed by Etienne Marchand,* vol.
         1. London: Longman and Rees. Reprint. Bibliotheca Australiana
         no. 23. New York: Da Capo Press, 1969.

Fogelson, Raymond D.
  n.d.   Person, Self, and Identity: Some Anthropological Retrospects, Cir-
         cumspects and Prospects. Unpublished manuscript.

Fornander, Abraham
  1918– *Hawaiian Antiquities and Folk-lore.* Memoirs of the Bernice P. Bishop
  1919   Museum, vol. 5. Honolulu: The Museum.

Forster, Georg
  1777   *A Voyage Round the World in His Brittanic Majesty's Sloop, Resolution, Com-
         manded by Captain James Cook, during the Years 1772, 3, 4, and 5,* vol. 2.
         London: B. White, J. Robson, P. Elmsley, and G. Robinson.

Fortes, M.
  1953   The Structure of Unilineal Descent Groups. *American Anthropologist*
         55:17–51.
  1959   Descent, Affiliation and Affinity. *Man* 59:193–197, 206–212.

Fosberg, F. R.
  1963a Disturbance in Island Ecosystems. In *Pacific Basin Biogeography,* edited
         by J. L. Gressitt, pp. 557–561. Honolulu: Bernice P. Bishop Mu-
         seum.
  1963b The Island Ecosystem. In *Man's Place in the Island Ecosystem,* edited by
         F. R. Fosberg, pp. 1–6. Honolulu: Bernice P. Bishop Museum.

Fox, A.
  1976   *Prehistoric Maori Fortifications.* Auckland: Longman Paul.

France, Peter
  1969   *The Charter of the Land: Custom and Colonization in Fiji.* New York:
         Oxford University Press.

Franco, R.
  1985   Samoan Perceptions of Work: Moving Up and Moving Around.
         Ph.D. diss., University of Hawaii.

Frank, A. G.
  1979 *Dependent Accumulation and Underdevelopment.* New York: Monthly
        Review Press.

Fraser, Douglas
  1962 *Primitive Art.* Garden City, New York: Doubleday.

Frazer, Sir James
  1922 *The Golden Bough.* Abridged. London: Macmillan.

Freeman, Derek
  1961 Review of *Social Stratification in Polynesia,* by M. Sahlins. *Man* 61:146–
        148.
  1964 Some Observations on Kinship and Political Authority in Samoa.
        American Anthropologist 66:553–568.
  1983 *Margaret Mead and Samoa: The Making and Unmaking of an Anthropological
        Myth.* Cambridge: Harvard University Press.
  1984 The Burthen of a Mystery. *Oceania* 54 (3): 247–254.
  1985 Reply to Shore. *Oceania* 55 (3): 214–218.

Friedman, Jonathan
  1981 Notes on Structure and History in Oceania. *Folk* 23:275–295.
  1985 Captain Cook, Culture and the World System. *The Journal of Pacific
        History* 20:191–201.

The Friend
  1854 Untitled Article. 3 (3): 17–18.

Frost, Alan
  1979 New Geographical Perspectives and the Emergence of the Romantic
        Imagination. In *Captain James Cook and His Times,* edited by Robin
        Fisher and Hugh Johnston, pp. 5–19. Seattle: University of Washing-
        ton Press.

Furet, François, and Jacques Ozouf
  1982 *Reading and Writing: Literacy in France from Calvin to Jules Ferry.* New
        York: Cambridge University Press.

Gailey, Christine Ward
  1983 Categories Without Culture: Structuralism, Ethnohistory and Ethno-
        cide. *Dialectical Anthropology* 8:241–250.
  1987 *Kinship to Kingship: Gender Hierarchy and State Formation in the Tongan
        Islands.* Austin: University of Texas Press.

Gallimore, Ronald, Joan W. Boggs, and Cathie Jordan
  1974 *Culture, Behavior and Education: A Study of Hawaiian Americans.* Beverly
        Hills, Calif.: Sage.

Gathercole, Peter
  1976 On a Maori Shell Trumpet at Cambridge University. In *Problems in
        Economic and Social Archaeology,* edited by G. de G. Sieveking, I. H.
        Longworth, and K. E. Wilson, pp. 187–199. London: Duckworth.

1979a   Changing Attitudes to the Study of Maori Carving. In *Exploring the Visual Art of Oceania,* edited by Sidney M. Mead, pp. 214–226. Honolulu: University of Hawaii Press.

1979b   Maori Godsticks and Their Stylistic Affinities. In *Birds of A Feather: Osteological and Archaeological Papers from the South Pacific in Honour of R. J. Scarlet,* edited by Atholl Anderson, pp. 285–295. BAR International Series no. 62. Oxford.

1986   Review of *Islands of History,* by Marshall Sahlins. *The Times Literary Supplement* (28 February): 224.

1988   The Contexts of Maori Moko. In *Marks of Civilization,* edited by Arnold Rubin, pp. 171–177. Los Angeles: Museum of Cultural History.

Gathercole, Peter, Adrienne L. Kaeppler, and Douglas Newton
1979   *The Art of the Pacific Islands.* Washington, D.C.: National Gallery of Art.

Geertz, Clifford
1980   *Negara: The Theater State in Nineteenth-Century Bali.* Princeton: Princeton University Press.

Geraghty, P.
1983   *The History of the Fijian Languages.* Oceanic Linguistics Special Publication no. 19. Honolulu: University of Hawaii Press.

Gerber, Eleanor Ruth
1975   Cultural Patterning of Emotions in Samoa. Ph.D. diss., University of California at San Diego.

1985   Rage and Obligation: Samoan Emotion in Conflict. In *Person, Self and Experience: Exploring Pacific Ethnopsychologies,* edited by G. M. White and J. Kirkpatrick, pp. 121–167. Berkeley: University of California Press.

Gifford, Edward W.
1929   *Tongan Society.* Bernice P. Bishop Museum Bulletin no. 61. Honolulu: The Museum.

1951   Archaeological Excavations in Fiji. *University of California Anthropological Records* 13:189–288.

Gilson, R. P.
1970   *Samoa 1830 to 1900: The Politics of a Multi-Cultural Community.* New York: Oxford University Press.

1980   *The Cook Islands 1820–1950,* edited by Ron Crocombe. Wellington: Victoria University.

Gladwin, Thomas
1972   Oceania. In *Psychological Anthropology,* edited by F. Hsu, pp. 135–171. Cambridge, Mass.: Schenkman.

Glasse, R.
1968   *Huli of Papua.* Paris: Mouton.

Gluckman, Max
1956   *Custom and Conflict in Africa.* Oxford: Blackwell.

Godelier, Maurice
1978   Infrastructures, Societies, and History (with CA Comment). *Current Anthropology* 19 (4): 763–771.

Goldman, Irving
1955   Status Rivalry and Cultural Evolution in Polynesia. *American Anthropologist* 57:680–697.
1957   Cultural Evolution in Polynesia, A Reply to Criticism. *Journal of the Polynesian Society* 66:156–164.
1958   Variations in Polynesian Social Organization. *Journal of the Polynesian Society* 66:374–390.
1960a The Evolution of Status Systems in Polynesia. In *Selected Papers of the Fifth International Congress of Anthropological and Ethnological Sciences,* edited by Anthony Wallace, pp. 255–260. Philadelphia: The University of Pennsylvania Press.
1960b The Evolution of Polynesian Societies. In *Culture and History,* edited by Stanley Diamond, pp. 687–712. New York: Columbia University Press.
1970   *Ancient Polynesian Society.* Chicago: University of Chicago Press.

Golson, J.
1959   Culture Change in Prehistoric New Zealand. In *Anthropology in the South Seas,* edited by J. D. Freeman and W. R. Geddes, pp. 29–74. New Plymouth, New Zealand: Thomas Avery and Sons.
1965   Some Considerations of the Role of Theory in New Zealand Archaeology. *New Zealand Archaeological Association Newsletter* 8:79–92.

Good, Carolyn G.
1980   The Rat Brothers: A Study of the Brother-Sister Relationship in Samoa. Master's thesis, University of California at Berkeley.

Goodenough, Ward
1955   A Problem in Malayo-Polynesian Social Organization. *American Anthropologist* 57:71–83.
1984   Margaret Mead and Cultural Anthropology. *Science* 220:906–908.

Goto, A.
1984   Marine Exploitation at South Point, Hawaii Island: An Aspect of Adaptive Diversity in Hawaiian Prehistory. *Hawaiian Archaeology* 1:44–63.

Graves, Nancy B., and Theodore D. Graves
1973   *Inclusive Versus Exclusive Behaviour in New Zealand School Settings.* Auckland: South Pacific Research Institute.

Graves, Theodore D., and Nancy B. Graves
1978a The Impact of Modernization on the Personality of a Polynesian People. *Human Organization* 37 (2): 115–135.
1978b *The Stress of Modernization in a Traditional Polynesian Society.* South Pacific Research Institute Research Report no. 18. Auckland.

1981   The Social Context of Drinking and Violence in New Zealand's Pub Settings. In *Social Drinking Contexts,* edited by T. Harford and L. Gaines, pp. 103–120. National Institute on Alcohol Abuse and Alcoholism Research Monograph no. 7.

1982   Patterns of Public Drinking in a Multiethnic Society. *Journal of Studies on Alcohol* 43 (9): 990–1009.

1983   The Cultural Context of Prosocial Development: An Ecological Model. In *The Nature of Pro-Social Development,* edited by Diane L. Bridgeman, pp. 243–264. London: Academic Press.

Green, Roger C.

1961   Moorean Archaeology. *Man* 61:169–173.

1963   *A Review of the Prehistoric Sequence of the Auckland Province.* New Zealand Archaeological Association Monograph no. 2.

1966   Linguistic Subgrouping Within Polynesia: The Implications for Prehistoric Settlement. *Journal of the Polynesian Society* 75:6–38.

1973   Tonga's Prehistoric Population. *Pacific Viewpoint* 14:61–74.

1974   Adaptation and Change in Maori Culture. In *Ecology and Biogeography in New Zealand,* edited by G. Kuschel, pp. 1–44. The Hague: W. Junk.

1979a   Early Lapita Art from Polynesia and Island Melanesia: Continuities in Ceramic, Barkcloth, and Tattoo Decorations. In *Exploring the Visual Art of Oceania,* edited by S. Mead, pp. 13–31. Honolulu: University of Hawaii Press.

1979b   Lapita. In *The Prehistory of Polynesia,* edited by J. Jennings, pp. 27–60. Cambridge: Harvard University Press.

1980   *Makaha Before 1880* A.D. Pacific Anthropological Records no. 31. Honolulu: Department of Anthropology, Bernice P. Bishop Museum.

1981   Location of the Polynesian Homeland: A Continuing Problem. In *Studies in Pacific Languages and Cultures in Honor of Bruce Biggs,* edited by J. Hollyman and A. Pawley, pp. 133–158. Auckland: Linguistic Society of New Zealand.

1982   Models for the Lapita Cultural Complex: An Evaluation of Some Current Proposals. *New Zealand Journal of Archaeology* 4:7–20.

1986   Some Basic Components of the Ancestral Polynesian Settlement System: Building Blocks for More Complex Polynesian Societies. In *Island Societies: Archaeological Approaches to Evolution and Transformation,* edited by P. V. Kirch, pp. 50–54. Cambridge: Cambridge University Press.

Green, Roger C., and J. Davidson, eds.

1969   *Archaeology in Western Samoa,* vol. 1. Auckland Institute and Museum Bulletin no. 6.

1974   *Archaeology in Western Samoa,* vol. 2. Auckland Institute and Museum Bulletin no. 7.

Green, Roger C., and M. Kelly, eds.

1970   *Studies in Oceanic Culture History,* vol. 1. Pacific Anthropological Records no. 11. Honolulu: Department of Anthropology, Bernice P. Bishop Museum.

1971   *Studies in Oceanic Culture History,* vol. 2. Pacific Anthropological Records no. 12. Honolulu: Department of Anthropology, Bernice P. Bishop Museum.

Green, Roger C., K. Green, R. Rappaport, A. Rappaport, and J. Davidson
1967   *Archaeology on the Island of Mo'orea, French Polynesia.* Anthropological Papers of the American Museum of Natural History 51 (2). New York.

Greiner, Ruth
1923   *Polynesian Decorative Designs.* Bernice P. Bishop Museum Bulletin no. 7. Honolulu: The Museum.

Grey, Sir George
1855   *Polynesian Mythology.* London: Murray.

Groube, L.
1967   Models in Prehistory: A Consideration of the New Zealand Evidence. *Archaeology and Physical Anthropology in Oceania* 2:1–27.
1971   Tonga, Lapita Pottery, and Polynesian Origins. *Journal of the Polynesian Society* 80:278–316.

Gruber, Jacob
1970   Ethnographic Salvage and the Shaping of Anthropology. *American Anthropologist* 72:1289–1299.

Gunson, Niel
1963   A Note on the Difficulties of Ethnohistorical Writing, with Special Reference to Tahiti. *Journal of the Polynesian Society* 71:415–419.
1965   Missionary Interest in British Expansion in the South Pacific in the Nineteenth Century. *The Journal of Religious History* 3:296–313.
1969   Pomare II of Tahiti and Polynesian Imperialism. *The Journal of Pacific History* 4:65–82.
1973   Visionary Experience and Social Protest in Polynesia: A Note on 'Ofa Mele Longosai. *The Journal of Pacific History* 8:125–132.
1975   Tahiti's Traditional History: Without Adams? *The Journal of Pacific History* 10:112–117.
1978   *Messengers of Grace: Evangelical Missionaries in the South Seas, 1797–1860.* New York: Oxford University Press.
1979   The Hau Concept of Leadership in Western Polynesia. *The Journal of Pacific History* 14:28–49.

Gunson, Niel, ed.
1978   *The Changing Pacific: Essays in Honour of H. E. Maude.* New York: Oxford University Press.

Haddon, A. C.
1901   On the Origin of the Maori Scroll Design. *Man* 31:68.

Hallowell, A. Irving
1955   *Culture and Experience.* Philadelphia: University of Pennsylvania Press.
1957   The Backwash of the Frontier: The Impact of the Indian on Ameri-

can Culture. In *The Frontier in Perspective,* edited by Walker Wyman and Clifton Kroeber, pp. 229–258. Madison: University of Wisconsin Press. Reprint. In *Beyond the Frontier: Social Process and Cultural Change,* edited by Paul Bohannan and Fred Plog, pp. 319–345. Garden City, N.Y.: Natural History Press, 1967.

1963   American Indians, White and Black: The Phenomenon of Transculturalization. *Current Anthropology* 4:519–531.

Hamel, J.
1982   South Otago. In *The First Thousand Years: Regional Perspectives in New Zealand Archaeology,* edited by N. Prickett, pp. 129–140. Palmerston North: New Zealand Archaeological Association.

Hamilton, Augustus
1901   *Maori Art.* Dunedin: Fergusson and Mitchell.

Handy, E. S. C.
1923   *The Native Culture in the Marquesas.* Bernice P. Bishop Museum Bulletin no. 9. Honolulu: The Museum.
1927   *Polynesian Religion.* Bernice P. Bishop Museum Bulletin no. 34. Honolulu: The Museum.
1930   *Marquesan Legends.* Honolulu: Bernice P. Bishop Museum.

Handy, E. S. C., and E. G. Handy
1972   *Native Planters in Old Hawaii: Their Life, Lore, and Environment.* Bernice P. Bishop Museum Bulletin no. 233. Honolulu: The Museum.

Handy, E. S. C., and M. K. Pukui
1972   *The Polynesian Family System in Ka'u, Hawaii.* Wellington: The Polynesian Society (first edition 1958).

Handy, E. S. C., and Jane L. Winne
1925   *Music in the Marquesas Islands.* Bernice P. Bishop Museum Bulletin no. 17. Honolulu: The Museum.

Handy, Willowdean
1922   *Tattooing in the Marquesas.* Bernice P. Bishop Museum Bulletin no. 1. Honolulu: The Museum.

Hanlon, David
1984   Review of *The First Taint of Civilization,* by Francis Hezel. *Pacific Studies* 8:142–145

Hanson, F. Allan
1970   *Rapan Lifeways: Society and History on a Polynesian Island.* Boston: Little, Brown.
1971   Nonexclusive Cognatic Descent Systems: A Polynesian Example. In *Polynesia: Readings on a Culture Area,* edited by Alan Howard, pp. 109–132. Scranton, Pa.: Chandler.
1973   Political Change in Tahiti and Samoa: An Exercise in Experimental Anthropology. *Ethnology* 12:1–13.
1982a   Book Review of *Historical Metaphors and Mythical Realities,* by Marshall Sahlins. *Journal of the Polynesian Society* 91:595–596.

1982b Female Pollution in Polynesia. *Journal of the Polynesian Society* 91:335–381.

1982c Method in Semiotic Anthropology or How the Maori Latrine Means. In *Studies in Symbolism and Cultural Communication,* edited by F. A. Hanson, pp. 74–89. University of Kansas Publications in Anthropology no. 14. Lawrence: University of Kansas.

1983 Art and the Maori Construction of Reality. In *Art and Artists in Oceania,* edited by Sidney M. Mead and Bernie Kernot, pp. 210–225. Palmerston North: Dunmore Press.

1987 Polynesian Religions: An Overview. In *Encyclopedia of Religion,* edited by M. Eliade, pp. 423–432. New York: Macmillan.

1989 The Making of the Maori: Culture Invention and Its Logic. *American Anthropologist.* In press.

Hanson, F. Allan, and L. Hanson
1983 *Counterpoint in Maori Culture.* London: Routledge and Kegan Paul.

Hanson, Louise, and F. Allan Hanson
1984 *The Art of Oceania: A Bibliography,* Boston: G. K. Hall.

Harfst, Richard
1972 Cause or Condition: Explanations of the Hawaiian Cultural Revolution. *Journal of the Polynesian Society* 81:437–471.

Harris, Marvin
1979 *Cultural Materialism: The Struggle for a Science of Culture.* New York: Random House.

Hawkesworth, John
1775 *Voyages to the Southern Hemisphere . . . Containing the Various Important Discoveries that were Made by the Hon. Commodore Bryon, Dr. Solander, Mr. Banks, and by the Captains Wallis, Carteret, and Cook.* London: R. Snagg.

Hawthorne, H. B., and C. S. Belshaw
1957 Cultural Evolution or Culture Change: The Case for Polynesia. *Journal of the Polynesian Society* 66:18–35.

Headrick, Daniel
1981 *The Tools of Empire: Technology and European Imperialism in the Nineteenth Century.* New York: Oxford University Press.

Healy, A. M.
1977 Review of *Ancient Tahitian Society,* by Douglas Oliver. *Oceania* 47:251–252.

Hecht, Julia
1976 *Double Descent and Cultural Symbolism in Pukapuka, Northern Cook Islands.* Ph.D. diss., University of Chicago.

1977 The Culture of Gender in Pukapuka. Males, Females and the Mayakitanga "Sacred Maid." *Journal of the Polynesian Society* 86:183–206.

1981 The Cultural Contexts of Siblingship in Pukapuka. In *Siblingship in Oceania,* edited by M. Marshall, pp. 53–77. Ann Arbor: University of Michigan Press.

Heelas, P., and Andrew Lock, eds.
1981 *Indigenous Psychology: The Anthropology of the Self.* London: Academic Press.

Heighton, Robert
1971 Hawaiian Supernatural and Natural Strategies for Goal Attainment. Ph.D. diss., University of Hawaii.

Henry, Teuira
1928 *Ancient Tahiti.* Bernice P. Bishop Museum Bulletin no. 48. Honolulu: The Museum.

Herbert, Walter
1980 *Marquesan Encounters: Melville and the Meaning of Civilization.* Cambridge: Harvard University Press.

Herskovits, Melville
1941 Some Comments on the Study of Cultural Contact. *American Anthropologist* 43:1–10.

Hexter, J. H.
1972 Fernand Braudel and the Monde Braudellien. . . . *Journal of Modern History* 44 (4): 480–539.

Heyerdahl, Thor
1950 *The Kon-Tiki Expedition by Raft across the South Seas,* translated by F. H. Lyon. London: Allen and Unwin.
1952 *American Indians in the Pacific: The Theory Behind the Kon-Tiki Expedition.* London: Allen and Unwin.
1958 *Aku-Aku, The Secret of Easter Island.* Chicago: Rand McNally.
1976 *The Art of Easter Island.* London: Allen and Unwin.

Heyerdahl, Thor, and Edwin N. Ferdon, Jr., eds.
1961 *Archaeology of Easter Island.* Monographs of the School of American Research, no. 24 (1). Santa Fe.

Hezel, Francis
1980 Review of *The Spanish Lake: The Pacific Since Magellan,* vol. 1, by O. H. K. Spate. *The Journal of Pacific History* 15:113–114.

Higgenbotham, H. N.
1984 *Third World Challenge to Psychiatry.* Honolulu: University of Hawaii Press.

Hind, Robert
1984 "We Have No Colonies": Similarities within the British Imperial Experience. *Comparative Studies in Society and History* 26:3–35.

Hiroa, Te Rangi. *See* Buck, Sir Peter

Hobsbawm, Eric, and Terrence Ranger, eds.
1983 *The Invention of Tradition.* New York: Cambridge University Press.

Hocart, A. M.
1927   *Kingship*. London: Oxford University Press.
1929   *Lau Islands, Fiji*. Honolulu: Bernice P. Bishop Museum.
1952   *The Northern States of Fiji*. London: Royal Anthropological Institute Occasional Paper no. 11.

Hogbin, H. I.
1934   *Law and Order in Polynesia*. New York: Harcourt, Brace.
1936   Mana. *Oceania* 6 (3): 241–274.

Holmes, Lowell
1983   A Tale of Two Studies. *American Anthropologist* 85:929–935.
1987   *Quest for the Real Samoa: The Mead/Freeman Controversy and Beyond*. South Hadley, Mass.: Bergin and Garvey.

Holmes, Tommy
1981   *The Hawaiian Canoe*. Hanalei, Kauai, Hawaii: Editions Limited.

Hommon, Rob J.
1976   The Formation of Primitive States in Pre-Contact Hawaii. Ph.D. diss., University of Arizona.
1980   Multiple Resources Nomination Form for Kahoʻolawe Archaeological Sites. On file at National Register of Historic Places, Washington, D.C.
1986   Social Evolution in Ancient Hawaii. In *Island Societies: Archaeological Approaches to Evolution and Transformation,* edited by P. V. Kirch, pp. 55–68. New York: Cambridge University Press.

Hooper, Antony
1970   Adoption in the Society Islands. In *Adoption in Eastern Oceania,* edited by V. Carroll, pp. 52–70. Honolulu: University of Hawaii Press.
1976   "Eating Blood": Tahitian Concepts of Incest. *Journal of the Polynesian Society* 85:227–241.
1981   *Why Tikopia Has Four Clans*. Occasional Paper no. 38. London: Royal Anthropological Society of Great Britain and Northern Ireland.

Hooper, Antony, and Judith Huntsman
1985   *Transformations of Polynesian Culture*. Auckland: The Polynesian Society.

Hooper, S. J. P.
1982   A Study of Valuables in the Chiefdom of Lau, Fiji. Ph.D. diss., University of Cambridge.

Hornell, James
1936   *The Canoes of Polynesia, Fiji, and Micronesia*. Bernice P. Bishop Museum Special Publication no. 27. Honolulu: The Museum.

Horrocks, Linley
1976   A Study of Intercultural Conflict: The Du Fresne Massacre at the Bay of Islands, New Zealand, 1772. *Artefact* (1) 1: 7–29.

Howard, Alan
1963   Land, Activity Systems and Decision-Making Models in Rotuma. *Ethnology* 2:407–440.

1964   Land Tenure and Social Change in Rotuma. *Journal of the Polynesian Society* 73:26–52.

1966   The Rotuman District Chief: A Study in Changing Patterns of Authority. *The Journal of Pacific History* 1:63–78.

1970   *Learning to Be Rotuman.* New York: Columbia University Press.

1972   Polynesian Stratification Revisited: Reflections on Castles Built of Sand (and a Few Bits of Coral). *American Anthropologist* 74:811–823.

1974   *Ain't No Big Thing: Coping Strategies in a Hawaiian-American Community.* Honolulu: University of Hawaii Press.

1979   Polynesia and Micronesia in Psychiatric Perspective. *Transcultural Psychiatric Research Review* 16:123–143.

1982a   Interactional Psychology: Some Implications for Psychological Anthropology. *American Anthropologist* 84:37–57.

1982b   Review of *Historical Metaphors and Mythical Realities,* by Marshall Sahlins. *American Anthropologist* 84:413–414.

1985a   Ethnopsychology and the Prospects for a Cultural Psychology. In *Person, Self, and Experience: Exploring Pacific Ethnopsychologies,* edited by G. M. White and J. Kirkpatrick, pp. 401–420. Berkeley: University of California Press.

1985b   History, Myth and Polynesian Chieftainship: The Case of Rotuman Kings. In *Transformations of Polynesian Culture,* edited by A. Hooper and J. Huntsman, pp. 39–77. Auckland: The Polynesian Society.

1986a   Book Review of *Kingship and Sacrifice: Ritual and Society in Ancient Hawaii,* by Valerio Valeri. *Journal of the Polynesian Society* 95:530–537.

1986b   Cannibal Chiefs and the Charter for Rebellion in Rotuman Myth. *Pacific Studies* 10:1–27.

1988   Hypermedia and the Future of Ethnography. *Cultural Anthropology* 3 (3): 304–315.

Howard, Alan, ed.
1971   *Polynesia: Readings on a Culture Area.* Scranton, Pa.: Chandler.

Howard, Alan, R. Heighton, C. E. Jordan, and R. G. Gallimore
1970   Traditional and Modern Adoption Patterns in Hawaii. In *Adoption in Eastern Oceania,* edited by V. Carroll, pp. 21–51. Honolulu: University of Hawaii Press.

Howard, Jane
1984   *Margaret Mead: A Life.* New York: Simon and Schuster.

Howard, John
1952   *Strange Empire: A Narrative of the Northwest.* New York: Morrow.

Howe, K. R.
1974   Firearms and Indigenous Warfare: A Case Study. *The Journal of Pacific History* 9:21–38.

1977   The Fate of the "Savage" in Pacific Historiography. *The New Zealand Journal of History* 11:137–154.

1979   Pacific Islands History in the 1980s: New Directions or Monograph Myopia? *Pacific Studies* 3:81–89.

1984   *Where the Waves Fall: A New South Sea Islands History from First Settlement to Colonial Rule.* Honolulu: University of Hawaii Press.
1985   Response. *Pacific Studies* 9:167–171.

Hubert, Henri, and Marcel Mauss
1978   *Sacrifice: Its Nature and Function.* Chicago: University of Chicago Press.

Hughes, P., G. Hope, M. Latham, and M. Brookfield
1979   Prehistoric Man-Induced Degradation of the Lakeba Landscape: Evidence from Two Inland Swamps. In *Lakeba: Environmental Change, Population Dynamics, and Resource Use,* edited by H. C. Brookfield, pp. 93–110. Paris: UNESCO.

Huntsman, Judith
1971   Concepts of Kinship and Categories of Kinsmen in the Tokelau Islands. *Journal of the Polynesian Society* 80:317–354.
1981a   Butterfly Collecting in a Swamp: Suggestions for Studying Oral Narratives as Creative Art. *Journal of the Polynesian Society* 90:209–218.
1981b   Complementary and Similar Kinsmen in Tokelau. In *Siblingship in Oceania: Studies in the Meaning of Kin Relations,* edited by M. Marshall. Lanham, Md.: University Press of America.

Huntsman, Judith, and Antony Hooper
1975   Male and Female in Tokelau culture. *Journal of the Polynesian Society* 84:415–430.
1976   The "Desecration" of Tokelau Kinship. *Journal of the Polynesian Society* 85:257–296.

Ihimaera, Witi Tame
1973   *Tangi.* Auckland: Heinemann.
1974   *Whanau.* Auckland: Heinemann.

'I'i, John Papa
1959   *Fragments of Hawaiian History,* translated by Mary Kawena Pukui. Honolulu: Bernice P. Bishop Museum.

Ingraham, Joseph
1971   *Joseph Ingraham's Journal of the Brigantine Hope on a Voyage to the Northwest Coast of America 1790–92,* edited by Mark Kaplanoff. Barre, Mass.: Imprint Society.

Irwin, G.
1981   How Lapita Lost Its Pots: The Question of Continuity in the Colonization of Polynesia. *Journal of the Polynesian Society* 90:481–494.

Ito, Karen
1985a   Affective Bonds: Hawaiian Interrelationships of Self. In *Person, Self and Experience: Exploring Pacific Ethnopsychologies,* edited by G. White and J. Kirkpatrick, pp. 301–327. Berkeley: University of California Press.
1985b   Ho'oponopono "To Make Right": Hawaiian Conflict Resolution and Metaphor in the Construction of a Family Therapy. *Culture, Medicine and Psychiatry* 9:201–217.

Jackson, Michael
   1972   Aspects of Symbolism and Composition in Maori Art. *Bijdragen tot de Taal-, Land- en Volkenkunde* 128:33–80.

James, K. E.
   1988   O, Lead Us Not Into "Commoditisation" . . . Christine Ward Gailey's Changing Gender Values in the Tongan Islands. *Journal of the Polynesian Society* 97:31–48.

Jarvie, I. C.
   1964   *The Revolution in Anthropology*. London: Routledge and Kegan Paul.

Jennings, Jesse, ed.
   1979   *The Prehistory of Polynesia*. Cambridge: Harvard University Press.

Jennings, J., and R. Holmer, eds.
   1980   *Archaeological Excavations in Western Samoa*. Pacific Anthropological Records no. 32. Honolulu: Department of Anthropology, Bernice P. Bishop Museum.

Jennings, J., R. Holmer, and G. Jackmond
   1982   Samoan Village Patterns: Four Examples. *Journal of the Polynesian Society* 91:81–102.

Jennings, J., R. Holmer, J. Janetski, and H. Smith
   1976   *Excavations on Upolu, Western Samoa*. Pacific Anthropological Records no. 25. Honolulu: Department of Anthropology, Bernice P. Bishop Museum.

Johansen, J. Prytz
   1948   *Character and the Structure of Maori*. Det Kgl. Dauske Videnskabernes Selskab, Historisk-Filologiske Meddelser. Bind 21:5.
   1954   *The Maori and His Religion in its Non Ritualistic Aspects*. Copenhagen: I Kommission Hos Ejnar Munksgaard.

Jordan, Cathy, et al.
   1977   *A Multidisciplinary Approach to Research in Education*. Technical Report 81. Kamehameha Schools. Honolulu: Bernice P. Bishop Estate.

Kaeppler, Adrienne L.
   1967a Preservation and Evolution of Form and Function in Two Types of Tongan Dance. In *Polynesian Culture History: Essays in Honor of Kenneth P. Emory*, edited by Genevieve Highland, Roland Force, Alan Howard, Marion Kelly, and Yosihiko Sinoto, pp. 503–536. Bernice P. Bishop Museum Special Publication no. 56. Honolulu: The Museum.
   1967b The Structure of Tongan Dance. Ph.D. diss., University of Hawaii.
   1971a Aesthetics of Tongan Dance. *Ethnomusicology* 15:175–185.
   1971b Eighteenth Century Tonga: New Interpretations of Tongan Society and Material Culture at the Time of Captain Cook. *Man* 6:204–220.
   1971c Rank in Tonga. *Ethnology* 10:174–193.
   1972   Method and Theory in Analyzing Dance Structure with an Analysis of Tongan Dance. *Ethnomusicology* 16:173–217.
   1975   *The Fabrics of Hawaii (Bark Cloth)*. Leigh-on-Sea, England: F. Lewis.

1976   Dance in Tonga: The Communication of Social Values Through an Artistic Medium. In *Communication in the Pacific,* edited by Daniel Lerner and Jim Richstad, pp. 15–22. Honolulu: East-West Center.

1978a   *"Artificial Curiosities" Being an Exposition of Native Manufactures Collected on the Three Pacific Voyages of Captain James Cook, R.N.* Bernice P. Bishop Museum Special Publication no. 65. Honolulu: The Museum.

1978b   Dance in Anthropological Perspective. *Annual Review of Anthropology* 7:31–49.

1978c   Melody, Drone, and Decoration: Underlying Structures and Surface Manifestations in Tongan Art and Society. In *Art in Society: Studies in Styles, Culture and Aesthetics,* edited by Michael Greenhalgh and Vincent Megaw, pp. 261–274. London: Duckworth.

1979a   Aspects of Polynesian Aesthetic Traditions. In *The Art of the Pacific Islands,* by Peter Gathercole, Adrienne L. Kaeppler, and Douglas Newton, pp. 77–95. Washington, D.C.: The National Gallery of Art.

1979b   *Eleven Gods Assembled: An Exhibition of Hawaiian Wooden Images.* Bernice P. Bishop Museum Miscellaneous Publication. Honolulu: The Museum.

1979c   A Survey of Polynesian Art with Selected Reinterpretations. In *Exploring the Visual Art of Oceania,* edited by S. M. Mead, pp. 180–191. Honolulu: University of Hawaii Press.

1980   Polynesian Music and Dance. In *Musics of Many Cultures,* edited by Elizabeth May, pp. 134–153. Berkeley: University of California Press.

1982   Genealogy and Disrespect: A Study of Symbolism in Hawaiian Images. *RES* 3:82–107.

1983   *Polynesian Dance: With a Selection for Contemporary Performances.* Honolulu: Alpha Delta Kappa.

1985a   Hawaiian Art and Society: Traditions and Transformations. In *Transformations of Polynesian Culture,* edited by Antony Hooper and Judith Huntsman, pp. 105–131. Auckland: The Polynesian Society.

1985b   Structured Movement Systems in Tonga. In *Society and the Dance: The Social Anthropology of Performance and Process,* edited by Paul Spencer, pp. 92–118. New York: Cambridge University Press.

1986   Cultural Analysis, Linguistic Analogies, and the Study of Dance in Anthropological Perspective. In *Explorations in Ethnomusicology: Essays in Honor of David P. McAllester,* pp. 25–33. Detroit Monographs in Musicology no. 9. Detroit.

1988   Hawaiian Tattoo: A Conjunction of Genealogy and Aesthetics. In *Marks of Civilization,* edited by Arnold Rubin, pp. 157–170. Los Angeles: Museum of Cultural History.

Kamakau, Samuel
1964   *Ka Po'e Kahiko: The People of Old,* edited by Dorothy Barrere. Honolulu: Bernice P. Bishop Museum.

1976   *The Works of the People of Old: Na Hana a ka Po'e Kahiko,* edited by Dorothy Barrere. Honolulu: Bernice P. Bishop Museum.

Kamehameha Educational Research Institute
  1983   Current Publication List. Honolulu: Kamehameha Schools.

Kantorowicz, Ernst
  1957   *The King's Two Bodies: A Study in Medieval Political Theology.* Princeton: Princeton University Press.

Kardiner, Abram
  1939   *The Individual and His Society.* New York: Columbia University Press.

Kardiner, Abram, et al.
  1945   *Psychological Frontiers of Society.* New York: Columbia University Press.

Kawharu, I. H.
  1975   *Orakei: A Ngati Whatua Community.* Wellington: New Zealand Council for Educational Research.
  1977   *Maori Land Tenure.* Oxford: Clarendon.

Keesing, Felix
  1928   *The Changing Maori.* New Plymouth, New Zealand: Thomas Avery and Sons.

Keesing, Felix, and M. Keesing
  1956   *Elite Communication in Samoa.* Stanford: Stanford University Press.

Keesing, Roger
  1984   Rethinking Mana. *Journal of Anthropological Research* 40 (1): 137–156.

Kellum-Ottino, M.
  1971   *Archéologie d'une Vallée des Iles Marquises.* Publications de la Société des Océanistes no. 26. Paris.

Kelly, Marion
  1967   Some Problems with Early Descriptions of Hawaiian Culture. In *Polynesian Culture History: Essays in Honor of Kenneth P. Emory,* edited by Genevieve Highland, Roland Force, Alan Howard, Marion Kelly, and Yoshihiko Sinoto, pp. 399–410. Bernice P. Bishop Museum Special Publication no. 56. Honolulu: The Museum.

Kelsey, Jane, and Warren Young
  1982   *The Gangs: Moral Panic As Social Control.* Wellington: Institute of Criminology.

Kent, Noel
  1983   *Hawaii: Islands under the Influence.* New York: Monthly Review.

Kernot, Bernie
  1981   An Artist in His Time. *Journal of the Polynesian Society.* 90:157–169.
  1983   The Meeting House in Contemporary New Zealand. In *Art and Artists of Oceania,* edited by Sidney M. Mead and Bernie Kernot, pp. 181–197. Palmerston North, New Zealand: Dunmore Press.

Kikuchi, W. K.
  1976   Prehistoric Hawaiian Fishponds. *Science* 193:295–299.

King, Michael
  1972   *Moko: Maori Tattooing in the 20th Century.* Wellington.
  1977   *Te Puea.* Wellington: Hodder and Stoughton.

Kirch, Patrick V.
1973   Prehistoric Subsistence Patterns in the Northern Marquesas Islands, French Polynesia. *Archaeology and Physical Anthropology in Oceania* 8:24–40.
1974   The Chronology of Early Hawaiian Settlement. In *Archaeology and Physical Anthropology in Oceania* 9:110–119.
1975   Cultural Adaptation and Ecology in Western Polynesia: An Ethnoarchaeological Study. Ph.D. diss., Yale University.
1977   Valley Agricultural Systems in Prehistoric Hawaii: An Archaeological Consideration. *Asian Perspectives* 20:246–280.
1978   The Lapitoid Period in West Polynesia: Excavations and Survey in Niuatoputapu, Tonga. *Journal of Field Archaeology* 5:1–13.
1979   *Marine Exploitation in Prehistoric Hawaii: Archaeological Excavations at Kalahuipua'a, Hawaii Island.* Pacific Anthropological Records no. 29. Honolulu: Department of Anthropology, Bernice P. Bishop Museum.
1981   Lapitoid Settlements of Futuna and Alofi, Western Polynesia. *Archaeology in Oceania* 16:127–143.
1982a   Advances in Polynesian Prehistory: Three Decades in Review. *Advances in World Archaeology* 1:51–97. New York: Academic Press.
1982b   The Impact of Prehistoric Polynesians on the Hawaiian Ecosystem. *Pacific Science* 36:1–14.
1983   Man's Role in Modifying Tropical and Subtropical Polynesian Ecosystems. *Archaeology in Oceania* 18:26–31.
1984a   *The Evolution of the Polynesian Chiefdoms.* New York: Cambridge University Press.
1984b   The Polynesian Outliers: Continuity, Change, and Replacement. *The Journal of Pacific History* 4:224–238.
1985   *Feathered Gods and Fishhooks: An Introduction to Hawaiian Archaeology and Prehistory.* Honolulu: University of Hawaii Press.
1986   Rethinking East Polynesian Prehistory. *Journal of the Polynesian Society* 95:9–40.
n.d.   Production, Intensification, and the Early Hawaiian Kingdom. In *Pacific Production Systems,* edited by D. E. Yen. Australian National University. In press.

Kirch, Patrick V., and T. Dye
1979   Ethnoarchaeology and the Development of Polynesian Fishing Strategies. *Journal of the Polynesian Society* 88:53–76.

Kirch, Patrick V., and M. Kelly, eds.
1975   *Prehistory and Human Ecology in a Windward Hawaiian Valley: Halawa Valley, Molokai.* Pacific Anthropological Records no. 24. Honolulu: Department of Anthropology, Bernice P. Bishop Museum.

Kirch, Patrick V., and Paul Rosendahl
1973   Archaeological Investigation of Anuta. Pacific Anthropological Records 21:25–108. Honolulu: Department of Anthropology, Bernice P. Bishop Museum.

Kirch, Patrick V., and M. Spriggs
  n.d.   A Radiocarbon Chronology for the Upper Anahulu Valley, Oahu.
          Hawaiian Archaeology, no. 2. Honolulu: Society for Hawaiian Archae-
          ology. In press.

Kirch, Patrick V., and D. E. Yen
  1982   *Tikopia: The Prehistory and Ecology of a Polynesian Outlier.* Bernice P.
          Bishop Museum Bulletin no. 238. Honolulu: The Museum.

Kirchoff, P.
  1955   The Principles of Clanship in Human Society. *Davidson Journal of
          Anthropology* 1:1-10.

Kirkpatrick, John
  1979   The Marquesan Notion of the Person. Ph.D. diss., University of
          Chicago.
  1981   Meanings of Siblingship in Marquesan Society. In *Siblingship in
          Oceania: Studies in the Meaning of Kin Relations,* edited by M. Marshall,
          pp. 17-51. Lanham, Md.: University Press of America.
  1983   *The Marquesan Notion of the Person.* Ann Arbor: UMI Research Press.
  1985   Some Marquesan Understandings of Action and Identity. In *Person,
          Self, and Experience: Exploring Pacific Ethnopsychologies,* edited by G. M.
          White and J. Kirkpatrick, pp. 80-120. Berkeley: University of Cali-
          fornia Press.

Kirkpatrick, John, and G. M. White
  1985   Exploring Ethnopsychologies. In *Person, Self, and Experience: Exploring
          Pacific Ethnopsychologies,* edited by G. M. White and John Kirk-
          patrick, pp. 3-32. Berkeley: University of California Press.

Kitching, Gavin
  1984   Imperialism: The Past in the Present. A Review Article. *Comparative
          Studies in Society and History* 26:72-82.

Kluckhohn, Clyde
  1951   Values and Value Orientations in the Theory of Action. In *Toward a
          General Theory of Action,* edited by Talcott Parsons and Edward Shils,
          pp. 388-433. Cambridge: Harvard University Press.

Kluckhohn, Florence R.
  1950   Dominant and Substitute Profiles of Cultural Orientations. *Social
          Forces* 28:376-393.

Kluckhohn, Florence R., and Fred Strodtbeck
  1961   *Variations in Value Orientations.* Evanston, Ill.: Ron Peterson.

Knapman, Bruce
  1976   Indigenous Involvement in the Cash Economy of Lau, Fiji, 1840-
          1946. *The Journal of Pacific History* 11:167-188.
  1985   Capitalism's Economic Impact in Colonial Fiji, 1874-1939. *The Jour-
          nal of Pacific History* 20:66-83.
  1987   Aid and the Dependent Development of Pacific Island States. *The
          Journal of Pacific History* 21:139-152.

Kohlberg, Lawrence
  1969   Stage and Sequence: The Cognitive-Developmental Approach to Socialization. In *Handbook of Socialization Theory and Research,* edited by D. Goslin, pp. 347–480. Chicago: Rand McNally.

Kooijiman, Simon
  1972   *Tapa in Polynesia.* Bernice P. Bishop Museum Bulletin no. 234. Honolulu: The Museum.
  1977   *Tapa on Moce Island, Fiji. A Traditional Handicraft in a Changing Society.* Mededelingen Rijksmuseum voor Volkenkunde no. 21. Leiden: E. J. Brill.

Koskinen, Aarne
  1953   *Missionary Influence as a Political Factor in the Pacific Islands.* Helsinki: Suomalaisen Tiedeakatemian Toimituksia Annales Academiae Scientiarum Fennicae.
  1957   On South Sea Islanders' View of Christianity. *Studia Missiologica Fennica* 1:7–16.
  1960   *Ariki the First Born: An Analysis of a Polynesian Chieftain Title.* FF Communications 181. Helsinki: Suomalainen Tiedeakatemia.
  1968   **Kite: Polynesian Insights into Knowledge.* Helsinki: The Finnish Society for Missiology and Ecumenics.

Krämer, Augustin
  1902– *Die Samoa Inseln: Entwurf einer Monographie mit besonderer Berucksichtigung*
  1903   *Deutsch-Samoas.* 2 vols. Stuttgart: Schweizerbart.

Kuykendall, Ralph
  1938   *The Hawaiian Kingdom,* vol. 1: *1778–1854, Foundation and Transformation.* Honolulu: University of Hawaii Press.
  1953   *The Hawaiian Kingdom,* vol. 2: *1854–1874, Twenty Critical Years.* Honolulu: University of Hawaii Press.
  1967   *The Hawaiian Kingdom,* vol. 3: *1874–1893, The Kalakaua Dynasty.* Honolulu: University of Hawaii Press.

Laboratory of Comparative Human Cognition
  1978   Cognition as a Residual Category in Anthropology. *Annual Review of Anthropology* 7:51–69.
  1979   What is Cultural About Cross-Cultural Cognitive Psychology? *Annual Review of Psychology* 30:145–172.

Laing, Ronald D.
  1965   *The Divided Self.* Baltimore: Penguin Books.

Langdon, Robert
  1969   A View of Ari'i Taimai's Memoirs. *The Journal of Pacific History* 4:162–165.
  1973   Review of *Beyond the Capes,* by Ernest Dodge. *The Journal of Pacific History* 8:225–226.
  1975   Ancient Tahiti, Without Benefit of a Lost Caravel: A Very Personal Review. *Pacific Islands Monthly* 45 (September): 48–49.
  1984   *Where the Whalers Went.* Canberra: Australian National University.

La Pérouse, Jean F. G. de
  1799   *A Voyage Round the World Performed in the Years 1785, 1786, 1787, and
          1788. . . .* 2 vols. Reprint. Bibliotheca Australiana no. 27. New
          York: Da Capo Press, 1968.

Laracy, Hugh
  1969   The First Mission to Tikopia. *The Journal of Pacific History* 4:105–109.
  1978   Review of *The Samoan Triangle: A Study in Anglo-American Relations,
          1878–1900,* by Paul Kennedy. *The Journal of Pacific History* 13:250–
          251.

Larssen, Karl Erik
  1960   *Fijian Studies.* Göteborg: Ethnografiska Museet.

Lātūkefu, Sione
  1968   Oral Traditions: An Appraisal of their Value in Historical Research
          in Tonga. *The Journal of Pacific History* 3:135–143.
  1974   *Church and State in Tonga.* Canberra: Australian National University.
  1977   Review of *Peter Dillon of Vanikoro,* by J. W. Davidson. *The Journal of
          Pacific History* 12:242–244.

Lavondés, H.
  1967   Observations on Methods Used in Assembling Oral Traditions in the
          Marquesas. In *Polynesian Culture History: Essays in Honor of Kenneth P.
          Emory,* edited by Genevieve Highland, Roland Force, Alan Howard,
          Marion Kelly, and Yosihiko Sinoto, pp. 483–500. Bernice P. Bishop
          Museum Special Publication no. 56. Honolulu: The Museum.

Leach, B. F., and H. Leach, eds.
  1979   *Prehistoric Man in Palliser Bay.* National Museum of New Zealand Bul-
          letin no. 21.

Leach, B. F., and G. Ward
  1981   *Archaeology on Kapingamarangi Atoll.* Dunedin, New Zealand: Depart-
          ment of Anthropology, University of Otago.

Leach, Edmund
  1954   *Political Systems of Highland Burma: A Study of Kachin Social Structure.*
          Boston: Beacon Press.
  1972   The Structure of Symbolism. In *The Interpretation of Ritual,* edited by
          J. S. La Fontaine, pp. 277–282. London: Tavistock.
  1985   Concluding Remarks. In *Transformations of Polynesian Culture,* edited
          by Antony Hooper and Judith Huntsman, pp. 219–223. Auckland:
          The Polynesian Society.

Leach, H.
  1979   *Evidence of Prehistoric Gardens in Eastern Palliser Bay.* National Museum
          of New Zealand Bulletin 21:137–161.
  1984   *1,000 Years of Gardening in New Zealand.* Wellington: A. H. and A. W.
          Reed.

Leaf, Murray
  1979   *Man, Mind, and Science: A History of Anthropology.* New York: Columbia
          University Press.

Lee, Dorothy Sara
1984   Music Performance and the Negotiation of Identity in Eastern Viti Levu, Fiji. Ph.D. diss., Indiana University.

Lee, Georgia
1986   Easter Island Rock Art: Ideological Symbols as Evidence of Sociopolitical Change. Ph.D. diss., University of California at Los Angeles.

Lemert, Edwin
1972   Forms and Pathology of Drinking in Three Polynesian Societies. In *Human Deviance, Social Problems, and Social Control,* edited by Edwin Lemert, pp. 218–233. Englewood Cliffs, N.J.: Prentice Hall

Lesher, Clara Rebecca
1937   The South Sea Islanders in English Literature 1519–1798. Ph.D. diss., University of Chicago.

Levin, Paula Frances
1978   Students and Teachers on Tubuai: A Cultural Analysis of Polynesian Classroom Interaction. Ph.D. diss., University of California at San Diego.

Levin, Stephanie Seto
1968   The Overthrow of the Kapu System in Hawaii. *Journal of the Polynesian Society* 77:402–430.

LeVine, Robert
1973   *Culture, Behavior and Personality.* Chicago: Aldine.

Levy, Robert
1966   Ma'ohi Drinking Patterns in the Society Islands. *Journal of the Polynesian Society* 75:304–320.
1967   Tahitian Folk Psychotherapy. *International Mental Health Research Newsletter* 9:12–15.
1969   On Getting Angry in the Society Islands. In *Mental Health Research in Asia and the Pacific,* edited by William Caudill and Tsung-yi Lin, pp. 358–380. Honolulu: East-West Center Press.
1970   Tahitian Adoption as a Psychological Message. In *Adoption in Eastern Oceania,* edited by V. Carroll, pp. 71–87. Honolulu: University of Hawaii Press.
1972   Personality Studies in Polynesia and Micronesia: Stability and Change. Working Paper. Social Science Research Institute, University of Hawaii.
1973   *Tahitians: Mind and Experience in the Society Islands.* Chicago: University of Chicago Press.
1983   Thoughts on a Tahitian University. *Pacific Perspective* 12 (1): 59–67.
1984   Emotion, Knowing and Culture. In *Culture Theory,* edited by R. Shweder and R. LeVine, pp. 214–237. New York: Cambridge University Press.
n.d.   Some of the Reasons Why Tahitians Are Bad Scientists. Unpublished manuscript.

Lieber, Michael D.
  1970   Adoption on Kapingamarangi. In *Adoption in Eastern Oceania,* edited by V. Carroll, pp. 158–205. Honolulu: University of Hawaii Press.

Lieber, Michael D., ed.
  1977   *Exiles and Migrants in Oceania.* Honolulu: University of Hawaii Press.

Linnekin, Jocelyn
  1974   Land Relations and the Status of Women in Post-Contact Hawaii. Manuscript. Hamilton Library, University of Hawaii.
  1983   Defining Tradition: Variations on the Hawaiian Identity. *American Ethnologist* 10:241–252.
  1985a   Book Review of *Kingship and Sacrifice: Ritual and Society in Ancient Hawaii,* by Valerio Valeri. *American Ethnologist* 12:788–790.
  1985b   *Children of the Land: Exchange and Status in a Hawaiian Community.* New Brunswick, N.J.: Rutgers University Press.
  1986   Book Review of *Kingship and Sacrifice: Ritual and Society in Ancient Hawaii,* by Valerio Valeri. *The Hawaiian Journal of History* 20:217–220.
  1987   Statistical Analysis of the Great Mahele: Some Preliminary Findings. *The Journal of Pacific History* 22:15–33.
  1988   Women and Land in Postcontact Hawaii: A Study in Gender and Social Change. Unpublished manuscript.

Linton, Ralph
  1924   The Degeneration of Human Figures Used in Polynesian Decorative Art. *Journal of the Polynesian Society* 33:321–324.
  1939   Marquesan Culture. In *The Individual and His Society,* edited by A. Kardiner, pp. 137–196. New York: Columbia University Press.
  1941   Primitive Art. *Kenyon Review* 3:34–51.
  1945   *The Culture Background of Personality.* New York: Appleton-Century-Crofts.

Linton, Ralph, and Paul Wingert
  1946   *Arts of the South Seas.* New York: Museum of Modern Art.

Loeb, E. M.
  1926   *History and Traditions of Niue.* Bernice P. Bishop Museum Bulletin no. 32. Honolulu: The Museum.

Loftus, Elizabeth, and Geoffrey Loftus
  1980   On the Permanence of Stored Information in the Human Brain. *American Psychologist* 35:409–420.

Love, Jacob Wainwright
  1979   Sāmoan Variations. Ph.D. diss., Harvard University.

Lundsgaarde, Henry, ed.
  1974   *Land Tenure in Oceania.* Honolulu: University of Hawaii Press.

Luomala, Katharine
  1955   *Voices on the Wind: Polynesian Myths and Chants.* Honolulu: Bernice P. Bishop Museum.
  1973   Moving and Movable Images in Easter Island Custom and Myth. *Journal of the Polynesian Society* 82:28–46.

Lutz, Catherine
  1985   Ethnopsychology Compared to What? Explaining Behavior and Consciousness Among the Ifaluk. In *Person, Self, and Experience: Exploring Pacific Ethnopsychologies,* edited by G. M. White and J. Kirkpatrick, pp. 35-79. Berkeley: University of California Press.

Lynd, R. S., and Helen Lynd
  1929   *Middletown: A Study in American Culture.* New York: Harcourt Brace.

McArthur, Norma
  1966   Essays in Multiplication. *The Journal of Pacific History* 1:91-105.
  1968   *Island Populations of the Pacific.* Honolulu: University of Hawaii Press.
  1978   "And, Behold, the Plague was Begun Among the People." In *The Changing Pacific: Essays in Honour of H. E. Maude,* edited by Niel Gunson, pp. 273-284. New York: Oxford University Press.

McCall, Grant
  1976   European Impact on Easter Island: Response, Recruitment and the Polynesian Experience in Peru. *The Journal of Pacific History* 11:90-105.

McCoy, P. C.
  1976   *Easter Island Settlement Patterns in the Late Prehistoric and Early Proto-Historic Periods.* International Fund for Monuments, Easter Island Committee, Bulletin no. 5.

MacDonald, Scott, and Ronald Gallimore
  1971   *Battle in the Classroom.* Scranton, Pa.: Intext.

McEwen, J. M.
  1966   Maori Art. In *An Encyclopedia of New Zealand,* vol. 2, 408-429. Wellington: Government Printer.

McGlone, M.
  1983   The Polynesian Deforestation of New Zealand: A Preliminary Synthesis. *Archaeology in Oceania* 18:11-25.

McKay, John, Bennett Hill, and John Buckler
  1984   *A History of World Societies,* vol. 2: *Since 1500.* Boston: Houghton Mifflin.

McKessar, C. J., and D. R. Thomas
  1978   Verbal and Non-Verbal Help-Seeking Among Urban Maori and Pakeha Children. *New Zealand Journal of Educational Studies* 13:29-39.

McLean, Mervyn
  1969a An Analysis of 651 Maori Scales. *Yearbook of the International Folk Music Council* 1:123-164.
  1969b Song Types of the New Zealand Maori. *Studies in Music* 3:53-69. Nedlands: University of Western Australia Press.
  1977   *An Annotated Bibliography of Oceanic Music and Dance.* Wellington: The Polynesian Society.
  1981   *Supplement: An Annotated Bibliography of Oceanic Music and Dance.* Auckland: The Polynesian Society.

McLean, Mervyn, and Margaret Orbell
1975   *Traditional Songs of the Maori.* Auckland: Auckland University Press.

McLeod, Norma
1957   The Social Context of Music in a Polynesian Community. Master's thesis, London School of Economics.
1972   Redundancy, Boredom and Survival. Paper presented at the Annual Meeting of the Society of Ethnomusicology, Toronto.

MacLeod, William Christie
1928   Celt and Indian: Britain's Old World Frontier in Relation to the New. Chapter 8. *The American Frontier.* Reprint. In *Beyond the Frontier: Social Process and Cultural Change,* edited by Paul Bohannan and Fred Plog, pp. 25–41. Garden City, N.Y.: Natural History Press, 1967.

MacPherson, C., and L. MacPherson
1985   Suicide in Western Samoa: A Sociological Perspective. In *Culture, Youth, and Suicide in the Pacific: Papers from an East-West Center Conference,* edited by Francis Hezel, Don Rubinstein, and Geoffrey White, pp. 36–73. Honolulu: East-West Center.

Malinowski, Bronislaw
1922   *Argonauts of the Western Pacific.* London: Routledge and Kegan Paul.
1935   *Coral Gardens and Their Magic, A Study of the Methods of Tilling the Soil and of Agricultural Rites in the Trobriand Islands.* 2 vols. New York: American Book Company.

Malo, David
1951   *Hawaiian Antiquities (Moolelo Hawaii),* translated by Nathaniel Emerson. Honolulu: Bernice P. Bishop Museum.

Marcus, George E.
1977   Succession Disputes and the Position of the Nobility in Modern Tonga. *Oceania* 47:220–241, 284–299.
1978a Land Tenure and Elite Formation in the Neotraditional Monarchies of Tonga and Buganda. *American Ethnologist* 5:509–534.
1978b Status Rivalry in a Polynesian Steady-State Society. *Ethos* 6:242–269.
1980a *The Nobility and the Chiefly Tradition in the Modern Kingdom of Tonga.* Memoirs of the Polynesian Society no. 42. Wellington.
1980b Role Distance in Conversations Between Tongan Nobles and Their "People." *Journal of the Polynesian Society* 89:435–453.
1981   Power on the Extreme Periphery: The Perspective of Tongan Elites in the Modern World System. *Pacific Viewpoint* 22:48–64.
1982   Review of *Historical Metaphors and Mythical Realities,* by Marshall Sahlins. *Journal of the Polynesian Society* 91:596–605.
1984   Three Perspectives on Role Distance in Conversations Between Tongan Nobles and Their "People." In *Dangerous Words: Language and Politics in the Pacific,* edited by D. L. Brenneis and F. R. Myers, pp. 243–265. New York: New York University Press.

Mariner, William
    1827   *An Account of the Natives of the Tonga Islands in the South Pacific Ocean.* . . . Compiled and Arranged by John Martin. 3d ed. 2 vols. Edinburgh: Constable.

Marsden, Maori
    1975   God, Man and Universe: A Maori View. In *Te Ao Hurihuri: The World Moves On. Aspects of Maoritanga,* edited by Michael King, pp. 191–219. Wellington: Hicks, Smith and Sons.

Marsella, A.
    1979   Cross Cultural Studies of Mental Disorders. In *Perspectives on Cross-Cultural Psychology,* edited by A. J. Marsella, R. Tharp, and T. Ciborowski, pp. 233–262. New York: Academic Press.
    1982   Culture and Mental Health: An Overview. In *Cultural Conceptions of Mental Health and Therapy,* edited by A. J. Marsella and G. M. White, pp. 359–388. Boston: Reidel.

Marshall, M.
    1981   *Siblingship in Oceania: Studies in the Meaning of Kin Relations.* Lanham, Md.: University Press of America.
    1984   Structural Patterns of Sibling Classification in Island Oceania: Implications for Culture History. *Current Anthropology* 25:597–637.

Martini, Mary, and John Kirkpatrick
    1981   Early Interactions in the Marquesas Islands. In *Culture and Early Interactions,* edited by Tiffany M. Field, A. M. Sostek, P. Vietze, and P. H. Leiderman, pp. 189–213. Hillsdale, N.J.: Erlbaum.

Mason, Leonard
    1959   Suprafamilial Authority and Economic Process in Micronesian Atolls. *Humanitiés Cahiers de l'Institut de Science Economique Appliquée* 5 (1): 87–118. Paris.

Mataira, Katerina
    1984   *Maori Arts of the South Pacific.* Raglan, New Zealand: Maori Artists and Writers Society.

Maude, H. E.
    1968   *Of Islands and Men: Studies in Pacific History.* New York: Oxford University Press.
    1971   Pacific History: Past, Present, and Future. *The Journal of Pacific History* 6:3–24.
    1973   James Wightman Davidson. *The Journal of Pacific History* 8:5–9.
    1981   *Slavers in Paradise: The Peruvian Labor Trade in Polynesia.* Canberra: Australian National University Press.

Mauss, Marcel
    1954   *The Gift: Forms and Functions of Exchange in Archaic Society.* Translated by Ian Cunnison. London: Cohen and West.

Mead, Margaret
    1928a *Coming of Age in Samoa.* New York: Morrow.
    1928b *The Maoris and Their Arts.* New York: American Museum of Natural History.
    1928c The Role of the Individual in Samoan Society. *Journal of the Royal Anthropological Society* 58:481–495.
    1928d The Tattooing Complex. In *Inquiry into the Question of Cultural Stability on Polynesia,* edited by M. Mead, pp. 71–81. New York: Columbia University Press.
    1929 The Samoan Kilt. *Journal of the Polynesian Society* 38:239.
    1930a *Growing Up in New Guinea.* New York: Morrow.
    1930b *The Social Organization of Manuʻa.* Bernice P. Bishop Museum Bulletin no. 76. 2nd ed., 1969. Honolulu: The Museum.
    1937 *Cooperation and Competition Among Primitive Peoples.* New York: McGraw-Hill.
    1956 *New Lives for Old.* New York: Morrow.
    1968 The Samoans. In *People and Cultures of the Pacific,* edited by Andrew Vayda, pp. 244–273. New York: Natural History Press.

Mead, Sidney M.
    1969 *Traditional Maori Clothing: A Study of Technological and Functional Change.* Wellington: Reed.
    1971a An Analysis of Form and Decoration in Polynesian Adze Hafts. *Journal of the Polynesian Society* 80:485–496.
    1971b The Development of the Decorated Meeting House in New Zealand. Unpublished manuscript.
    1975 The Origins of Maori Art: Polynesian or Chinese? *Oceania* 45:173–211.
    1983 Te Toi Matauranga Maori mo nga Ra Kei Mua: Maori Studies Tomorrow. *Journal of the Polynesian Society* 92:333–351.
    1984 Nga Timunga me nga Paringa o te Mana Maori: The Ebb and Flow of Mana Maori and the Changing Context of Maori Art. In *Te Maori: Maori Art From New Zealand Collections,* edited by S. M. Mead, pp. 20–36. New York: Harry N. Abrams.

Mead, Sidney M., ed.
    1984 *Te Maori: Maori Art from New Zealand Collections.* New York: Harry N. Abrams.

Mead, Sidney M., L. Birks, H. Birks, and E. Shaw
    1973 The Lapita Pottery Style of Fiji and Its Associations. Polynesian Society Memoir no. 38. (In *Journal of the Polynesian Society* 82 [3 and 4].)

Meleisea, Malama
    1985 Review of *Where the Waves Fall: A New South Sea Islands History from First Settlement to Colonial Rule,* by K. R. Howe. *Pacific Studies* 9:147–149.

Melville, Herman
    1876 *Typee.* New York: Harper.

Mercer, P. M.
1979 Oral Tradition in the Pacific: Problems of Interpretation. *The Journal of Pacific History* 14:130–153.

Metge, Joan
1964 *A New Maori Migration: Rural and Urban Relations in Northern New Zealand.* London: Athlone.
1976 *The Maoris of New Zealand: Rautahi.* London: Routledge and Kegan Paul.

Métraux, Alfred
1937 Relief Carving on Stone in Polynesia. *Ethnos* 2:340–344.
1940 *Ethnology of Easter Island.* Honolulu: Bernice P. Bishop Museum.

Minturn, Leigh, and William L. Lambert
1964 *Mothers of Six Cultures.* New York: Wiley.

Moerenhout, Jacques-Antoine
1837 *Voyages aux Iles du Grand Ocean* . . . . 2 vols. Paris: A. Bertrand.

Molloy, B. P.
1967 Changes in Vegetation. In the *Waimakariri Catchment,* edited by J. Hayward. New Zealand: Lincoln College.

Monberg, Torben
1967 An Island Changes Its Religion: Some Social Implications of the Conversion to Christianity on Bellona Island. In *Polynesian Culture History: Essays in Honor of Kenneth P. Emory,* edited by Genevieve Highland, Roland Force, Alan Howard, Marion Kelly, and Yosihiko Sinoto, pp. 565–589. Bernice P. Bishop Museum Special Publication no. 56. Honolulu: The Museum.
1976 Ungrammatical "Love" on Bellona (Mungiki). *Journal of the Polynesian Society* 85:243–255.

Moorehead, Alan
1966 *The Fatal Impact: An Account of the Invasion of the South Pacific, 1767–1840.* New York: Harper and Row.

Morgan, Lewis H.
1871 *Systems of Consanguinity and Affinity of the Human Family.* Washington, D.C.: Smithsonian Institution.

Morison, Samuel Eliot
1921 *The Maritime History of Massachusetts: 1783–1860.* Cambridge, Mass.: Riverside Press.

Morrell, W. P.
1960 *Britain in the Pacific Islands.* Oxford: Clarendon Press.

Morris, Nancy
1976 Ka Loea Kalaiaina, 1898; A Study of a Hawaiian Language Newspaper as a Historical Reference Source. Master's thesis, University of Hawaii.

Morton, Harry
1982 *The Whale's Wake.* Honolulu: University of Hawaii Press.

Moulin, Jane
    1979   *The Dance of Tahiti.* Papeete, Tahiti: C. Gleizal.

Moyle, Richard
    1971   Samoan Traditional Music. Ph.D. diss., University of Auckland.
    1972   Samoan Song Types. *Studies in Music* 6:55–67. Nedlands: University
            of Western Australia Press.
    1978   A Preliminary Analysis of Lau Music. In *Lau-Tonga 1977.* Royal
            Society of New Zealand, 17:23–38.
    1987   *Tongan Music.* Auckland: Auckland University Press.

Murdock, George P., ed.
    1960   *Social Structure in Southeast Asia.* Viking Fund Publications in Anthro-
            pology no. 29. New York: Wenner-Gren.

Murdock, George P., Clellan Ford, Alfred Hudson, Raymond Kennedy, Leo
Simmons, and John Whiting
    1950   *Outline of Cultural Materials.* 3d ed. New Haven: Human Relations
            Area Files.

Murphy, Jane
    1976   Psychiatric Labelling in Cross-Cultural Perspective. *Science* 191:
            1019–1028.

Musée de l'Homme
    1972   *La Découverte de la Polynésie.* Paris: Musée de l'Homme.

Nayacakalou, R. R.
    1975   *Leadership in Fiji.* New York: Oxford University Press.

Neich, Roger
    1977   Historical Change in Rotorua Ngati Tarawhai Woodcarving Art.
            Master's thesis, Victoria University, Wellington.
    1983   The Veil of Orthodoxy: Rotorua Ngati Tarawhai Woodcarving in a
            Changing Context. In *Art and Artists In Oceania,* edited by Sidney M.
            Mead and Bernie Kernot, pp. 245–265. Palmerston North: Dunmore
            Press.
    1984   Processes of Change in Samoan Arts and Crafts. In *Development in the
            Arts of the Pacific,* edited by Philip J. C. Dark, pp. 16–47. Pacific Arts
            Association Occasional Paper no. 1.

Newbury, Colin
    1976   Rediscovering Tahiti, Review of Douglas Oliver's Ancient Tahitian
            Society. *The Journal of Pacific History* 11:244–247.
    1980   *Tahiti Nui: Change and Survival in French Polynesia 1767–1945.* Hono-
            lulu: University of Hawaii Press.
    1982   Book Review of *Historical Metaphors and Mythical Realities,* by Marshall
            Sahlins. *Journal of the Polynesian Society* 91:606–608.

Nicholls, John G.
    1978   Development of Causal Attributions for Success or Failure in Maori
            and Pakeha Children. *Developmental Psychology* 14:687–688.

Nicol, John
    1822   *The Life and Adventures of John Nicol, Mariner.* Edinburgh: William Blackwood.

Obituary (for David Malo)
    1853   *The Polynesian.* November 5, 10 (26): 101.

Oceanus (pseud.)
    1814   Letter to the Editor. *The Naval Chronicle* 31:380–382.

Ochs, Eleanor
    1982   Talking to Children in Western Samoa. *Language and Society* 11:77–104.
    1986   *Culture and Language Acquisition: Acquiring Communicative Competence in a Western Samoan Village.* New York: Cambridge University Press.

Ochs, Eleanor, and B. Schieffelin
    1983   *Acquiring Conversational Competence.* London: Routledge and Kegan Paul.
    1984   Language Acquisition and Socialization: Three Developmental Stories and Their Implications. In *Culture Theory,* edited by Richard Shweder and R. LeVine, pp. 276–320. New York: Cambridge University Press.

Ogan, Eugene
    1984   History, Political Economy, and Hawaiian Identity. *American Ethnologist* 11:189–190.
    1985   Review of *Where the Waves Fall,* by K. R. Howe. *American Historical Review* 90:209–210.
    n.d.   Intellectual Voyages in the South Seas. Review of *Islands of History,* by Marshall Sahlins. Unpublished manuscript.

Oliver, Douglas
    1961   *The Pacific Islands.* Garden City, N.Y.: Doubleday and Company.
    1974   *Ancient Tahitian Society.* 3 vols. Honolulu: University of Hawaii Press.
    1978   Norms of Tahitian Land Tenure: Ancient and Modern. In *The Changing Pacific: Essays in Honour of H. E. Maude,* edited by Niel Gunson, pp. 110–127. New York: Oxford University Press.
    1981   *Two Tahitian Villages: A Study in Comparisons.* Laie, Hawaii: The Institute for Polynesian Studies.
    1984   A "New" Approach to Pacific History. *Honolulu Star-Bulletin/Advertiser* (1 July): C12.
    1985   Response. *Pacific Studies* 8:108–112.

Olson, S. L., and H. F. James
    1984   The Role of Polynesians in the Extinction of the Avifauna of the Hawaiian Islands. In *Quaternary Extinctions: A Prehistoric Revolution,* edited by Paul S. Martin and R. G. Klein, pp. 768–780. Tucson: University of Arizona Press.

Orans, M.
    1966   Surplus. *Human Organization* 25:24–32.

Orchiston, D. Wayne, and Linley Horrocks
    1975   Contact and Conflict: The Rowe Massacre in Early Protohistoric
            New Zealand. *Historical Studies* 65:518–538.

Ortner, Sherry
    1974   Is Female to Male As Nature is to Culture. In *Women, Culture and Society*, edited by M. Rosaldo and L. Lamphere, pp. 67–88. Stanford:
            Stanford University Press.
    1981   Gender and Sexuality in Hierarchical Societies: The Case of Polynesia and Some Comparative Implications. In *Sexual Meanings: The Cultural Construction of Gender and Sexuality*, edited by Sherry Ortner and
            Harriet Whitehead, pp. 359–409. Cambridge: Cambridge University
            Press.
    1984   Theory in Anthropology Since the Sixties. *Comparative Studies in Society and History* 26:126–166.
    1985   Review of *Islands of History*, by Marshall Sahlins. *New York Times Book Review* (9 June): 26–27.

Ottino, Paul
    1965   *Ethno-histoire de Rangiroa.* Papeete: O.R.S.T.O.M.
    1967   Early *'Ati* of the Western Tuamotus. In *Polynesian Culture History: Essays in Honor of Kenneth P. Emory*, edited by Genevieve Highland,
            Roland Force, Alan Howard, Marion Kelly, and Yoshihiko Sinoto, pp.
            451–481. Bernice P. Bishop Museum Special Publication no. 56.
            Honolulu: The Museum.
    1970   Adoption on Rangiroa Atoll, Tuamotu Archipelago. In *Adoption in Eastern Oceania*, edited by V. Carroll, pp. 88–118. Honolulu: University of Hawaii Press.
    1973   *Rangiroa: Parente Étendue, Résidence et terres dans un atoll Polynésien.* Paris:
            Éditions Cujas.

Panoff, M.
    1965   La Terminologie de la Parente en Polynésie: Essai d'Analyse Formelle. *L'Homme* 3:60–87.

Parsonson, G. S.
    1967   The Literate Revolution in Polynesia. *The Journal of Pacific History* 2:39–57.

Pawley, A. K.
    1966   Polynesian Languages: A Subgrouping Based on Shared Innovations in Morphology. *Journal of the Polynesian Society* 75:39–64.
    1967   The Relation of Polynesian Outlier Languages. *Journal of the Polynesian Society* 76:259–296.
    1972   On the Internal Relationships of Eastern Oceanic Languages. Pacific
            Anthropological Records 13:1–142. Honolulu: Department of Anthropology, Bernice P. Bishop Museum.
    1979   Proto-Oceanic Terms for People: A Problem in Semantic Reconstruction. Unpublished manuscript, Department of Anthropology,
            University of Auckland.

1981   Melanesian Diversity and Polynesian Homogeneity: A Unified Explanation for Language. In *Studies in Pacific Languages and Culture in Honour of Bruce Biggs,* edited by J. Hollyman and A. K. Pawley, pp. 269–309. Auckland: Linguistic Society of New Zealand.

1982   Rubbish-Man, Commoner, Big Man, Chief? Linguistic Evidence for Hereditary Chieftainship in Proto-Oceanic Society. In *Oceanic Studies,* edited by J. Siikala, pp. 33–52. Transactions of the Finnish Anthropological Society no. 11. Helsinki.

Pearce, Roy Harvey
1988   *Savagism and Civilization: A Study of the Indian and American Mind.* Berkeley: University of California Press.

Pearson, W. H.
1969   European Intimidation and the Myth of Tahiti. *The Journal of Pacific History* 4:199–217.

1970   The Reception of European Voyagers on Polynesian Islands, 1568–1797. *Journal de la Société des Océanistes* 26 (27): 121–153.

1972   Hawkesworth's Alterations. *The Journal of Pacific History* 7:45–72.

Pene, John Te Maapi
1983   A Report on Worker Cooperative Possibilities. Working Paper, Department of Psychology. Hamilton: University of Waikato.

Petersen, Glenn
1982   *One Man Cannot Rule a Thousand: Fission in a Ponapean Chiefdom.* Ann Arbor: University of Michigan Press.

Phelps, Steven
1976   *Art and Artifacts of the Pacific, Africa and the Americas.* London: Hutchinson.

Polanyi, Karl
1968   *Primitive, Archaic, and Modern Economies: Essays of Karl Polanyi.* New York: Anchor Books.

Pomare, Eru W.
1980   *Maori Standards of Health.* Wellington: Medical Research Council of New Zealand.

Portlock, Nathaniel
1789   *A Voyage Round the World; But Most Particularly to the North-West Coast of America. . . .* London: Stockdale. Reprint. Bibliotheca Australiana no. 43. New York: Da Capo Press, 1968.

Poulsen, J.
1968   Archaeological Excavations on Tongatapu. In *Prehistoric Culture in Oceania,* edited by I. Yawata and Y. Sinoto, pp. 85–92. Honolulu: Bernice P. Bishop Museum.

Price-Williams, Douglas R.
1975   *Explorations in Cross-Cultural Psychology.* San Francisco: Chandler and Sharp.

Prickett, N., ed.
  1979   *Prehistoric Occupation in the Moikau Valley, Palliser Bay.* National Museum of New Zealand Bulletin 21:29–47.
  1982   *The First Thousand Years: Regional Perspectives in New Zealand Archaeology.* Palmerston North: New Zealand Archaeological Association.

Pukui, Mary Kawena, and Samuel N. Elbert
  1971   *Hawaiian Dictionary.* Honolulu: University of Hawaii Press.

Pukui, Mary Kawena, E. W. Haertig, and Catherine Lee
  1972   *Nana I Ke Kumu (Look to the Source),* vol. 1. Honolulu: The Queen Lili'uokalani Children's Center, Lili'uokalani Trust.
  1979   *Nana I Ke Kumu (Look to the Source),* vol. 2. Honolulu: The Queen Lili'uokalani Children's Center, Lili'uokalani Trust.

Quimby, George
  1972   Hawaiians in the Fur Trade of North-West America, 1785–1820. *The Journal of Pacific History* 7:92–103.

Quirós, Pedro Fernandez
  1904   *The Voyages of Pedro Fernandez de Quirós, 1595–1606.* Vol. 1, translated and edited by Clements Markham. London: Hakluyt Society.

Ralston, Caroline
  1978   *Grass Huts and Warehouses: Pacific Beach Communities of the Nineteenth Century.* Honolulu: University of Hawaii Press.
  1979   Review of *Friendly Islands: A History of Tonga,* by Noel Rutherford. *The Journal of Pacific History* 14:126–127.
  1984   Hawaii 1778–1854: Some Aspects of Maka'ainana Response to Rapid Cultural Change. *The Journal of Pacific History* 19:21–40.
  1985   Review of *Where the Waves Fall: A New South Sea Islands History from First Settlement to Colonial Rule,* by K. R. Howe. *Pacific Studies* 9:150–163.
  n.d. a Changes in the Lives of Ordinary Women in Early Post-Contact Hawaii. In *Family and Gender in the Pacific,* edited by Margaret Jolly and Martha MacIntyre. Cambridge: Cambridge University Press. In press.
  n.d. b Polyandry, "Prostitution," "Pollution": The Problems of Eurocentrism and Androcentrism in Polynesian Studies. In *Crossing Boundaries,* edited by Marie de Lepervanche et al. Sydney: Allen and Unwin. In press.

Ralston, Caroline, and Nicholas Thomas, eds.
  1987   Sanctity and Power: Gender in Polynesian History. *The Journal of Pacific History* 22 (3 & 4).

Ramsey, Peter D. K.
  1983   Successful and Unsuccessful Schools: A Study in South Auckland. *Australian and New Zealand Journal of Sociology* 19:272–304.

Ramsey, Peter D. K., et al.
  1981   *Tomorrow May Be Too Late. Final report of the Schools with Special Needs Project.* Hamilton: University of Waikato.

Ranby, Peter
  1979   *What Do Maori Children Think of Themselves?* *Set Number One.* Wellington: New Zealand Council for Educational Research.

Raspe, P.
  1973   The Breeding Structure of a Polynesian Isolate. Master's thesis, University of Auckland.

Reid, A. C.
  1983   The Chiefdom of Lau: A New Fijian State Built Upon Lakeban Foundations. *The Journal of Pacific History* 18:183–197.

Renfrew, C.
  1984   *Approaches to Social Archaeology.* Cambridge: Harvard University Press.

Rigby, Barry
  1973   Private Interests and the Origins of American Involvement in Samoa, 1872–1877. *The Journal of Pacific History* 8:75–87.

Riley, T.
  1975   Survey and Excavations of the Aboriginal Agricultural System. Pacific Anthropological Records 24:79–115. Honolulu: Department of Anthropology, Bernice P. Bishop Museum.

Ritchie, Barbara
  1983   A Sense of Place in Society: The Role and Significance of the House in Tonga. Master's thesis, University of Cambridge.

Ritchie, James
  1956   *Basic Personality in Rakau.* Wellington: Victoria University College.
  1960   *Values in Personal and Social Change.* Master's thesis, The Library, Victoria University, Wellington.
  1963   *The Making of a Maori.* Wellington: A. H. and A. W. Reed.

Ritchie, Jane
  1957   *Childhood in Rakau.* Wellington: Victoria University College.
  1964   *Maori Families.* Wellington: Victoria University.
  1977   *Tamariki Maori.* Hamilton: University of Waikato.
  1978   *Chance To Be Equal.* Picton: Cape Catley.

Ritchie, Jane, and James Ritchie
  1970   *Child Rearing Patterns in New Zealand.* Wellington: A. H. and A. W. Reed.
  1978   *Growing Up in New Zealand.* Sydney: George Allen and Unwin.
  1979   *Growing Up in Polynesia.* Sydney: George Allen and Unwin.
  1981a   Child Rearing and Child Abuse: The Polynesian Context. In *Child Abuse and Neglect: A Cross-Cultural Perspective,* edited by Jill Korbin, pp. 186–204. Berkeley: University of California Press.
  1981b   *Spare the Rod.* Sydney: George Allen and Unwin.

Roberts, Helen H.
  1926   *Ancient Hawaiian Music.* Bernice P. Bishop Museum Bulletin no. 29. Honolulu: The Museum.
  1932   Melodic Composition and Scale Foundations in Primitive Music. *American Anthropologist* 34:79–107.

Robertson, George
  1973   *An Account of the Discovery of Tahiti: From the Journal of George Robertson, Master of the H.M.S.* Dolphin, edited by Oliver Warner. London: Folio Press.

Robinson, Ronald
  1972   Non-European Foundations of European Imperialism: Sketch of a Theory of Collaboration. In *Studies in the Theory of Imperialism,* edited by Roger Owen and Bob Sutcliffe, pp. 117–142. London: Longman.

Robley, H. G.
  1896   *Moko, or Maori Tattooing.* London: Chapman and Hall.

Rogers, Garth
  1976   *Kai and Kava.* Ph.D. diss., University of Auckland.
  1977   The Sister Is Black: A Consideration of Female Rank and Power in Tonga. *Journal of the Polynesian Society* 86:157–182.

Roggeveen, Jacob
  1970   *The Journal of Jacob Roggeveen,* edited by Andrew Sharp. Oxford: Clarendon Press.

Rohner, R. P.
  1975   *They Love Me, Love Me Not.* New Haven, Conn.: HRAF Press.

Roscoe, Paul
  1988   Population Pressure, Population Density, and Political Evolution in the Pacific: Towards a Demographic Dimension to Practice Theory. Unpublished manuscript.

Rose, Roger G.
  1971   The Material Culture of Ancient Tahiti. Ph.D. diss., Harvard University.
  1980   *Hawai'i: The Royal Isles.* Bernice P. Bishop Museum Special Publication no. 67. Honolulu: The Museum.

Rosendahl, P. H.
  1972   Aboriginal Agriculture and Residence Patterns in Upland Lapakahi, Island of Hawaii. Ph.D. diss., University of Hawaii.

Roth, George Kingsley
  1934   The Manufacture of Barkcloth in Fiji (Vitu Levu). *Journal of the Royal Anthropological Institute* 64:289–303.

Routledge, David
  1985   Pacific History as Seen From the Pacific Islands. *Pacific Studies* 8:81–99.

Royal Anthropological Institute of Great Britain and Ireland
  1951   *Notes and Queries.* London: Routledge and Kegan Paul.

Rubinstein, Don
  1983   Epidemic Suicide Among Micronesian Adolescents. *Social Science and Medicine* 10:657–665.

Rubinstein, Don, and Geoffrey White
1983 Bibliography on Culture and Mental Health in the Pacific Islands. Manuscript on file at the East-West Center, Honolulu.

Rutherford, Noel
1971 *Shirley Baker and the King of Tonga.* New York: Oxford University Press.

Rutherford, Noel, ed.
1977 *Friendly Islands: A History of Tonga.* New York: Oxford University Press.

Sahlins, Marshall
1958 *Social Stratification in Polynesia.* American Ethnological Society Monograph. Seattle: University of Washington Press.
1963 Poor Man, Rich man, Big Man, Chief: Political Types in Melanesia and Polynesia. *Comparative Studies in Society and History* 5:285–303.
1968 *Tribesmen.* Englewood Cliffs, N.J.: Prentice-Hall.
1972 *Stone Age Economics.* Chicago: Aldine.
1976 *Culture and Practical Reason.* Chicago: University of Chicago Press.
1981a *Historical Metaphors and Mythical Realities: Structure in the Early History of the Sandwich Island Kingdom.* Association for Social Anthropology in Oceania Special Publication no. 1. Ann Arbor: University of Michigan Press.
1981b The Stranger-King: Dumézil among the Fijians. *The Journal of Pacific History* 16:107–132.
1983a Other Times, Other Customs: The Anthropology of History. *American Anthropologist* 85 (3): 517–544.
1983b Raw Women, Cooked Men, and Other "Great Things" of the Fiji Islands. In *The Ethnography of Cannibalism,* edited by P. Brown and D. Tuzin, pp. 72–93. Special Publication, Society for Psychological Anthropology, Washington, D.C.
1985 *Islands of History.* Chicago: University of Chicago Press.

St. George, Alison
1978 Perceptions, Expectations and Interactions: A Study of Teachers and Pupils in Five Ethnically Mixed Classrooms. Ph.D. diss., University of Waikato.
1983 Teacher Expectations and Perceptions of Polynesian and Pakeha Pupils and the Relationship to Classroom Behaviour and School Achievement. *British Journal of Educational Psychology* 53:48–59.

Salmond, Anne
1975 *Hui: A Study of Maori Gatherings.* Wellington: A. H. and A. W. Reed.
1978 Te Ao Tawhito: A Semantic Approach to the Traditional Maori Cosmos. *Journal of the Polynesian Society* 87:5–28.

Sapir, Edward
1929 The Unconscious Patterning of Behavior in Society. In *Selected Writings of Edward Sapir, Culture Language and Personality,* edited by David G. Mandelbaum, pp. 544–559. Berkeley: University of California Press.
1934 Emergence of a Concept of Personality in a Study of Cultures. *Journal of Social Psychology* 5:410–416.

Scarr, Deryck
   1972   Creditors and the House of Hennings: An Elegy from the Social and
          Economic History of Fiji. *The Journal of Pacific History* 7:104–123.

Scheper-Hughes, Nancy
   1984   The Margaret Mead Controversy: Culture Biology and Anthropo-
          logical Enquiry. *Human Organization* 43 (1): 85–93.

Schieffelin, B., and Eleanor Ochs
   1986   Language Socialization. *Annual Review of Anthropology* 15:163–191.

Schilt, R.
   1984   *Subsistence and Conflict in Kona, Hawaii: An Archaeological Study of the
          Kuakini Highway Realignment Corridor.* Department of Anthropology
          Report no. 84-1. Honolulu: Bernice P. Bishop Museum.

Schneider, David
   1968   *American Kinship: A Cultural Account.* Englewood Cliffs, N.J.: Prentice-
          Hall.
   1972   What is Kinship All About? In *Kinship Studies in the Morgan Centennial
          Year,* edited by P. Renning, pp. 32–63. Washington, D.C.: Anthro-
          pological Society of Washington.
   1976   The Meaning of Incest. *Journal of the Polynesian Society* 85:149–169.

Schoeffel, Penelope
   1978   Gender, Status and Power in Samoa. *Canberra Anthropology* 1 (2): 69–
          81.
   1979   Daughters of Sina. Ph.D. diss., The Australian National University.

Scribner, Sylvia, and Michael Cole
   1973   Cognitive Consequences of Formal and Informal Education. *Science*
          182:553–559.

Seaton, S. Lee
   1974   The Hawaiian Kapu Abolition of 1819. *American Ethnologist* 1:193–
          206.

Seaver, Joan
   1984   Some Observation on the Arts Today in the Navel of the World. In
          Development in the Arts of the Pacific, edited by Philip J. C. Dark, pp.
          49–70. Pacific Arts Association Occasional Paper no. 1.

Segall, Marshall H.
   1979   *Cross-Cultural Psychology.* Monterey, Calif.: Brooks Cole.
   1983   Aggression in Global Perspective: A Research Strategy. In *Aggression
          in Global Perspective,* edited by Arnold P. Goldstein and Marshall H.
          Segall, pp. 1–43. New York: Pergamon.

Service, Elman
   1955   Indian-European Relations in Colonial Latin America. *American
          Anthropologist* 57:411–425.

Shawcross, W.
   1967   An Investigation of Prehistoric Diet and Economy on a Coastal Site
          at Galatea Bay, New Zealand. *Proceeding of the Prehistoric Society*
          33:107–131.

1970   Ethnographic Economics and the Study of Population in Prehistoric New Zealand: Viewed Through Archaeology. *Mankind* 7:279–291.

1972   Energy and Ecology: Thermodynamic Models in Archaeology. In *Models in Archaeology,* edited by D. L. Clarke, pp. 577–622. London: Methuen.

Shennan, Jennifer

1981   Approaches to the Study of Dance in Oceania: Is the Dancer Carrying an Umbrella or Not? *Journal of the Polynesian Society* 90:193–208.

1984   *Maori Action Song; Waiata Kori, Waiata A Ringa.?* Wellington: New Zealand Council for Educational Research.

Shineberg, Dorothy

1967   *They Came for Sandalwood: A Study of the Sandalwood Trade in the South-West Pacific 1830–1865.* Melbourne: Melbourne University Press.

Shore, Bradd

1976a   Adoption, Alliance, and Political Mobility in Samoa. In *Transactions in Kinship: Adoption and Fosterage in Oceania,* edited by I. Brady, pp. 164–199. Honolulu: University of Hawaii Press.

1976b   Incest Prohibitions, Brother-Sister Avoidance, and the Logic of Power in Samoa. *Journal of the Polynesian Society* 85:275–296.

1977   *A Samoan Theory of Action: Social Control and Social Order in a Polynesian Paradox.* Ph.D. diss., University of Chicago.

1979   Ghosts and Government: A Structural Analysis of Alternative Institutions for Conflict Management in Samoa. *Man* n.s., 13:175–199.

1981   Sexuality and Gender in Samoa: Conceptions and Missed Conceptions. In *Sexual Meanings: The Cultural Construction of Gender and Sexuality,* edited by S. Ortner and H. Whitehead, pp. 192–215. Cambridge: Cambridge University Press.

1982   *Sala'ilua: A Samoan Mystery.* New York: Columbia University Press.

1983   Paradox Regained: Freeman's Margaret Mead and Samoa. *American Anthropologist* 85:935–944.

1984   Response to Derek Freeman's Review of *Sala'ilua: A Samoan Mystery. Oceania* 55 (3): 218–223.

1985   Polynesian Worldview: A Synthesis. Unpublished manuscript.

n.d.   Samoan Worldview Literally: Images and Reflections. Unpublished manuscript.

Shortland, Edward

1856   *Traditions and Superstitions of the New Zealanders.* 2d ed. London: Longman, Brown, Green, Longmans and Roberts.

Shweder, Richard

1979–   Rethinking Culture and Personality Theory. *Ethos* 7:225–311, 8:60–
1980   94.

Shweder, Richard, and Robert LeVine, eds.

1984   *Culture Theory.* New York: Cambridge University Press.

Silverman, M.
    1969   Maximize Your Options: A Study in Symbols, Values, and Social Structure. In *Forms of Symbolic Actions,* edited by R. Spencer, pp. 97–115. Proceedings of the 1969 Annual Spring Meeting, American Ethnological Society. Seattle: University of Washington Press.

Simmons, David
    1976   *The Great New Zealand Myth: A Study of the Discovery and Origin Traditions of the Maori.* Wellington: Reed.
    1983   Moko. In *Art and Artists of Oceania,* edited by Sidney M. Mead and Bernie Kernot, pp. 226–243. Palmerston North: Dunmore Press.
    1984   Te Rarangi Taonga. In *Te Maori: Maori Art from New Zealand Collections,* edited by Sidney Mead, pp. 175–235. New York: Harry N. Abrams.

Sinoto, Y. H.
    1966   A Tentative Prehistoric Cultural Sequence in the Northern Marquesas Islands, French Polynesia. *Journal of the Polynesian Society* 75: 287–303.
    1970   An Archaeologically Based Assessment of the Marquesas Islands as a Dispersal Center in East Polynesia. Pacific Anthropological Records 11:105–132. Honolulu: Department of Anthropology, Bernice P. Bishop Museum.
    1979   The Marquesas. In *The Prehistory of Polynesia,* edited by Jesse Jennings, pp. 110–134. Cambridge: Harvard University Press.
    1983   An Analysis of Polynesian Migrations Based on the Archaeological Assessments. *Journal de la Société des Océanistes* 39:57–67.

Skinner, H. D.
    1923   *The Morioris of Chatham Island.* Honolulu: Bernice P. Bishop Museum.
    1924a   Origin and Relationships of Maori Material Culture and Decorative Art. *Journal of the Polynesian Society* 33:229–243.
    1924b   Review of *Polynesian Decorative Designs,* by Ruth H. Greiner. *Journal of the Polynesian Society* 33:138–141.
    1974   *Comparatively Speaking: Studies in Pacific Material Culture 1921–1972.* Dunedin: University of Otago Press.

Smith, Bernard
    1960   *European Vision and the South Pacific 1768–1850: A Study in the History of Art and Ideas.* New York: Oxford University Press.
    1979   Cook's Posthumous Reputation. In *Captain James Cook and His Times,* edited by Robin Fisher and Hugh Johnston, pp. 159–185. Seattle: University of Washington Press.

Smith, C.
    1961   A Temporal Sequence Revised from Certain *Ahu.* In *Archaeology of Easter Island,* edited by T. Heyerdahl and E. N. Ferdon, Jr., pp. 181–220. Monographs of the School of American Research, no. 24 (1). Santa Fe.

Smith, Howard
  1975   The Introduction of Venereal Disease into Tahiti: A Re-examination. *The Journal of Pacific History* 10:38–45.

Smith, Jean
  1974   *Tapu Removal in Maori Religion.* Memoirs of the Polynesian Society no. 40. Wellington: The Polynesian Society.
  1981   Self and Experience in Maori Culture. In *Indigenous Psychologies: The Anthropology of the Self,* edited by P. Heelas and Andrew Lock, pp. 145–159. London: Academic Press.

Sorrenson, M. P. K.
  1982   Polynesian Corpuscles and Pacific Anthropology: The Home-made Anthropology of Sir Apirana Ngata and Sir Peter Buck. *Journal of the Polynesian Society* 91:7–27.

Sparrman, Anders
  1953   *A Voyage Round the World with Captain James Cook in H.M.S.* Resolution. London: Robert Hale.

Spate, Oskar H. K.
  1977   Prolegomena to a History of the Pacific. *Geographia Polonica* 36:217–223.
  1978   The Pacific as an Artefact. In *The Changing Pacific: Essays in Honour of H. E. Maude,* edited by Niel Gunson, pp. 32–45. New York: Oxford University Press.
  1979   *The Spanish Lake.* Canberra: Australian National University Press.
  1980   A Savage Culture Dissected (Review of *Islands and Beaches,* by Greg Dening). *Canberra Times* (11 October): 22.
  1983   *Monopolists and Freebooters.* Canberra: Australian National University Press.
  1985   Review of *Where the Waves Fall: A New South Sea Islands History from First Settlement to Colonial Rule,* by K. R. Howe. *Pacific Studies* 9:163–167.

Spears, John
  1910   *The Story of the New England Whalers.* New York: Macmillan.

Spindler, George D., ed.
  1978   *The Making of Psychological Anthropology.* Berkeley: University of California Press.

Spiro, Melford E.
  1951   Culture and Personality: The Natural History of a False Dichotomy. *Psychiatry* 14:19–46.

Spitz, P.
  1978   Silent Violent: Famine and Inequality. *International Review of Social Science* 30 (4): 867–892.

Spoehr, Florence
  1963   *White Falcon: The House of Godeffroy and Its Commercial and Scientific Role in the Pacific.* Palo Alto, Calif.: Pacific Books.

Spriggs, M.
    1981   Vegetable Kingdoms: Taro Irrigation and Pacific Prehistory. Ph.D.
            diss., Australian National University.

Stackpole, Edouard
    1953   *The Sea-Hunters: The New England Whalemen during Two Centuries 1635–*
            1835. New York: Lippincott.
    1972   *Whales and Destiny: The Rivalry between America, France, and Britain for*
            Control of the Southern Whale Fishery, 1785–1825. Amherst: University of
            Massachusetts Press.

Stanley, Julian C., ed.
    1972   *Preschool Programs for the Disadvantaged.* Baltimore: Johns Hopkins Uni-
            versity Press.
    1973   *Compensatory Education for Children, Ages 2 to 8.* Baltimore: Johns
            Hopkins University Press.

Starbuck, Alexander
    1878   *History of the American Whale Fishery from its Earliest Inception to the Year*
            1876. Part IV of the Report of the U.S. Commission on Fish and
            Fisheries. Washington. Reprint. 2 vols. New York: Argosy-Antiquar-
            ian, 1964.

Steadman, D. W., and S. P. Olson
    1985   Bird Remains from an Archaeological Site on Henderson Island,
            South Pacific. *Proceedings of the National Academy of Sciences* 82:6191–
            6195.

Steinen, Karl von den
    1925–   *Die Marquesaner und Ihrer Kunst.* 3 vols. Berlin: Darunter Zahlreichen.
    1928   Reprint. New York: Hacker Art Books, 1969.

Stevenson, Christopher
    1984   Corporate Descent Group Structure in Easter Island Prehistory.
            Ph.D. diss., Pennsylvania State University.
    1986   The Socio-Political Structure of the Southern Coastal Area of Easter
            Island: A.D. 1300–1864. In *Island Societies: Archaeological Approaches to*
            Evolution and Transformation, edited by P. V. Kirch, pp. 69–77. Cam-
            bridge: Cambridge University Press.

Stevenson, Karen
    1981   *Artifacts of the Pomare Family.* Honolulu: The University of Hawaii Art
            Gallery.

Stewart, C. S.
    1970   *A Visit to the South Seas, in the U.S. Ship* Vincennes, *During the Years*
            1829 and 1830. . . . New York: Praeger.

Stillman, Amy Kuʻuleialoha
    1982   The Hula Kuʻi: A Tradition in Hawaiian Music and Dance. Mas-
            ter's thesis, University of Hawaii.

Stocking, George
    1983   *Observers Observed: Essays on Ethnographic Fieldwork.* Madison: Univer-
            sity of Wisconsin Press.

Stone, L.
   1969   Literacy and Education in England, 1640–1900. *Past and Present*
           42:69–139.

Straus, Murray A., Richard J. Gelles, and Suzanne K. Steinmetz
   1980   *Behind Closed Doors.* New York: Anchor Press.

Strauss, W. Patrick
   1963   *Americans in Polynesia, 1783–1842.* East Lansing: Michigan State Uni-
           versity Press.
   1981   Review of *Islands and Beaches,* by Greg Dening. *American Historical
           Review* 86:906.

Suggs, R. C.
   1960   *The Island Civilizations of Polynesia.* New York: Mentor Books.
   1961   Archaeology of Nuku Hiva, Marquesas Islands, French Polynesia.
           Anthropological Papers of the American Museum of Natural History 49 (1).

Sutton, D.
   1980   A Culture History of the Chatham Islands. *Journal of the Polynesian
           Society* 89:67–93.

Tagupa, William
   1973   Review of *Ancient Tahitian Society,* by Douglas Oliver. *Journal de la
           Société des Océanistes* 29:380.
   1981   Review of *Islands and Beaches,* by Greg Dening. *Pacific Studies* 4:202–
           204.

Tatar, Elizabeth
   1982   *Nineteenth Century Hawaiian Chant.* Pacific Anthropological Records
           no. 33. Honolulu: Department of Anthropology, Bernice P. Bishop
           Museum.

Te Awekotuku, Ngahuia
   1981   The Sociocultural Impact of Tourism on the Te Arawa People of
           Rotorua, New Zealand. Ph.D. diss., University of Waikato.

Terrell, Jennifer
   1982   Joseph Kabris and his Notes on the Marquesas. *The Journal of Pacific
           History* 17:101–112.

Terrell, John
   1967   Galatea Bay: The Excavation of a Beach-Stream Midden Site on
           Ponui Island in the Hauraki Gulf, New Zealand. *Transactions of the
           Royal Society of New Zealand* 2 (3): 31–70.

Tharp, Roland G., and Ronald Gallimore
   1979   The Ecology of Programs Research and Evaluation. *Evaluation Studies
           Review Annual* no. 4:36–60.
   1982   Inquiry Process in Program Development. *Journal of Community Psy-
           chology* 10:103–118.

Thilenius, Georg
   1902   *Ethnographische Ergebnisse aus Melanesien . . . I . . . Die Polyneischen
           Inseln an der Ostgrenze Melanesiens.* Erhardt Karras, Halle. Abh. der
           Kaiserl. Leopold-Carolina Deutsche Akademie der Naturforscher,
           vol. 80.

Thomas, Allan
   1981   The Study of Acculturated Music in Oceania: "Cheap and Tawdry
          Borrowed Tunes?" *Journal of the Polynesian Society* 90:183–191.
   1984   Pokihi: The Box Drum of the Tokelau Islands. In *Development in the
          Arts of the Pacific,* edited by Philip J. C. Dark, pp. 71–75. Pacific Arts
          Association Occasional Paper no. 1.

Thomas, David R.
   1975   Cooperation and Competition among Polynesian and European
          Children. *Child Development* 46:948–953.
   1978   Cooperation and Competition Among Children in the Pacific Islands
          and New Zealand: The School as an Agent of Social Change. *Journal
          of Research and Development in Education* 12:88–96.
   1979   Teacher Expectations and the Oral Language Performance of Maori
          and Pakeha Children. Manuscript on file at Psychology Department,
          University of Waikato.

Thomas, Nicholas
   1986   'Le Roi de Tahuata': Iotete and the Transformation of South Mar-
          quesan Politics, 1826–1842. *The Journal of Pacific History* 21:3–20.
   1987   Unstable Categories: *Tapu* and Gender in the Marquesas. *The Journal
          of Pacific History* 22 (3): 123–138.

Thompson, Chris
   1971   Fijian Music and Dance. *The Fiji Society Transactions and Proceedings*
          11:14–21.

Thompson, Laura
   1940   *Southern Lau, Fiji: An Ethnography.* Bernice P. Bishop Museum Bulletin
          no. 162. Honolulu: The Museum.

Thrum, Thomas
   1918   Brief Sketch of the Life and Labors of S. M. Kamakau, Hawaiian
          Historian. *Twenty-Sixth Annual Report of the Hawaiian Historical Society,*
          pp. 40–61. Honolulu: Paradise of the Pacific Press.

Tiffany, Sharon W.
   1975a The Cognatic Descent Groups of Contemporary Samoa. *Man*
          10:430–447.
   1975b Giving and Receiving: Participation in Chiefly Distribution Activi-
          ties in Samoa. *Ethnology* 14:267–286.

Tiffany, Sharon W., and W. W. Tiffany
   1978   Optation, Cognatic Descent, and Redistributions in Samoa. *Ethno-
          logy* 17:367–390.

Tilly, Charles
   1978   Anthropology, History, and the Annales. *Review* 1 (3/4): 207–213.

Tippett, Alan Richard
   1968   *Fijian Material Culture: A Study of Cultural Context Function and Change.*
          Bernice P. Bishop Museum Bulletin no. 232. Honolulu: The Mu-
          seum.

Trask, Haunani-Kay
  1983   Cultures in Collision: Hawaii and England, 1778. *Pacific Studies* 7:91–117.
  1985   Review of *Islands of History*, by Marshall Sahlins. *American Ethnologist* 12:784–787.

Tuggle, H., and P. Griffin, eds.
  1973   *Lapakahi, Hawaii: Archaeological Studies*. Asian and Pacific Archaeology Series no. 5. Social Science Research Institute, University of Hawaii.

Tuggle, H., and M. J. Tomonari-Tuggle
  1980   Prehistoric Agriculture in Kohala, Hawaii. *Journal of Field Archaeology* 7:297–312.

Turnbull, John
  1813   *A Voyage Round the World, in the Years 1800, 1801, 1802, 1803, and 1804 . . . .* 2d ed. London: A. Maxwell.

Turner, Victor
  1974   *Dramas, Fields, and Metaphors: Symbolic Action in Human Society.* Ithaca, N.Y.: Cornell University Press.

United States Children's Bureau Division of Research
  1964   Psychiatric Problems of Adopted Children. *Child Welfare* 43:137–139.

Valentine, Charles
  1963   Social Status, Political Power, and Native Responses to European Influence in Oceania. *Anthropological Forum* 1:3–55.

Valeri, Valerio
  1982   The Transformation of a Transformation: A Structural Essay on an Aspect of Hawaiian History (1809–1819). *Social Analysis* 10:3–41.
  1985a *Kingship and Sacrifice: Ritual and Society in Ancient Hawaii.* Chicago: University of Chicago Press.
  1985b The Conqueror Becomes King: A Political Analysis of the Hawaiian Legend of 'Umi. In *Transformations of Polynesian Culture*, edited by Antony Hooper and Judith Huntsman, pp. 79–103. Auckland: The Polynesian Society.
  1987   Response (to John Charlot's Review of *Kingship and Sacrifice*, by Valerio Valeri). *Pacific Studies* 10 (2): 148–214.

Vancouver, George
  1798   *A Voyage of Discovery to the North Pacific Ocean and Round the World . . . Performed in the Years 1790, 1791, 1792, 1793, 1794, and 1795. . . .* London: Robinson and Edwards. Reprint. Bibliotheca Australiana no. 31. New York: Da Capo Press, 1967.

Van Tilburg, Jo Anne
  1986   Power and Symbol: The Stylistic Analysis of Easter Island Monolithic Sculpture. Ph.D. diss., University of California at Los Angeles.

Vayda, Andrew Peter
  1956   Maori Warfare. Ph.D. diss., Columbia University.

Walker, Ranginui
  1987   *Nga Tau Tohetohe.* Auckland: Penguin Books.

Wallace, Anthony F. C.
  1970   *Culture and Personality.* New York: Random House.

Wallerstein, Immanuel
  1974   *The Modern World-System: Capitalist Agriculture and the Origins of the Euro-
         pean World-Economy in the Sixteenth Century.* New York: Academic Press.
  1979   *The Capitalist World-Economy.* New York: Cambridge University Press.

Walter, Michael A. H. B.
  1978a The Conflict of the Traditional and the Traditionalized: An Analysis
         of Fijian Land Tenure. *Journal of the Polynesian Society* 87:89–108.
  1978b An Examination of Hierarchical Notions in Fijian Society: A Test
         Case for the Applicability of the Term "Chief." *Oceania* 49:1–19.

Ward, John
  1950   *British Policy in the South Pacific (1786–1893).* Sydney: Australasian
         Publishing Co.
  1966   The British Territories in the Pacific. In *The Historiography of the British
         Empire-Commonwealth: Trends, Interpretations, and Resources,* edited by
         Robin Winks, pp. 197–211. Durham, N.C.: Duke University Press.

Ward, R. Gerard, ed.
  1972   *Man in the Pacific Islands: Essays on Geographical Change in the Pacific
         Islands.* Oxford: Clarendon Press.

Wardwell, Allen
  1967   *The Sculpture of Polynesia.* Chicago: The Art Institute.

Watson, Karen
  1972   The Rhetoric of Narrative Structure: A Sociolinguistic Analysis of
         Stories Told by Part-Hawaiian Children. Ph.D. diss., University of
         Hawaii.
  1975   Transferable Communicative Routines: Strategies and Group Iden-
         tity in Two Speech Events. *Language in Society* 4:53–72.

Watson-Gegeo, Karen, and Stephen Boggs
  1977   From Verbal Play to Talk-Story: The Role of Routines in Speech
         Events Among Hawaiian Children. In *Child Discourse,* edited by
         S. Ervin-Tripp and C. Mitchell-Kernan, pp. 67–90. New York: Aca-
         demic Press.

Watt, Sir James
  1979   Medical Aspects and Consequences of Cook's Voyages. In *Captain
         James Cook and His Times,* edited by Robin Fisher and Hugh Johnston,
         pp. 129–157. Seattle: University of Washington Press.

Webb, M. C.
  1965   The Abolition of the Taboo System in Hawaii. *Journal of the Polynesian
         Society* 74:21–39.

Webster, S.
  1975   Cognatic Descent Groups and the Contemporary Maori: A Prelimi-
         nary Reassessment. *Journal of the Polynesian Society* 84:121–152.

Weiner, Annette B.
  1983   Ethnographic Determinism: Samoa and the Margaret Mead Contro-
          versy. *American Anthropologist* 85:909–919.
  1985   Inalienable Wealth. *American Ethnologist* 12 (2): 210–227.

Weisler, M., and P. V. Kirch
  1985   The Structure of Settlement Space at Kawela, Molokai, Hawaiʻian
          Islands. *New Zealand Journal of Archaeology* 7:129–158.

Weisner, Thomas S.
  1982   Sibling Interdependence and Child Caretaking: A Cross-Cultural
          View. In *Sibling Relationships: Their Nature and Significance,* edited by
          Michael E. Lamb and Brian Sutton-Smith, pp. 305–327. Hillsdale,
          N.J.: Erlbaum.

Weisner, Thomas S., and Ronald Gallimore
  1977   My Brother's Keeper: Child and Sibling Caretaking. *Current Anthro-
          pology* 18:169–190.

Wendt, Albert
  1977   *Pouliuli.* Honolulu: University of Hawaii Press.
  1983a   Contemporary Arts in Oceania: Trying to Stay Alive in Paradise As
          an Artist. In *Art and Artists of Oceania,* edited by Sidney M. Mead and
          Bernie Kernot, pp. 198–209. Palmerston North, New Zealand: Dun-
          more Press.
  1983b   Three Faces of Samoa: Mead's, Freeman's and Wendt's (Review of
          *Margaret Mead and Samoa: The Making and Unmaking of an Anthropological
          Myth,* by Derek Freeman). *Pacific Islands Monthly* (April): 10–14, 69.

West, Francis
  1973   James Wightman Davidson. *The Journal of Imperial and Commonwealth
          History* 2:114–117.

Westervelt, W. D.
  1915   *Legends of Gods and Ghosts (Hawaiian Mythology).* Boston: Geo. Ellis.

White, G. M., and J. Kirkpatrick, eds.
  1985   *Person, Self, and Experience: Exploring Pacific Ethnopsychologies.* Berkeley:
          University of California Press.

White, John
  1887–   *The Ancient History of the Maori, His Mythology and Traditions.* Wel-
  1890   lington: G. Didsbury.

Whiting, John W. M.
  1969   Methods and Problems in Cross-Cultural Research. In *Handbook of
          Social Psychology,* vol. 2, edited by G. Lindzey and E. Aronson, pp.
          693–728. Cambridge, Mass.: Addison-Wesley.

Whiting, John, and Beatrice Whiting
  1980   A Strategy for Psychocultural Research. In *The Making of Psychological
          Anthropology,* edited by George D. Spindler, pp. 41–61. Berkeley: Uni-
          versity of California Press.

Willett, Frank
  1983   The Hunterian Museum: Its Founder and Its Ethnographic Collec-
          tion. *Museum Ethnographers Group Newsletter,* no. 14:10–15.

Williamson, Robert W.
  1924   *The Social and Political Systems of Central Polynesia.* 3 vols. Cambridge: Cambridge University Press.
  1933   *Religious and Cosmic Beliefs in Central Polynesia.* Cambridge: Cambridge University Press.

Williamson, Robert W., and R. Piddington
  1939   *Essays in Polynesian Ethnology.* Cambridge: Cambridge University Press.

Wilson, James
  1799   *A Missionary Voyage to the Southern Pacific Ocean . . . in 1796, 1797, 1798.* London: T. Chapman.

Wolf, Eric
  1982   *Europe and the People Without History.* Berkeley: University of California Press.

Yawata, I., and Y. H. Sinoto, eds.
  1968   *Prehistoric Culture in Oceania.* Honolulu: Bernice P. Bishop Museum.

Yen, D. E.
  1961   The Adaptation of the Kumara by the New Zealand Maori. *Journal of the Polynesian Society* 70:338–348.
  1973   The Origins of Oceanic Agriculture. *Archaeology and Physical Anthropology in Oceania* 8:68–85.
  1974   *The Sweet Potato and Oceania.* Bernice P. Bishop Museum Bulletin no. 236. Honolulu: The Museum.
  1984   Easter Island Agriculture in Prehistory: The Possibilities of Reconstruction. Paper presented at the First International Congress on Easter Island and East Polynesia. Easter Island.

Yen, D. E., P. V. Kirch, P. Rosendahl, and T. Riley
  1972   Prehistoric Agriculture in the Upper Valley of Makaha, Oahu. Pacific Anthropological Records 18:59–94. Honolulu: Department of Anthropology, Bernice P. Bishop Museum.

Young, John
  1982   Response of Lau to Foreign Contact: An Interdisciplinary Reconstruction. *The Journal of Pacific History* 17:29–50.

Young, P. Lewis
  1980   Destruction of Vision (Review of *Islands and Beaches,* by Greg Dening). *Australian Book Review* (December): 31–32.

CONTRIBUTORS

Robert Borofsky is associate professor of anthropology at Hawaii Loa College and Book Review Forum editor for *Pacific Studies*. He has carried out research in Pukapuka, Cook Islands from 1977 to 1981 resulting in the book *Making History: Pukapukan and Anthropological Constructions of Knowledge* (1987). Besides his concern with Polynesia, he is interested in the anthropology of knowledge and the culture of nursing. Borofsky is currently at work on two books: "Contact and Change," dealing with the impact of Polynesians and Westerners on each other, and "Pacific Issues in Historical Perspective," an edited volume with David Hanlon. In 1988–1989 he was a Fellow at the Institute of Culture and Communication, East-West Center.

Alan Howard is professor of anthropology at the University of Hawaii. He has conducted research among Hawaiian-Americans and has participated in a project focused on health and migration among Samoans. He is currently engaged in a long-term research project on the culture history of Rotuma (Republic of Fiji), where he did fieldwork initially in 1959–1961. His major publications include *Learning to be Rotuman* (1970) and *Ain't No Big Thing: Coping Strategies in a Hawaiian-American Community* (1974).

Adrienne L. Kaeppler is curator of oceanic ethnology at the National Museum of Natural History/Museum of Man, at the Smithsonian Institution, Washington, D.C. From 1967 to 1980 she was an anthropologist on the staff of the Bernice P. Bishop Museum in Honolulu, Hawaii. She has carried out field research in Tonga, Hawaii, Tahiti, Easter Island, the Solomon Islands, New Guinea, and Japan. Her research focuses on the interrelationships between social structure and

353

the arts, especially dance, music, and the visual arts. She has published widely on these subjects and is currently finishing two books on cross-cultural aesthetics and Hawaiian dance and ritual. Kaeppler's major publications include *The Fabrics of Hawaii (Bark Cloth)* (1975), *Artificial Curiosities* (1978), *Eleven Gods Assembled* (1979), and *Polynesian Dance* (1983).

Patrick V. Kirch is professor of anthropology at the University of California, Berkeley and curator of oceanic archaeology in the Lowie Museum. He has also held appointments as archaeologist at the Bernice P. Bishop Museum and director of the Burke Museum at the University of Washington. Kirch has carried out extensive archaeological as well as ethnoecological fieldwork throughout the Pacific, including major projects in Hawaii, Tonga, Samoa, Futuna, 'Uvea, Tikopia, Anuta, and Mussau. Among his principal works are *Tikopia: The Prehistory and Ecology of a Polynesian Outlier* (1982, with D. Yen); *The Evolution of the Polynesian Chiefdoms* (1984); *Feathered Gods and Fishhooks: An Introduction to Hawaiian Archaeology and Prehistory* (1985); and *Niuatoputapu: The Prehistory of a Polynesian Chiefdom* (1988).

John Kirkpatrick is currently senior research associate with Community Resources, Inc. in Honolulu, Hawaii and teaches in the Ethnic Studies Program of the University of Hawaii. He has conducted fieldwork in French Polynesia, Hawaii, and Micronesian Yap. His research with Marquesans focused on cultural understandings of social life and psychology. Kirkpatrick has written *The Marquesan Notion of the Person* (1983) and several papers on Marquesan society and culture. He has also edited *Person, Self, and Experience: Exploring Pacific Ethnopsychologies* (1985) with Geoffrey M. White. Recently he has done studies of ethnicity and the social impacts of development in modern Hawaii.

George E. Marcus is professor and department chair of anthropology at Rice University. He is serving as inaugural editor for the journal *Cultural Anthropology*. He coauthored, with Michael Fischer, *Anthropology as Cultural Critique* (1986) and is coeditor, with James Clifford, of *Writing Culture: The Poetics and Politics of Ethnography* (1986). Since his fieldwork in Tonga during the 1970s, he has pursued an interest in the comparative study of contemporary non-Western monarchies as well as of Polynesia as fully integrated into a regime of historic modernity. In 1988–1989 Marcus completed a year as Scholar at the Getty Center for the History of Art and the Humanities.

Jane and James Ritchie hold professorships at the University of Waikato and are New Zealand's leading experts in child development.

She is more the psychologist; he the anthropologist. In what is really a linked series of eight books they have reported their own research, summarized that of others, and commented on the New Zealand and Pacific world of childhood and culture. Among their many publications are *Growing Up in New Zealand* (1978), *Growing Up in Polynesia* (1979), and *Spare the Rod* (1981). James Ritchie is currently with the Centre for Maori Studies and Research engaged in action anthropology with Maori tribal groups, chiefly on economic development and political empowerment. Jane Ritchie directs the Centre for Women's Studies and Research.

Bradd Shore is associate professor of anthropology at Emory University. His major fieldwork was carried out in Western Samoa from 1972 to 1974, resulting in numerous papers and the book *Sala'ilua: A Samoan Mystery* (1982). Shore's Polynesian research has dealt with topics ranging from kinship analysis, cosmology, and social control to conceptions of person and gender. More recently, his work has focused on cognitive implications of the culture concept. He is currently working on a book entitled "Culture in Mind: Cognitive Foundations of Cultural Knowledge." In 1988–1989 Shore was a Fellow at the Center for Advanced Study in the Behavioral Sciences.

GENERAL INDEX

Acculturation, 98. *See also* Modernization
Adoption, 74–77, 87, 104, 112; compared with American patterns, 74, 75 n. 15, 94, 135 n. 4; and fosterage, 94 n. 13; rates, 4, 75–77, 94 n. 14; and social alliances, 86, 87, 94 n. 17. See also *social organization under specific islands*
Aesthetics, 10, 279; changing patterns of, 237, 280; defined, 213; indigenous perspectives on, 216, 220; study of, 217–218, 220, 232, 238 n. 1; underlying structures of, 220–222, 230. *See also* Art; *headings under specific islands*
Affiliation, 98, 100
Aga, 80, 91, 94, 149, 172
'Aha, 152, 153, 172
Ahu, 41, 42, 171
Ahupua'a, 42, 45
'Aiga, 56, 57–58, 88, 188, 194
'Aiga potopoto, 57–58
Ali'i, 157, 194, 196, 224, 280
Alofa, 93, 280
Aloha, 93, 119
America, 75, 133, 181, 215, 284
Amio, 80, 91, 94, 149, 172
Ancestral Polynesian Society, 20–23, 186; basis for deductions about, 20, 21
Andesite line, 14
Aneityum, 39
Anger. *See* Conflict; Emotional expression
Anuta, 26, 36, 67, 74, 227, 288; geography of, 15, 67; prehistory of, 26, 27, 277

Ao, 147, 226
Appropriation, 257–258, 261, 269; European perspectives on, 250, 251–256, 259, 272 n. 9; and European property, 250–260, 269, 272 n. 9; Polynesian perspectives on, 251, 256–260, 273 n. 10; and violence, 261–262, 264–265, 267
Archeology, 13, 14, 45, 46. *See also* Prehistory; *headings under specific islands*
Ari'i, 44
Ariki, 106, 144, 159
Aroha, 106, 110
Aropa, 67, 93
Art, 213, 217, 231, 232, 286; and association of verbal and visual modes, 217–218, 220; comparative analysis of, 215, 216; defined, 213; exhibitions of, 239 n. 7; modern approaches to, 220–232; past approaches to, 212–220; and reconstructing social organization, 279; and society, 213; traditional, 217, 222, 234–236; underlying structures of, 230. *See also* Aesthetics; *headings under specific islands*
Atafu, 72
'Ati, 53–54
Atolls, 72, 75, 290
Australia, 284
Australian High Commission, 235
Austral Islands, 232
Australs, 15
Austronesian, 17, 137

NAME INDEX

Alia Matua, 176
Alia-Tama, 176
Alkire, 290
Allen, 17
Ambrose, 18
Ammerman, 33
Anderson, A. J., 36, 39
Anderson, B., 168
Anderson, J., 215
Archey, 214
Ausubel, 125
Auwai, 242
Awatere, 281
Ayres, 36

Babadzan, 231
Baessler, 212
Baker, 134
Bakhtin, 183
Balfour, 212
Banks, 251, 252, 255, 257, 272, 273
Barnes, 53
Barrau, 16
Barrow, 214
Bass, 250, 263
Bastian, 212
Bateson, 101, 118
Beaglehole, E., 3, 49, 60, 96, 97, 98, 99,
    111, 116, 119, 130, 158, 271
Beaglehole, J. C., 241, 251, 252, 254,
    255, 256, 257, 259, 264, 265, 266, 270,
    272, 273, 274, 275
Beaglehole, P., 49, 96, 97, 98, 99, 111,
    158
Beasley, 212

Beggerly, 39
Bellwood, 14, 23, 32, 40
Belshaw, 62
Bernard, 135
Best, 6, 143, 144, 146, 159, 172, 173, 212,
    214, 239
Biersack, 85, 271
Biggs, 4, 21, 114
Boenchea, 251, 255, 262, 267, 272, 274
Boggs, 109, 112, 113, 114, 115, 116,
    134
Bonk, 13, 14, 27
Boon, 186
Borofsky, 89, 103, 104, 115, 116, 117,
    118, 125, 130, 231, 245, 270, 271, 273,
    274, 280
Bott, 70, 79, 85, 90, 138, 176, 181, 222
Bougainville, 248, 249, 251, 252, 253,
    254, 255, 262, 267, 270, 272, 273, 274,
    291
Bourdieu, 59
Boutilier, 248
Boutin, 255
Bowden, K., 263, 272
Bowden, R., 182
Bowles, 119
Brady, 74, 75, 78, 87, 94, 104, 271, 289
Braudel, 284
Brenneis, 193
Brigham, 212, 214
Brookfield, 37
Brooks, 77
Buck, 2, 99, 158, 212, 214, 229
Buckler, 270
Burney, 241, 273

367

Production Notes

This book was designed by Roger Eggers.
Composition and paging were done on the
Quadex Composing System and typesetting
on the Compugraphic 8400 by the design
and production staff of University of
Hawaii Press.

The text typeface is Baskerville and
the display typeface is Goudy Bold.

Offset presswork and binding were done by
Vail-Ballou Press, Inc. Text paper is
Writers RR Offset, basis 50.